PRINCIPLES OF
FAMILY
PSYCHIATRY

PRINCIPLES OF
FAMILY
PSYCHIATRY

by

JOHN G. HOWELLS

M.D., F.R.C. Psych., D.P.M.

**Director, The Institute of Family Psychiatry
The Ipswich Hospital, Ipswich, England**

BRUNNER/MAZEL, *Publishers* • New York

Published by BRUNNER/MAZEL, INC.
64 University Place, New York, N.Y. 10003

Library of Congress Cataloging in Publication Data

Howells, John G
   Principles of family psychiatry.

   Includes bibliographies and index.
   1. Family psychotherapy. I. Title. DNLM: 1. Family
therapy. WM430 H859p
RC488.5.H64   616.8'915   73-90298
ISBN 0-87630-089-1

To

Ola

David, Richard, Cheryll and Roger

PREFACE

As people have moved through time they have discerned the effects of environmental hazards upon themselves. The most obvious and compelling hazards are physical. The more discerning individuals have been aware of less obvious but no less damaging hazards that spring from the pattern of psychic communication between people. A time has been reached in our history when many of the physical hazards are under some control; we now turn to comprehend and control the psychic hazards.

As people, alone or in family groups, meet noxious psychic events, some people are damaged by them and, once damaged, tend to become tenant to the noxious forces and perpetuate their expression through time. This book is concerned with the understanding of the aetiology and management of this psychopathological process.

It may help the reader if the main principles underlying the construction of this book were outlined. These are:

1. The family is taken as the element in society most useful as the basic unit in clinical work. Hence, the term "family psychiatry." The family, and not the individual as is traditional, is the patient. Thus, such terms as "adult psychiatry," "child psychiatry," and "geriatric psychiatry" are discarded. This emphasis on the family is in tune with emphasis given to it in the framework of long-standing societies as, for instance, in Europe, and also in the enormous experiments in social construction in the U.S.S.R., the U.S.A., and the People's Republic of China.

2. Pathological phenomena are divided into the psychic and organic parts of the whole organism, and this is the underlying principle of the nosology used here.

Nomenclature supports nosology by going back to first principles. Thus, the term *psychonosis* covers psychic pathology and replaces the incorrect term "neurosis" (literally, disorder of neurone), and the term *encephalon-*

osis covers cerebral organic pathology and replaces the incorrect term, hitherto employed, of "psychosis" (literally, disorder of psyche).

Again, "emotional" (truly psychic) are differentiated from "mental" symptoms (truly organic manifestations of cerebral dysfunctioning).

Process (endogenous) schizophrenia is sharply delineated from non-process schizophrenia. Process schizophrenia, covered by the new term *encephalo-ataxia,* is considered a part of the encephalopathies. Non-process schizophrenia is regarded as a severe form of *psychonosis* (neurosis in the old terminology).

This book is largely concerned with psychonosis.

3. While accepting for practical purposes the usefulness of considering the psychic and organic functions of the organism separately, we must still regard these as two interacting parts of the whole. It is an essential principle here to practice pananthropic medicine (medicine of the whole person.) This is in conformity with the true nature of medicine (its field is that of *disease,* literally "not at ease," or, technically, "a morbid process" of any sort), which has always been concerned with both mind and body and tried from its earliest recorded history to explain the interaction between the two.

A tendency to equate medicine with organic pathology alone springs from an unawareness of medical history; paying undue attention to the early success of medicine in the organic field; ignoring the effects on the soma of noxious psychic events as dire as death itself, and the effects on the psyche of noxious physical agents; failing to treat somatic pathology produced by psychic trauma; and denying the patient under treatment by psychic methods the benefits of alleviating organic agents.

Today we witness the start of a movement which will ultimately match the early success of medicine over organic pathology with equal success over psychopathology.

4. In conformity with the procedures of medicine, much weight is given to diagnosis (discernment). Only by an understanding of psychopathology in general can rational, effective procedures be devised to reverse and contend with the pathological process. In a particular case, only by a correct discernment of the pathological process can effective management be executed. Hence, the emphasis here on Family Diagnosis. Amongst other matters, it leads to careful *differentiation of the indicators of a pathological process from the pathological process itself.*

5. Psychopathology here starts from a *tabula rasa.* The doctrines of interpretive schools are eschewed. It is held that only the events themselves are important; the actual experience is all and its revelation as it happened to the organism is the aim of diagnostic procedures. This leads here to basing understanding on the principles of Experiential Psychopathology.

6. Benexperiential Therapy is the natural outcome of Experiential Psychopathology. Psychic changes in organisms, healthy or pathological, are the result of experience. Thus, to effect an improved change in a given psychopathological process calls for a re-experience to the advantage of the psyche—hence Benexperiential Therapy and its employment here in a number of ways.

7. The organism participates in a pattern of transaction with psychic forces outside itself. This pattern of forces or vectors can operate to the organism's advantage or disadvantage. The understanding of the adverse pattern can be termed Vector Psychiatry. Fortunately, the pattern is capable of control, and its control to effect improvement of a particular organism is termed Vector Therapy.

8. That control of a pattern of vectors is possible opens a new field of therapy, and one that could resolve psychonosis in a few generations. Psychonosis is preventable; cure is more difficult, but more knowledge may make this possible also. To control and change the pattern of vectors of one organism is Vector Therapy. To control and change the pattern of vectors of a whole society is the basis of a Salutiferous, or health-promoting, Society.

It may also be useful for the reader to be acquainted with the order of presentation of the material on family psychiatry. The main tenets of family psychiatry are covered in the "Introduction to Family Psychiatry" (Section I). There follows a section on the characteristics of the family—"The Anatomy of the Family" (Section II). "Nosology" (Section III) is considered next, as it is an essential introduction to a description of "Family Psychopathology—Experiential Psychopathology" (Section IV). Thus, a basis has been supplied for an outline of "Family Diagnosis" (Section V) which leads inevitably to "Family Therapy" (Section VI). "Special Aspects of Family Psychiatry" (Section VII) comes next and the book closes with a suggested framework for "The Organisation of a Family Psychiatric Service" (Section VIII). Because of the limitations of space, case illustrations are brief. Each is selected to demonstrate one principle only; to speculate on any other elements of the case illustration is unwise.

The book grew from two previous publications in the family field: *Family Psychiatry* (1963) and *Theory and Practice of Family Psychiatry* (1968). It leans heavily upon profitable transactions between the author and attendees at annual courses held at the Institute of Family Psychiatry—the course for medical practitioners held each spring for the last 20 years, and the June course for psychiatrists. It gained from the day-to-day interaction over the last 25 years between colleagues at the Institute. Throughout, it is nourished by the endeavour to help hapless patients who optimistically pander to our urge to serve; only in recent years can it be said that our clumsy efforts have led to measurable improvement.

This book is addressed more particularly to the psychiatrist (healer of the psyche) than to the neuropsychiatrist. Thus only a small part of it is concerned with encephalonosis (psychosis, to employ the old terminology). It is not a textbook, but an outline of principles. Detail will be filled out by companion volumes.

Montaigne (*Essays.* Bk. III, Ch. 2) said, "Men are apt to believe what they least understand." A conscious effort has been made to avoid mysticism and pseudointellectualisation and to rely on directness and basic English whenever possible, in the belief that the book will be read by those knowledgeable enough to share ignorance, face limited truths, and be concerned with building from small but sure foundations.

J. G. H.

ACKNOWLEDGEMENTS

Some of the material in this book is based on the author's previous work published in *Theory and Practice of Family Psychiatry* and in volumes of the *Modern Perspectives in Psychiatry* series. Permission to use this material has kindly been granted by the publishers, Churchill Livingstone.

It is a pleasure to acknowledge my great indebtedness to Maria-Livia Osborn. Her role of respected conferee has been an invaluable source of consultation for clarifying obscurities in my ideas. The literary work, preparation of the book, and index have benefitted from her enthusiasm and expertise.

TABLE OF CONTENTS

xiii

I
INTRODUCTION TO FAMILY PSYCHIATRY

The Family as a Social and Clinical Unit

All phenomena in the cosmos have equal significance—whether cloud, music, mathematician, caterpillar, or the Socratic method. All are essential, interdependent elements in the plan of the universe, the cosmic design. Thus the individual, family, and society have equal significance per se. However, in a particular set of circumstances at a moment in time one element may take on special significance—a warship in wartime has a value over a passenger ship which would not appertain in time of peace; but as essential phenomena, a warship and a passenger ship have equal significance.

In one aspect of the cosmic plan, the emotional life of people, the family, at this moment in history has a special significance. People, it seems, live in families—sociologists and anthropologists agree that this is almost universal. That society has empirically come to use this pattern must be based on good grounds. Some of the reasons for the family pattern of social life are easy to understand. The family offers the protection of group living; it satisfies the complementary requirements of male and female; offspring are fitted for social living by membership in a group; the family is a manageable small group in the vastness of society; it is a unit that can survive economically. If the family had not occurred spontaneously, it would have had to be invented.

Humanity flows in a continuous stream from the past, through the present, into the future and might, at a superficial glance, be thought to be made up of individuals. Closer observation, however, shows that these individuals cluster and coalesce into groups—families. These groups expand, elements split off from them, come together as adult males and females, and new groups are formed. Through these groups, the families, humanity propagates itself and nurtures and trains the elements that make new groups.

3

Hence the family is the most significant group in society and can claim to be the basic unit on which society is built.

The family then is the biological cell of society. When people leave their factories in the evening, they pour into the highways, slip into the side streets, and filter down the lanes until they enter the pathway to a house, pass inside and join a family. Not only is the family the unit today—but it will be tomorrow. Families make more families. An offspring breaks off from a family, links with an offspring of another family in society, and a new family unit is born.

For the psychiatrist, the significance of this small group, the family, is this: not only is the family unit responsible for emotional health—it is also responsible for emotional ill-health. As the concern of the psychiatrist (*psyche iatros*—healer of the psyche) is with psychic harmony, it follows that he must take the family as the object of his efforts. Thus family psychiatry replaces individual psychiatry. It must be emphasised that to practice family psychiatry does not denigrate either the individual or society, nor does it exclude working with the individual or society. It is a matter of working with the significant biological unit for a particular purpose at a moment in history. It should lead to the well-being of the individual and of society.

Should the family not be the significant functional unit in society, then family psychiatry would not be appropriate. This occurs today in a small number of cultures and it has been so in the past. Julius Caesar (1), at the time of his first invasion of England, had it reported to him that the strange Celts of that island lived in groups of ten men who shared all the women and children of this group. Here a "ten-man group" psychiatry would have been appropriate, as this was the functional group.

It might be asked why medicine, psychiatry, sociology, and ecclesiastical and legal authorities, etc., have used the individual as the functional unit hitherto. The most relevant fact is probably that the practitioner in all these callings is an individual. He identifies with his like. Especially in travail one identifies with the victim. So an emotional predisposition is reinforced by training programmes usually planned by individuals. To this is added the difficulty of grasping group phenomena. This difficulty is largely artificial, as the individual in fact has a long contact with group phenomena—his family—but his training restricts and hampers his natural aptitude. By nature and experience the individual is a family element and behaves as such.

The above postulate that the family is the optimum unit in clinical practice can be tested by taking a number of apparent exceptions to the general rules.

1. It might at first be thought that an unmarried person during his own therapy should be considered in isolation from a family. However, he may still be living in his preceding family and his pathology may be an integral part of his family pathology. This could be so even when he is living at some distance from the family, e.g., at a university. Furthermore, should his parents be dead, not only may he have to contend with his extended family, but also the genesis of his pathology may lie in his preceding family. One can never escape the influence of the preceding family, as it lies within one-self; this influence interacts with the present environment and is a factor that must be clarified, estimated and resolved. Again, even though one is apparently single, an informal relationship with another person may be so intimate that whatever its legality the relationship de facto constitutes a family; an uncommon example is that of two homosexuals apparently single, but living so intimately as to constitute a family unit.

The following case illustrates a typical situation of a single person. A Roman Catholic priest presents with acute anxiety, agitation, insomnia and loss of weight. At first glance he might seem to be reacting to his recent decision to leave the Church. However, his problem is more fundamental. Should he leave the Church, the possibility of marriage is open to him (a young lady is already cherished) but there is an emotional obstruction to his intention—he cannot believe that he is sexually mature. He believes that the expression of his immaturity is demonstrated by an obsession to seek out and examine illustrations of naked sexual organs. His present handicap, it is soon revealed, is the result of past experiences in his own family. His parents carried prudery to an extreme, as shown by one memory of himself as an infant sitting in the bath, a stranger coming into the room, and his mother hastily hiding his sexual organs. His sexual organs and those of others became the object of great curiosity tinged with guilt. He accepted the dictates of loving parents to be good by joining the Church, but his equally strongly dictated obsessive curiosity also has to be satisfied. The origin of his problem is in the family; it is resolved by therapy turning around family events. Relief opens the way to another family of his own making.

2. Akin to the situation of a single person, can be quoted the instance of a family which has become so fragmented as to be a group of individuals going their own individual ways but apparently living as a family, although having ceased to operate as a group. Are these individuals free of the family? It is unlikely. They must contend always with the influence of their preceding families within themselves; they may have actual links with their extended preceding families; they may not be as free of their present loosely knit family as they imagine; and some of them may already have become

informally united with other persons so as to constitute de facto other families.

3. What of a sick individual who moves into an otherwise healthy family, e.g., a child brought up by grandparents and now rejoining his parents. Is he, too, to be thought of in the context of family management? It must be so. His pathology turns around his preceding family—his life with his grandparents. His future turns around the capacity of his new family to contend with him. The family approach is essential. The family may have accepted him back for motives of its own. The family may become ill or, conversely, it may be the agent to produce health in him. The family cannot escape involvement. The family is still the significant unit.

4. Not all family members are sick to the same degree. The interplay of factors from the past with present life experiences producing pathology do not affect each member equally. Could one strikingly sick member of the family be considered in isolation? The situation of an illegitimate adolescent boy rejected by his mother and stepfather might be such an instance. But the source of his pathology lies in this family. The manifestations of his pathology are a reflection of this family's way of life. His destructive behaviour is at its strongest within his family. He can only be understood as an integral part of that family. The family is still the significant unit. Indeed, he may need the help of a carefully selected therapeutic foster family.

5. It may be contended that a member brought up outside his natural home may not need consideration as a family element. In the United Kingdom only six children in 1,000 are brought up in the care of the authorities (2), often in substitute families, either a foster home or an artificially created family within a hostel. The psychopathology of such children has therefore to be understood against these anomalous substitute families. For a small number, however, the family unit, as one understands it, does not exist—exceptionally, one may be brought up in a very large group of children with tenuous attachments to parent figures. Here the child has had no preceding family as one normally understands it. (We must, however, bear in mind the tendency of large groups to break up into smaller functionally optimum groups which give a near family experience). Therefore there can be no estimation of a preceding family. Instead, diagnosis turns around an understanding of a relationship within a very large group and the term "family" for this group may not be appropriate. "Large group," or "hostel," or "village" psychiatry would be appropriate nomenclature. This is a rare event and is resolved when the patient has become a member of a family of his own making.

6. An even rarer experience may be that of an individual who has enjoyed no fellow feeling from anyone as a child—whether it be family, substi-

tute family, near family, or large group. Complete physical separation from everyone must be very rare if only because he must be fed to survive. Minimum contact and maximum deprivation might occur within a large house, with disinterested parents, fleeting brief relationships with many servants, and dispatch to boarding school at an early age. Edith Sitwell (8) seems to have had only two rather tenuous positive relationships in her childhood—with a peacock and with a footman. Wordsworth's childhood may have been similar. But both came to have close attachments to siblings later in life and Wordsworth went on to found a family. Exceptionally, these two people may have had no customary family unit in their childhoods (unless a brother, a footman and a peacock, a loosely knit group, can be embraced within the term), but they too were part of a family group in adulthood—and family living has obvious difficulties for those who have never experienced such a group in the past.

7. Should physical and mental handicaps in an individual be treated in the context of the family? Instances might be individuals suffering from mental retardation, cerebral palsy, epilepsy, schizophrenia, blindness and diabetes. They must certainly be treated in the context of the family on a number of counts. Firstly, the family may have caused the handicap—e.g., the unwanted child of a mother suffers a greater number of hazards during pregnancy and birth and these can lead to handicaps; some families produce accident proneness and thus disability; harsh families inflict physical damage on their children; or hostile families do not take the customary care to protect their children. Secondly, families may aggravate an existing handicap—e.g., epileptics have more seizures and need stronger medication at times of family turmoil; unloving families do not have the interest to train children to find ways around a disability. Thirdly, the handicap has family repercussions—e.g., it may influence the amount of time to be spent at home by a parent; the possibilities of employment, finance, etc. Fourthly, the management of the handicap is family business—frequently the deciding factor in asking for institutional care is the emotional capacity of a family to manage the handicapped. Indeed it can be argued that every physical illness must be considered as a constituent part of family life. The most aetiologically physical of conditions, such as an epidemic infection or cancer, still affect the individual's family life and his care may turn around an estimation of family capacity. Lastly, families have their own very personal myths in relation to illness and death.

From the above it can be seen that it is exceedingly rare for the family not to be the significant functional unit in the understanding and management of emotional illness (and indeed physical illness). That this should be so is not surprising. It appears that throughout time, and in most cultures today, people have spontaneously elected to live in family groups. To regard an individual in isolation is a negation of one of the essential truths about a group. The truth is that a group is a polydynamic system and any event within that system affects every other element within it; that is the essential nature of a system. Of course, none of this discussion precludes using individual methods of diagnosis and treatment as part of the total programme of family management.

Family Psychiatry: General Formulation

Psychiatry is the field of medicine concerned with the study of abnormal psychic states.

Family Psychiatry (3, 4) is a system of theory and practice of psychiatry whereby the family is taken as the unit to be evaluated and treated. The family is the patient.

Thus the custom of taking the individual as the unit becomes obsolete; this applies to any aspect of individual psychiatry—child, adolescent, adult, or geriatric psychiatry. In family psychiatry the sick individual, whatever the age, is taken to be an index of a sick family; attention moves from the individual to the family, which becomes the patient.

The family is regarded as an organism in its own right. Like the individual, it has a structure, lines of communication within itself, characteristics of its own, and most important, a mind of its own. Thus family psychiatry asserts the existence of a group psyche or "collective psyche" of the family. The family's collective psyche is as real an entity as the individual's psyche. The procedures of investigation are aimed at exposing the collective psyche; the processes of treatment have as their target the harmonising of the collective family psyche functioning. Throughout, family psychiatry is concerned with the family group psyche.

The general aim of family psychiatry is to accept a sick, disordered family and to produce a healthy, co-ordinated family. The family is the biological cell of society. Families breed more families. Sick families tend to breed more sick families; reversing this phenomenon could transform the level of society's emotional health over a number of generations.

The family is the unit throughout clinical practice. Taking the family as the unit, in the author's system, applies to the programme of referral, to the elucidation of symptomatology, to the description of psychopathological processes, to the procedures of investigation, to the recording of data and to the techniques of therapy.

The referral programme is planned to cover the whole family, either initially or ultimately. The ideal referral is that of the whole family from the start. However, an individual of any age or clinical category can be the presenting patient; a dyad, e.g., husband and wife or parent and child, can be the propositus; or a part of the family may be the identified problem. But wherever the clinician starts in the family, he moves to involve the rest of the family and ends with the whole family as his patient.

Indicators, symptoms and signs, of dysfunction may appear at any point, and usually at many points, in the family's structure. Attention to the indicators in an individual family member is not enough. Assessment of the indicators must embrace every dimension of the whole family.

The psychopathological process to be understood lies, not in the individual alone, but in the substance of the family collective psyche. Thus, to established theory must be added communications theory, general systems theory, and the theory of mechanics. The family consists of a number of individuals with a polyadic communication pattern. These communications added together are but a part of the group psyche; the whole also has many properties of its own, for the whole is more than the sum of its parts. As the family is a polydynamic system, any event at any point within the system affects the rest of the system. As the family system moves through time, it is subject to experiences, some benevolent and constructive, and some noxious and destructive. The understanding of the dysfunction caused in the family system by noxious experiences is the task of experiential psychopathology.

The procedures of investigation, family diagnosis, must uncover the functioning and dysfunctioning of the total family group in all its dimensions. The liabilities are revealed as well as the assets that have to be mobilised in treatment. A central feature of family psychiatry is to illuminate the understanding of the family process under investigation by a study of the processes of the family units that contributed to its formation, the preceding families, i.e., the family units of the two parents. The key to understanding the present often lies in the past.

A frame of reference is required for a description of a family. From clinical experience it has been found that a useful account can be based on a consideration of the family in five dimensions: (1) Dimension of the Individuals, (2) Dimension of Internal Communication, (3) Dimension of General Psychic Properties, (4) Dimension of External Communication, (5) Dimension of Physical Properties.

Recording data applicable to an individual is not enough. Instead, the record embraces the dynamic history of the family in its five dimensions as it flows from the past through the present into the future.

The unit in management and treatment, family therapy, is the family. Benexperiential psychotherapy is pursued with the collective group psyche.

But equally effective and complementary therapy becomes possible within and without the family system, arising from an estimation and rearrangement of its vectors—vector therapy. Social action in a planned and precise fashion opens the way to a health-promoting, salutiferous society.

A vignette of a family in travail will demonstrate the value of the above in clinical practice.

A middle-aged man, sent by his family doctor, presents at a psychiatric clinic with a threatened perforation of his gastric ulcer. Exploration reveals him as an anxious, agitated man bothered by insomnia and nightmares and lacking attention at work. Further family exploration exposes the fact that his wife is chronically depressed, migrainous, frigid, irritable, difficult, and suicidal at times; their child of three is backward in speech, lethargic, eczematous, clinging and given to periodic bouts of weeping. Examination of the dimension of the individuals thus exposes the presence of three emotionally sick family members, and not just the presenting family member.

The marital relationship is one of tension, irritability, and verbal abuse; physical intercourse, at one time satisfactory, has ceased. The mother-child relationship is one of mutual hostility and rejection. The father-child relationship is positive to a just-adequate degree. Thus two out of three relationships in the dimension of internal communication are unsatisfactory.

Fragmentation has occurred in the family—father and child are opposed to mother. Father has taken on the whole parenting role. Anger and recrimination is the characteristic mood of the family. Thus there is failure in the dimension of the family's general psychic properties.

The family, partly due to lack of finance and partly from its misery, isolates itself from the community. Thus its operations in the dimension of external communication are deficient.

Father's work problems have led to loss of productivity bonus and debts have accumulated; the physical health of all three family members is poor; there is failure in the dimension of physical properties.

Emotional disorder in this family dates from the conception of the child. Pregnancy was for the mother a saga of disinterest, severe vomiting and delayed childbirth. She was severely depressed for three weeks following the birth and has been chronically depressed ever since. The child is clearly unwanted by her; it is the product of an unrevealed and unloving passing relationship outside marriage.

Analysis of this not exceptional picture of a dysfunctioning family leads to the following conclusions:

1. The man of the family is the presenting patient. He comes with a gastric ulcer, whose pain could not be overlooked. But on careful examina-

tion his personality is seen to be disturbed as a whole—he is also anxious, agitated, troubled in sleep and failing at work. There are both physical and psychic symptoms. Typically, he complains of the obvious, painful, and by now dangerous physical symptom; he overlooks the equally significant mood changes in himself.

2. All three individuals prove to be equally in need of help. Of the three, he is perhaps the healthiest. The wife's condition is serious. The child will be irrevocably damaged in time and will fail later at her most exacting tests—as wife and mother. Failure to examine the family would have left two of its members without help. Indeed, help to the father alone might have made him a more effective antagonist in the marital battle and led to his wife's destruction.

3. This family is sick as a whole—not just each member individually. There is dysfunction also in all four other dimensions. In the dimension of internal communication two of its three basic relationships are faulty. In the dimension of general psychic properties it is fragmented. It is isolated in its dimension of external communication. It is failing in its dimension of physical properties. The sick man was an index of a sick family.

4. The referral programme calls for coverage of the whole family, for the family is the patient.

5. The psychopathological process at work involves the whole substance of the family; the individual is but a part of the whole. Every shifting event brings change throughout the family. The collective group psyche is disordered.

6. Indicators, symptoms and signs, appear at many points, in all its dimensions. Thus, assessment of the indicators calls for an examination of the whole family in each of its five dimensions.

7. The procedures of investigation must extend to an examination of the family in all its five dimensions—family diagnosis. Not only its liabilities but also its assets must be evaluated—the positive father-child relationship being one here. The reactions of the individuals and thus their relationships depend upon their experiences in the past—in their own families as children. Mother is vulnerable to fleeting masculine charm. Father, coming from a large, warm, closely knit family, relates easily to children—even when not his own. Clues to management arise from the understanding of the past—this is the golden road to therapy, e.g., father should be encouraged to continue in the main parenting role.

8. Data recording must present a picture of the family in its five dimensions in a continuous form through time, from the past through the present into the future—the preceding, present, and succeeding families.

9. The processes of therapy (family therapy) must be directed to the whole family. But family diagnosis must come before family therapy—both

parts of the system of family psychiatry. Family group therapy—one aspect of family therapy—could, for example, allow mother to express her guilt, have it expurgated by the husband and therapist, and allow her to accept the child, not as an unwanted representation of a disappointing man in her extramarital liaison, but as an innocent child. With mother's co-operation and understanding, the anguish of the troubled mother-child relationship can be relieved by foster care during the day when father is unable to give emotional support, and by father accepting the main parenting role when he is at home. Both changes are aspects of vector therapy, another part of family therapy.

10. Resolution of this family disorder creates a climate for the healthy development of the child, a part founder of one of the next generation of families. So family therapy on a large scale makes its contribution to the improvement of the families to come, and hence the improvement in the emotional health of future generations in society.

Misconceptions about the Nature of Family Psychiatry

Family psychiatry should not be confused with another approach—the psychiatry of the individual in his family. This latter is individual psychiatry and it evolved in this fashion. Starting from concern with an individual patient, the realization developed that the individual can only be understood and helped if his family is seen and assessed. Thus the spouse and perhaps the children are also seen. The aim throughout, however, is to use the family to help the *individual*. The focus of attention is the individual and the family is an adjunct in his management; the patient is the individual. The reverse is true in family psychiatry. The family is the focus and the individual an adjunct; the patient is the family. In family psychiatry the sick individual is regarded as an index of a sick family and thereafter interest moves to the whole sick family. Furthermore, in family psychiatry the aim is to produce a healthy family, and inevitably the individuals become and remain healthy in consequence. Family psychiatry is not concerned with the individual *and* his family, but with the whole family, of which individuals are part.

In clinical practice, unless great care is exercised, there is often a slipping back to an individual approach. This may be due to identification with the individual, utilisation of techniques applicable to individuals, economy in facilities, misunderstanding of the theory, inertia of the clinical organisation and, lastly, not always being able to cover the whole family. If the latter difficulty arises, as it does, the clinician is still in a stronger position utilising the family psychiatric model than reverting to the traditional individual approach. Faced with only one family member, he can, by continually interpreting material in the context of the whole family, make a more realistic appraisal of affairs, manage the situation in such a way that communication with the family is not impaired, leave the door open to more family involvement later and bring partial help to the whole family rather than just a part of it. Attention to the individual alone is not only ineffective, but, as will be seen later, it can be positively damaging in some circumstances.

A typical illustration of the "individual and family psychiatry" approach is the great attention given to the family of the person suffering from encephalo-ataxia (schizophrenia in the old terminology). Some workers believe that anomalies of family functioning are responsible for the development of encephalo-ataxia. At this point no comment is made about the veracity of this concept; it has been discussed elsewhere (5) and will again be discussed later. Given the above thesis, it follows that attempts should be made to remove the anomalous family functioning so that the patient can recover his health. The focus of attention is the individual, and the family is an adjunct to be changed so as to bring health to one family member, whatever the cost to the rest of the family. Leaving aside whether or not such therapy is effective, it can be seen that this approach is the negation of family psychiatry. The family is used to change the individual. In family psychiatry it is axiomatic that as the family is the focus, it should be changed, its health should be achieved, and the health of the individual is but an element in the health of the whole family.

Allied to the above misconception is the notion that family psychiatry is particularly applicable to the management of encephalonosis (psychosis in the old terminology). Leaving aside again the question of whether encephalonosis is a product of family psychopathology and even the value or otherwise of family group therapy in these conditions, it must be emphasised that there is no doubt that psychonosis (neurosis in the old terminology) frequently arises from family psychopathology and that it is the commonest condition dealt with in clinical practice. To limit family work to encephalonosis (psychosis) is to miss the opportunity to bring relief or cure to the commonest, most disabling, and yet most responsive condition in clinical practice—psychonosis (neurosis).

Another misconception is to assume that family psychiatry is more applicable in child psychiatry than in the psychiatry of any other age group. This, again, is the negation of family psychiatry. Perhaps children are associated with family care; but without adults there would be no family. All members of the family of any age group, child, adolescent, adult, aged, are elements of the family, with equal value. Thus family psychiatry replaces psychiatry of the individual—of any age group. Practitioners treating patients in all age groups are encouraged to embrace family psychiatry and shift the emphasis of their work from the individual, of any age group, to a total family approach.

When emphasis is given to the family in the children's field, practice rarely extends as far as family psychiatry. At its most limited, total emphasis is placed on the intrapsychical functioning of the child and little value given to environmental influences. Phantasies are thought to be more important than ongoing trauma. The child is regarded as sick in himself; parents require help or guidance in the management of a sick child. This is the classical, old-time child guidance or *child psychiatry*. Sometimes the involvement of the parents in the child's illness is perceived, but this perception is often limited by concentrating on the mother-child relationship alone—*child and mother psychiatry*. Less often, attention is given to the involvement of father and mother in the child's condition—*child and parents psychiatry*. An advance from this position sees the child as a part of a situation that includes siblings as well as parents. All these practices are, of course, individual psychiatry. The child is the focus and the patient.

A large conceptual jump is now required to reach family psychiatry. Here the family is the focus and the patient, and the presenting child is taken as an index of a sick family; thereafter he is given no more emphasis, but no less, than the rest of the family members and all the dimensions of the family. Even should attention be given to all the family members, they collectively make up only one dimension of the family. Family psychiatry is concerned with all the dimensions. The above practice is limited to an introduction to the family through a referred child. When all age groups can be referred, the full clinical service of *family psychiatry* is reached. (Occasionally a psychiatric service limits itself to one channel of referral, e.g., child or adult, while moving on to practice psychiatry based on the whole family and thus "child and family psychiatry" or "adult and family psychiatry" might be an adequate description of the service, but not of its philosophy.)

Again, family therapy can be confused with family psychiatry. Family therapy, treatment of the family, is but one part of family psychiatry, which is a broad approach calling, in addition, for new programmes of referral, appraisal of psychopathology, and procedures of investigation. To add to the confusion, the term "family therapy" is sometimes used in a limited way as if it were synonymous with family group therapy—a technique in psychotherapy whereby the whole family meets together for treatment. This technique, however, is but one part of a family therapy, family treatment, programme. It is better to utilise the term "family therapy" to cover that aspect of family psychiatry concerned with all treatment techniques and to utilise the term "family group therapy" for the therapy of the family as a group—a part only, as will be seen later, of family therapy.

Interest in the family sometimes extends only to a study of specific events in the family background of the patient which may be linked to his illness. Exploration unearths such events as divorce, "broken" homes, hospital admission, death of relatives, mobility of the family, etc. This is a very limited family approach. Family psychiatry cannot give significance to specific events in isolation from the whole family group dynamic process. Events unique to individuals can only be weighed against a particular family background; in one, divorce is a tragedy, in another, a great opportunity.

Some Advances in Theory

A new system gives an opportunity for rethinking much of the theoretical basis of psychiatry. Family psychiatry is a system for the practice of psychiatry, and the material produced by it could be handled on the framework of any of the existing schools of psychopathology. However, by its very nature, taking a different organism (the family instead of the individual) as its unit, it highlights some of the deficiencies of the existing schools. Since the pages ahead will catalogue some of the new insights that change present theory, some illustrations only will be given here.

Advances in psychopathology are striking—they point to the need to understand present family functioning in the light of events in the preceding families; to the importance, not of nuclear incidents in family events, but of long-protracted continuous influences; to the inability to explain and encompass extra-personal psychic influences by present theory and thus the requirement to extend theory to embrace general systems theory, communication theory and mechanistic considerations, naturally with proper caution; to the determination of symptom formation as the inevitable consequence of intra-family dynamics.

Given the understanding of long-protracted events, symptom formation, individual behaviour and family behaviour become clear as the consequences of these real events. *Interpretation* is no longer required—only the understanding of obvious events. Symbolism and phantasy interpretation are discarded. Events speak for themselves. The experience is all. Thus the psychopathology of choice is represented by experiential psychopathology. A brief formulation will be made in this volume, but a longer discussion will be found in a companion volume.

That experiential psychopathology adequately explains emotional illness, but fails to give an aetiological explanation for organic psychosis, gives new insight into the nosology of psychiatry (6). The division must be made between psychiatry proper, concerned with psychonosis, and neuropsychiatry, whose field is encephalonosis. The confusion of terminology and its consequences are discussed in Section III.

Later, attention will be drawn to the implications of the total family approach for the theory of child care. The traditional view that children, and young children in particular, are exclusively brought up by a mother in one unique, close, continuous relationship is shown by the data of the Ipswich Thousand Family Survey to be false. This view has always been challenged by everyday observation, but the entrenched views of experts die hard. The data now speak for themselves. A child is a group animal—from conception. He requires and normally receives the tender support and care of his whole group. He has a relationship to a number of people. He benefits, and this is essential to his safety, by one of the assets of group living—there is always a substitute for another person. Thankfully, he rarely receives just one unique relationship. The theory of one unique continuous mother-child relationship is obsolete. A child's relationships are discontinuous—mother now, father next, brother next, and even grandfathers give their contribution. He is the happy recipient of a galaxy of warm protective feelings. The theory of the irreplaceability of a continuous relationship is obsolete. The overriding importance given to mother is modified by the realization that she is, due to the cultural pattern, the foremost provider in a group of providers.

From the above spring insights of great practical importance. Is fathering different from mothering? There are clearly more likenesses than differences—so that one can substitute for the other. This is of great clinical value as it offers the opportunity for reorganising predominant care within the family—a major plank in the platform of vector therapy. Is natural parenting essentially different from care by an uncle or a grandmother? Clearly similarities outnumber differences. Thus again vector therapy makes substitution possible. Is natural parenting essentially different from foster parenting? Again there are more similarities than differences. So here we have another opportunity for vector therapy. Is damage done by the number of changes of relationship or by their poor quality? Clearly it is the latter, for a child is seen to benefit from a number of changes of good quality—his usual experience. Thus we learn not to avoid changes, but to pay attention to quality of relationships, a principle of value in vector therapy. And is separation of child from mother (or, why not, from father) always harmful, or is it deprivation that is the danger? Although a direct study in 1955 (7) exploded the cruel doctrine of "no separation," misconception still surrounds the separation hypothesis, and it is a sad fact that practice is still often based on it.

Vector psychiatry, with its emphasis on the identification and assessment of emotional or psychic forces or vectors, offers fruitful new opportunities for therapy, as will be seen later. Hitherto, attention was focused on intra-psychic vectors. These are not overlooked, as they make a continuous inter-action with extrapsychic vectors. Furthermore, in turn the intra-family vectors integrate with the extra-family vectors in society and make a pattern of adjustable forces extending from the person to society. Herein lie great new possibilities for treatment.

Practical Advantages of Family Psychiatry

Within families there are see-saw movements; as one member of a family becomes more secure another becomes less so. This is a continually fluctu-ating situation. For example, a father, aggressive and belligerent, leaves his family because of the marital friction induced by the mother protecting her children from his violence. Mother cannot tolerate the break and the hus-band returns. Father must now be placated by the wife, who fears another break. Father's violence to the children continues unabated and the children become physical and emotional wrecks. The transactional pattern of vectors has changed to the disadvantage of the children, but to the advantage of the adults.

Treatment of one member of the family is a deliberate intervention in the transactional pattern. For example, for the sake of one individual, a therapist applies psychotherapy to the anxious, work-shy son of a widow. After intensive therapy five days a week for two years the boy improves, but his mother becomes a permanent patient in a mental hospital because of chronic depression; the therapist has stumbled into the conflict between mother and son, sided with the son, upset the balance in the son's favour, and therapy ends as it began—with one sick and one healthy family member.

The traditional individual approach, then, is a blind, unknowing, insensi-tive interference with this transactional pattern. It may be constructive by good fortune, but usually it is nothing but a blundering, stumbling interven-tion—an elephant in a tea shop. Clearly, as an individual is but an integral part of a whole, the whole must be understood before attempting any change. This speaks for a total family approach.

An occurrence all too common in individual psychiatry is to find that the person who came from the family is the one least in need of help. Insight is highly correlated with disturbance; the less the insight the greater the disturbance, as a general rule. Thus when insightful members of the family seek help, giving attention to them alone leaves sicker members of the family unseen. All elements of the family are equal in their right to receive help. Indeed, to help one member alone brings little benefit in the long run; once the support of the therapist is withdrawn, the dynamics revert, and the individual takes up his old position. To see the whole family and to give equal weight to all its elements is to the advantage of the whole family.

When there is family turmoil, often it is one person who comes for help (mechanisms that explain his coming will be discussed later). Left behind are equally sick if not sicker family members. For example, a wife's frigidity is so marked that she seeks help. Her symptom arises from marital disharmony resulting in depression in the husband. Such is the tension in the household that one child fails at school and the other develops asthma. All four are reacting to one situation, but have a high chance of being dealt with separately. The gynaecologist will refer the wife to one psychiatrist; the family physician will send the husband to another; the children's physician will despatch the children to a child psychiatrist. Thus, three different services can be working independently and ineffectively to the solution of one basic situation. In all probability, the total situation will never emerge in any service. Such happenings are wasteful and uneconomical for, by and large, the information required to help one member of the family is precisely the information required to help another. For these considerations also a total family approach is to be advocated, for it is economic in its use of resources.

Treatment turns around empathy, understanding, and mutual confidence between therapist and the treated. But this can be sabotaged by the absent family members. To them, the therapist often appears to be allied to the family member under treatment, and thus opposed to the rest of the family. This becomes starkly clear if management of a marital problem is dealt with by seeing only one member of the partnership. Covert hostility towards the therapist develops in the unseen member. Conversely, a relationship with the whole family arouses collaboration and co-operation in treatment. Furthermore, to be denied the help of all the family members usually seriously limits the value of the diagnostic process. It is no less than astonishing how an account given by one family member has to be modified in the presence, or with the active participation, of the rest of the family. To be loyal and responsive to a group of individuals is no new experience to a therapist—this is the basis of his life experience in his own family.

If it is accepted that a sick person represents a sick family, it will be clear that if therapy assists the sick individual only, at the end of his treatment he will still be in a sickness-producing milieu. Usually, he reverts and the effort is wasted. Health and harmony in the whole family will of themselves be a guarantee of continuing good health for its members. Furthermore, they guarantee that its representatives going forth into the future have within them the empathy to contribute to the formation of healthy succeeding families. Families make families. Sick families tend to make sick families. Healthy families tend to make healthy families.

As frequently happens in new developments, new techniques emerge. Family psychiatry is no exception. Later it will be seen how new referral programmes became necessary, family group diagnosis came on the scene, new family projective procedures appeared, family group therapy evolved, and vector therapy transformed the therapeutic scene. These are but a few of the new techniques to be discussed later.

Lastly, family psychiatry has brought new opportunities for preventing emotional ill-health. As has been said, sick families make more sick families. We must break into the vicious circle. Healthy families now guarantee the healthy families of the future. But it can only be a slow process of evolution. Two main hopes are now open to us. Firstly, the family itself can be given an increasing measure of health and harmony through vector therapy —thus it will steadily add to the increasing harmony of society. But, secondly, society itself can be changed through the devices of the health-promoting society, the salutiferous society. The interaction of improving family and improving society will escalate over generations to a near ideal standard of emotional health.

Family psychiatry offers a new system of practice; experiential psychopathology gives a new understanding of psychopathology; vector psychiatry supplies new opportunities in therapy and prevention.

REFERENCES

1. CAESAR, J. *De Bello Gallico*. Translated by H. J. Edwards (1971). London: Heinemann.
2. Department of Health & Social Security (1973). Children in care in England and Wales 1972. London: H.M.S.O.
3. HOWELLS, J. G. (1963). *Family Psychiatry*. Edinburgh: Oliver & Boyd.
4. HOWELLS, J. G. (1968). *Theory and Practice of Family Psychiatry*. Edinburgh: Oliver & Boyd; New York: Brunner/Mazel.
5. HOWELLS, J. G. (1968). Family psychopathology and schizophrenia. In: Howells, J. G. (ed.) *Modern Perspectives in World Psychiatry*. Edinburgh: Oliver & Boyd; New York: Brunner/Mazel.
6. HOWELLS, J. G. (1971). Classification of psychiatric disorders. In: Howells, J. G. (ed.) *Modern Perspectives in Adolescent Psychiatry*. Edinburgh: Oliver & Boyd; New York: Brunner/Mazel.
7. HOWELLS, J. G., and LAYNG, J. (1955). Separation experiences and mental health. *Lancet, ii*, 285.
8. SITWELL, E. (1965). *Taken Care of: An Autobiography*. London: Hutchinson.

II

THE ANATOMY OF THE FAMILY

General Considerations

Definitions

The *Oxford English Dictionary* offers the following definitions of the family: (i) "The body of persons who live in one house or under one head, including parents, children, servants, etc."; (ii) "The group consisting of parents and their children, whether living together or not; in wider sense, all those who are nearly connected by blood or affinity"; (iii) "A person's children regarded collectively"; (iv) "Those descended or claiming descent from a common ancestor."

The first definition conforms most closely to modern ideas of the "nuclear family." The "nuclear family," sometimes termed the "elementary family," can be defined as a sub-system of the social system, consisting of two adults of different sexes who undertake a parenting role to one or more children. Hereafter, the "nuclear family" will be referred to as the "family." The "family of orientation" is often used to designate the nuclear family in which a person has, or has had, the status of a child, and the term "family of procreation," that in which a person has, or has had, the status of a parent. The limitations of these two terms in family clinical work will be referred to later; in clinical work it is necessary to contend with a chain of families and thus the terms preceding, present and succeeding families are more useful. When authority is based on a male as head of the family, we speak of a "patriarchy," and when on a female, of a "matriarchy."

The term "extended family" is used to refer to any grouping, related by descent, marriage or adoption, which is broader than the nuclear family and which conforms closely to the second definition of the *Oxford Dictionary*. "Lateral" extension of the family would embrace uncles, aunts, cousins, etc., while "vertical" extension of the family would embrace two or more generations.

23

A family exists for a particular purpose in the social context in which it finds itself, and is shaped by this fact. The unit may be a small or large nuclear family, a nuclear family extended laterally or vertically or both, an extended family large enough to merit the term "clan," or it may, rarely, melt into a community that regards itself as the effective unit.

In psychiatry, a blood tie is of secondary importance in a family to an emotional tie, e.g., a servant giving intimate care of the children may have more significance for them than the natural parents. Thus in clinical practice the concept of the family has to be widened to take account of this.

Universality

Murdock (6) expresses it as his view that the family is a basic group in all human cultures. He substantiates this by a study of 250 representative cultures in which he found no exception to his view. This confirms the conclusions of Lowie (4) in an earlier study.

Variants

Attempts to prove the historical development of the family through various forms to the present highly regarded nuclear family have failed. The form of the family is its response to its social background.

An extended family, sometimes termed a "joint" family, consists of two or more nuclear families. Among the Hindus, for example, may be found an extended family consisting of kinsmen over three or four generations and their wives and offspring. It constitutes a perpetual corporation owning property generation after generation, and not dissolving after the death of every husband. When descent is dependent on the female side of the family, it is termed matrilineal, when on the male, patrilineal. In some extended families, where many women may be present, the word meaning mother is used by the child to refer to other women around him as well. Thus, it is as if the child were brought up by many mothers—plural mother upbringing.

A polygamous family is dependent on plural marriage. There are two or more nuclear families having one married partner in common. In polygyny there is marriage of one man with more than one woman simultaneously. It may be due to economic factors, or as a means of ensuring an heir. By Koranic law, for example, a man may have four wives. The Mormons of Utah practised polygyny until 1890. In polyandry one woman is married simultaneously to more than one man. This is usually associated with matrilineal descent and matriarchy. When the co-husbands are brothers, it is known as Adelphic polyandry. Sometimes the family is informal, the woman being visited by a succession of men and dwelling alone with her children. Amongst the Nayar of Malabar, the women lived together in a joint family of several mothers and their children. Hobhouse, Wheeler and Ginsberg (2) found monogamy in 66 societies, polygamy in 409 societies (polygyny in 378 and polyandry in 31).

Murdock (5) states that of 192 societies studied, 47 (24%) normally have a nuclear family, 92 (48%) possess some form of extended family, and 53 (28%) have polygamous, but not extended, families. In developed societies the percentages may be quite different.

Many societies have had institutions founded to extend the family in time, to avoid its dissolution at the death of one of the spouses. Levirate is a practice by which a widow is inherited by her deceased husband's successor; it is found amongst ancient Hebrews and in parts of Africa. Sororate is a practice by which a wife is replaced by a sister if she dies or is barren. It is still practiced by some primitive people today.

Variants have their counterpart in modern society, close examination of which shows the diversity of family forms and that the nuclear family is not universal. The Ipswich Thousand Family Survey showed that in a typical town in the U.K. 87.96% live as nuclear families, 6.02% as extended families, and 6.02% as anomalous families. The commonest type of family was the nuclear family with two children. The anomalous group contained families of great interest and diversity: e.g., fathers alone nurturing children; mothers alone with children; mother together with grandmothers or grandfathers nurturing children; brothers and sisters bringing up younger siblings; two homosexuals bringing up children, etc. These modern variants are of great research interest and test many of the hypotheses concerning family functioning. Clinical practice tends to be based on an idealised concept of the family, an ideal often stemming from personal prejudice or personal experience of the clinical worker, and usually conforming to the model of the nuclear family. Atypical family formations are not necessarily unhealthy. The real issue is not the structure of the family, but whether the needs of the family are being met.

Functions

There is much agreement amongst authorities on the functions of the family, which are usually taken to be: (i) the satisfaction of the affectional needs of the family members; (ii) the satisfaction of sexual needs by reproduction; (iii) the protection, upbringing and socialisation of children; (iv) the material maintenance of the members of the family by forming an economic unit; (v) other, normally subsidiary, functions that may have a political, ritual, or religious connotation. The emphasis given to each function is not only a matter of variation amongst individual families, but is influenced also by class, community and cultural considerations. The family is a flexible unit.

That family members have affectional needs has become clearer as more study was given to personality. Hitherto it was given less prominence and is still excluded from some lists of family functions. Man does not live by bread alone. While his educational and social aspirations may be met elsewhere, his affectional needs are satisfied through his intimates, his fellow family members. Their responses make for harmony, or disharmony that may amount to emotional illness. His present experiences in his family of procreation are vital, but no less important is his past life in his family of orientation, the preceding family. And the two are linked.

The family permits satisfaction of sexual needs leading to the procreation of children. Such children are usually of legitimate status, their family affiliation being known, so that they can enjoy the advantages coming from this. In nearly all societies, sex within marriage is privileged and protected by taboos and permissions which vary greatly, but aim to foster the right sexual expression for that society. That sex is not the sole factor in marriage and family is suggested by the fact that sexual liaison is frequently allowed without the need for marriage; in Murdock's study (6) of 250 societies, only 54 forbade liaisons between non-relatives. Furthermore, sexual liaison is frequently allowed outside marriage; in the same study a majority of societies allowed liaison between a married man and his female relatives.

Children result from sexual experience and have to be reared by the family, which appears to offer the best milieu for their upbringing that can be devised in most, but not all, societies. It supplies the care of two adults— an insurance against the loss of one. The adults are of different sexes, thus allowing adjustment to both sexes. When the child is the product of a profound act of affectional co-operation, it is cherished as an expression of this and protected thereby. However, the family, while the commonest, is not the only unit for child rearing. Other methods are practised, e.g., communal or the semi-communal upbringing of the Kibbutz, and these could even be modified or changed in the future. The child has a number of requirements and as long as they are met, the method employed can fit the social system.

The family must provide material maintenance for its members—food, clothing, warmth, shelter, protection and recreation. The two adults are complementary—the wife in Western society is busy with the home and child care, while the husband labours to keep them. This model is being increasingly adjusted as more wives take up an occupation. Nuclear families, or a number of families linked by kinships, may form strong economic units that lead to mutual prosperity. As the parents support the children, so the children may support the aged parents later on. But nature is flexible. As long as the family is maintained, it may even allow reversal of work roles, or work by both.

Optimum Size of the Family

Little thought has been given to the question of what is the ideal size of the family to carry out its functions. Very large families break up into smaller groups. This may be because there is a limit to the capacity of an individual to pay constant attention to a number of emotional influences; an individual family member may be able to respond only to a few others in a given time. If so, research has yet to be definite about this. The smaller the family, the more concentrated the emotional influences from the small number of people involved. If these influences are beneficial, all is well. Should they be adverse, there is no escape. The larger the family, the more dilute the influences, but with the advantage that each individual has a far wider choice in his relationships, and is thus able to acquire those relationships which suit him best.

The child is in a group situation from the moment of birth, and benefits from this. Definite knowledge on the spacing of children might show what is a manageable load on the parents and to what extent older children can supplement the parental care of the younger children. Usually, a large number of young children is an economic strain on a family, while a large number of older children makes for a prosperous economic unit.

The Future of the Family

At first, study of the family tended to be an appraisal of its material and economic aspects. Poverty was a real problem. With its conquest, more attention was given to matters of child rearing and reproduction. More recently, the family as an affectional unit has become a focus for study. A number of researchers in industrial countries see a decline in family functioning, others see an improvement. Kluckhohn (3) represents the former view: ". . . the traditional philosophy of the family has been threatened in recent decades. Both in Europe and in the United States, the function of protection for the aged, the infirm, and the distressed is being taken over more and more by the state. Greatly increased geographical mobility, changed patterns in regard to employment of married women, and other economic developments make it possible to regard this long-established functional continuity as still a constant. Under modern urban conditions, both men and women can enjoy opportunities (which previously were easily accessible only in family life) without surrendering their independence or assuming family responsibilities."

On the other hand, Fletcher (1) maintains that in all true respects the family strength has been improved. He states that there is now a far more satisfactory and refined provision for the needs of the family than in the pre-industrial period or in early industrial Britain, when women were considered inferior, women and children were frequently exploited within or outside the family, and conditions in the home were deplorably inadequate. He goes on, "There is little doubt, then, that the essential functions of the family, centred upon sexual relationships, parenthood and homemaking, are far more satisfactory in modern standards than they were in the family of the distant or the recent past." He states that the position of the family has been strengthened in its non-essential functions, too; for instance, both parents, husband and wife, are now more responsible members of society than they ever were in the past.

Furthermore, the economic functions of the family have improved. Today expert advice is much more readily available to the family. The husband has security of tenure protected by his trade union or professional organisation. The child in the family has far more educational opportunities than ever before, more of his life is ordained by society as a whole, he is healthier and, if he is handicapped, has better care. Recreational opportunities are greater for the whole family.

Similarly, Parsons and Bales (7) have argued that despite divorce and related phenomena, Americans were marrying on an unprecedented scale. They have also been having children in increasing numbers, and they have been establishing homes for themselves, as family units, on a very large scale. This, they feel, would not seem to indicate irresponsibility.

Civilisations change their character with time, and modern society is no exception. Industrialisation has brought a decline in the importance of inherited wealth and, with it, social mobility as the class structure narrows. There is greater physical mobility with great waves of emigration and immigration. Women earn their own living. Knowledge explodes old superstitions and faiths, and new morals and ideals take their place.

It would be helpful if there were means of estimating by agreed signs of family disorder whether a family system was working well or not. Knowledge is lacking and some of the indices employed are patently unreliable. For instance, is a high divorce rate a sign of health or ill-health? Divorce figures are difficult to interpret. It occurs more frequently among the childless and in the early years of marriage. But marriage may be as much under strain in its later years, with the parents keeping together for the sake of

the children. Does this make for successful child rearing, or is it a danger
to it? Is not divorce an attempt to break up an unhealthy unit in order to
recreate healthy ones? Similarly, is a high birth rate a sign of family stability
or a sign of family disorganisation? Again, does physical mobility lead to
loss of support from the extended family, or is it a gain to be independent
from an extended family, should it be malevolent?

Families are resilient. The main functions of the family are so fundamental that, however social circumstances change, means are found to
carry them out. Young and Wilmott (8) give such an instance when they
describe the movement of families from a long-established community in
East London to a new estate outside. Child rearing in London was dependent on an extended family system, which made the maternal grandmother mother's principal aid in the care of the children. Outside London,
mother's principal aid became the previously neglected father. In either
event the children received care. Family resilience is highly correlated with
family emotional health; thus breakdown at acculturisation may be an index
of family ill-health rather than a product of the change.

REFERENCES

1. FLETCHER, R. (1962). *The Family and Marriage*. London: Penguin.
2. HOBHOUSE, WHEELER, and GINSBERG. Quoted by Kluckhohn, C. In: Bell, N. W.,
   and Vogel, E. F. (eds.) (1960) *The Family*. Glencoe, Ill.: The Free Press.
3. KLUCKHOHN, C. (1949). *The Family in a Democratic Society*. New York: Colum-
   bia Univ. Press.
4. LOWIE, R. N. (1920). *Primitive Society*. New York.
5. MURDOCK, G. P. (1949). *Social Structure*. New York: Macmillan.
6. MURDOCK, G. P. (1960). The universality of the nuclear family. In: Bell, N. W.,
   and Vogel, E. F. (eds.) *The Family*. Glencoe, Ill.: The Free Press.
7. PARSONS, T., and BALES, R. F. (1955). *Family: Socialization and Interaction Process*. Glencoe, Ill.: The Free Press.
8. YOUNG, M., and WILMOTT, P. (1957). *Family and Kinships in East London*. London: Macmillan.

Conceptualisation of the Family

Introduction

Humanity flows through time. It leaves the Past, reaches the Present, and runs on into the Future. This is a dynamic process of which we are a part, and which we perceive from within the process. The essential, basic unit for humanity is a small group, the family, in the time-space continuum. As times passes, this unit throws off fragments, individuals, who break off from the family to form new families; and these again pass on into time repeating the process.

These coalescing groups, the families, need description. Categorisation is essential so that an understandable portrayal can be communicated to others. A frame of reference is required which can take account of the separate parts of the family as well as the family as a whole.

The family is an everchanging, flowing, dynamic entity. To grasp change as it happens is usually beyond our conceptualisation. Therefore we freeze the family process at one moment in time, usually our first contact with the family, and describe what we see. We must be careful to add life to this static picture.

Life development is not smooth, nor is human development—hence pain, anguish and incompetence. For the clinician, description is more than a theoretical exercise. He needs a conceptual framework for sick families that will allow clinical assessments to be made, therapy to be planned, and the outcome to be predicted. Furthermore, a psychiatrist has to pay special attention to the psychic aspects of the family. It must be confessed that the psyche is a concept not easy to describe. Psychic phenomena are real enough. We cannot deny the existence and force of psychic events, even if we find it difficult to describe them. For the population at large the difficulty is even greater. They find it difficult to grasp the significance of psychic

30

matters. It may be due to the fact that such matters are inherently subtle, or just unfamiliar, or it may be that the failure to grasp, lack of insight, is a quality of a disturbed population.

An Analysis of Conceptual Models

Hill and Hansen (2), looking upon the family as sociologists, state, "Conceptual frameworks are elusive and abstract; indeed, some students have found them to be almost ephemeral." They go on to analyse many studies of conceptual models of the family, from which they identify five main conceptual frameworks:

1. *The interactional approach.* In this approach the family is a unit of interacting persons, each occupying a position within the family and having a number of assigned roles. It has focused on the internal aspects of the family, but neglected consideration of the family as an entity in relation to the community.

2. *The structure-function approach.* In this approach the family is viewed as a social system, one of the many components of the complete social system (society). At best, this approach studies the functions performed by the family in society. This framework, to date, has tended to emphasise the statics of structure and to neglect change and dynamics.

3. *The situational approach.* Situational analysis studies the situation itself, or the individual overt behaviour in response to the situation. Rather than emphasise interaction, like the interactionalists, situationalists turn to the study of the family as a social situation for behaviour. The family is seen as a unit of stimuli acting towards a focal point (e.g., a child).

4. *The institutional approach.* This is strongly allied with historical analysis. Institutionalists emphasise the family as a social unit, in which individual and cultural values are of central concern. This approach is concerned with broad sweeps of time, and not with individual acts, interacts or transacts.

5. *The developmental approach.* Family developmentalists view the family as an arena of interacting personalities, intricately organised internally into paired positions. The approach furnishes an opportunity for the accretion of generalisations about the internal development of families, from their formation in the engagement and wedding to their dissolution in divorce or death.

This study illustrates the difficulty and complexity of the task of conceptualisation. To be satisfactory, a framework must encompass essential elements from the five approaches.

Nosological Classifications

The dictates of clinical work have led to a number of clinicians attempting to work out classifications of family structure and functioning. Being based on clinical work, they are largely concerned with pathology. Their usual aim is to arrive at a family diagnosis, so that the pathology of the family can be described in meaningful terms. An account of some of these classifications may be found in a previous work (3).

A study of the requirements of the clinical situation, and experience, would suggest that a satisfactory conceptual framework must embrace the following:

1. The individual as an amalgam of the physical and psychic; his whole functioning in health and disease, at all times of life.

2. Reciprocal interactions in the family involving individuals, dyads, family coalitions, and the whole family.

3. The family as a small group with a structure and properties—roles, leadership patterns, qualities, standards, etc.

4. The family as a sub-system of society and endowed with social properties. The family is an entity in a field of forces in life space and thus there is a transactional process that includes all family elements, the extended family, community, culture and society.

5. The physical structure of the family.

6. The historical development of the family. Thus, the time sequence of Past, Present and Future.

7. The family as a unit of change—its dynamism, its flow, the process.

8. Family functioning and dysfunctioning, health and pathology.

9. Flexibility to allow for different sizes, states and conditions.

10. Practicality that allows the framework to be expanded for research and contracted for the dictates of day to day clinical work.

The categorising of healthy families into a small number of types is likely to be unfruitful. Such an approach has failed in the description of the personality of individuals. The variety of individuals is infinite. A more satisfactory approach is to take a known number of diameters—e.g., honest/dishonest, able to concentrate/inattentive, intelligent/dull, sociable/withdrawn, etc.—and describe the individual according to his known performance on many of these diameters. The results, due to the great variation in performance, do not allow of typology. No system is as yet completely acceptable, as there is disagreement about the selection of the diameters and some are still to be identified. A family is even more varied and complex than the individual and is also likely to elude categorisation into a small number of conventional types.

Haley (1) describes an experiment in typing and identifying normal families. The results were not encouraging. Parents and one child discussed a neutral subject for about two minutes, with the conversation ranging from amiable discussion to argument. Eighteen such two-minute segments were randomized on a tape recording. Four family research groups in the country were asked to listen to the tape recording and estimate for each segment which kind of family was conversing. Of the 40 experienced family workers tested, none guessed better than chance, even though as a group these people reported having treated over 2,000 families. One research group which did do better than chance was asked to take the test again, and did not succeed any better than the other groups on the second try. Several laymen were also asked to listen and make their guesses; they did slightly better than experienced family people but did not do better than chance.

Labelling sick families using the traditional terminology of psychiatry is also to be avoided. Labelling has the disadvantage of concentrating upon one element, which has come into focus by chance, and thus giving that element disproportionate attention. In individual psychiatry, for instance, such labels as anxiety neurosis, obsessional neurosis, depression, etc., have focused upon the presenting symptom in the individual, and this practice has led to a situation where the symptom itself is regarded as the illness, and scarce attention is given to the rest of the psychopathological processes within the individual. Such labels limit description. It is the whole pathological psychic *process* in individual, family and society which has to be understood and described and then re-patterned to bring health, efficiency and competence into the individual, family and social system.

It is suggested that the above ten requirements can be satisfied in a 15-dimensional approach to the family (3) and replace previous categorisation of the family. Five dimensions are each described at three consecutive time periods, the Past, the Present and the Future. The five are: the Dimension of the Individuals, the Dimension of Internal Communication, the Dimension of General Psychic Properties, the Dimension of External Communication, and the Dimension of Physical Properties.

The family, like the individual, is a psycho-somatic entity. Its psyche and soma are an indivisible whole. Therefore psychosomatiatria—the medicine of mind and body—applies to it, i.e., pananthropic medicine.

The family, like an individual, is a fragment of the cosmos with an endowment. This endowment is its physical and psychic apparatus. The apparatus has properties that can be developed to its potential. The developing agent is experience. Experience embraces all that happens, both physical and psychic. Experience in harmony with the apparatus releases its potential in a way that leads to good functioning. Experience in disharmony with the apparatus leads to dysfunction. Trained observers are able to pick out indicators of dysfunction, i.e., to diagnose.

In our present state of knowledge psychic phenomena are less easy to ascertain than physical. This causes confusion as to what phenomena are labelled psychic or physical. The differentiation is made here while accepting the close interaction between the two and the philosophical possibility that both sets of phenomena are basically the same.

Each of three organisms, Individual, Family, Society, has (i) somatic and (ii) psychic components. In the case of Family and Society there are collective somatic and psychic properties. Each organism has possessions. Each organism has elements. Each organism lives in a physical environment. Each organism has a communication pattern, internal and external, and this pattern has somatic and psychic components.

The above properties can be listed singly or in various combinations. If we consider the organism family, it has:

(1) General somatic properties.
(2) General psychic properties.
(3) Family possessions.
(4) A physical environment.
(5) A family communication pattern—(a) internal and (b) external. Somatic and psychic.
(6) Elements, i.e., a number of individuals. Somatic and psychic.

Therefore, in practice we can have five convenient dimensions involving:

(1) Physical: (a) somatic part [(1) above].
             (b) possessions [(3) above].
             (c) physical environment [(4) above].
(2) Internal communication pattern. Somatic and psychic [(5a) above].
(3) External communication pattern. Somatic and psychic [(5b) above].
(4) General psychic properties [(2) above].
(5) Individuals [(6) above].

As the physical past of the family is generally obvious and easily understood, it will be dealt with in one dimension. That part of the family which is largely psychic, however, needs fuller discussion and will be considered under four dimensions: the individuals; the internal transactions of forces; the external transaction of forces; general psychic characteristics. This is an arbitrary division of the largely psychic part. The division might have been done differently, and elements do not always fit tidily into place. However, this division has the merit of being based on function and is useful in clinical practice. It has all the merits and demerits of an arbitrary but useful division of the body into physiological systems.

It follows from the above that the family can be considered in five dimensions—four largely psychic (that of the individuals, that of internal communication, that of general psychic properties, that of external communication) and one to cover most of the physical part of the family. It is understood, of course, that both dimensions of communication have a somatic apparatus and that the dimension of individuals has a somatic component. However, we shall be largely concerned with the psychic aspects of these dimensions in family psychiatry.

The analysis of a simple three member family is taken for illustration.

1. The *Dimension of the Individuals* can be represented diagrammatically as follows:

Each individual's physical and psychic experience as a functioning and dysfunctioning social being is evaluated from conception through its intra-uterine experience to birth, infancy, childhood, adolescence, adulthood, old age and death. The reversed triangle emphasises the importance of the past in its influence on their psychic structure.

2. But the individual is not a motionless monument. He relates all the while to others within the family group. Father interacts with mother, mother with father, father with the child and the child with father, mother with the child and the child with the mother. Parts of the family interact with the individual and other parts. This, then, is a dynamic situation. Minute by minute, hour by hour, day by day, we have the cut and thrust

of daily living. The *Dimension of Internal Communication* covers this internal dynamic situation and is depicted in a simplified form as follows:

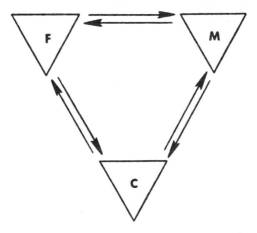

3. The family members form a small group and thus all that is true of small group dynamics will also be true of the family. The family will have characteristics common to all small groups and also special characteristics of its own. The *Dimension of General Psychic Properties* can be diagrammatically represented as follows:

G

4. This dynamic group of individuals in its material circumstances interacts with the community, and the community in turn interacts with the family. This interaction normally takes place at two levels, the level of the individual and the level of the group.

The individual reacts with the extended family outside, with friends, neighbours, workmates, schoolmates, chance acquaintances, and all these individuals in turn react on the individual in the family. But more than this, the group as a whole reacts with the social system as a whole. In the social system the family is expected to subject itself to the dictates of society. To the family, the social system is symbolised by the term "they"—"they" being the subtle, intangible community or public opinion. All the while, "they" formulate principles and precepts which are imposed upon the family. "They" convey what "they" feel about this or that issue through the mass media of communication, the press, wireless, television, etc. All the while, the family is under the scrutiny of "they" and feels impelled to conform to "their" standards.

The *Dimension of External Communication* can be represented by the following diagram:

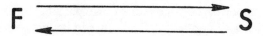

5. The family also has a physical structure. In addition to the collective somas of the individuals, it has possessions and a physical environment, e.g., it has a house of a certain size in a particular neighbourhood, with a garden, or otherwise; a diet of known quality and quantity; an income of a certain size; recreational facilities, etc. The *Dimension of Physical Properties* can be diagrammatically represented by:

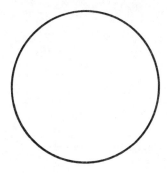

It is now possible to bring together the five dimensions:

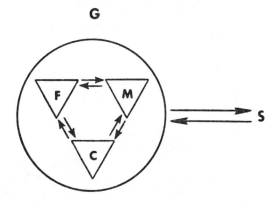

It is understood, of course, that in as diffuse and complex an organism as a family, there cannot be exact boundaries between dimensions, and the same applies to the individual and society.

Usually a family description starts with the Present in its five dimensions. To understand the Present in the light of what has gone on before then requires a description of the Past in five dimensions. The family's history starts at the moment of courtship of the parents. Ideally, it should be completed with a description of the Future in its five dimensions; a family dies when the last of the parents dies. In our present stage of knowledge the Future is only predictable within crude limits, e.g., that a university career is possible, a marriage breakdown likely, or financial difficulties a probability. The complete 15 dimensions can be represented as follows:

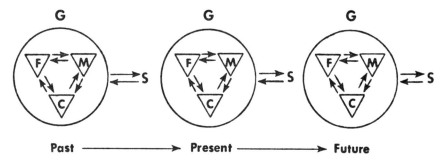

A family, like an individual, shows elements of health and sickness at the same time. To identify the healthy elements will be very important at the stage of treatment. Thus the family description must include details of health and pathology in its 15 dimensions.

Family description should thus be based upon 15 dimensions encompassing the dynamic flow through time as a healthy and pathological unit. Labels are avoided. The *process* is all important.

The Family as a System

The whole is more than the sum of its parts. The whole has properties attributable to it alone. A family group has some of the characteristics of a system—an organised whole or in a fuller definition, "a whole composed of parts in orderly arrangement according to some scheme or plan" (*Oxford English Dictionary*).

The attempt to relate our knowledge of simple mechanical systems to the understanding of living systems is a laudable one. But the family is of such complexity as not to be completely understandable with our present knowledge; the same would apply to other living systems such as individuals and societies. However, mathematical considerations are a real part of family evaluations. A family of three is a different entity from a family of four. Such obvious mathematical considerations cannot be denied. But, while some phenomena in the family can be evaluated in quantitative terms, other phenomena cannot; e.g., two families may differ from one another by having two children rather than one—the difference is quantitative. Two families with two children, however, may differ markedly from each other in that in one the second child is acceptable to the parents, while in the other the second child is rejected. The difference between these two families cannot be evaluated quantitatively—there is a qualitative difference.

Similarly some of the tenets of systems theory are valuable in certain respects, but greatly limited in others; e.g., in a completely mechanical system the responses of elements can be predicted, but in the family, its elements, the individuals, are so complex, discriminating, and capable of such a wide repertoire of actions, that their responses are not predictable. Again, the very openness of the family system allows of continuous change due to input and output. The "steady state" is so hypothetical as to be invalid in practical terms. Indeed the family expects to change as it grows and works towards its targets. Yet again, a family system has, almost always, areas of special relevance, so that purely mechanical and quantitative considerations cannot apply; e.g., not all family members may be equally disturbed, as some historical experience, perhaps to be born a boy when a girl was required by the family, has made for special vulnerability. Nevertheless, some analogies are valid between systems and families, and general systems theory should be encouraged to make its special contribution. But it is not to be assumed that the mere labelling of an old perplexity by a new term clarifies the problem; e.g., for man to be regarded as an example of "progressive individualisation" does not explain man.

General systems theory, in its quest for the principles of organisation common to all systems, is again to be applauded. In psychiatry it may have to take the form of a modified systems theory, to elucidate what is common between understood simple mechanical systems and the family. The value of this procedure is that we can start from the known. It will be a step in the proper aspiration of general systems theory to delineate the organisation of the whole cosmos.

The family has to respond at times as a whole. We know it functions and can function well. Thus it needs not only an organisation, but also an organising centre of control. In the individual this is found in his psyche. In the family it is found in its collective group psyche. The family has a mind. The family is a somato-psychic organism.

A major gain of the mechanistic approach to the family has been the awareness of the pattern of internal and external forces that besets the family. These forces are vectors. Defining, weighing, and utilising these forces can be termed vector psychiatry. The use of this knowledge for a specific purpose—therapy—is termed vector therapy.

Each dimension of the family will now be discussed in turn. The first four represent largely psychic aspects of the family and the fifth embraces the physical. The order for discussion is as follows:

(1) Dimension of the Individuals
(2) Dimension of Internal Communication
(3) Dimension of General Psychic Properties
(4) Dimension of External Communication
(5) Dimension of Physical Properties

These lead to a description of the "Diachronic Course of the Family."

REFERENCES

1. HALEY, J. (1972). Critical overview of present status of family interaction research. In: Framo, J. L. (ed.) *Family Interaction*, p. 27. Springer.
2. HILL, R., and HANSEN, D. A. (1960). The identification of conceptual frameworks utilized in family study. *Marriage and Family Living, 22,* 299.
3. HOWELLS, J. G. (1968). *Theory and Practice of Family Psychiatry*. Edinburgh: Oliver & Boyd; New York: Brunner/Mazel.

The First Dimension:
The Dimension of the Individuals

General

The individual is a psychic and somatic organism. Like the family he is a subject for pananthropic medicine, the medicine of the whole person. Individuals may be of any age group from infancy to the senium and of either sex. To give a complete description of the individual would merely cover ground already familiar to the reader. Thus only a brief summary is presented here.

The individual is born with an endowed organic fabric. This is supplemented when it acquires additional qualities from the environment. It is of great importance to distinguish between the endowed and acquired parts of the person, while at the same time emphasising that they are interrelated.

The endowment consists of a number of interrelated systems, each of which has an apparatus with inherent properties of a given capacity. All the systems together make up the total capacity of the person. The system most apposite to psychiatry is the central nervous system; this will later merit more coverage.

Experience acts on the endowment and produces a number of additional characteristics. It is useful to differentiate between properties dependent on endowment and characteristics dependent on experience. The possible acquired characteristics are largely, but not completely, the same for all individuals, but their quality and degree vary from person to person as experience is unique to each person.

The harmonious interaction of experience and endowment leads to optimum functioning and to signs of well-being. The disharmonious interaction of experience and endowment leads to signs of dysfunction or disorder. It is these indicators of disorder which the person may complain of (symptoms) or which are apparent to others (clinical signs).

41

The capacities or potentials of a system are not realised at the same age; maturation takes place at varied speed. The appreciation of hunger is present at birth; sexuality blossoms during adolescence. The capacity for abstract thought ripens at about the age of ten or so.

Many of the physical properties of an individual are determined by the genetic constitution, e.g., height, colour of eyes, intelligence. Some essentially genetically determined properties may still be influenced by the environment, physical and psychic, e.g., low height, by malnutrition. Even gender roles can be changed by environmental pressure; it has been demonstrated, for instance, that hermaphrodite children, proven cytologically to be male, can, under the dictation of parental pressure, behave as girls—even to the point of it being dangerous for any attempt to be made to enforce the biological sex. Acquired characteristics are determined almost completely by the environment, e.g., temperament, attitudes, interests, beliefs and emotional illness.

The total *aim* of the organism is laid down by the cosmic plan; to satisfy this is inevitable. A number of subsidiary aims are forced upon us, e.g., to reproduce, to respond to an infant, to eat, etc. These aims can be fulfilled by the apparatus with its given properties—within its given capacity. An aim is essential to an apparatus, otherwise it will not be used. However, capacity sets a limit on the achievement of the aim, e.g., a man can run but not fly. The stage reached is determined by the capacity of a particular apparatus, together with the effect of experience.

Many motivations are general and shared by all, but ultimately the individual develops personal targets. For example, while all people like to be secure, this security is achieved by people through different ends—by the accumulation of money, by academic success, by subordinating oneself to the will of others, etc.

Many factors arising from experience will affect achievement of aims— may exaggerate, minimise, or distort them.

A conflict can arise between two aims, e.g., to have a baby or to look after a sick husband, and from this can arise trauma to the self or others.

Perhaps the ultimate aim of an organism is to function harmoniously in all its systems, to work towards its aims to the limit of its capacities and thus to fulfil the cosmic plan to its optimum. When this is achieved, the organism is healthy, functioning harmoniously and efficiently, satisfying its aims within its capacities and aware of all the feeling tones of this achievement—happy, joyful, secure and self-assured.

It is not relevant here to give a detailed account of the whole of a person's endowment; but it is worthwhile to dwell at greater length on the central nervous system, which is linked so closely with psychic functioning.

The Endowed Brain and Nervous System

The brain could well be called the "servant of the psyche."

Linked to the brain are the central nervous system, the autonomic nervous system and the endocrine system, and these in turn are linked to all other body systems. Thus, psychic influences through the brain and its linked systems can affect any part of the body. Rarely does psychic functioning or dysfunctioning fail to do this.

The cerebrum, with its associated nervous system, is a major system of the soma, with an elaborate apparatus, some general properties, a capacity, an aim and a "feeling tone" or mood. It is subdivided into a number of local areas, each with its apparatus, properties and capacity; in addition, some areas are associated with a feeling tone or mood.

Some of the major subdivisions serve certain main properties, such as sensation, perception, memory, thought, imagination, motor expression, vocalisation. Intelligence is a measure of the capacity of the thought apparatus. Other areas are associated with special properties, such as sleep, hunger, musical appreciation, estimation of depth, self-image, pain; and some with a feeling tone, such as sexuality, anger, laughter, elation, depression. The divisions or centres can be co-ordinated to function together as a whole or part.

The psyche is dependent on the efficient working of the brain. The brain supplies machinery for the reception of meaning from others and also for the expression of meaning to others. The mechanisms of communication will shortly be described. The sensations through one of the five senses, or an amalgam of senses, pass to the perceptual interpretative apparatus of the brain. Recent work suggests that subliminal perception is an additional property and does not exclude the possibility of extra-sensory perception also. At the perceptual areas, presumably by consulting previous experience located in the memory, meaning is given to sensations and they become percepts. These pass to the thought apparatus; consultation with the memory can continue. Furthermore, it is possible to formulate creative and original material from the basic material supplied by perception and memory, hence the term imaginative thought (internal experience). It is here that interpretation is of the highest complexity—previous memories are consulted, appropriate selection made, a matching and checking on previous experience, i.e., introspection, imaginative thought, creative formation, decision-making and apposite emotions are matched to ideas. The raw material of perception, or the original material of imaginative thought, may now need transmission to others. It passes out through the motor areas and motor nerves of the brain. Meanings are most elaborately and quickly communicated through the voice and auditory apparatus. But non-verbal communication, of course, is also highly developed and capable of subtle expression. This complex machinery of thought can be interrupted and disorganised by such clinical conditions as acute intoxication and, probably, by encephalo-ataxia (schizophrenia).

There is proof of the existence of an autonomic system that controls a number of somatic activities in an automatic fashion, e.g., temperature and sleep. To have such an apparatus is clearly of great value, as repetitive basic functions can proceed without continual attention. It would seem that, equally, many of the higher functions of the brain can operate *automatically* or without attention. Responses of a complex character can be automatic, e.g., a typist working at high speed can type automatically without even being aware of the content of the words. At any moment attention can take over and the automatic activity ceases, calling for much greater effort of concentration. Such automatic responses are clearly of great value. They have often in the past been termed "unconscious"—better to use functional terms such as "automatic." When the functions of the higher brain stem are in operation, awareness is possible and the individual can give attention to whatever interests him. Awareness, it is clear, is a function of the higher brain stem, and not of the cerebral cortex. This complex apparatus needs rest, and so awareness disappears with sleep, natural or artificial. Given "awareness," activities are either (i) autonomic or (ii) controlled. As has been said, these terms are preferred to such terms as "unconscious" and "conscious." Attention demands the ability to concentrate on one element of sensation, and therefore, one must be able to inhibit or block the remainder.

While this complex machinery of the brain is essential for reception and transmission of psychic activity, it does not of itself encompass that activity. The "higher" capacities of imagination and motivation appear to transcend the functions of local areas as we now understand them. While we do not dare to claim the final elucidation of the nature of psychic activity, it is not unreasonable to regard it as the more refined, subtle, and ultimate expression of activity in the total cerebral apparatus. Such a view, of course, leads to an organic view of the psyche, but nevertheless one of such subtlety in comparison with the well-understood cerebral activity associated with obvious properties, as to amount to a qualitative difference, such as would be accepted in comparing a crude noise with a concerto.

This complex cerebral system either controls or is linked with all other body systems. It is easy, therefore, to accept the physical concomitants of psychic activity—the physical well-being associated with harmonious psychic functioning and the physical trauma produced by disharmonious psychic functioning. On the harmonious side, we can appreciate the rapid pleasurable physical reaction produced by the sight of a loved partner, the relaxed sleep of the secure, the laughter of the merry, and the elation of success. On the disharmonious side, we can understand the blush of shame, the stoop of guilt, the lined face of anxiety, the loss of tone in depression; some of these are accentuated to asthma, gastric ulceration, migraine and many life-threatening disabilities. It is also possible to understand how psychic activity can "charm" warts, bring a swelling to a ring finger when infidelity is mentioned, and influence sensation, temperature or activity in one small part of the soma.

Lastly, the apparatus has a feeling tone or *mood*. There is a capacity for self-awareness—a built-in "governor" that gauges the function of the organism. This is the most elusive part of the organism. Somatic activity, it seems, evaluates somatic activity. We are aware of its work in feeling tones or moods—pleasurable, e.g., a pleasurable response to a child, or painful, e.g., anguish. It is the counterpart of physical well-being or of pain. We are more aware of painful than pleasurable moods. The former indicate disharmony; there is fear of consequences and thus a need to be mindful of maintaining harmony in the organism. Similarly, a motorist soon forgets and takes for granted the hum of his well-functioning engine, but a sudden backfire immediately causes alarm and the desire to find and eliminate the dysfunction. A mood is non-verbal and more primitive than thought. It is a non-verbal internal communication of awareness of cerebral activity.

Some of the moods apply to the organism as a whole and are an indication of the working of the whole psyche and its whole cerebral apparatus; e.g., faced by the possibility of stress, there is an anticipation of trauma by the organism—it may be attacked, and this is reflected in the mood of "anxiety." The loss of a loved person gives rise to a feeling tone termed "grieving." If the "idea of self" is weakened, there is a feeling tone of "unworthiness." Should the "idea of self" feel that it is to be blamed, there is a feeling tone of "guilt."

Some moods are more localized and attached to a system and realisation of its aims, e.g., the pleasurable feeling tone of responding to a child—the parental feeling; satisfaction at sexual intercourse—sexual feeling; laughter, etc. The centres do not control the mood, but the mood uses the correct centre or centres. Sometimes these centres may function inappropriately, e.g., cerebral injury may cause uncontrollable laughter when the person experiences no such humorous mood, or a mood can be provoked by the stimulus of an electrode. Sometimes the response involves a number of centres working together—many permutations of possible feelings are involved. Thus there may be great complexity and subtlety of mood, e.g., the pathos of a clown. A massive stimulus can exhaust the mood centres, e.g., there is usually a limit to a burst of laughter. Moods are antipathetic, e.g., joy and grief; love and hate; security and anxiety; sexual attraction and sexual revulsion; guilt and innocence, etc. Moods are also graded; there can be degrees of each. They are very responsive to the mood of others and so alert and warn the self.

Moods can be influenced by thought, or be controlled by it at times. One may experience the mood of sleepiness, give way to its dictates, or overrule it and so remain awake. Moods can be influenced by experience. Some families make their members angry, or submissive, or anxious, or volatile. Again, children often use the crying centre, but adults are expected to keep "a stiff upper lip." The property and its apparatus are endowed, but experience influences the use of capacity.

Moods can be employed as a part of the coping mechanisms. Anger stimulates anger and there is a rapid, primitive, overwhelming reaction. This has the value of speed and strength, but the drawback of being ill-directed or inappropriate. Thus, except in dire circumstances, it is best used at the behest of thought.

In speech, moods may be linked to "emotive" words that by common usage have come to bear special representation of mood. Words can be patterned in an emotive way in poetry or prose and convey more mood than is strictly covered by the words themselves. Similarly, mood can be conveyed in art.

Acquired Characteristics

From conception onwards, the environment interacts with the endowment of the individual. His properties begin to develop and grow to the limit of their capacity and are governed by their endowed rate of maturation. The family is the environment overwhelmingly most important as the platform of experience.

Of the characteristics acquired by the person, none is more important than *attitudes*. An attitude is the assumption of an opinion in relation to an object or thought. Attitudes dictate the quality of the communication to others and in turn the response to the communication of others. Some attitudes are so strongly held as to be termed *beliefs*. Some are concerned with ethical matters and are termed *values*. Some convey the aspirations, ambitions, targets, *aims* of the person. Attitudes may be more centred in particular areas than others and are thus termed *interests*.

The quality of a person's collective values is termed his *character,* e.g., religious, kindly, etc. Those values that dictate and control final action are collectively termed his *conscience*. *Temperament* denotes a person's predominant moods, e.g., anxious, melancholic, etc.

Knowledge is acquired through ability, utilising opportunities presented to the individual by the techniques of learning and, in the widest sense, through experience. Knowledge is formal, taught by the didactic agencies; experience is acquired in the process of living. The latter is of much greater depth and significance than the former; it embraces all that goes on between the individual and his material and emotional surroundings. In time we shall know a great deal more about "experience." Akin to acquiring knowledge is the acquisition of *skills*.

Development of the Individual

Each individual passes through a number of epochs in his course from conception to death. It must be stressed that these are not necessarily discordant or stressful. Mishaps, dysfunction, misfortune are matters that call for help and thus come to attention. A whole epoch, such as adolescence, for instance, may come to be regarded as inevitably stressful, when a careful examination of all adolescents reveals that most pass happily and comparatively uneventfully from childhood to adulthood.

The physical frame begins to develop with conception and reaches full form but not full size by birth. At this moment the body is nine months old and already has experienced the intra-uterine environment with its vicissitudes—physical and psychic. Recent work suggests that the foetus may be influenced by physical and emotional factors in utero—and at times will be in hazard thereby. The field has been extensively reviewed by Montagu (1) and by Stott (4). That emotional changes in the mother may be significant for the state of the infant is suggested by the work of Sontag (2), who found that maternal emotion, or fatigue, produces a marked effect on foetal activity, and that very active foeti tend to be light in weight and to show a minimum of fat storage. Some experimental work by Spelt (3) suggests that an infant in utero can be conditioned to vibration; thus it may possibly be conditioned as well to other stimuli from within and without the mother.

Infancy follows life in utero, a stage that must be for most an uneventful passage from inside the mother into the open life of the family· again it should be mentioned that the foetus has truly been a family member from conception though carried by its mother. And, of course, an infant is nine months old at birth. That the child is nurtured by the whole family is a fact of such importance as to deserve extra discussion. This will be found in a chapter entitled "Families Nurture Children" in the section on "Special Aspects of Family Psychiatry." Once outside the mother, if not before, life experience predominantly in the family begins to exert a powerful influence on the individual. Infancy is a time of dependency, breast-feeding, and toilet training.

Infancy passes to childhood, with its developing vocalisation, locomotion and play, and on to the child of school age as education begins. It is not useful to use psychoanalytical terms such as latency, which are based upon fancied stages of sexual development. Childhood ends with the physiological signs of puberty, earlier in girls than in boys.

Early adolescence, from about 12 to 15, with its menstruation and increasing peer friendships, can probably be separated from the late adolescence of 15 to 18 insomuch as each stage has a different set of predominant interests. Sexuality becomes prominent in adolescence and passes from an interest in the self to shifting relationships for the opposite sex to a largely steady interest in one member of the opposite sex.

Adolescence gives way to young adulthood with courtships, marriage, pregnancy, parenthood and an expanding family. Middle adulthood brings an established career; grown-up children, often with children of their own; the menopause; and, as the family contracts, a return to the original marital partnership. At this time can come a reassessment of the marriage and, for the woman, a desire for an occupation outside the home. Late adulthood is the time for retirement, declining powers, dependency, bereavement and death.

Each epoch may bring its discordance between experience and the developing person. The stresses fall conveniently into two groups: (i) those that can arise at any time, e.g., death of a spouse, loss of employment, injury, etc.; and (ii) those especially associated with a particular epoch, e.g., special stresses of childbirth arising from an unwanted pregnancy, spouse jealousy, sibling rivalry, etc. But of course the epoch may be uneventful.

The time from conception to early adulthood is spent in the Preceding Parent Family. Thereafter, the time is spent in the Presenting Family, as will be discussed later.

Male and Female

Curiously, much attention is given to the dissimilarities between the sexes, but little attention to the far more numerous similarities. Even in physique there are many more similarities than there are differences. Again, qualities like mothering and fathering have far more likenesses than differences. However, some differences are established, e.g., more males are conceived than females; males have a higher death rate in early life; males are physically stronger; females display the menstrual cycle; females carry the foetus; females can feed the infant on the breast. In some societies, the male is the main breadwinner and the female the homeminder, but there is great cultural variation and even reversal of roles; each sex tends to have different job preferences, but this is far from absolute. Although there are exceptions, men tend to excel in the arts and in the sciences; some social interests, hobbies, and activities tend to be dissimilar, but many are shared.

Clinical Implications

The individual, family, and society are all phenomena of equal importance. Family psychiatry does not suggest that the individual is unimportant, but merely emphasises that the neglected family and society are equally important. The individual may be the first family element to come to attention. The individual deserves help in his own right. There is need for careful assessment of the individual and for improved precision in this. He has his own unique features, rights, and obligations. He is not, however, the best unit for clinical work. The family has much more merit, for reasons already given.

REFERENCES

1. MONTAGU, M. F. ASHLEY (1962). *Pre-Natal Influences.* Springfield, Ill.: Charles C Thomas.
2. SONTAG, L. W. (1941). The significance of foetal environmental differences. *Amer. J. Obstet. Gynec. 42,* 996.
3. SPELT, D. K. (1948). The conditioning of the human foetus in utero. *J. exp. Psychol., 38,* 338. In: Howells, J. G. (ed.) *Theory and Practice of Family Psychiatry.* Edinburgh: Oliver & Boyd; New York: Brunner/Mazel.
4. STOTT, D. H. (1969). The child's hazards in utero. In: Howells, J. G. (ed.) *Modern Perspectives in International Child Psychiatry.* Edinburgh: Oliver & Boyd; New York: Brunner/Mazel.

The Second Dimension:
The Dimension of
Internal Communication

Introduction

From his earliest beginning Man was made aware of the hazards of his physical surroundings—a fall could hurt, a snake could bite, a whirlpool could drown him. Therefore, it was natural that he should band together with others to manage his surroundings with greater safety and effectiveness. But here came another revelation—this interaction with other humans was hazardous also. Even today we have yet to reach a level of harmony that can make every interaction painless. Psychic interactions, then, can bring satisfaction or disappointment, pain or suffering, security or danger. The world of the emotions can be as treacherous and destructive as the physical world. Man has hardly begun to make his psychic environment safe.

Psychic trauma comes from psychic sources—other human beings. Man is at his most vulnerable in his formative years, his first 15 years or so, and this is precisely the time he spends mostly in his family. The family is the milieu that bears most directly on him for a continuous period while his personality is being formed. His family is the crucible wherein he and his family to come are forged. Hence the importance of the family. A man will interact with more than his family, but his family interactions will usually be overwhelmingly the most meaningful to him.

The interaction between persons has not received the same degree of attention from psychopathologists as have the intra-personal processes of the individual. Thus it deserves longer consideration here.

Interaction includes consideration of two linked entities, communication and relationship.

Communication, in the psychic field, is concerned with the process of connection between persons. Communication includes (i) the somatic means for the passage of information, i.e., the process of communication,

50

and (ii) the meaning or message passed between persons. Thus, in communication we study what is passed and how it is passed.

Relationship is the standing of one person to another. In psychological and psychiatric work, special attention is given to the kind of feeling between people; a qualitative judgment is involved, e.g., hostile, dependent, etc.

The interaction starts and ends with the persons involved having standing to one another, i.e., a relationship. Persons start with standing to one another, a meaning to be passed is formulated, the meaning is passed through the process of conveyance, the meaning is received, the standing between the persons is altered. Thus three elements are involved, the standing (relationship), the meaning (message), and the process of conveyance.

The above is true of the simple interaction between two people. In the family, however, the communications usually involve a number of people and the term "transaction" is more appropriate. Transaction implies a web or pattern of interactions, a field of forces, a polydynamic system. Thus, discussion will embrace a consideration of communication, of relationship, and of the family as a polydynamic system.

While the standing between individuals and the meanings conveyed between them have received some attention from psychopathologists (although less so than the intrapsychic life of the individual), less attention has been given to the process of conveying meaning between people. Also, there has been even less interest in non-verbal, as against verbal, communication. What follows is an attempt to redress the balance.

Communication

Communication denotes conveyance between people. It includes consideration of the meaning, message, or information that is conveyed and the process of conveyance, the apparatus, the channels. It applies in a conveyance between one person and another, e.g., husband and wife, or between one person and group, e.g., husband and part of his family. What is said here is also relevant to the consideration of external family communication.

The purpose of communication is to influence others, to react to the present situation, to gain security by mutual support, to receive from others all those elements essential to maturation, existence and security.

Meaning

Communication is concerned with the emission, transmission and admission of meaning. The meaning conveyed may arise directly from the sender, or he may be the means for indirect communication from others; e.g., father's views of a child may be conveyed to the child through the mother. In addition to a message, instructions for its interpretation are conveyed; the part of communication that deals with interpretation is termed meta-communication.

The cues, signs and messages conveyed from one individual to the other may be simple, e.g., a smack to a child, or complex, e.g., the tearful acceptance of good news. They are sometimes difficult to discern; a slight intonation of voice can, by cultural habit, convey to another person feelings of interest, affection, or empathy. There may be reason to suppose that in infancy relationships are more likely to be conveyed by simple cues, involving one of the basic senses. It is possible that the mere physical handling of the child by a parent can, over a period of time, begin to have special meanings to the infant; we infer that this is so from the case of a child "playing up" when the mother wishes to go out in the evening—even though the mother appears to have gone through the usual repertoire of movements, the child has picked up mother's anxiety. In the course of the child's development, the cues, or meanings, understood by him become more complex or subtle.

Signs are representations. A symbol, e.g., a word, allows conceptualisation by representing an entity. Semeiotics, the science of signs, concerns itself with events in their function as symbols. Within it there are three fields: (i) syntactics, which is concerned with the relationships of symbols to other symbols; (ii) semantics, which deals with the relations of signs to the events or objects they purport to designate; and (iii) pragmatics, which is the science of the relation of signs to their human interpreters. The pragmatic aspects of language interest the psychiatrist most.

Language is but one channel of communication by the use of words, but it is the primary one in human communication. Linguistics studies phonology, which describes the sounds made when people talk; morphology, which describes the grouping of these sounds into syllables; and syntax, the description of the organisation of words and syllables into utterances. None of these fields are concerned with meaning in language, which is the field of semantics.

Signs, symbols, words, messages, often have an added meaning. An intonation may suggest irony, sarcasm, or cynicism. The intensity of the communication may give added meaning—a whisper may denote secrecy; a shout, alarm. The timing of messages in communication may give added meaning, as may the sequences of messages. Emotion may add meaning to a message and give it a special significance. Words and actions may have a meaning given to them by the total situation—e.g., silence, the absence of verbalisation, may be very meaningful in some contexts. Similarly, a social situation imposes meanings—the role of the individual, the rules of the situation, and what is expected—e.g., in one context a smack of a certain magnitude on a child's bottom may be a sign of the greatest hurt and humiliation, in another a smack of the same magnitude is a sign of play.

Messages may be distorted by the sender, or by the receiver, or by the process of transmission. Expectations, wishful thinking, prejudices, play their part in distortion at either end. The recipient tends to give to the words of others the same meaning which they have for him.

The flow of meaning between one person and another may be security-producing, positive, beneficial, constructive; or it may be insecurity-producing, negative, hurtful, threatening and destructive. Meanings passing between individuals have infinite capacity to help or hurt, to produce health or sickness. They have special force when emanating from persons of particular significance to the individual—those persons in his immediate family circle, and those around him in his formative years. The essential matter is the meaning given to the signs in terms of the security and self-respect of the recipient. In the past, excessive attention has been given to the intrapsychic events set in motion by the admission of meanings at a single moment in time (the nuclear incident). It has been overlooked that communication is often a continuous process, e.g., communication between parent and child. More important than being beaten by a father on a particular day is the fact that one has to live every day with the sort of father given to beating. Modification of the stressful meanings can resolve situations and bring relief. Resolution is attempted in psychotherapy, when a counteracting relationship is brought into the situation. It is also an aspect of vector therapy, which changes the original stressful meaning by changing its character, its direction, the time over which it operates, or its strength.

Process of communication

The process of communication involves emission, transmission and admission. In sequence there is a stimulus, sensation, percept, memory, thought, motor expression and feedback (which allows opportunity for correction and clarification). Many elements are employed—physical, nervous, hormonal and chemical; one form may change into another, e.g., physical sound into the chemistry of a neurone. Proprioception is concerned with stimuli arising within the individual or the group; enteroception, with stimuli arising outside the indivdual or the group.

We may expect that meaning be conveyed through the five senses (auditory, visual, olfactory, tactile and gustatory), or through extra senses not yet identified, or through the combination of a number of senses.

Hearing and articulation permit the use of sounds which can be used as symbols to conceptualise meaning. Of sound, words are frequently used and have generally accepted meanings—allowing of subtle, sophisticated expression of meaning unique to man. Semantics is concerned with the study of such meanings in language. Sounds may have meaning without word formation, and some may have an intense, primitive, biological appeal, e.g., a cry of pain.

Visual sense and manual skill allow of pictorial representation of meaning in writing, drawing, painting, modelling, carving, etc. Words can be articulated and expressed pictorially in writing. This is especially valuable when meaning needs to be conveyed to someone not present. Intense meaning can be conveyed from a distance, e.g., a guilt-inducing letter from parent to child.

Touch is probably next in importance in human communication and has tended to be undervalued. It is employed in the expression of intense meaning, e.g., the parent's handling of a child, belligerence between persons, sexual expression between couples, and the expression of love through a kiss, handholding and fondling. Tactile sensation is an amalgam of the sensation of touch, temperature, pressure and vibration.

The olfactory sense is not usually well developed in humans. It finds its greatest usefulness in the selection and tasting of food. It offers pleasure, as in the smell of a rose, or repugnance, as in the fumes of an unventilated room. It can reach great emotional intensity, e.g., the perfume of the beloved. Man has learned to employ animals with a better developed olfactory sense, e.g., police dogs in detection.

Taste is the least developed sense in the human, but it plays a major part in the intake and choice of food.

A great deal may be conveyed even by the use of one sense, such as touch. Critchley (3) relates that the old time post office telegraphists continually using Morse code could, at the same time, convey personal characteristics at great distance to the receiving telegraphist. But each sense has its limitations.

That meaning is often conveyed through an amalgam of perceptual stimuli is suggested by some work on such a simple creature as the mouse. Barnet (2), having surveyed the evidence to show that a handled mouse withstood stress better than unhandled controls, reports, "At first some emphasis was laid, at least by implication, on the need to stroke the stimulated animal, but recently the emphasis has been put more on the mere fact of handling." The human, even more than the animal, has complex, sophisticated meanings to convey. Thus, he usually employs an amalgam of senses, sometimes all at great intensity.

In early infancy, touch, sound and taste play a pre-eminent part. Smell may also be operative, but to assess the part it plays is difficult. At one time disproportionate importance was given to the feeding experience in children, and to the breast as the point of communication. It is being realised that the whole waking experience, coinciding with the feeding experience, is of more significance. Vision comes later and drawing and writing become possible with increasing manual dexterity. The child, like primitive man, makes much use of direct manual expression in drawing. With the advent of abstract ideas, increasing use has to be made of combinations of senses to express their complexity and subtlety.

Much of human communication is verbal, but in recent times increasing study is being devoted to non-verbal communication. Non-verbal communication has been the subject of comment by Ruesch (10). Broadly speaking, he divides non-verbal forms of communication into three distinct categories:

1. Sign language, which includes all those forms of codification in which words, numbers and punctuation signs have been supplanted by gestures; these vary from the simple gesture of the hitch-hiker to such complete systems as the language of the deaf.

2. Action language, which embraces all movements not used exclusively as signals, e.g., acts such as walking and drinking. For these not only serve personal needs, but they also constitute statements to those who perceive them.

3. Object language, which comprises all intentional and non-intentional displays of material things, e.g., machines, architecture, art objects, the human body. These objects not only have material substance, but also an object language.

Meanings are continually conveyed between people, but some of them may not be consciously perceived by the participants, if recent work on subliminal perception is correct. This supposition may be of great significance to communication theory, psychotherapy and social psychiatry.

More knowledge is required about the capacity of the individual for communication; there must be limits. A person subject to hurt for long enough ceases to cry as the point of exhaustion is reached. It may explain spontaneous recovery from, for example, depression, when the centre for its expression becomes exhausted.

Study must pay increasing attention to the time factor in communication. Possibly, rarely, an overwhelming stress acting over a short period of time may have permanent ill effects—the nuclear incident so significant in outmoded psychotherapy. Trauma acting over long periods of time may be a commoner situation and have more permanent ill effects.

In acute and chronic psychosis, temporary or permanent interruption of brain functioning by physical agents plays havoc with communication. In encephalo-ataxia (schizophrenia) there may be similar central, intracerebral, interruption of communication, and not extra-cerebral, as is suggested by some psychopathologists.

Relationship

The standing of one person to another, continually altering due to communication, can be described on various parameters—the position in space, in terms of age, in gender role, in economic terms, in physical characteristics, in educational terms, in ethical terms, etc. In psychology and psychiatry, the concern is to describe the standing between them in emotional terms—hence, terms such as anxious, dependent, dominating, clinging, overprotective, aggressive, timid, sensitive, encouraging, possessive, guilty, hostile, disliking, ignoring, tolerant, fearful, jealous, affectionate, sulky, irritable, refusing, rebuking, demanding, threatening, punishing, interested, depriving, secretive, rejecting, etc.

Thus a number of terms are commonly employed to outline the standing of one person to another. Some variables may, psychologically, be more fundamental than others, e.g., those that indicate security or insecurity, love or hatred. Sometimes there is a dichotomy into those indicating a positive attitude and those indicating a negative one—an individual can be positive on one parameter, but negative on another. Until there is greater knowledge about the essential qualities and their rank order in a relationship, the assessments of relationships will be inadequate and thus there will be small agreement among authorities. This area must be of prime concern for psychopathologists wishing to advance in an orderly and objective fashion.

In the meantime, a number of schedules have been devised to assess and describe relationships and some of these will be mentioned in the section on "Family Diagnosis." It will be necessary to take into account the entities common to the many roles that an individual can simultaneously play, e.g., as a person, as a husband, as a male, as a politician, etc. It is urgent to bring precision into this field, because the link between one person and another carries those essential elements of meaning that make for emotional health or sickness. Precision here is as important as in the description of intrapsychic events. Equal weight may be given to intra- and extrapsychic events; the second have suffered comparative neglect.

A complete description of a relationship includes (i) a description of each individual involved in the relationship, e.g., an element might be "not normally aggressive"; (ii) a description of the standing of one person to another at that time, e.g., an element might be "highly aggressive to Mr. X."; (iii) a description of the effects of the relationship on each person involved in it, e.g., an element might be "great anxiety produced in Mr. X." An analysis of the second and third descriptions will clearly show the "meanings" conveyed between two people in that situation.

In a verbal interaction:

1. One can make a statement to convey benevolent ideas about the other. Such ideas can be obvious or subtle.

2. One can make a statement to convey noxious ideas about the other. Such ideas can be obvious or subtle.

3. One can make a statement to convey information, facts, opinions—about self, or others, or things, or events, true or untrue (known or unknown to self).

4. One can ask a question—genuinely seeking information, or to support or attack.

5. (3) and (4) may be mixed, e.g., appear to be merely informative, but also contain criticism or encouragement.

6. One can make an exclamation that covers (1) through (4)—of interest, of disbelief, of encouragement, of neutrality, to emphasise, to negate, to confuse.

7. Silences may indicate (1) or (2).

(1) and (2) may be analysed as follows:

a subject who sends the statement of meaning	I
an object who receives the statement of meaning	you
a verb that describes the meaning conveyed	hate

Non-verbal interaction can mirror all the above.

Family Transaction—The Family as a Polydynamic System

As the member of a group, a family member finds himself involved in a complex pattern of interactions within it. He is, in fact, an element in a field of forces. Furthermore, he and his family are involved in a complex pattern of interactions with the community outside the family (to be discussed shortly). The term transaction now becomes relevant. The study of fields of forces, vector psychology, was of interest to psychologists in the thirties, but it has since suffered comparative neglect. Kurt Lewin (7) was the leader of a movement which had a great deal to say in its "field theory" about the organisation of society. The work of Lewin was not specifically applied to the family group. The family, however, is a sub-system of society and considerations of vector psychology are relevant to it. Thus a brief digression will be made to consider vector psychology, before relevant aspects of it are applied to the family group.

Kurt Lewin held that mathematics and Galileian physics were the basis of dynamic psychology—even social psychology. A central view in his philosophy was that the context or situation in which the behaviour occurred was as important as the object: "Only by the concrete whole which comprises the object and the situation are the vectors which determine the dynamics of the event defined." The vector is a directed quantity, and, as such, force is a vector. In psychology the concern is with emotional forces. Thus vector psychology can be defined as "a representation of the play of the various tensions and forces within the life space." The internal vectors in the object are not to be neglected, e.g., the relationship of a part to the whole. The object can be the individual. Lewin was also concerned with valence—the demand value of a stimulus: "With all these, however, there remain certain critical properties of the psychobiological environment still undescribed. Objects are not neutral to the child, but have an immediate psychological effect on its behaviour. Many things attract the child to eating, others to climbing, to grasping, to manipulation, to sucking, to raging at them, etc. These imperative environmental facts—we shall call them valences (*Aufforderungscharaktere*)—determine the direction of the behaviour. Particularly from the standpoint of dynamics, the valences, their kind (sign), strength and distribution, must be regarded as among the most important properties of the environment."

Today we must regard vector psychology as a useful corrective to dynamic individual psychiatry, which rests on vague definition of elements and speculative ideas of processes. It can be applied to the individual, to society, and now to the family. Within the individual, its concepts might be applied to memory, perception, thought and motivation; e.g., recall in memory might be described in terms of the valence or demand value or meaninglessness of the message to be recalled. By an amalgamation of Lewin's views, gestalt psychology, cybernetics and communication theory, it might be possible to construct a model of the internal mental processes of an individual just as useful, dynamic and meaningful as that of the dynamic psychopathologists. One can proceed from the individual, with his internal vector qualities, to the group, with its external (to the individual) qualities, to the society and its external (to the group) qualities, to the culture and its external (to culture) qualities. All four are significant.

Vector psychology may have its limitations. The procedures of physics, concerned as they are with the handling of quantities, may fall short when qualities have to be considered.

A family is a field of forces, and thus some of the concepts of vector psychology, mathematics and physics may apply to it. Within the family can be identified a number of interactions making up a complex transaction. The possible interactions may be summarized as follows:

Individual $\longleftrightarrow$ Individual

Individual $\longleftrightarrow$ Dyad

Individual $\longleftrightarrow$ Coalition of family members,
                                i.e., part of a family.

Individual $\longleftrightarrow$ Rest of family

Dyad $\longleftrightarrow$ Dyad

Dyad $\longleftrightarrow$ Coalition

Dyad $\longleftrightarrow$ Rest of family

Coalition $\longleftrightarrow$ Coalition

Coalition $\longleftrightarrow$ Rest of family

The basic family individual interactions will be fully discussed shortly.

The dyads, triads, tetrads, coalitions in the family vary greatly. Examples would be a parental constellation of father and mother making a dyadic interaction with the child; this, as much as the mother-child relationship, can have a powerful influence on the personality of the child. A dyad, again, could consist of two female members of the family, mother and daughter, who interact with a male, father. The mother and maternal grandmother may form a constellation dependent on blood tie and interact with father. It must be noted that each interaction is reciprocal. Furthermore, in addition to direct influences, account must be taken of indirect influences, e.g., father may have mother as his agent in inflicting trauma on the child. Again, any element in interaction with another may simultaneously be interacting with a third element or more. The complexity of the possible interactions is considerable. The family is truly a polydynamic system.

Basic Individual Interactions in the Family

An interaction involves two people.

The direct person-to-person interactions within the nuclear family are: (i) father to mother and mother to father; (ii) father to child and child to father; (iii) mother to child and child to mother; (iv) child to child. The reciprocal father-child relationship may be a father-son or father-daughter relationship. The reciprocal mother-child relationship may be either a mother-son or mother-daughter relationship. The reciprocal child-child relationship may be brother-brother, sister-sister, or brother-sister.

It is to be noted that each relationship is reciprocal and involves two communications, e.g., husband-wife and wife-husband. The reciprocality of the relationship can be overlooked; e.g., much emphasis may be given to the fact that a mother is disrupting the emotional life of the child, forgetting that the child is also disrupting the emotional life of the mother.

Each individual, as will be discussed in the chapter on "The Dimension of General Psychic Properties," plays a number of roles in the family and these influence the interaction. The husband-wife interaction may be in addition the interaction of person to person, male to female, father to mother, business associate to business associate. The father-daughter interaction may in addition be person to person, male to female, and adult to child.

Some of the interactions in the family have received disproportionate attention—in particular, the marital interaction and the mother to child interaction. One of the contributions of family psychiatry is to redress the balance. The father to child, or the child to child interactions, in a particular set of circumstances, may be more significant than the mother to child.

All these interactions, and not only the mother to child relationships, make a contribution to the health of the family and of the child, its representative in the future. Equally, they can all make a contribution to the pathology of the family and of the child.

Each of the four basic interactions will now be given fuller discussion.

The husband-wife interaction

Between the adults of different sexes the major interaction is that of husband-wife. But within it are also fundamental person to person elements, male to female elements and, later, father to mother elements. These in special circumstances may take precedence over the husband to wife interaction.

Marriage has been defined by Murdock (8) as being "a complex of customs centering upon the relationship between a sexually associating pair of adults within the family. Marriage defines the manner of establishing and terminating such a relationship, the normative behaviour and reciprocal obligations within it, and the locally accepted restrictions upon its personnel." Marriage can be formal or informal. Formal means that it has a legal or statutory basis, and informal means there is no statutory basis. In Rome at the time of Justinian, it was possible for a marriage to last only as long as the partners in it mutually agreed to keep together. The informal living together of man and woman may be just as significant emotionally as the formal arrangement.

The purposes of marriage, usually the first step in founding a family, are similar to some of the purposes of the family—to satisfy affectional needs, sexual gratification, economic co-operation, and the opportunity to have children. But a marriage can exist satisfactorily without the latter.

Marriages may be monogamous, and in general this is more likely to occur when the normal sex ratio is not disturbed. Polygamy (plural marriage) is commoner than monogamy if all societies are considered. Kluckhohn (6) states that monogamy is found in only 66 societies, as against polygyny in 378 and polyandry in 31. Polygyny is the marriage of one man to two or more women. This union may be informal, e.g., in ancient Egypt marriage was no bar to the right to have concubines, who were, however, inferior in status to the legal wife. Polyandry, the marriage of one woman to two or more men, is rare.

The reasons for marriage are many, from a superficial economic arrangement to an intense personal fulfilment. The choice of a partner may be left to chance, e.g., in some Catholic countries a man may marry any girl from an orphanage to fulfil a religious vow. Such marriages can be successful, as both partners may approximate to the norm of the population and be free of adverse motivation. In Scotland, at one time, a chance meeting at a fair was followed by a trial marriage for a year. A marriage may be arranged by the family of a partner or those of both partners; this was customary in Britain, and still applies in many countries today. These are often successful because there is a deliberate choice of one another by the preceding families; this may enhance the possibility of complementarity. There is a tendency to marry into the same social class and to those of similar interests. Prestige may be sought through a husband's social position, or a wife's beauty. The need for economic security may weigh heavily in some situations.

The tendency of like to marry like has been supported by a study by Slater and Woodside (11). They reviewed early work on the assortive mating and, after comparing a group of neurotic soldiers and their wives with a control sample, concluded that there is a high degree of similarity, including a neurotic predisposition between husband and wife. The expected frequencies of psychiatric illness in married pairs were studied by Penrose (9) and Gregory (4), who found that the incidence of married couples, both of whom were ill in a psychiatric sense, was in the order of eight or nine times the expected value.

Toman's (12) studies drew attention to influences from the past. He tested the following hypotheses. In divorced couples: (i) Older siblings married more frequently to older siblings, and younger siblings to younger siblings. (ii) A larger number of parents come from like-sexed sibling configurations. (iii) Early loss of family members is more prevalent. The underlying assumptions for these hypotheses are, other things being equal: (i) The optimum situation is one in which partners are unlikely to get into conflict over their rights of seniority, etc. (ii) Individuals having opposite-sex siblings are used to the other sex and have less difficulty in accepting their marriage partner. (iii) The death of a parent or a sibling may make an individual slightly more ready to discontinue relationships of his own accord, or to choose in the first place those which would not last.

Family work certainly emphasises that the experiences in the preceding parent family may play a major part in the choice of partners. Subtle but powerful family emotional influences may be at work in partner selection. An individual gathers from his family and his life experience an image of the ideal partner; when image and reality coincide there is "love at first sight." Furthermore, in the partner may be attractive reflections of an idealised father or mother or sibling or previous wife. Or the partner may be the counterbalance to the type of person the family made one become. Behind the choice of a husband or of a wife, there may be the dictates of a father, or a mother, or of both, determining what kind of marriage is acceptable to them. Rebellion against the expected dictates can play an equally important part. The partner, again, may satisfy an emotional need for security, affection, parenting, domination, subjection or pity.

There are correlates with successful marital relationships—absence of psychonosis, common interests, unselfishness, shared targets, an ability to be realistic and to adjust to new situations, emotional satisfaction, sexual satisfaction, shared social class, shared economic ambitions, shared satisfaction in children, an ability to tolerate differences, to share responsibility, to mix with others, and harmony with the extended family on both sides. Most of these factors are correlated with emotional health.

Marriages may break down. In the United States of America the divorce rate is approximately one divorce for every three to four marriages. Some marriages do not break down despite marital disharmony of severe degree;

partners keep together in unhappiness and conflict, which can lead to severe physical and emotional ill-health and to ultimate destruction in suicide or homicide. It might well be asked, "Why is it that some unsatisfactory marriages do not break up?" There is no single answer. Partners may keep together due to economic need, e.g., a mother with many dependent children; for "the sake of the children," because the fears of life outside marriage are greater than the anxiety within, or loss of personal prestige might be too great; because religious beliefs might make divorce impossible; or because of some basic needs which are met despite the heavy emotional cost. Some make their escape only to marry a new partner in the image of the last, and so involve themselves once again in a futile and destructive struggle.

A marriage, being the most intimate form of shared life, is the strictest test of the ability to sustain an emotional interaction with another person. Thus marriage breakdown is highly correlated with psychonosis, the quality of the sexual relationship being the most reliable guide to the quality of the marital relationship. An emotionally stable partner is usually able to sustain a partner with psychonosis of a severe degree. Two psychonotic partners rarely find satisfaction, though for reasons previously mentioned they may stay together.

A marriage may break down because the original reason for it, superficial or fundamental, may have disappeared. A more desirable partner to fulfil the emotional needs may appear. Conflict with the partner who represents a disliked father, mother, sibling, or idea may reach a point when life together is impossible. Children may change the family dynamics and produce intense rivalry in a partner. Harmony in marriage results from the mutual harmony of the two preceding parent families. Disharmony is not due to the clash of individuals, but to the battle between the two families that they represent.

Marital stress in clinical practice reveals itself in four groups of indicators: (i) those indicative of incompatibility, in day to day interaction, e.g., quarreling, physical violence, etc.; (ii) those indicative of sexual disharmony, e.g., frigidity; (iii) those indicative of psychonosis in one or both partners, e.g., psychosomatic symptoms, depression; (iv) those indicative of encephalo-ataxia (schizophrenia). The last is an incidental presentation, as encephalanosis in a partner is well tolerated unless a paranoid system involves the other partner and leads to suspicion and strife.

Howells (5) showed that of 40 persons presenting at a marital problem clinic, 23 people were in the category of incompatibility, seven people showed sexual disharmony, eight people exhibited signs of emotional illness, and two people suffered from encephalo-ataxia (schizophrenia).

Parent-child interaction

Two main interactions are included here—the father-child and the mother-child. Each is reciprocal. Each can be a reciprocal relationship with either a male or female child. Each participant has an adult or child role and a gender role. Thus pairs can also interact reciprocally in adult-child, male-female, male-male, or female-female relationships. Each interaction can make a contribution to health—or to pathology. To identify the mother-child relationship alone as responsible for health or pathology is a gross limitation of the true situation. Fathering is a much neglected area, and thus more attention is given to it later in the section on "Special Aspects of Family Psychiatry."

Children may result from design or accident. Baird (1) found that of 226 women, 53 had 76 unwanted children—30% more than the desired number. If by accident, they may still be accepted and loved, but the chance of rejection is greater. Planned children have a greater chance of acceptance, but some may still be rejected. There are degrees of acceptance as there are degrees of rejection. An illegitimate child may be fully accepted, but due to the likely adverse circumstances surrounding his birth, he has a greater chance of rejection than a child conceived in a legal union. Children are usually an expression of the mutual love and appreciation operating between the parents. In other situations the children are an economic necessity, especially male children. Children may be conceived in a host of circumstances less favourable to their future acceptance; e.g., they may be an attempt to repair a failing marriage, or an effort to bring relief to a psychonotic parent, or a means of making the wife dependent on the husband, or a substitute for a lost parent or husband or sibling or child, or a means of emotional gratification to the mother, who may then discard the child when it becomes demanding; or they may be wanted as a support in old age, or as a social requirement, or as a duty in the light of religious ideals.

The meaning given to the child in the emotional life of the parent is of paramount importance in determining the attitude of the parent to the child. The meaning is not constant, but fluctuates with the life experience of the parents and can vary from extreme rejection to joyful acceptance, or vice versa. The meaning starts at conception, is reinforced in the mother when movement of the child in utero is experienced, and again at the child's birth. Usually the child is imbued with strong identification with the loved or unloved partner. In addition it is invested with feelings associated with other intimate figures in the life of the parent—grandparents, siblings and friends. At birth, it often becomes the most highly prized object in the life of the parents and thus an object for anxiety, should they be anxious.

The sex gender of the child may be a factor in the meaning given to it by the parent, e.g., for economic reasons, family tradition, or the emotional requirements of the parent, a son may be preferred. The child is also invested by the parent with the feelings dictated by previous life experience in relation to its gender. Parental attitudes may be latent until the child's gender role becomes more evident in adolescence.

The parent-child relationship is recognised as being of vital importance to the satisfactory nurturing of the child. Not only are the child's physical needs largely dependent on it, but so is his intellectual life, his character and the formation of his ideals. Of predominant interest to family psychiatry is the fact that the psychic influences determining psychic health or illness spring mostly from this relationship. Thus the parent-child relationship is strongly echoed in the child's later person-person, adult-adult, husband-wife, father-mother and parent-child relationships. Furthermore, his whole family experience is stamped on him. The child's paramount importance is the fact that he carries his family into the future; he represents his family in its union with another family.

The child has importance to the life experiences of the parent; the child-parent relationship is as vital as the parent-child relationship. A child, in the parents' eyes, often represents the partner and other loved or hated figures. It also allows an expression of creativeness in living form, the fascination of growth in its multitudinous aspects, the intimacy of a responding being, the vicarious delight in the child's achievements, and the satisfaction of social approval.

More attention has been given to the influence of the parent on the child than to the influence of the child on the parent. A child's reaction to a parent is not that of blind obedience to an idealistic phantasy of a parent; this is only seen in children with no parent or parents. A normal child reacts to the reality of the parent. Real bonds replace magical bonds. He responds to real persons. Unlike the parent, whose attitudes and behaviour are fixed by time, the child is more flexible and plastic. The child has real needs—to be parented—and this he will accept from anyone able to give it. He needs *a* parent more than he needs *the* parent.

The child's own attitude to a parent is not a reflection of that parent's attitude alone. A child is nourished by a group situation and his reaction may be dictated in part by this; e.g., an angry mother does not necessarily provoke anger in a child, as the child may not imitate her but imitate his tolerant father and grandfather and respond to his mother with tolerance.

A child, as his equipment is more rudimentary, cannot understand nor emit sophisticated meanings at first. He may even have difficulty in expressing quite strongly held views in words. Hence the need to study his behaviour, especially as experienced in play. One of the dangerous assumptions often made is that the child thinks, evaluates and judges like an adult.

Sibling-sibling interaction

The reciprocal interaction may be brother-brother, sister-sister, or brother-sister.

The importance of the sibling-sibling interaction as an element in family life has probably been grossly underestimated. The Ipswich Thousand Family Survey makes this strikingly apparent. (See Table I). In the child's first ten years the time spent relating to siblings is more than the time spent relating to father, and almost equal to that spent relating to mother. The first year, naturally, is an exception, as children of that age in the sample were less likely to have siblings. The greatest amount of relating is on Saturday and Sunday, when children are not at school; over the ten year period this rose from 18.62% for the average day to 21.36% on Saturday and 20.09% on Sunday.

Most children have at least one sibling. One-child families amounted to only 15.5% of the sample of 1,000 families. The average number of children per family was 2.7. The commonest family was that of parents with

TABLE I

PATTERN OF RELATING OVER TWENTY-FOUR HOURS
BY AGE OF CHILD (WHOLE SAMPLE)

Age of Child	% RELATING TIME		
	Mother	Father	Sibling
1	25.84	12.10	12.81
2	26.72	12.05	16.26
3	25.99	12.97	20.03
4	25.16	13.62	21.27
5	26.85	12.25	19.97
6	21.38	12.57	19.32
7	22.50	12.85	17.94
8	20.38	13.64	19.27
9	19.04	13.02	18.87
10	19.89	11.88	19.58
AVERAGE	23.45	12.71	18.62

two children—40% of families, while 44.5% had more than two children. Only 11% of families had more than four children—striking testimony to the decrease in the large family in the western world.

The one-child family is thus uncommon and the great majority of children will be brought up in interaction with at least one sibling; the child has an equal chance of his sibling being of the same or opposite sex.

The child-child relationship is usually harmonious and adds to the emotional and social life of each, but it can be traumatic due to a number of factors. Disparity of age can be a strain. There is much to suggest that if the disparity is one to two years, the children develop little rivalry and regard themselves as a pair not far removed from a twin relationship. A disparity in age of from two to five years appears to produce the increasing opportunity for rivalry, while a longer gap reduces rivalry, as presumably the older sibling is secure enough not to feel threatened by the younger. Unwise parental management—thrusting a new infant on the child without warning, overprotecting a sibling, not allowing participation by one child, and giving heavier punishment to one child—may set up hostility between siblings. Furthermore, one sibling, for reasons significant in the emotional life of the parent, may be preferred to another, which again sets up rivalry. If rivalry is dictated by parental attitude, then the sibling-sibling relationship tends to be worse in their presence.

In most families and at most times, especially in harmonious families, siblings are a great support to one another. The younger in particular benefit from the stimulating company of an older sibling—a spur to social and intellectual development. In disharmonious families, while the tendency to destructive sibling interaction is more likely, there are exceptions. Occasionally siblings will form a tightly knit group against the parents. In extreme instances they may even bring one another up alongside, but with minimal communication with, the parents; this is the likely outcome of the rejection of all the children. Linkages between children can also occur in other circumstances—older children may skip forming a partnership with a near sibling because of rivalry and partner a younger sibling. Anyone left out of this process will be isolated or have a special relationship with a parent.

In some situations in civilised communities, and as a matter of custom in some primitive communities, the child may be brought up by its older siblings. Not only are there "little mothers" in families, but also "little fathers."

Sex differences in siblings can enrich the life experience of each. A boy acquires attitudes towards females from his sister as well as from his mother —and frequently from the female friends of his sister.

Clinical Implications

Signs of family disorder may appear first or most markedly in one of the basic interactions of the family. This may be the marital, parent-child, or sibling-sibling relationship. Thus the clinical service should make it possible for a dyad from the family to present itself with their mutual problem.

The family diagnostic process must evaluate any signs of disruption in the dimension of internal communication. In general the signs are seen either as excessive or turbulent interaction, e.g., quarrelling, or the reverse —a reduction which can lead to withdrawal and stoppage of communication, e.g., absence of sexual intercourse. In addition, the participants themselves may show any of the signs of emotional illness arising from the communication difficulties. As a part of the total exploration of the family, a useful procedure from time to time is that of the dyadic diagnostic interview. Similarly, the techniques for the psychiatric evaluation of relationships may also be applicable. Family therapy must take the dysfunctioning of dyads into account. In conjunction with this technique, dyadic interview therapy, bringing a couple together for therapy, is a useful technique. In the Prior Present Family and again in the declining phase of the family, it is the only group therapy that is applicable. Again, in vector therapy it becomes crucial to evaluate the family transaction and to explore ways of changing it to produce health—as part of the management of the whole internal and external system of interactions.

REFERENCES

1. BAIRD, D. (1967). Sterilisation and therapeutic abortion in Aberdeen. *Brit. J. Psychiat., 113,* 701.
2. BARNET, S. A. (1961). Behaviour and needs of infant mammals. *Lancet, i,* 1067.
3. CRITCHLEY, M. (1942). Aphasic disorders of signalling. *J. Mt. Sinai Hosp., 9,* 363.
4. GREGORY, I. (1959). Husbands and wives admitted to mental hospital. *J. ment. Sci., 105,* 457.
5. HOWELLS, J. G. (1963). *Family Psychiatry,* p. 31. Edinburgh: Oliver & Boyd.
6. KLUCKHOHN, C. (1960). In: Bell, N. W., and Vogel, E. F. (eds.). *The Family.* Glencoe, Ill.: The Free Press.
7. LEWIN, K. (1935). *A Dynamic Theory of Personality.* New York: McGraw-Hill.
8. MURDOCK, G. P. (1949). *Social Structure.* New York: Macmillan.
9. PENROSE, L. (1944). Quoted by Kreitman in *Psychiat. Q.,* Supplement No. 18, 161.
10. RUESCH, J., and KEES, W. (1956). *Nonverbal Communication: Notes on the Visual Perception of Human Relations.* Berkeley and Los Angeles: Univ. of California Press.
11. SLATER, E., and WOODSIDE, M. (1951). *Patterns of Marriage.* London: Cassell.
12. TOMAN, W. (1959). Family constellation as a basic personality determinant. *J. indiv. Psychol., 15,* 199.

The Third Dimension:
The Dimension of
General Psychic Properties

The family is a small group of people and therefore everything that applies to small group structures and dynamics must apply also to the family. While the family has characteristics in common with all other small groups, it has also special characteristics of its own. (i) It is made up of a diverse group of individuals—males and females, adults, adolescents, and children of either sex, whose age range may span two or three generations. (ii) The relationships within the family are more intense than in any other group of society. Hence their significance for health or illness. (iii) The family normally has a long collective history. Its life is a continuous flow from the distant Past, into the Present, and on to the Future. (iv) The family has certain distinct properties; it usually shares one language, one religion, one social class, one house and one income. (v) It has special functions, providing as it does for the affectional needs and the economic requirements of its members, for the sexual satisfaction of the marital couple, and the procreation and upbringing of children. (vi) It is a fundamental sub-system of society and it is recognized as such.

Recent years have seen an increasing interest in the study of groups in all sections of society—industry, education, youth associations, agriculture, voluntary societies, religion, hospitals, armed services, etc. The family is the most obviously important small group, and yet it has been comparatively neglected.

This dimension is concerned with the acquired attributes of the family produced by the interaction between the family and its experience. Thus it has some characteristics in common with the general characteristics of an individual (1–6 below) and some in addition because of its group structure (7–14 below). Since these general characteristics can lead to harmonious functioning of the family or to dysfunction, this dimension is of special importance to psychopathology.

Characteristics in Common with Individuals

1. *Attitudes.* As with the individual, these are of overwhelming importance in that they dictate communication—offensive and defensive, constructive and destructive, loving and hating.

Many attitudes are shared by the family members. Some of the strongest are never expressed verbally, e.g., the absence of discussion of a subject, perhaps discussion of affection, serves to emphasise how lacking awareness of it can be. Some attitudes are strongly held and might be termed *beliefs.* Others have been held in the preceding families, perhaps for generations, and assume the quality of *traditions.* Some of the beliefs are fictional and could thus be termed *myths,* e.g., that mother cannot drive the car; the family may affect this pretence for motives of its own.

Some families develop strongly shared *interests,* e.g., they are all interested in sport; in other families individuality is encouraged. The choice of interests may be immensely diverse in families due to many factors.

Values and morals are the standards that guide action. They arise in society and are a means of ordering its functioning to the advantage of all. They are often imperfect and transitory. Previous families impart them to their young who carry them forward in time; the imparting may not be verbal and formal, but by example. Sometimes the young rebel against the family by rebelling against its mores; they have no more powerful weapon than to be hostile to the family by rejecting its most cherished values; the more rigidly these are held by the family, the greater the satisfaction of damaging them. Families with rigidly held morals often produce the most persistent delinquents. Family members can clash over values.

Aims are sometimes termed goals, targets, ambitions, motivations. Many are forced on the family by biology, e.g., all must eat. Some are the product of the previous families, e.g., poor economic conditions may provoke an interest in economic success; and some aims are acquired by fortuitous circumstances in the life of the family. Differing aims held by family members can lead to conflict and potent trauma within the family. Families whose members develop shared aims tend to be cohesive and successful even if antisocial.

Some attitudes are very strongly held and virtually unchangeable; these tend to have a long history and to come from the preceding family. They may hardly be recognized by either the family or the individual; but these attitudes guide them in fundamental matters such as care of children, independence from others, self confidence and acceptance of loss without any formal acknowledgment of them.

Differing attitudes held strongly by conflicting family members can lead to situations of destructive trauma within the family. *This fact is at the roots of psychopathology.*

2. *Character.* The more prominently held values, morals, and principles of a family could be termed its character. Thus character arises from attitudes, resulting in a respectable family, a selfish family, an honest family, etc. Some workers have even attempted classification of families in this form. This is a very limited approach to family classification because (i) these values shift with time, and (ii) it labels a family by a description of only one element in it.

3. *Conscience.* This also arises from attitudes. Allied to morals is the matter of family conscience. Morals and conscience are the more strongly held collective values. They dictate the behaviour of families and are consulted when action is contemplated. To disregard conscience is to lead to a feeling of unworthiness or guilt; this can be so potent as to lead to destruction of the unworthy self ("I can't live with myself") by an individual, or severe and even destructive censure by the rest of the family.

4. *Temperaments.* These are the families' predominant moods. Families may present characteristic moods—gay, aggressive, affectionate, sad, etc. Essentially these are varying flavours of love and hate. Again, the attempt has been made to classify families by its predominant mood, temperament. Such classifications are unsatisfactory as (i) the moods shift and change, and (ii) only one modality in the family is considered and this grossly limits description.

5. *Skills.* These may determine external *tasks* or *vocation.* Family members may have skills in common or they may complement one another. Skills may be a biological gift to a particular family member or be acquired by habit and contact from the previous or present family.

6. *Knowledge.* This may have many qualities—academic or practical, general or specialised, shared or individual. Conflicting attainments can cause clashes within the family.

Characteristics Due to Group Status

7. *Control.* The family unit must have an ordered existence to achieve its goals. This can be imposed by a benevolent or malevolent leadership, by combinations of family members, or by a democratic process of collective decision. Thus power can flow to a person, a dyad, or a coalition. Rules are framed to maintain order—or to impose discipline.

Even in a democracy, there can be *leadership*—invested in one person or in one group by a free collective will. The leadership can change depending on the situation that is being experienced. Leadership may be overt or covert. *Decisions* are arrived at by processes of discussion particular to a family or by the opinion of a leader, or dictator. There should be a balance between leadership and democracy.

Parents may impose their will on the younger members and convey the art of dictatorship which is passed on to the succeeding families and to society.

8. *Roles.* These are the parts the family members play in the family drama.

Some are special to the small group of family—a man may have a part to play as a male, father, husband, breadwinner, lover, etc.; a woman operates as a female, mother, wife, etc.

Some roles are shared with all small groups—some family members are cast in the role of diplomat, placator, arbiter, scapegoat, provocateur, punisher, supplicant, etc.

Tasks are minor roles assigned to family members—one person wakes the family, another collects the fuel, a third answers the door, etc.

Roles can be *flexible,* e.g., father and mother take turns in bathing the infant.

Roles can be *reversed,* e.g., father, instead of mother, bathes the infant.

9. *Arrangement.* This describes the cohesiveness of a family. Does it operate as a cohesive whole, or is it fragmented, or split into two or more parts? Are these parts in agreement or opposition? Partnership and coalition and alignments are made and broken with every fleeting moment—but agreement on basic issues may be strong between some members, while they are free to disagree on superficial matters. Study of the family needs to ask not only who is in alignment, but also on what issues its members agree or disagree.

10. *Conflict.* This can arise between elements of varying size within the family due to contrary attitudes concerning beliefs, traditions, aims, interests and values. From the clash come threat, trauma, and insecurity. The strongest clashes occur over basic, often unexpressed, attitudes coming from preceding families. Protagonists are met by antagonists. Attitudes are so ingrained as not to have reached the awareness of their protagonist—or even the antagonist. Allies are called in on either side.

The participants are reactors while some family members, sometimes the children, remain as observers. But observers record data and pass judgment. Observers can be powerful helpers to the family diagnostician in family interviews. Conflict may be temporarily or permanently resolved by exhaustion, concession by one side, arbitration and, less often, by constructive resolution.

11. *Autonomy of the person.* While family psychiatry focuses attention

on the family, it does not deny the rights, functions and obligations of an individual. An individual needs his own identity if he is to function optimally in the group. The group must allow opportunities for this to develop. Later he must function in society as the family's representative, form a union with another, and found a new family.

12. *The daily pattern.* This is unique for each family, although there may be many shared patterns in localities, races and cultures. The very rituals and mannerisms of the family bring a feeling of predictability and thus security. Everyone knows what to expect; it is familiar and comforting —even if sometimes damaging. People cling to home, for it is an understood and predictable entity, as compared with unfamiliar alternatives.

13. *The family climate.* Families have an atmosphere, climate, flavour. It is composed of recognisable positive elements and unrecognized negative elements. The latter are as important as the former. The latter make it difficult to analyse and describe the climate. People may say "there is tension," or "I felt an atmosphere," or "I had a feeling of disquiet."

Although experienced in picking up positive phenomena, even well trained observers may find it difficult to describe the unexpressed, e.g., no hostility—but an absence of thoughtfulness, no harsh comment—but no encouragement when it is appropriate. In addition, the climate may be difficult to discern because of contrived deception. The family member, or the family as a whole, is adept at hiding true attitudes from others and even at forging false ones. The onlookers pick up confused signals, leading to a feeling of the unexpected, the unpredictable, and thus the insecure.

14. *Efficiency.* A family has a capacity for meeting its day to day requirements, for achieving its aims, and living in harmony with society. This is dependent on the collective gifts and abilities of the family members, its cohesion, its realisable targets and its leadership.

Clinical Implications

This dimension of general psychic properties is the stuff of psychopathology. It is here that we look for the signs of trauma arising from clashing attitudes that are often stamped on it by the preceding families. Its assessment calls for a direct meeting with the family—family group diagnosis. Its elucidation may supply the key to therapy through a change produced by beneficial experience on its basic attitudes—benexperiential psychotherapy.

The Fourth Dimension:
The Dimension of
External Communication

Introduction

The family interacts with society and society interacts with the family. Thus we need to consider the family, interaction, and society. The family is under discussion. Interaction was described in the chapter devoted to the "Dimension of Internal Communication"; communication consists of (i) the meaning conveyed and (ii) the somatic means of communication, and ends in a relationship, the standing between two objects. We need therefore to consider the number and types of possible interactions between the family and society; the family or any of its parts can interact with society and any of its parts. Society is a new element here and therefore also merits some description.

The above dictates that we first briefly consider society and follow with a discussion of the possible interactions.

The Social System

The study of the development of parts, or of the whole, of the social system is the concern of historians. The study of the functioning of society is the field of sociologists. Much is being learned about the basic functioning and structures of society through the study of primitive communities by social anthropologists. Cultural anthropology is now often distinguished from social anthropology. It deals with cultural systems rather than with social ones; with the relations, that is, among items of culture, sometimes called "culture traits."

Society, like the individual and the family, is a psychosomatic organism. There is a physical structure (social soma) and a social psyche. A great deal more is known about society's physical structure than about the social psyche.

Society performs a number of functions for the family. A family may gain protection from the community against the ill effects of either another family or another community. Individuals and families need the satisfaction and security of identifying with units larger than themselves. Furthermore, a community furthers economic production; much can be achieved which is impossible in smaller units; specialisation is assisted. Again, society makes it possible to pool services and facilities. For example, goods can be supplied through a market system possible only on a large scale; a church can cater for a number of families, a school for a large number of children. Biologically, marriage is possible outside the family or clan. The individual and family profit from the collective wisdom of a larger group and from values and customs passed down the generations.

Physical structure

Society consists of individuals, families, neighbourhoods, communities and cultures. The neighbourhood consists of those people living in close proximity to the family. The community is larger and embraces those people living in a particular township or area. The culture consists of those with common beliefs or customs; it can include a tribe, a country or several countries. In addition to people, society has its possessions, and lives in a physical environment.

Social psyche

This consists of (i) the psyche of individuals and families within it, which has already been discussed; (ii) the transactions between all the elements in society—our particular concern is that between the family and its immediate society, and this will be discussed later; and (iii) its general characteristics—which will now be discussed more fully.

The general characteristics of society can, as with the family, be considered in two groups—those held in common with individuals (1–6 below), and those common to groups (7–15 below; one is additional to those of the family). These characteristics are the result of the effect of experience on mankind through time.

Characteristics in Common with Individuals

1. *Attitudes*. These, including beliefs, traditions, myths, interests, values and aims, are multiple and complex. They are often irrational and self-destructive. They are borrowed by the family. Society may be unaware of the attitudes that influence it.

As in the family, *values* and *morals* are often imperfect and transitory. The mass is often neither moral, wise nor just. Democracy is limited by these facts. Some sections of society may have a vague social conscience—often wayward, uncertain and indefinite. Values influence legislation and exert a strong influence on the family.

Contrary attitudes lead to conflict between segments of society, and the family is one such segment. Conflict precipitates threat, insecurity and trauma.

2. *The ethos*. This arises from attitudes. The principles, standards, beliefs and mores of society collectively make up its character, disposition or ethos. These values are acquired by cultures, communities, families and individuals within society by the processes of learning and by experience. There is great social "pressure" on everybody to conform to the accepted value systems of the culture. Failure to conform leads to banishment, disciplinary action, loss of prestige or loss of security. To conform brings appreciation, prestige and security. When the values are wrong, it takes nonconforming pioneers to persuade people to alter them and to demonstrate and institute new values. A society changes its values with extreme reluctance.

3. *Social conscience*. This also arises from attitudes. Its predominant, sacred values exert a strong pressure to conform and, when threatened or confused, society falls back on what it regards as its essential values. These influence its choice of religions and beliefs held within the religions.

4. *Temperaments*. These are society's predominant moods. They can be remarkably volatile, e.g., as seen in mob panic. They are much influenced by events and their interpretation by leaders or leadership groups. Some large groups, e.g., national groups, are held to have a characteristic temperament. This is an open question, for it is certainly true that there can be great diversity within such a national group. Naturally, a large group undergoing the same experience, e.g., defeat in war, can share the same predominant feelings, e.g., bitterness, an amalgam of inferiority and aggression.

5. *Skills*. In society there is great variation of skills depending upon geography, resources, training and inclinations.

6. *Knowledge* is continually increasing and of great complexity. It veers towards the material; society is woefully inadequate as to knowledge of its own psychic functioning.

Characteristics in Common with Groups

7. *Control*. For its general well-being, society enforces standards on its members. The strongest control is subtle—the suggestion effect of the

group, threat of loss of appreciation and prestige, the paths of least resistance, the introjection of authority as a supportive figure, the pressures of class, economic groups, the clan, etc. Furthermore, nature exerts its own discipline—not wearing clothes in a cold climate leads to suffering or death.

Society exerts explicit control through formal legal codes; these are normally the "will of the people" and change with varying conditions and the acquisition of knowledge. There is informal control through religious standards, conventions, customs and traditions. Allied to control is leadership. This may be based on religion, education, income or class. Sometimes control is by a combination of class, tradition and heredity—the establishment. Leadership may be dictatorial or democratic. Sometimes it is expressed through the activity of a group, e.g., the clergy, or a trade union, or an elected town council. These groups in turn have their leaders. Leadership is linked to power—the share given to the individual or group in shaping or controlling activity, policy, and its rewards in society.

8. *Social roles.* As an individual has a standing or place in a family, so he has one assigned to him in society. Within the family he may be husband and father; in society he has many more roles—male, consumer, citizen, etc. Some roles are dependent upon groupings in society, e.g., snob, based on class; baker, based on occupation; pupil, based on education; priest, based on religion; voter, based on political affiliation; consumer, based on economics; thief, based on legislation; etc. Roles are allotted by others; thus there is a giver as well as a recipient, and without the giver there is no role. Role acting or playing is a determinant of interaction between the giver and the recipient.

An individual may be asked to enact one or more roles simultaneously, and these roles may be in conflict with one another. Roles may be ascribed, e.g., by age, or sex; may be achieved, e.g., headteacher; may be adopted, e.g., leader; or may be assumed, e.g., a part in a play. Roles may be modified, e.g., leader becomes an adviser, or reversed, e.g., teacher becomes a pupil.

9. *Arrangement.* There are many possible alignments, groupings and fragments. Social groupings are dependent on a number of factors, e.g., politics—communist, socialist, republican, conservative, etc.; education—day school, boarding school, university, etc.; religion—Baptist, Roman Catholic, Hindu, etc.; occupation—teacher, clergyman, tailor, etc. An individual may belong to a number of groups, e.g., a teacher who is a republican, a graduate who is a practising Buddhist. Each group has its leaders, conventions, practices and standards, and imposes discipline on its members.

Prestige may conform closely to economic classes; but there are exceptions, e.g., aristocracy may, due to death duties and other reasons, become poor, but still maintain a prestigious position in society. The working class may acquire wealth and a high standard of living, but still have a low prestige value in some societies. It is usual, however, for income grouping to be closely related to occupational grouping; e.g., a labourer the world over is in a low economic group; a lawyer usually acquires at least a middle or upper middle economic grouping. Income influences standards of living —housing, education, leisure and health.

The class ranking of individuals and families in society is often on a three point scale—upper (aristocracy), middle (professional), and lower (working) classes. Hereditary, economic, occupational and religious factors operate in determining the class to which an individual belongs. In some societies, the middle, or professional, class hardly exists. In a few societies differences between classes may be hardly noticeable, while in others the differences are very marked, e.g., in feudal societies. Class differentiation can change with time. Social class can exert considerable pressures on the behaviour and values of families and individuals belonging to it, e.g., on the child-rearing practices, education and work aspiration, partner selection in marriage, etc.

10. *Conflict.* This is ever present, in some form or another, and arises among society's elements because of differences in attitudes, beliefs, aims, interests and values. Protagonists, antagonists, allies, arbiters and observers all play their parts.

11. *Autonomy of individual and family.* Each individual and family fights to maintain its identity, rights and autonomy in the face of social pressures.

12. *The daily pattern or way of life.* There are basic elements in common throughout groups in society, but they show great variation in detail.

13. *The social climate.* Societies, like families, have an atmosphere or flavouring. Great pressures can be exerted by the unexpressed, informal and "unwritten laws."

14. *Efficiency.* This reflects society's capacity to run its day-to-day affairs, to achieve its targets, and to maintain harmony. This is dependent on the collective gifts and abilities of its members, their cohesiveness, targets, resources and leadership.

15. *Social mobility.* Industrialization, wealth, wars and mechanical means of transport have led to accelerated social mobility. People leave rural areas for the higher standards of living in industrialised areas. Wars can lead to the mass exodus of people. Wealth encourages travel. The car, railways, ships and air transport make movement an easy matter. The future, it can be confidently predicted, will bring greater mobility and thus more mixing of peoples. Much may be lost or gained by mobility, depending on its circumstances. Loss may be in terms of giving up support of relatives and friends, isolation, the clash of cultural roles and values, the problems of

language. Gain may be in terms of escape from traumatic relatives and friends, emergence from isolation, and the acquisition of new and ·better values. Much has yet to be understood about migration. This is sometimes the prerogative of the healthy, stable, balanced and enterprising. Sometimes it constitutes the escape of the unstable and the weak, who reap another disillusionment in their new community. Failure of integration may not be the fault of the selection, but of the individual. Usually the healthy family or individual has a remarkable capacity for adjustment.

Family-Society Interactions

These interactions can be portrayed as follows:

FAMILY   SOCIETY

Individual ⟷ Individual or Family or Society

Part of Family ⟷ Individual or Family or Society

Family Group ⟷ Individual or Family or Society

Every interaction is reciprocal. Part of the family means a couple or several members, but not all family members. Family in society stands for a family other than the Presenting Family and includes families related by blood ties or others. Society stands for neighbourhood, community, culture or the whole of humanity. The interaction can be with a special group in society, e.g., religious, political, administrative, economic, educational, etc. There may be a large number of simultaneous interactions. Some of the interactions may come from indirect influences—one group influences another, which in turn influences a third.

As within the family, every interaction elsewhere involves a standing between the two entities involved in the interaction, i.e., a relationship which can have a feeling tone and be described by its characteristics. Also involved in the interaction is communication—meanings are conveyed through the channels of communication.

The Presenting Family, its parts, or an individual family member interacts with an individual in society, a family in society, or a part or the whole of society. Thus further discussion is required of the interactions with individuals in society of prime interest to a family; then with the family of greatest concern to the Presenting Family—the extended family; and, lastly, with society.

The interaction of an individual family member, a dyad, a coalition, or the whole family with the individual members of the community involves relationships with individual members of the extended family, neighbours, friends, workmates, schoolmates and chance acquaintances. *Relatives* have a potent influence—even from a distance. *Friends* can exert strong influences, especially when they are neighbours; depending upon the degree of intimacy and the length of contact, they can have an influence as powerful as that of relatives. *Neighbours* have a role not only as intimates, but also as a reflection of "neighbourhood" opinion. *Schoolmates and teachers* are usually in touch with the individual school-child for one third of his waking life during his school years. A *work* situation for male or female can be harmonious or traumatic depending on the relationships involved. *Casual acquaintances* are many; trauma, if it occurs, is more likely to be due to a marked impact working over a short period. Chance acquaintances are often accepted as being the mouthpieces of collective community opinion. All these interactions are reciprocal.

The family's interaction may be with its *extended family* in vertical extension to an older or younger generation, or in its lateral extension to siblings. There may be both. The total grouping may be large enough to merit the term "clan" or "tribe." Relatives harbour the collective opinion of "the family." By right, they have an intimacy with the individual which is denied to others. They may be in life-long contact with the family and previous traumata may be reinforced by present actions.

It is convenient to think about interactions with and in society in terms of fields of forces. This matter has already been discussed in the chapter on the "Dimension of Internal Communication." Sociologists often prefer to talk of the field of transaction. The transactional approach denotes a whole web, pattern, or matrix of activity. The interactional approach denotes activity between two organised bodies. The transactional approach is the better representation of events within the family group, or within society.

Any element in the family can interact with any group of society— neighbourhood, community, culture, or special groupings. Each in turn interacts with the family. "They" is a term which represents the subtle, intangible, ever present, collective public or social opinion. Communication media like newspapers, radio and television all try, with varying degrees of distortion, to convey this opinion to people at large. The family feels under the scrutiny of "they," it is conscious of the standards expected by "they," and tends to be insecure if not attuned to "they."

Beliefs about many matters that are termed cultural come to a particular family in two ways: (i) from the preceding parent families, which have also been subjected to cultural pressure; and (ii) from the cultural inter-action now. Of the two influences the first is the greatest. But the second may modify the first to some extent with the result that family traditions are modified over the generations. The end behaviour depends on the competing strengths of the influences. As families are faced with the same essential situations in all cultures, these have many elements of belief and behaviour in common; there is more similarity than dissimilarity. But as situations have some variations, it follows that the expressions may show variations of emphasis from culture to culture. To study these variations is of great value. It can be seen that what appears to be fixed and immov-able is capable of variation. What are assumed to be unconvertible truths are seen to be adjustable. The function of a piece of behaviour may become more evident—usually as a necessary adjustment to a given environment. Examples of cultural belief that affect families are as follows: the last daughter may be expected to look after aged parents; sons do not marry until their sisters have married; fathers are the family leaders; success is measured in material wealth; children should be physically punished; the aged are respected; there must be overt display of feeling; divorce is a disgrace; etc.

Two of the interactions between family and society need further con-siderations because of their frequency and influence—these are the in-teractions with workmates and schoolmates.

Adult members of the family spend a considerable portion of their wak-ing life in a *work* situation. This is again a transactional field. Interactions include management-foreman, foreman-worker, and worker-workmate. To produce harmony in these interactions makes for less stress, lower sick-ness rate and greater productivity. Work situations apply increasingly to mothers. Mothers can profit from going out to work. This practice has always been customary in some areas and there is no evidence to suggest that it causes any increase in emotional illness or delinquency in family members. The alleged ill effects on the children of mother going out to work have been greatly exaggerated. Mothers usually take care to pro-tect their children during separation. Indeed, the very disturbed mother brings profit to herself and the child, attenuating the disharmony between them by going out to work. The child profits if he is given good substitute care, and the mother profits by relief from a traumatic situation, by mix-ing with others, and by gaining encouragement from succeeding at her work. She is likely to be a better mother because of the work experience.

Important interactions in the *school* transactional system are head-teacher-teacher, teacher-parent, teacher-child, and child-schoolmate. The teacher is a key figure. To produce harmony in these interactions can compensate the child for deficiencies in his family, widen his emotional experience, strengthen his emotional state and improve his achievements.

Clinical Implications

The signs of dysfunction in the dimension of interaction between family and society may be the cause of referral of a family. The family or society, but usually the family, takes the initiative. It may at first rely on its own resources, later mobilise or consult clan resources and lastly turn to resources in the community. To help themselves, communities set up facilities to ameliorate family disorder. Society has concentrated on the eradication of the obvious problems of physical ill-health. It can readily see the involvement of social factors in the aetiology of physical illnesses; periodic reminders come in the form of epidemics that handicap large sections of the population. It has therefore often taken large scale social action against physical ill-health.

Mental disorder has received less attention and, again, concentration has been on the more obvious conditions of encephalonosis and mental retardation. Emotional disorder has suffered even greater neglect.

The signs of dysfunction in family-society interaction fall into three main groups:

1. Signs in the interaction itself—either excessive or reduced activity, e.g., aggression, exploitation, delinquency, etc., on the one hand, or isolation and withdrawal on the other.

2. Signs in the family, e.g., alcoholism, drug addiction.

3. Signs in society, e.g., civil war.

The last requires discussion. A society, like the individual or family, can be sick in its own right. It can manifest signs of this, such as punitive legislation, inappropriate attitudes, outmoded beliefs, disruption, strife between groups, etc.

The above signs must not be confused with signs exhibited by families, but thought to be social problems, e.g., child neglect, delinquency, alcoholism, divorce, promiscuity, suicide, illegitimacy, drug addiction, etc. These are social only insomuch as they are widespread. But they do not respond to social action such as economic measures, legal reform, or ethical prompting. This is because they are not social in pathogenesis—they are results of family dysfunction manifested in the behaviour of individuals. That this is so becomes immediately apparent in a close study of severely pathogenic families—the so-called "problem families."

For example, a problem family displayed a large number of signs of emotional disorder, including what is often termed a "social problem"—child neglect. This mother neglected her children. The following emotional causes emerged: (i) The birth of the children was the result of the mother's emotional need to have a baby from which she could have affection. (ii) The children were immediately rejected when they made demands upon the mother as toddlers and the mother would want another baby. (iii) The mother was continually tense and therefore inattentive, irritable, impatient and explosive, with consequent trauma to the children. (iv) At other times the mother felt guilty about her own behaviour and therefore became unreasonably overprotective and denied the children beneficial social contacts. (v) She projected onto her own children her unsatisfactory feelings about the maternal grandmother who brought her up.

To take another example, in a problem family of a higher income group the following pathogenesis emerged. The wife was a life-long extreme alcoholic—to the point that her liver and kidneys had been so badly damaged that her life was threatened. Yet her alcoholism was inevitable in the set of family conditions in which she found herself. Her adolescence was spent in a cold, rejecting preceding family and she clearly remembers being invited to a frighteningly formal party held by her parents. She felt shy, embarrassed and unwanted. The footman came by with a tray of champagne. Hurriedly she picked up a glass, winced, gulped, and in a few minutes the confidence so lacking before flowed into her. She had discovered the temporary elation of alcohol. Her waywardness was a continuing irritation to her parents and they solved it by shifting the responsibility to another by "marrying her off" to an elderly, respectable, well-connected widower. So began a life of unrelenting boredom and frustration with a well-meaning husband who tried, with every good intention, to control her. Alcohol became a balm, an essential support against an intolerable emotional environment.

Delinquency, similarly, has an invariable factor in its background—a family milieu that breeds resentment, bitterness and hostility to others. At first expressed within the family, as the individual emerges in society in adolescence these feelings are converted into hostility to society. Society in turn takes over the cold punitive moralising attitude of the family and guarantees the reinforcement of hostility.

Thus we should not confuse family-induced behaviour expressed in society, pseudo-social problems, with the true pathological behaviour of society. The first responds to amelioration of family situations, the second to social action on a large scale.

Investigation of family pathology must include an assessment of the dimension of external communication. This interaction emerges in family group diagnosis and some of its features are reflected in the interaction between the diagnostician, a representative of a family in society, and the family. This is a confrontation between two families rather than two people.

Account must be taken of the dimension of external communication in family therapy. Sick families contribute to social dysfunction as sick units in the total system of society. Their amelioration cannot fail to improve the standard of social functioning. Equally, a sick society bears heavily on all families, and an improvement in the level of social functioning brings health-promoting forces to bear on families. This principle lies behind the concept of the salutiferous society; large-scale measures change the pattern of social functioning so as to promote healthy emotional living.

The Fifth Dimension:
The Dimension of Physical Properties

This dimension consists of: (i) the physical constitution of the family group in a state of health or sickness; (ii) its physical possessions, in particular its home; some of these physical possessions could be regarded as belonging to society, but used by the family—it is convenient to consider them here; (iii) the physical environment—climate, geography, etc. [(iii) does not require discussion.]

The physical properties of a family are the easiest to catalogue. But like every dimension of the family, the physical dimension is responsive to the total life of the family. When there is dysfunction, it is reflected in the family's physical health and in its possessions. That possessions can be affected is glaringly obvious in the so-called "multi-problem" or "hard-core" family.

The Family's Physical Constitution

The elementary family group usually consists of two parents and one or more children. The group has male and female members amongst its adults and its children. Family members may be of any age from infancy to senium. The family group may be formal, with a legalized marriage between the parents, or informal. To the elementary family may be added: (i) relations, such as grandparents, siblings of parents, cousins of the children, etc.; (ii) others, such as servants, lodgers, governesses, nannies, etc.

In an evaluation of a family, account should be taken of such matters as:
1. *Race.*
2. *Colour*—be it black, brown, yellow, white or mixed.
3. *Social Class.*
4. *Economic Class.*
5. *Size.* Table II shows the distribution of children in 1,046 families in the Ipswich Thousand Family Survey. There were a total of 2,853 children.

85

The average number of children per family was 2.71. The largest single group of families (36.9% of families) had 2 children. Thus the most common family structure is that of 4 people. Only 11% of families had more than 4 children.

TABLE II

IPSWICH THOUSAND FAMILY SURVEY

NUMBER OF FAMILIES BY SIZE		
Number of Children	Number of Families	Total Number of Children
One	162	162
Two	418	836
Three	247	741
Four	104	416
Five	46	230
Six	42	252
Seven	10	70
Eight	7	56
Nine	10	90
Total	1046	2853

6. *Build*—whether all or some approach the average, or whether they are small or pygmy in stature, or large and giant.

7. *Sex Distribution*—the number of males and females in young and old.

8. *Age Distribution.*

9. *Special Characteristics,* e.g., auburn hair in all or some family members.

10. *Type*—nuclear, extended, or anomalous. The Ipswich Thousand Family Survey showed that approximately 88% of families were nuclear, 6% extended, and 6% anomalous. As families are reluctant to reveal anomalous states, it is believed that the latter is an underestimate; there are indications that 10% would be a truer figure and thus the number of nuclear families is reduced to 82%.

11. *Physical Health and Sickness*—as will be seen under Family Diagnosis, signs of physical sickness can be a common finding in disturbed families. It can involve the whole or part of the family or just an individual member. In addition to that sickness which may arise by chance, the trauma of family life in disturbed families may precipitate psychosomatic symptoms; hence the imperative need for emotional and physical states to be considered as an indivisible whole. Occasionally, severe physical illness may of itself be a source of stress within the family; well-adjusted families, however,

appear to manage sickness better than disturbed families. Some families have an idiosyncracy for a particular sympton, e.g., obesity, or enuresis, or a particular disease, e.g., asthma; in addition to any genetic or constitutional component, these may result from shared learned responses to stress.

A fuller discussion of the physical health of the family would be more appropriate to a book on organic pathology, so the reader is referred to that source. It is sufficient to emphasise here that each member of the family has a cerebral apparatus, the servant of psychic functioning; and these individual cerebral organic systems can come together and function as a collective whole in family group endeavour.

Physical Possessions

In many areas of the world the physical and material needs of the family have yet to be fully met. There are also many areas where they are over-met —as if the quest for material satisfaction went on under its own momentum despite satiation. Due to the intangibility of emotional phenomena, man beset by disharmony, dysfunction and unhappiness assumes that the solutions still lie in the tangible, understandable, material sphere. Thus material comfort becomes an end in itself; disillusionment results, but the quest continues. Man realises that he does not live by bread alone, but matters of the psyche have been hitherto difficult to grasp. Material want can lead to dysfunction and material poverty. Thus there is an interplay of physical and emotional phenomena.

The family's requirements are influenced by the background, geographical, cultural and social, in which the family lives.

District

A family cannot function without support from the community, and, indeed, the modern family enquires about facilities before moving into an area. Stores easily reached are essential to the housewife, and a substantial part of her time will be spent in them. Banking, hairdressing, garage, postal and laundry facilities are all needed by the family. There will be also a demand for a place of worship with all its associated activities. Schools have to be accessible, as well as recreational facilities for children, such as playground, swimming pool and playing fields. Adults are prepared to travel to satisfy their need for entertainment—theatres, cinemas, concert halls, clubs, restaurants, etc.; all contribute to the life of the family. In well-developed communities the family will rely on local facilities for water, electricity, telephone, sewage disposal, road maintenance and police protection.

Local facilities are usually in the care of a district authority, organised by paid officials and under the control of a democratic body elected by those living in the area. That this is an incorruptible, just and efficient organisation is probably more immediately important to the family for its comfort and security than the quality of national government.

Dwelling

The nature, size and construction of this is dictated by the family functions that take place there. These include protection from the weather, sleeping, feeding, drinking, child care, washing of clothing, personal hygiene, sanitation, care of the sick, storage, study and recreation.

The family needs protection against the elements—wind, rain, heat and cold—and climate determines the mode of construction. In cold countries rooms are smaller, as they require heating. Intense heat dictates shade and cool rooms. A combination of wind and cold calls for an igloo. Great wind forces families underground.

The family base is its dwelling, which usually requires two main areas—a living area and a sleeping area. It may vary greatly in size and sophistication, from a simple hut to a caravan, a flat, a house, or a many-roomed mansion. The accommodation should be adequate for the size of the family. Paradoxically, the greater the number of children, the less able are the parents to afford adequate accommodation, as was shown by a survey of 1,000 families (3, 4) in an urban area in Great Britain, which demonstrated that families with young children lived in smaller dwellings with fewer amenities. In the families studied, 56.8% of the households lived in three rooms or less; 59.6% lived in "flats" or "rooms." In a previous survey, the same investigation team found that accomodation was often very deficient; e.g., one in nine families were overcrowded (one person in three if each member of the family was counted as an individual); one house in seven was structurally inadequate. Bossard (1) has evolved a Spatial Index for Family Interaction for relating floor space to inter-relationship within the household.

In the dwelling the family needs certain obvious facilities, like water and a source of artificial power, electric or gas, for light and warmth and cooking. Other requirements include furniture and utensils, toys and books. The more essential furniture are tables, chairs, beds and storage fittings. A radio and television set are both found nowadays, even when many other essentials might be absent. Little study has been given to the effect of colour in the home; the use of colour probably reflects the family's personality. A garden, for pleasure or food production, is usually annexed to the house in rural or semi-rural areas. In the absence of a garden, children play either in the street or in the nearest organised playground.

A neglected subject, until the coming of the aeroplane, was the effect of noise on the family. Harsh noises are distracting and irritating; but many people find continuous music from a radio a desirable accompaniment to family life.

Some domestic activities turn around the care of children—feeding, bathing, playing, occupying, protecting and nursing them. In most societies the care of children is a group activity, with all members participating, but the mother is usually the leader, especially with infants, and is supported by the husband, by the grandparents, and by the child's siblings. Exclusive care of children by the mother is unusual.

Families vary in the time they allot to essential tasks. When food and other necessities are plentiful and easily obtained, more time is available for relaxation; in farming communities, there are times demanding intense activity, generally followed by slack periods; in civilized areas, the hospitals will take over the care of the very sick, and the schools will relieve parents of their children for part of the day. In wealthy areas the machine has made domestic tasks easier and less time-consuming; this is especially so where the standard of living has been raised for all income groups, and thus servants have become scarce.

At home, too, the sick must be nursed; the sick and hurt make for the home, which usually supplies protection, care and rest. Other activities in the same home include attention to personal hygiene, sanitation, the making, repairing and washing of clothes, the cleaning of the house and the storage of goods.

Food

Food and its preparation is an essential home activity. In many parts of the world food does not reach families in quantities sufficient for their needs —this despite the surplus of products in other countries. Often, although food is adequate in amount, the diet is badly balanced. In the study of an urban area already referred to, 6.5% of the children were inadequately fed —food being either deficient in amount or in quality. Water is as essential as food; in some areas supplies can be spasmodic, meagre and impure.

Clothing

Clothing is required for protection from the elements, and when this need has been met, surplus effort goes into making it decorative; in areas of great wealth, clothing has become highly sophisticated. The Newcastle study showed that in the families studied, 4.6% of the children were inadequately clad.

Transport

Transport has become mechanised in industrial nations. The mule and horse have given way to bicycle, motorcycle and car; in some areas it is commonplace for a family to have at least two cars. Its main uses are for work, shopping and recreation.

Income

The whole family's material state may be dependent on the income provided by the work of the husband alone, or by that of the husband and wife, or of all family members. In the Western world, more women are now employed outside the house. The Ipswich Thousand Family Survey showed that, in 1971, in a typical English town, the percentages of mothers with children who went to work were as follows:

TABLE III

PATTERN OF WORK BY MOTHERS

Full Time (38)	3.6%
Part Time—Day (148)	14.1%
Part Time—Evening (33)	3.1%
Night Work (5)	.5%
Not Working (822)	78.6%

The income may be unequally distributed between the family members, and this may lead to what is termed "secondary poverty." Furthermore, the income, even if fairly distributed, may be inefficiently deployed, a characteristic of problem families. Again, the earning capacity of a family member may depend more on his emotional balance than on training and ability.

Recreation

In the young child this takes place almost exclusively at home. In the older child playmates join the child and there is more outside activity, but its own siblings are still more likely to be its constant companions. In the adolescent, gang activities become common and most of this takes place at a distance from the home. Adults look for recreation within the home and in the locality. In highly developed societies the range and sophistication of recreation is great.

Most families aspire to an annual holiday, but the length and luxury of this varies greatly. The holiday is a particularly important feature of family life, as in some busy households it is the longest uninterrupted time together. Holidays are not always periods of enjoyment; even the period of Christmas may be remembered for its strife.

Education

Much of this takes place at home—early skills are acquired from parents; formal school teaching is supported by coaching at home; interest in learning is a reflection of family attitudes; success may be dependent on family support and encouragement. Recent experience suggests that inability to attend school is a family failure as often as it is an aversion to school.

Clinical Implications

Physical health can clearly be influenced by material surroundings. Lack of warmth, water or food can threaten life. Lack of cleanliness leads to disease; overcrowding promotes the spread of infection; lack of sleep predisposes to ill-health. Dietary deficiencies are linked to well recognized deficiency diseases. Hare and Shaw (2) found that rates of physical and mental ill-health increased with family size.

Mental health can also suffer. Acute and sub-acute toxic confusional states may result from dietary deficiencies, impure water, and from poisoning by lead toys. These cases are clear cut. But what are the effects of adverse conditions on emotional health? Poor conditions, for instance, make care of the child more difficult and lead to fatigue, which in turn causes irritability. Children sleep less readily when there is much noise. One living room does not allow the possibility of escape when tensions arise; it also does not allow study or play to be separated from the main family activities. In overcrowded conditions, parental quarrels cannot be hidden from the children. Lack of outdoor play facilities adds to the overcrowding. Inadequate diet results in listlessness and irritability. Families lose status in the clan and in the community when their conditions are bad. Lack of privacy for the parents in sexual activities may lead to the frustration of abstinence, or expose the children to the witnessing of sexual intimacies.

While we accept that physical conditions can affect the emotional health of families, it seems that of far greater significance in the lives of families is the effect of emotional health on its physical state. Emotional ill-health affects the material dimension of the family in two broad ways—it imposes too high or too low standards.

In some families material prosperity replaces emotional harmony. The family seeks happiness by acquiring wealth, advancement in employment, reputation, success and position. Its very insensitivity to others and its introverted self-interest may be advantageous in its quest for power, which it equates with security. Society abounds with leaders of great psychopathogenicity. In turn they set wrong targets from their privileged position. Some achieve the ultimate in material gain only to commit suicide in disillusionment.

The converse is as true. A family can underachieve. Its efficiency may be severely handicapped by its psychopathogenicity; mechanisms arising from this can render it a social cripple. Not only may there be an inability to advance, there may also be a sharp fall down the social and economic scale. Nowhere is this more apparent than in the study of highly pathogenic families. What is unclear in healthy or moderately healthy families, becomes starkly clear in the very disturbed. These so-called problem families, or multiple-handicapped families, or hard-core families, present themselves to social agencies with social failure. Their titles suggest the frustration of agencies in dealing with them. They are termed "problem" because however advantageous the circumstances surrounding the family, they fail to solve their own difficulties; "multiple handicapped" denotes the variety and multitude of their handicaps; "hard-core" denotes how resistant they are to change. Some of society's greatest social problems are cradled in these families—child neglect, delinquency, alcoholism, sloth, poor work records, etc.

Problem families are of such interest that a chapter is devoted to them in the section on "Special Aspects of Family Psychiatry."

REFERENCES

1. BOSSARD, J. H. S. (1951). A spatial index for family interaction. *Amer. sociol. Rev.*, *16*, 243.
2. HARE, E. H., and SHAW, G. K. (1965). A study in family health: (1) Health in relation to family size. *Brit. J. Psychiat.*, *111*, 461.
3. MILLER, F. J. W., COURT, S. D. M., WALTON, W. S., and KNOX, E. G. (1960). *Growing up in Newcastle upon Tyne*. London: Oxford Univ. Press.
4. SPENCE, J., WALTON, W. S., MILLER, F. J. W., and COURT, S. D. M. (1954). *A Thousand Families in Newcastle upon Tyne*. London: Oxford Univ. Press.

The Diachronic Course
of the Family

Time is important in Family Psychiatry, in two respects. Firstly, the family courses through time and is greatly influenced by this fact. Secondly, in psychopathology time span plays a large part in the setting up of psychopathological processes and therefore it should be given a correspondingly important part in its eradication, i.e., in treatment. It is the former that requires our attention here. The course of the family through time will be mapped out.

The Historical Course of Families

The one-generation model

The family, like the individual, has a history. This extends from courtship to the death of the last parent of a given family. The course of the family moves through a number of phases, each of which is reflected in changing structure and function:

1. Two representatives from different families—to be termed later, preceding parent families—meet at a point in time. The union may be tentative and break up, or be consolidated. The union continues until it is legalised by marriage. This is the *phase of courtship* in premarriage.

2. The adults in the family continue alone from marriage until tne birth of the first child. This is the *phase of early partnership* in marriage and ends at the start of the family's expansion.

3. The family, usually, now moves into a period of continuing expansion as more children are added to its numbers. This phase ends with the birth of the last child. This is the *phase of expansion.*

4. The family continues with no addition to its numbers out the phase ends when the first child moves out to live elsewhere or to found his own family. This is the *phase of consolidation.* Harris (1) points out that a

mother with a nicely spaced family (i.e., two years between births) cannot expect to spend less than ten years with pre-school children at home, nor less than eleven years with the last child at school and no pre-school children.

5. Decline of numbers now sets in as all the children leave and the founders of the family find themselves alone as a couple. This is the *phase of contraction.* The mother cannot usually expect to lose the youngest child by marriage until 25 years after she became pregnant with the first. The point at which they lose this last child is of profound significance for the couple as their major activity, as parents, has gone.

6. Life of the family continues with the founders together again as a couple. This is the *phase of final partnership.* If the mother married at 21, Harris (1) explains, she will only be 46 at the marriage of her last child. Assuming retirement at 60 she will have 14 years of working ahead of her. Following retirement she will on average have a further 15 years of life.

7. Then one partner and then the next dies. This is the *phase of disappearance;* the family is no more—except that it lives again through its representatives in other families. Each of these representatives is an embodiment of the family itself—irretrievably stamped by the family and destined to perpetuate that family and act out its dictates.

Diagrammatical representation is as follows:

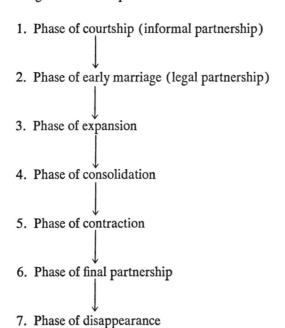

1. Phase of courtship (informal partnership)

2. Phase of early marriage (legal partnership)

3. Phase of expansion

4. Phase of consolidation

5. Phase of contraction

6. Phase of final partnership

7. Phase of disappearance

It is essential to the understanding of each phase to appreciate that each phase as it arises evokes in each parent the memories of that phase in the preceding parent families. The children, in turn, in the succeeding children families, will be seen to recreate experiences in each phase in the image of their own experiences in that phase of their preceding families.

Each of these phases has profound significance clinically. Certain events are only possible at a particular phase in the family's history. For example, in the phase of expansion, husband and wife undertake entirely new roles as parents instead of spouses, which may wreck the partnership; conversely, the phase of final partnership brings the partners together again after years as parents to undertake a forgotten role—as spouses rather than as parents.

In the *first phase,* the phase of courtship, the partners must contend with the partner-selection pressure from the preceding families; give over autonomy while retaining some independence; prepare for a coming marriage; prepare for and experiment with a mutually satisfying sex life; and obtain, if possible, complete or substantial freedom from the preceding family.

In the *second phase,* that of early marriage, significant features are: a sporadic contact with the partner becomes a permanent one; sex compatibility has to be achieved; relatives have to be given their proper significance in the life of the partners; preparation for children; a high standard of living with both partners usually at work; interdependence is a reality; imposing expectant attitudes on to the partner; continuing to "work through" the influence of preceding families.

In the *third phase,* that of expansion, features are: a fall in the standard of living unless wife's earning loss is compensated by higher earnings by husband; agreement about conception, pregnancy, child care; rivalries between parents and children and between children; new roles as parents as well as spouses; greater interdependence; problems of birth control; one or the other parent's overinvolvement with the children, with resulting strain on the marriage. Childbirth is such an important nodal point in the history of the family that a chapter is devoted to it in the section on "Special Aspects of Family Psychiatry."

In the *fourth phase,* that of consolidation, features are: the problems of school, adolescence, university, heterosexuality in the children; high earning power required of one or both parents; greater independence of children; generation clash with children and their contemporaries.

In the *fifth phase,* the phase of contraction, features are: loss of involvement in children; need for new interests by wife; increasing economic prosperity.

In the *sixth phase,* that of final partnership, features are: freedom of wife to go to work; loss of involvement in children by both parents; new roles as spouses rather than parents; high economic status; height of career for husband.

In the *seventh phase,* that of disappearance, features are: retirement with lower economic state and prestige; generation clash with grandchildren; increasing dependency on others; maximum contact time between partners; problems of bereavement; loneliness; loss of partner; death. Old age, a neglected subject, is given a chapter in the section on "Special Aspects of the Family."

When the clinician meets the family, the presenting family, it will be at some stage of its history, which can be at any of the phases. At this point in time—now, the family is termed the "Immediate Family." Exploration will be required of the past history of this family from its formation to date. This period is termed the "Prior Family." From the moment of contact with the family its life continues, partly in touch with the clinician, and also subsequently. This is termed the "Continuing Family." Thus there are three periods of exploration of the presenting family.

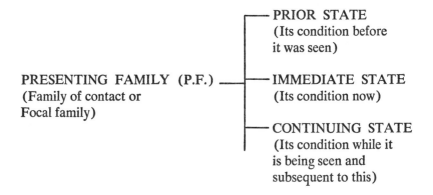

PRESENTING FAMILY (P.F.) ——
(Family of contact or
Focal family)

— PRIOR STATE
(Its condition before
it was seen)

— IMMEDIATE STATE
(Its condition now)

— CONTINUING STATE
(Its condition while it
is being seen and
subsequent to this)

The multi-generational model

In its dynamic course through the space-time continuum humanity is teased out into chains of intertwining families. In family psychiatry, evaluations have to embrace chains of at least three generations of families—occasionally more. It is emphasised again that the understanding of a family must be in terms of the families from which it was formed—this is a central truth of family psychiatry.

Harris (1) asserts that the family is typically three-generational. About 39% of all old people, 65 years old or over, in the U.S.A. have great-grandchildren and are thus members of four-generational families. Divergence towards two-generational families is less common and is said to be only 7% of old people with children in the U.S.A., and 12% in the U.K.

It has been customary and satisfactory in sociology to name families in terms of their contribution to the individual; e.g., the family in which the individual acts as a child is termed its "family of orientation"—sometimes "family of origin"; the family in which the individual takes on the status of a parent is termed its "family of procreation." The classification based on the individual is unsatisfactory in a system centred on the whole family and takes no account of the next-generation families or of remote families in the chain.

Thus the following classification is offered. The family under study, the point of first contact in the chain of families, is termed "the Presenting Family." It can be described in detail by its seven phases and five dimensions. The next previous families in the chain are termed "the Preceding Parent Families" and are two in number—the previous family of father and the previous family of mother, i.e., the family in which each was brought up as a child. Each of these in turn can be considered and described as it functions in its seven phases and in its five dimensions. The families two generations back are termed "the Preceding Grandparent Families." These are the families where the grandparents were brought up as children. They are four in number, the two paternal grandparent families and the two maternal grandparent families.

The families that follow the presenting family are termed "the Succeeding Children Families"; the numbers depend on the number of children and each receives a contribution from a "Collateral Family" (to be described later). These succeeding children families are families where the children of presenting families are the parents and their formative agents. Each can be described in its seven phases and in its five dimensions. Subsequent generations of families can be termed—"the Succeding Grandchildren Families." These are families where the grandchildren of the presenting family are the parents and their formative agents.

Later this framework will be used as the basis of the clinical exploration of families. In any description of a chain of families the point of departure should be the presenting family (see diagrams on the following pages).

Alongside each generation of families are to be found contemporary families. These are of two types: (i) those *related* to the families under investigation, consanguineal if there is a blood tie, and affinal if there is a marriage tie; and (ii) those who are *unrelated;* these normally supply partners to the families under investigation so that succeeding families can be formed. When referring to a contemporary family it is convenient to

WRITTEN REPRESENTATION OF CHAIN OF FAMILIES

PRECEDING GRANDPARENT
FAMILIES   FATHER (2)   MOTHER (2)

(Previous families where
grandparents of Presenting
Family were children)

PRECEDING PARENT
FAMILIES   FATHER   MOTHER

(Previous families where
parents of Presenting Family
were children)

PRESENTING _____⟨ PRIOR STATE
FAMILY (P.F.)   IMMEDIATE STATE
                                      CONTINUING STATE

(Focal family or
family of contact)

SUCCEEDING CHILDREN
FAMILIES

(Where children of Presenting
Family are parents)

SUCCEEDING
GRANDCHILDREN
FAMILIES

(Where grandchildren of
Presenting Family are parents)

refer to the family in the chain to which it is contemporary. Naturally, in clinical work concern is only with those contemporary families of clinical significance to the chain of families under study.

The system adopted for describing families has aetiological value. The history of the preceding parent family while the parent of the presenting family lived in it is of great importance for our understanding of the presenting family. Its subsequent history after the parent left is usually less important, as it has no aetiological significance now for the presenting family—unless still tied to it. Occasionally, the preceding parent family may still have direct influence on a presenting family, e.g., if the presenting family lives with the father's or mother's preceding family.

DIAGRAM OF FIVE-GENERATION FAMILY MODEL

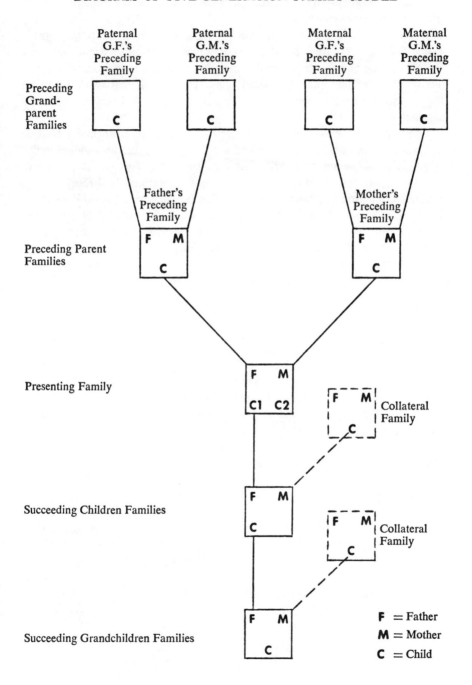

Similarly, contemporary related families are of little consequence unless of emotional significance to the presenting family. Indeed a contemporary unrelated family might be of greater importance if it had emotional significance for the presenting family, e.g., it might be in close friendship with the presenting family. In general, however, related contemporary families are more significant than unrelated ones. Thus in clinical work selection for investigation is dependent on the requirement of being emotionally significant.

Sometimes the preceding parent family changes structure in its course, e.g., mother dies and stepmother and surviving father set up a new family. This is significant and is described as a part of the history of the preceding family. Again, a child may leave his parents' home and be brought up in another contemporary home, e.g., adoptive home, foster home, his sister's home, etc. Therefore these must be described in his history of preceding parent family as they are significant. Thus occasionally the preceding parent family is an amalgam of a sequence of families.

The term "Composite Family" may be used to cover the nuclear family together with additional families; if they live in the same household they may be termed the "Domestic Group Family."

Abbreviations

It is normally more precise to use terms such as husband's sister rather than aunt—or to refer to the individual by name, e.g., Mary, or to use both designations, e.g., Mary, husband's sister.

Starting from the husband and wife, individuals within families can be abbreviated as follows:

Husband's Paternal Grandfather	Husband's Maternal Grandfather	Wife's Paternal Grandfather	Wife's Maternal Grandfather
H.P.G.F.	H.M.G.F.	W.P.G.F.	W.M.G.F.
Husband's Paternal Grandmother	Husband's Maternal Grandmother	Wife's Paternal Grandmother	Wife's Maternal Grandmother
H.P.G.M.	H.M.G.M.	W.P.G.M.	W.M.G.M.
Husband's Father	Husband's Mother	Wife's Father	Wife's Mother
H.F.	H.M.	W.F.	W.M.
	Husband H	Wife W	

Children can be referred to by numbers, e.g., C1, C2, C3, etc., or by name.

It is also possible to use abbreviations for generations by the use of + or − with numbers, e.g., Presenting Family = PF.

PF − 2 (Preceding Grandparent Generation)

PF − 1 (Preceding Parent Generation)

PF + 1 (Succeding Children Generation)

PF + 2 (Succeeding Grandchildren Generation)

Conclusion

A general framework is offered for the description of the family. This is based on a schema of the historical development of the family over a chain of generations. The history of a particular family in the chain passes through seven phases.

Conceptualisation of the family is dependent on the use to be made of it. What is appropriate for clinical purposes may be of no value in a different context. Thus the framework adopted must lead to meaningful clinical findings and useful clinical practices.

The family, like the individual, has a physical structure. This determines a dimension of physical properties. As a group, the family has general psychic characteristics. This determines the dimension of general psychic properties. Embraced within the latter are a number of entities, individuals, with psychological characteristics of their own. These are of sufficient clinical significance as to merit a dimension of individuals. Within the system of the family group lies a pattern of internal communication between its parts. Thus is identified a dimension of internal communication. Lastly the family group has a pattern of external communication with entities outside itself; it is convenient to separate the internal and external patterns and so found a dimension of external communication.

Any family in any phase or generation can thus be described in detail under five dimensions, four psychic and one physical, which are:

(1) The Dimension of the Individuals.

(2) The Dimension of Internal Communication.

(3) The Dimension of General Psychic Properties.

(4) The Dimension of External Communication.

(5) The Dimension of Physical Properties.

Clinical Implications—The Influence of Preceding Families

The individual who goes forth into the future as a representative of the preceding family is an epitome of that family. As surely as a piece of cake carries almost all the ingredients of the whole cake, so does an individual member of the family carry almost all the ingredients of his family. Some, and only some, differences may be due to his uniqueness as a person—just as the piece of cake has a shape of its own, different from the whole. Even his differences from the rest of the family are the product of the family, e.g., he may fight his family and adopt attitudes different from theirs—but they caused him to adopt this posture.

As he goes forth into time in search of his partner with whom to found a new family, his preceding family has already laid down the rules, sequence, course, aims of his quest—even the reasons for an unsuitable choice. Only some actions are possible for him—to meet the multiferous dictates of the family or to rebel against them. Chance and opportunity will play their part and he can only work out the will of the family within their confines. Given the maximum possible opportunity, he will act out the family's will to the absolute. A too obviously sexy partner would scandalise the sexual morality of the family and is taboo; a "modern miss" clashes with the conservatism of the family and is taboo; a boyish girl threatens the homo-sexual apprehensions of the family and is taboo. If he wishes to rebel, then all these become the desirable qualities in a mate. What has been formalised in thought may allow a course that opposes the family; but the automatic ingrained elements follow the family path as if guided by its radar. So often one hears the remark "I thought I was with his father" or "I catch myself behaving just like my father."

Choice of partner is controlled by the image of the opposite sex painted by the family over the years—who they say is desirable and who is not. Thus qualities are apprehended in the partner that meet the family dictates. Error can occur at this point. The seeker can "imagine" that the other possesses the desired qualities, but, due to insufficient time, artificial sur-roundings, or deliberate deception by the other, the judgement may go astray. After the marriage come the great "awakening," marital strain and collapse.

The experience in the preceding family may dictate specific qualities in the partner. For example, the loved father, weak and mother-dominated, may be taken as the model of the desirable; the husband, his own father's copy, allows the wife to take the dominant wife role taught by mother. There will be mishap if the husband proves to have hidden at that time unrevealed sources of opposition—a cruel awakening. Again, an unloved father, weak and mother-dominated, may not serve as a desirable model and the opposite is sought or a model based on some male more admirable than father. So, in the marriage, choices are made remarkably like parental figures in preceding marriages, or starkly different. Greater knowledge of the mechanisms at work could lead to more accurate matching of marriage partners. Sufficient experience with many members of the opposite sex in adolescence allows for the informal matching process to take place.

Some of the rules of selection are as follows:

People tend to imitate what they like, to improve on what they dislike.

The greater the harmony of the preceding family, the more flexible its product and the greater the capacity to adjust to a psychonotic partner. The psychonotic partner may have the assistance not only of the spouse but also the spouse's preceding family.

Partners can be alike and different; but if they are in harmony then they are likely to be alike in basic qualities.

An offspring tends to imitate the behaviour of the parent of the same sex in matters appropriate to the behaviour of that sex gender.

The opposite-sex parent may dictate some attitudes of the person in the same sex role; e.g., it is mothers who wish their boys to be masculine, and the more feminine the mother the more interested she is in the male and hence desires masculinity in her boys.

Liking a parent of the opposite sex may cause one to tend to select a partner in that image or in a part of it.

Disliking a parent of the opposite sex may cause one to tend to look for a partner with opposite properties from that parent.

A person tends to choose a partner in accord with his family's life style.

A person who is critical of his family's life style tends to marry someone from a family who can compensate for this.

These rules, involving as they do conformity and rebellion, imitation and rejection, can lead to interesting results. For example, the grand-daughter's husband is found to be wild like her grandfather; the sequence of events is as follows: grandfather is wild; his son, the father, rejects his behaviour and is timid; his daughter rejects the behaviour of her unloved father and seeks an opposite; her selection is that of a wild husband.

Sometimes the mechanisms are more obscure in that they also include attitudes towards the siblings; e.g., admiration of an elder brother who becomes a father substitute; admiration of a sister who becomes the model of a wife (the daughter also carries ingredients of the parents); rejection of an unloved sister. It has sometimes been argued that the brother-sister relationship plays a larger part in partner selection than the parent-child relationship—because the brother-sister age gap is more like that in the marriage. In practice there appears to be more emphasis on attitudes to parents than to siblings.

But the choice of partner is only the first intervention of families. Each partner brings into the marriage fixed attitudes, roles, interests, beliefs, values, conscience, temperament and skills. Some of these are basic elements, e.g., view of a father's role, ideas on the discipline of children, self-confidence in a particular situation, dishonourable behaviour, sexual conduct, areas of imagined threat, etc. Each must act on the dictates of the family and a clash can ensue with other family members, especially over basic issues. Two thieves can live in harmony, but it is unlikely that an honest man and a thieving woman will agree. Many of the basic qualities are hidden, unknown to the protagonist and sometimes hardly discerned by the antagonist. Thus conflict occurs without the participants knowing the nature of their conflict. Given considerable emotional health, a partner may have resilience and a capacity to adjust. The more psychonotic the partner the less the flexibility. Given two psychonotic partners, the adjustment is minimal.

Out of conflict will come an attempt at adjustment and at coping, and the coping mechanisms themselves will be distorted by the way in which the preceding family has forged them. The choice of indicator, again, may arise from the presenting family, or may be the re-establishment of an indicator from the preceding family. The preceding family can dictate the psychonosis and its indicators just as the presenting family can reawaken and reinforce these patterns from the past.

It follows from the above that an understanding of what happens in the presenting family can be greatly enhanced by the understanding of the two preceding families. In turn the presenting family will be making its inevitable contribution to the succeeding families.

REFERENCE

1. HARRIS, C. C. (1969). *The Family. Studies in Sociology*. London: Allen & Unwin.

III
NOSOLOGY

GENERAL CONSIDERATIONS

From time to time, with each upsurge of knowledge, clinicians have attempted reclassifications. Their history is too lengthy for review here. Starting with a *tabula rasa* and in the belief that any attempt at classification is worthwhile, a tentative new model is now put forward. This new model (i) is based on the aetiological modality, (ii) accepts the division of psychiatry into two main fields dependent respectively on psychic and organic pathology, (iii) caters for all age groups in one classification and (iv) is served by terms bereft of the distorting influences of "common usage." This classification, like every communication on the subject, is limited by the absence of final truth in psychiatry.

In this section we shall be concerned with the classification of abnormal states in the individual. As will be seen later, in the discussion of psychopathology, the classification is equally valid for abnormal states in the family.

At first, traditional nomenclature will be employed. Later in the chapter this will give way to suggested new terminology.

The Value of Taxonomy

It is appropriate to ask here: Why should one classify any phenomena? It is a purposeless exercise unless it has value. The attributes of categorisation have through long practice proved to be: (i) the aid it gives to the understanding of phenomena by generalising from data; (ii) the more effective control it gives over phenomena, which in turn can lead to improvement; (iii) the assistance to more accurate prediction of the course

107

of the phenomena. Phenomena can be assessed from many vantage points and classified by many modalities; the most appropriate is the one that most adequately serves a given purpose at a particular moment in time. The classifier must be knowledgeable about the material he intends to classify if he is to establish a worthwhile system and be able to test the practicability of his formulations. Taxonomy (tax, τάξις order; nomy, νομός law) then, the science of classification, has value.

Why classify in medicine? Classification by the orderly assembly of data may expose instances that have affinity and are meaningful as a group; light may be thrown on the nature and locus of dysfunction; therapy may come to have a logical and therefore useful basis; more precise evaluation of treatment becomes possible; research can be planned in a manner relevant to its purpose; research data are more easily comparable; areas of ignorance may be exposed. Thus classification is a tool for the essential purpose of medicine, to relieve suffering, and to produce harmonious functioning by treatment. Nosology (nosis, νόσος disease; logy, λόγος word), the classification of diseases and a branch of taxonomy, has value.

Data in medicine, as elsewhere, can be categorised by many modalities, e.g., the age of the patient; degree of physical disability; degree of social disability; body build; size of head, shape of hand; response to therapy; prognostic value; or even by a mathematical abstraction of easy digestion using a computer, etc. The overriding factor in the selection of a modality for classification is that it be the one most appropriate to the purpose in mind. Experience has amply demonstrated the special value of a nosology based on certain aetiology; such a classification has the virtue of leading to certain treatment, the end result of medical endeavour. The elucidation of the nature of cerebral syphilis as an infection, for instance, led to the utilisation of the appropriate powerful therapeutic agents and to measures to control and prevent this disorder.

The Present Position in Psychiatry

Classification of psychiatric disorders on a useful aetiological model calls for precision and agreement in three main areas in all of which at present there are deficiencies. The first area includes the identification of indicators of dysfunction (i.e., signs and symptoms), agreed criteria for evaluating these, and a systematic procedure for investigating the presence of such indicators. The second area includes the correct grouping of states of dysfunction to produce meaningful syndromes. Rawnsley et al. (22) after an international diagnostic exercise concluded that, at the level of sub-categories of diagnosis, international variations in usage are so great as completely to vitiate comparisons between countries; for instance, U.S. psychiatrists diagnosed schizophrenia much more frequently than U.K. psychiatrists, but the reverse was true of depression. Kramer et al. (16) came to similar conclusions. The third area includes agreement over the definitions of all the terms and categories employed in nomenclature.

The supreme example of the monumental waste and frustration produced by inability to agree on diagnostic criteria is the research field of schizophrenia. Langfeldt (18), a distinguished researcher and nosologist, wrote in this connection: "However, in spite of the thousands of investigations, thus far no conclusion has been borne to the point of universal authority by further investigation. This circumstance is, in part, due to the fact that there is no agreement on the characteristics of the schizophrenic disorders." Bleuler (2), with his definition of "schizophrenia," extended the term to include the vaguer concept of psychosis, and this in turn has come to embrace any major deviation of behaviour, regardless of aetiology. Only a handful of papers define their criteria so as to show beyond doubt that they deal with "genuine" schizophrenia. The result is great doubt on the interpretation of findings. In the genetics of schizophrenia, for example, there has already been a sharp change of opinion—concordance rates in twin studies of schizophrenia are not what geneticists a few years ago claimed them to be. Perhaps the criteria are different. Who knows? Is it possible, for instance, that many of the patients included in the category of schizophrenia in the early studies were advanced neurotics; the strong correlations amongst family members would be understandable, as neurosis is eminently a familial disorder, but by communication rather than by inheritance. Howells (11) is forced to regard the research on the family psychopathology of schizophrenia as unproven, as in no instance was there an adequate criterion of schizophrenia; the data suggested that the researchers were studying atypical schizophrenia, probably severe neurosis (psychonosis).

The starting point in any consideration of the present classificatory scheme for mental disorder must be Stengel's exhaustive review (1959) (26) carried out for the World Health Organisation, together with his more recent critical summaries (27, 28). Some of the issues in the nosology of mental disorders were explored at a conference held under the auspices of the American Psychopathological Association in 1959—Zubin (1961) (37). This led to a cross-national study—Kramer et al. (1969) (16). The W.H.O. has also set up a working party for a ten-year period and laudably this group has also based their work on the study of case material. Stengel (26) reviews 58 different systems. Special mention must be made of the outstanding historical review of nosology by Karl Menninger in the closing pages of *The Vital Balance* (19). The International Classification of Diseases (I.C.D.) is the most widely employed system, but it is regarded with general dissatisfaction. The I.C.D. has a number of unsatisfactory features. It is based on concepts that are often outdated. It is a compromise between many conflicting movements and traditions. But its most serious limitation is that it is based on a large number of different modalities which causes it to be an illogical, disorderly, confusing hotch-potch. This latter point can be demonstrated by listing some of the modalities employed. The numbers refer to the categories in the I.C.D.:

Age—with childbirth—294.4; behaviour disorders of childhood 308; involutional melancholia 296.0.

Agent—alcoholic psychosis 291; alcoholism 303; infection 292; trauma 293.5.

Organ—brain 292; skin 305.0.

Symptoms—schizophrenia 295; neurosis 300; sexual deviation 302.

Social Behaviour—exhibitionism 302; antisocial 301.7; transient situational 307.

Degree—mental retardation 310–315.

Temporal—acute paranoid reaction 298.3; episodic excessive drinking 303.0; acute schizophrenic episode 295.4.

Obstacles to Agreement

The question of diagnosis is bedevilled by the inability to establish agreed criteria for the definition of clinical categories. Some of the inherent difficulties will be catalogued. Some of these are beyond our control. Others are capable of modification.

1. When there is exact knowledge, definitions present less of a problem. Ignorance on many essential matters presents a real problem for psychiatry. Nevertheless, classification still falls behind the available knowledge.

2. It is clearly shown in Rayner's study (23) that the use of the term "psychosis" is generally equated with highly abnormal or unusual behaviour. Highly abnormal behaviour also occurs in neurosis. Acute anxiety or anguish can precipitate a number of acute symptoms which are as bizarre and extreme as those in psychosis. Neurotic behaviour may be just as disruptive and damaging as psychotic behaviour, if not more so. Careful examination, however, reveals that the abnormal behaviour in neurosis is different from psychotic behaviour. In the absence of careful examination many severe conditions of neurosis are liable to be labelled "psychotic."

3. There are misjudgements that spring from personal training and experi-

ence. Individual psychiatrists see what they are trained to see. At one extreme psychiatrists may have a background of training and experience in mental hospitals and are oriented towards psychosis; psychopathology may be ill-understood, if recognised at all. Thus, there is a tendency to label highly abnormal behaviour demanding hospital admission as "psychotic" irrespective of the basic clinical picture. Thus psychosis is overdiagnosed. At the other extreme, psychiatrists may have a background in psychopathology and rarely see psychosis. Often they follow the fashion of regarding extreme states as psychotic—when acquaintance with psychotics would have exposed the qualitatively different clinical picture. Thus for both reasons psychosis tends to be overdiagnosed. This argues for a comprehensive training with experience in both fields.

4. Every vocation has a heritage and so has psychiatry. Misconceptions tend to go unchallenged and come to have the status of myths. Yet, practitioners in the past were even more ignorant than ourselves and therefore even less able to arrive at satisfactory criteria. For instance, Stierlin's examination (30) of Bleuler's concept of schizophrenia (2) exposed it as an attempt to integrate viewpoints from Kraepelin, Freud and Simon, leaving a confusing heritage. Thus we must continually re-examine the assessments of the past.

5. To base clinical requirements on hospital rather than on community practice can give a very wrong impression of clinical needs. Hospital practice may suggest the preponderance of psychotic material; community practice, the reverse.

6. Neurosis is more readily diagnosed if a direct link between the stress and the reaction can be established. Due to the exigencies of medical practice, time is limited. Thus often either no attempt is made to explore psychopathology or no time is available. Therefore neurotic conditions may be overlooked. Particular examples are: conditions of paranoia with deep suspicion can be precipitated by anxiety and even by deafness; they are often interpreted to mean a psychotic state. Post-puerperal depression is an area that has recently come under the close scrutiny of psychopathologists and what were previously thought to be endogenous psychotic depressions are now seen in the main to be reactive neurotic states.

7. Symptoms can be shared by syndromes with a quite different aetiology. Dyspnoea may be due to anaemia or a pneumothorax. Equally, the depersonalisation of an agitated panic-stricken person may have a different basis from the bizarre depersonalisation of a schizophrenic.

8. Hasty examination may cause the observer not to notice qualitative differences in common symptoms. The detachment of the lovelorn is quali-

tatively different from the detachment due to the stupor of catatonic schizophrenia or that of diabetic coma.

9. Symptoms can be elevated into clinical syndromes. For example, "enuresis," though a symptom, is often classed as a disease. "Catatonia" is a symptom rather than a clinical category. "Withdrawal" or "autism" as a symptom may be due to preoccupation, depression, catatonic stupor or diabetic coma, but it is not itself a clinical syndrome. Slavish categorisation by the initial or presenting symptom will in particular lead to the above abuse. Thus investigation may stop short of an examination that would have revealed further signs of dysfunction, and an incomplete picture is obtained.

10. A great disadvantage to psychiatry has been the breakup of its practice into age groups—infant, child, adolescent, adult and geriatric psychiatry. Thus, the flow of psychopathology from infancy to old age is not always comprehended. The temper tantrums of the infant become the awkwardness of the schoolboy, the delinquency of the adolescent, the criminal behaviour of the adult and the malevolent contrariness of the aged. As it is one process, the essential nomenclature should be the same. The late development of adolescent psychiatry has been particularly damaging as it sets up a gap between child and adult psychiatry. Terms associated with age periods—e.g., infantile psychosis, puerperal psychosis, climacteric psychosis, involutional melancholia—tend to establish discrete syndromes occurring at these periods and obscure the need to define the aetiological picture. Sometimes the conceptions of the practitioners of one age group are imposed upon that of another, when a total appreciation would have produced conclusions meaningful for all age groups and to the benefit of each.

11. Terms may be misleading. Strömgren (32) has pointed out that "amentia" in the United Kingdom is synonymous with mental retardation but in continental Europe it is used for a specific form of delirium. Again, ideas may be shared by clinicians but the term employed for the idea may be different, e.g., "psychogenic psychosis" in Denmark, "constitutional psychosis" in Norway, and "reactive psychosis" elsewhere. Some words are borrowed from everyday language, e.g., "confusion," and tend to be imprecise. A term, which by the concepts of one era sounds adequate, becomes inadequate with increasing knowledge, e.g., "split mind" may have satisfied clinicians in Bleuler's day, and "schizophrenia" was acceptable; but today the term hardly covers the central signs of this state of psychosis. Words coined to denote a particular category may be borrowed and used to cover related conditions, e.g., Korsakov's psychosis was first used to describe a state arising in alcoholic dementia but was later employed for similar states elsewhere in organic dementia.

ISSUES IN CLASSIFICATION

The Medical Heritage

Medicine has a long history of grappling with classificatory systems for morbid phenomena and has arrived at a general plan which is satisfactory in its field of operation. Psychiatry should thus profit from medicine's long experience. The definition of disease is as follows (dis-ease = without ease). "A disease is the sum total of the reactions, physical and mental, made by a person to a noxious agent entering his body from without or arising within (such as micro-organism or a poison), and injury, a congenital or hereditary defect, a metabolic disorder, a food deficiency, or a degenerative process. These cause pathological changes in organs or tissues which are revealed by characteristic signs and symptoms. Since a particular agent tends to produce a pathological and clinical picture peculiar to itself, although modified by individual variations in different patients, a mental concept of the average reactions or a composite picture can be formed which, for the convenience of description, is called a particular disease or clinical entity. But a disease has no separate existence apart from a patient, and the only entity is the patient" (*Butterworth's Medical Dictionary*). Thus to delineate a clinical category there has to be an agent, a fabric which is disrupted by the agent and signs of the fabric's dysfunction. To identify the complete morbid process is to establish a clinical diagnosis. Feinstein's recent re-examination (7) of the procedures of clinical judgement does not quarrel with this system but he calls for greater refinement and precision.

Before we discuss in turn the agent, the fabric, the signs and the diagnosis, some mention must be made of the phenomenology of psychiatry. Some would deny that there are meaningful signs of disturbances of psychic functioning. But there is no doubt that guilt at the murder of a mother is as much a phenomenological entity as a broken leg resulting from a fall. Dysfunction of the psyche manifests itself by anomalous behaviour which incapacitates, causes discomfort, pain and anguish and makes the individual seek relief, or makes the onlooker seek relief on his behalf. Hence the need for a psychiatrist (psyche, ψυχή mind; iatros, ἰατρός healer).

The Agent. As the result of long experience, five groups of harmful agents have been recognised in medicine. These are (i) infective, (ii) neoplastic, (iii) congenital and hereditary, (iv) metabolic and degenerative, (v) traumatic.

Included in group (v) is emotional or psychic trauma which is overwhelmingly common, of great force of impact, capable of dire consequences and of influencing every component of the soma. Psychic stress usually comes from a psychic source, i.e., another person.

The Fabric. Harmful *organic* agents may disrupt any tissue in the body. The tissue of prime concern to the psychiatrist or neuropsychiatrist is the encephalon (brain). Manifestations of the dysfunctioning of the encephalon are termed "mental symptoms" and may come within the purview of the psychiatrist. In general the effects of organic agents on the encephalon are well documented. They may strike at the encephalon directly, or indirectly through the products of somatic dysfunction elsewhere.

Psychic agents may also strike at the fabric of the psyche and any part of the soma, including the encephalon.

Sometimes the two groups of reactions, organic and emotional, coexist, e.g., a physical blow may not only do direct physical damage, but may also arouse a psychic reaction by its threat value.

The "process" precipitated in the organ by the harmful agent is of course different from the signs of pathology. The misfire of a motor car is a useful sign of machine failure, but it is not an adequate description of the disturbed combustion in the engine. Pathological processes in the soma are now largely, but not completely, understood. Pathological processes in the psyche are less understood. The greater the ignorance, the more conflicting the views. Truth does not nourish speculation.

The Indicators. An increase in functioning per se is not a sign of dysfunction, e.g., a rapid pulse rate in a runner is a sign of excellent functioning.

Signs may be shared by a number of different clinical categories, e.g., dyspnoea can accompany carcinoma of the chest, anaemia, or cardiac disease. A sign can be shared by emotional or physical disorders; dyspnoea can occur in anxiety and in physical disorders. The signs of organic disorder are so well known that they do not need categorising here.

Psychic trauma impinging on an individual releases two clusters of indicators of dysfunction. (i) Physical (termed psychosomatic.) They may affect one organ alone, e.g., precipitating asthma, or a number of organs together, as in hypertension with colitis and migraine. The brain is not exempt and there may be dysfunctioning of the encephalon, e.g., migraine or epilepsy. (ii) Psychic changes. The indicators of psychic stress are rarely, if ever, monosymptomatic.

A number of indicators appear in each group and indeed, it is rare for both clusters not to be involved. But only careful and global examination will expose this fact. Too often examination stops at the presenting symptom.

The Diagnosis (διάγνωσις = *discernment*). The isolation of the indicators of disorder calls for a systematic investigation in a meaningful way because, over time, careful endeavour in a field shows that particular signs are significant and these are incorporated in the plan of investigation. If the plan of investigation fails to examine for the significant signs, then it will fail to elicit these signs. In psychiatry there is disagreement over what is significant and individual systems of examination are inadequate and incomplete. This is especially true in the psychic field.

Having been elicited, the indicators may be grouped together with the disrupted fabric and the responsible agent in a meaningful way and so be formed into a syndrome, a disease category. Hence the diagnosis is made. It is usually necessary to take account not only of the nature and degree of the indicators, but also of their historical development. It is relevant to point out that diagnoses are made by the presence of positive indicators of disorder and not by the absence of indicators. Frequently psychiatrists are encouraged by physicians to assume that the absence of physical indicators must denote a psychiatric disorder. The latter can only be diagnosed by positive indicators pointing to psychiatric disorder. The diagnosis implies a pathological process provoked by a known agent in a particular site or sites and leading to characteristic indicators. Ideally, it leads to a logical plan of treatment.

Psychic and Somatic States

For centuries, with fluctuating clarity, attempts have been made to divide mental phenomena into those that result from dysfunction of psyche and those that spring from dysfunction of brain activity. In the 16th century Felix Platter (21) in Europe and Timothie Bright (3) in England and in the 17th century Richard Burton (1605) (4), Willis (1621–1675) (35) and Sydenham (33) all recognised emotional states. Hunter and Macalpine (13) recount that in 1600 in England there were practitioners licensed by the Bishops to practise on melancholy (neurosis) and on the mad (psychosis). Emotional disorder was well understood at this time (Howells and Osborn) (12). Harvey's discovery of the circulation (9) in the early 17th century unleashed an era of intensive preoccupation with physiological activities; psychiatry survived only inasmuch as it dealt with insanity (psychosis), the demands of which could not be ignored. Psychiatrists became alienists largely divorced from the medical field. The end of the 19th century saw the reawakening of interest in psychic dysfunction. That trend continues apace today. There is general acceptance that psychiatry has two areas of activity—emotional dysfunction and brain dysfunction. This is not accepted in all quarters where severe emotional disorder is believed to extend into psychosis.

One of the end results of lack of clarity over criteria is the tendency to confuse the signs of psychic dysfunction, e.g., anxiety, anguish, guilt, agitation, with signs of brain dysfunction, memory defects, confabulation, disorientation, hallucinations, perceptual anomalies, etc. The last group are known to spring from damage to areas of the brain, the first are not. The two groups of symptoms on careful examination are qualitatively different —but equally incapacitating to the individual.

An equally great, and hardly credible, cause of bewilderment is that the clinical term employed to denote morbid disorder of mind, i.e., neurosis, suggests a disorder with an organic basis. Conversely, the term used to denote morbid disorder of the brain, psychosis, suggests a psychic basis. Can this be so? Remarkably, close study shows that this is so. Indeed the terms are virtually reversible.

The term neurosis is derived from the Greek—νεῦρον neuron (nerve) which, with its suffix -osis (nosis—disorder), thus means a "nerve disorder," i.e., a somatic condition. That this is so can be seen from the writings of the clinician who first used the term—Cullen, in 1776 (5). In his "Synopsis Nosologiae Methodicae" he proposed to comprehend under the title of Neuroses "all those preternatural affections of sense or motion which are without pyrexia as a part of the primary disease, and all those which do not depend upon a topical affection of the organs, but upon a more *general affection of the nervous system* . . . of such diseases I have established a class, under the Title of Neuroses. . . ." [Author's italics]. Thus his class "Neurosis" was intended to have a somatic basis. But in time the term came to mean the reverse of Cullen's intention—it came to denote morbid states based on psychic dysfunction. An attempt at compensation was to add the prefix "psycho" to neurosis, making psychoneurosis, which led to the absurdity "psychic disorder of nerve." Thus does haphazard "common usage" bring inexactitude.

The term psychosis is also derived from the Greek—ψυχή psyche, mind, which, with its suffix -osis (nosis—disorder), thus means "disorder of mind," i.e. psychic condition. Psyche is employed in the "Iliad" and meant "breath." It came to mean "the breath of life" or the principle of life itself. Later it stood for mind, soul or spirit. Today it stands for mind. First employed by Von Feuchtersleben (8) in 1845, it was not a widely used term in psychiatry before the early 20th century, being preceded by "insanity" and used interchangeably with it until about 1930. In the checkered and confused career of the term "psychosis," as carefully followed by Rayner

(23), it seems that the condition was diagnosed not always by its phenomenology but by the degree of abnormal behaviour, i.e. its severity. Once more we can see arising the difficulty already mentioned, that of equating severely abnormal behaviour with psychosis and extending it to cover the equally extreme but qualitatively different behaviour of neurosis. Thus again we find a central term in psychiatry coming by "common usage" to mean its precise opposite.

Briefly, consideration must be given to terms used more or less synonymously with neurosis and psychosis. For the first there is "mental disorder." Mental comes from the Latin—*mens* (the mind). Unfortunately, this term, owing to incorrect "common usage," embraces also symptomatology of brain dysfunction, e.g., memory loss. Thus its use is not advocated. "Emotional disorder" has the disadvantage that there is no satisfactory definition of "emotional," which probably forms only a part of psychic activity. For psychosis there are "madness," "insanity" and "lunacy," all with evident disadvantages. "Madness," over a number of centuries, has lost all precise meaning and at worst is a term of abuse. "Lunacy" is derived from "moon sickness" thought to be associated with the moon in the mediaeval span of interest in astrology; it is too inexact for contemporary usage. "Insanity" is derived from the Latin *insanus,* i.e., not sound (unsound in mind). Its direct meaning—unsoundness of mind—is thus the reverse of its commonly employed meaning and is no alternative to "psychosis." It seems that we are far from the era of astrology in time but not in nomenclature.

In seeking acceptable terms to cover conditions of psychic and somatic origin the first possibility is to reverse the terms "psychosis" and "neurosis." There would be the evident disadvantage of confusion, and in any event the term "neurosis" describes a "disorder of nerve" rather than a "disorder of brain." It would seem essential to go back to first principles. A common basis for both conditions in Greek or in Latin might seem desirable. Brain from a Latin derivation would force the term "cerebrum" upon us; unhappily, it has ceased to mean brain but stands for the cerebral hemispheres by "common usage." Greek is more helpful. We are offered "encephalon" (encephalos, ἐγκέφαλος, marrow within the head, brain) which stands for brain. Thus, by adding the suffix -nosis (morbid process) to the above, a morbid process of brain neatly becomes encephalonosis.

A matching Greek term is now needed for the morbid psychic processes. Phrenosis is a possibility. Phrenic is derived from the Greek term for diaphragm, which area was thought to be the seat of the emotions. Thus phren (phren, φρήν, mind) came to stand for mind. Frenzy, derived from it, at first covered emotional disturbance, but unfortunately the term soon became identified with mental disturbance, e.g., phrenitis stood for delirium.

The term also has an unhappy link with phrenology. Another Greek term for mind is psyche, ψυχή. Psychosis is unthinkable because of the confusion it would cause. Psychopathology (psyche, ψυχή, mind; pathy, πάθος, morbid process, λόγος, discourse) would fit, but regrettably, it has a special meaning in contemporary forensic practice. Greek, however, is accommodating. The suffix -nosis (from νόσος, disease) stands for a morbid process. Thus disorder of psyche becomes psychonosis.

So we have our preferred terms—encephalonosis (morbid process of brain) and psychonosis (morbid process of mind). These will now be employed with the old terms in parentheses.

Areas for Delineation

Before a finer sub-classification of psychonosis (neurosis) and encephalonosis (psychosis) can be attempted, some attention must be paid to some diagnostic categories which present difficulty in classification.

It will be noted that the issues in the first six categories turn around differentiating extreme behaviour characteristic of psychonosis (neurosis) from psychosis. Instead of being labelled psychonosis (neurosis) they are all regarded as atypical schizophrenia and thus included under encephalonosis. The high incidence of affective disorders in the relations of such patients would be in conformity with the view that the patients suffer from psychonosis (neurosis).

1. Pseudo-neurotic schizophrenia. This condition was described by Hoch and Polatin in 1949 (10). It is a borderline state which causes problems in diagnosis. The characteristic features are a variety of psychic symptoms, chaotic sexuality, transient hallucinations and a good prognosis. One is forced to come to the conclusion that these conditions are usually states of psychonosis (neurosis).

2. Schizo-affective psychoses. These were described by Kasanin in 1933 (15). Their principal feature according to Kasanin was "characterised by a very sudden onset in a setting of marked emotional turmoil with a distortion of the outside world. . . . The psychosis lasts a few weeks to a few months and is followed by a recovery." The similarity to pseudo-neurotic schizophrenia is evident. In time the condition came to stand for mixed affective and presumed schizophrenic states. In clinical practice it appears that, given time, it is possible to disentangle psychopathology in such patients and come to the conclusion that they are all essentially psychonotic (neurotic) states. Indeed, the very existence of affect is not indicative of a diagnosis of schizophrenia in that one of the characteristic features of this condition is the absence of *affect* in the patient.

3. Psychogenic psychoses. A Danish psychiatrist, Faergeman (6) has described these conditions in some detail and the term is widely used in Scandinavia. Sometimes the term "reactive psychosis" or "ambulatory psychosis" or "constitutional psychosis" is used with the same meaning. The term psychogenic psychosis is useful in that it emphasises that extreme behaviour can occur as a result of emotional stimuli. But the term "psychosis" is unfortunate in its present connotation. One is forced again to accept that these conditions are essentially psychonotic states (neurotic). They appear to present extreme, unusual, bizarre variants of neurosis. Some patients react in an unexpected way and this may be dependent upon their unusual childhood experiences. Reactive psychoses in the Russian classifications are associated with psychonoses (neuroses).

4. Schizophreniform psychoses. These conditions were described by Langfeldt in 1937 (17). Langfeldt distinguishes "genuine schizophrenia" from an atypical form termed schizophreniform. Other terms applied to psychoses which are equivalent to "genuine" are "process," "central" and "nuclear." The symptoms in Langfeldt's "genuine" class are close to those regarded by Schneider (24) as of prime importance in the diagnosis of schizophrenia. The atypical schizophreniform psychosis, like "non-process" psychosis, has a good prognosis; Stephens and Astrup (1963) (29) verified this for "non-process" psychosis. It would appear that these conditions represent typical, puzzling, or bewildering conditions of psychonosis (neurosis).

5. Paranoia. Our increasing knowledge of psychopathology has shown that this condition can be set up in states of anxiety and can even reach an extreme degree, e.g., a bitter, disabled man up against, and thwarted by, authority. The suspicions and delusions are explicable in terms of real life situations. In the absence of other signs denoting schizophrenia, paranoia existing alone invariably indicates a psychonotic (neurotic) state.

6. Severe stress conditions. It is reasonable to wonder whether severe stress can cause dysfunctioning of the brain and thus produce encephalonosis. Such an hypothesis is reasonable and must be considered in the genesis of schizophrenia, but it needs verification. It would seem that most of the states described, e.g., phobic reaction, are reversible, and in this event it would seem better to regard the phenomenology as being indicative of a severe psychic reaction, i.e., severe psychonosis (neurosis).

Slight anxiety may cause anguish, an increased pulse rate, sweating of the skin, etc. Therefore very extreme anxiety would be expected to create an even more severe reaction. This reaction may be exaggerated by the fact that the somatic changes (e.g., thyroid, or adrenal secretion) may of themselves set up a toxic state. Thus the condition could be regarded as a psychosomatic disorder within psychonosis (neurosis).

7. Paraphrenia. This has come to mean schizophrenia occurring in the aged. It has the disadvantage of implying a separate aetiology from schizophrenia occurring in other age groups and is a term best deleted from clinical practice.

8. "Borderline" and "latent" psychoses. These terms have as little value as would the terms "latent" or "borderline" pneumonia. A condition either is or is not.

9. Psychopathy. Strictly defined this term means pathological states of mind or morbid conditions of mind. However, it, together with such terms as psychopathic states, has come to mean an antisocial or sociopathic individual and it has a special meaning in forensic psychiatry. Such an individual, if at variance with the society in which he lives, is abnormal or sick. That is to say his dysfunction has been caused by emotional stress and his behaviour is a part of his defensive reaction to it. Few would now accept Morel's (20) implication of constitutional moral degeneracy. As will be seen later in the discussion of psychonosis, this condition must properly form a part of psychonosis.

10. Character disorders. Among these it is usual to include such conditions as homosexuality, sexual deviations and alcoholism. Clarification may come through a brief discussion of alcoholism. Habitual drinking of a social kind, although it may not be conducive to the well being of the soma, cannot be regarded as a psychiatric disability. Indeed, should the habitual drinking take on a severe degree, it might still, strictly speaking, not be regarded as a psychiatric disability. However, for an individual to indulge in extreme habitual drinking threatening his own welfare is usually per se an indication of an emotional disorder. Experience shows that severe alcoholism indicates an emotional disorder and that the excessive drinking is part and parcel of the individual's reaction to stressful events in his life experience.

11. Multiple diagnoses. These may arise in two circumstances: (i) a justifiable doubt about a diagnosis when two or more possibilities may be listed; (ii) because there is a truly mixed condition, e.g., a neurosis (psychonosis) accompanied by amphetamine intoxication, i.e., psychonosis and encephalonosis together.

Elements of a Satisfactory Classification

From the discussion so far it is possible to identify the conditions for the satisfactory classification of syndromes in psychiatry.

1. As far as possible, and certainly within its main divisions, the classification should be based on one modality.

2. The most purposeful modality in medicine is that based on aetiology.

3. The classification should be applicable to all age groups.

4. There should be precise definition of all terminology. There is much advantage in using, as far as possible, terms derived from classical Greek because of its universal usage, especially in medical terminology. Words should fit as closely as possible to the ideas they represent while it is recognized that often a word can only approximate to the idea that it represents. Emotive words such as lunacy, idiocy, etc., should be kept to a minimum.

5. Practicability in the clinical field is essential.

6. The classification should be capable of existing alongside classifications based upon secondary modalities, e.g., degree of disorder, measures of social adjustment, measures of intellectual deficit.

7. Multiple diagnoses should be possible.

8. Miscellaneous terms should be kept to a minimum.

9. The classification should be easily adjusted in the light of changing concepts of aetiology in psychiatry in the course of time.

PSYCHONOSIS

Definition

Psychonosis is defined as a morbid process of mind (psyche, ψυχή, mind; nosis, νόσος, disorder).

The essential process in psychonosis is that the psyche suffers the trauma of psychic noci-vectors, with the result that there is disruption of its functioning and indication of dysfunction is seen in signs and symptoms. Psychic events are phenomena but we do not here need to go into a discussion of the form of the psyche. Psychonosis is a disorder of the acquired part of the psyche, described later under psychopathology.

Stress

The psychic trauma may be of two varieties: (i) it may be a stress specific to an individual, a stress that has an especially destructive meaning for him, because of his sensitisation to the stress; (ii) a general stress to which most people are susceptible. The impact of the trauma is greater if the personality is more vulnerable because of previous adverse traumatic experiences.

Psychopathology

This consists of more than the manifest indicators, the signs and symptoms, in the same way the symptoms of thyrotoxicosis do not give a complete picture of the process going on within the fabric of the thyroid gland.

The process, psychopathology, is complex and diffuse and has been a matter for discussion among psychopathologists for many generations: The ways of describing psychopathology are legion, e.g., Freudian, Jungian, behavioural, phenomenological, etc. There is no general agreement. The matter is discussed under experiential psychopathology.

Indicators

When these result from a subjective evaluation they are termed symptoms; when from an objective evaluation, signs.

These can conveniently be divided into two clusters, namely (i) the psychosomatic group, (ii) the psychic group.

The first, the psychosomatic group, includes all those signs of organ dysfunction. One or more systems of the body, including the central nervous system, may be implicated at any one time.

The second group includes all those signs of change of psychic state, e.g., anxiety, depression, apathy, obsession, phobic states, etc; and those defensive reactions such as timidity, withdrawal, and assertive changes of behaviour such as temper tantrums, awkwardness, antisocial behaviour, etc.

It is characteristic of psychonosis that it is never monosymptomatic; indeed it is pathognomonic (characteristic) of psychonosis that it always manifests itself in a number of indicators. Furthermore it can be said that rarely does the symptomatology present in one of the above two groups alone. There is usually a total disturbance of the personality which embraces elements in both groups, but which becomes apparent only on close and complete examination.

It might be asked why this truth is sometimes overlooked. This is because there has been a tendency to classify according to the presenting sign and not to proceed to a complete examination of the psyche. Hence such terms as anxiety, hysterical, obsessional, neurasthenic, and depressive states are used. This is categorisation by the presenting sign and should be avoided. Indeed it would leave us at the era of the mediaeval practitioners who labelled such symptoms as "fever" and "melancholie" as clinical disorders.

The inability to agree about psychopathology has imperceptibly shifted attention to describing the process in terms of the signs; this is illusionary as the signs are a mere index and no more. Further knowledge may not allow categorisation of the psychopathological process. On the other hand, it may reveal that it is as clear cut as the inflammatory process, is confined to one system, the psyche, and has variations in its expression which are dependent on the life situation, i.e., symptoms and signs are governed by the demands and dictates of the life situation in the past and the present.

Diagnosis

The aim of classification is to produce order that leads to more useful treatment. It would seem that in the field of psychonosis (neurosis) any classification based upon the character of the stress, or the psychopathological process, or the symptomatology alone limits rather than helps. As so many factors are involved when an individual in his life situation meets stress, a simple categorisation of the result is not possible and indeed limits the appreciation of this experience. Thus it is better to rely upon a descriptive account which outlines: (i) the source and nature of the trauma; (ii) the characteristics of the individual; and (iii) the indicators of dysfunction which are apparent.

In practice there may be virtue in using *secondary evaluations*. The *degree* of severity of the psychonosis may be considered, e.g., mild, moderate and severe. The degree should be an index of the incapacity of the individual in his life situation at that time; some persons are so handicapped as to remain largely in the same degree of incapacity throughout their lives. The *speed of onset* may be another useful secondary evaluation, e.g., acute (sudden) or chronic (insidious).

A brief diagnosis could read: A married female aged 40 under marital stress has a severely incapacitating and acute psychonosis in which she manifests lack of concentration, anxiety, depersonalisation, frequent haemorrhage and dermatitis, irritability and angry outbursts. This could be expanded by greater detail in each area or abbreviated to "Psychonosis— acute and severe."

Should the unit under consideration be the family rather than the individual, the same procedure is effective for then the process in the group psyche of the family needs description.

Psychopathy

It has already been stated that psychopathy and character disorders present special problems and that both conditions are best classified under psychonosis (neurosis).

The psychopath is an individual faced with an intolerable life situation which has provoked a psychonosis (neurosis) and by the nature of the life situation it has also provoked antisocial or asocial behaviour. Unfortunately the severity of his symptoms leads to concentration on his antisocial behaviour. But by proceeding to a full assessment of personality it is possible to see that there are manifestations of a total personality disturbance. Classification by the presenting symptom has in this area been a major limiting factor in the appreciation and management of this disability.

Personality Disorders

In this group are included terms to denote types of personality, e.g., paranoid, affective, hysterical, explosive, etc. Terms such as paranoid and hysterical have a clinical connotation and really describe mild degrees of psychopathology. There would be an advantage in reserving clinical terms for clinical states and classifying personality traits on a non-clinical scheme such as one of a number devised by psychologists.

Child Psychiatry

Any useful final classification must embrace all age groups from infancy to old age. The child interacts with a situation, largely but not completely within his family; the adult is involved in the same basic situation. Both child and adult manifest, flavoured by age, the same changes. Age must influence the expression of symptoms as development affects the equipment of expression, e.g., speech is susceptible during its formative period in early childhood; again, an infant can have a temper tantrum but not rob a bank.

Child psychiatry has suffered a number of historical misfortunes from which it is rapidly emerging. Dependence on paediatrics led to focusing on the individual with a bias to neuropsychiatry that limited the evaluation of the child's interaction with parental and family psychopathology; indeed child psychiatrists often had no experience of adult psychopathology. The late development of adolescent psychiatry accentuated the isolation of child psychiatry; from this springs the tendency not to see the link between child and adult psychiatry and its common denominators and hence a reluctance to use common terms. Furthermore it led to a tendency to regard childhood manifestations of psychonosis (neurosis) as being less dangerous than the adult forms when they are equally so. Psychonosis (neurosis) in the infant is not only widespread but can be severe and even lead to sudden death, as for example in severe deprivatory psychic states. The dependence of the services on school authorities led to (i) limited experience with the under-fives; (ii) an attenuated awareness of the strength and primary influence of family dynamics.

Comment on some terms employed in the children's field is necessary for clarification. It is noticed that terms such as "normal variation" describe mild transient psychonosis, "adaption reaction" and "reactive disorder" describe moderate psychonosis, and "personality disorder," severe and persistent psychonosis. Thus terms denoting the degree of severity of the disorder (i.e., mild, moderate and severe) would be more suitable. "Habit" or "developmental" disorders, because of their imprecision, hardly deserve to be retained. To regard enuresis as a "developmental disorder," as it commonly occurs in childhood, is as useful as regarding gastric ulceration as a developmental disorder as it occurs in adulthood. There is of course no room for such terms as "maladjusted" in the clinical field as this term is a vague reference to social adaptability. The "hyperkinetic syndrome" describes a child whose restlessness is produced by the coercion and restriction of his environment and is usually seen only in a severe psychonosis.

Relationship of Psychonosis to the International Classification of Diseases (I.C.D.)

A number of categories listed in the 8th revision, 1965, would fall under psychonosis: Neurosis 300; Reactive depressive psychosis 298.0; Reactive excitation 298.1; Reactive confusion 298.2; Acute paranoid reaction 298.3; Paranoia 297.0; Reactive psychosis unspecified 298.9; Sexual deviation 302; Alcoholism 303; Drug dependence 304; Physical disorders of presumably psychogenic origin 305; Transient situational disturbances 307; Behaviour disorders of childhood 308; Mental retardation (with psycho-social deprivation) 310–315.8.

ENCEPHALONOSIS

Definition

Encephalonosis is defined as a disorder or morbid process of brain (encephalos, ἐγκέφαλος, brain; nosis, νόσος, disease). It is a disorder of the organic sub-stratum, endowment, of the psyche.

The term includes all disorders of brain but as it has not been employed in other directions it can be reserved for those conditions seen in psychiatric practice. Encephalonosis is a disorder set in being by an organic agent acting on the organ, the brain, resulting in a number of well defined signs and symptoms.

Agents

Traditionally in clinical practice these are grouped into five types: (i) infective, (ii) neoplastic, (iii) congenital and hereditary, (iv) metabolic and degenerative, (v) traumatic (including psychic stress). The agent involved influences the pathology and thus the ultimate signs.

Pathology

The influence of the agent on the organ may be either direct, i.e., primary, or indirect, i.e., secondary. In the secondary group the agent affects some organ in the body which in turn sets up a toxic agent which influences brain functioning, e.g., adrenalin of the suprarenal gland may influence brain functioning. The pathology depends upon the area of the brain damage together with the nature of the agent and the duration of its action.

Indicators

These include hallucinations, illusions, disorientation, emotional lability, perseveration, echolalia, amnesic symptoms, etc. Signs may be common to a number of syndromes. They are commonly covered by the term "mental." However they are different from the indicators of psychonosis (neurosis) in that (i) they are qualitatively distinct, and (ii) once established they are largely unaffected by changes in the psychic environment.

Diagnosis

As the organic agent plays a part in determining the organic process, there is merit, indeed it is usual, to classify these conditions according to the five groups of agents, i.e., infective, neoplastic, genetic, degenerative and traumatic. Although the division is not complete, some states have an acute onset and tend to be reversible and others have a slow or chronic course and tend to be irreversible. Thus classification can proceed by two main divisions—acute and chronic—and each may be subdivided into five categories according to the agent. In addition there are conditions of unknown aetiology—cryptogenic (crypto, κρυπτός, hidden; -genic, γένεσις, origin) encephalonosis. Incidentally, the term "amentia" and the term "dementia" are best avoided as they imply disorders of mind (*a* = absence; *de* = out of; *mens* = mind).

Conditions can be further subdivided according to their *severity*, e.g., conditions of intellectual retardation could be subdivided into groups of severity such as mild, moderate and severe. Similarly, conditions can be graded according to the degree of social disability; for example, employable, unemployable, etc.

Cryptogenic (of unknown origin) States

There are two conditions in psychiatry sometimes covered by the term "functional" which deserve special consideration; these are (i) schizophrenia and (ii) manic-depressive disorder. The term cryptogenic is preferable to functional in that it has an aetiological connotation.

The condition to be referred to later as encephalo-ataxia (schizophrenia) is a continuing challenge to psychiatrists. Its symptomatology by its nature, novelty and complexity lays claim to being the most fascinating syndrome in medicine. Countless researchers have laid siege to it without its final resolution. Though it forms but a small percentage of psychiatric disorders, it is yet of major concern because of the severity and permanence of its disability. So that there be no confusion it must be made clear that in this section the condition under discussion is "nuclear," "process," "genuine," "essential" schizophrenia.

As Rayner (23) recalls, the term schizophrenia was coined by Bleuler as a compromise to meet the organic-pathologists and psycho-pathologists and stands for "split mind." This term might have some slight advantage in the early phases of schizophrenia, inasmuch as some aspects of reality are retained and thus the individual seems to be functioning at two levels. However, recent work has shown with little doubt that the central feature of schizophrenia is not the splitting of the mind, but its disorganisation. Thus a term should be employed to indicate disorganisation, disorder or confusion. Such a term would be encephalo-ataxia (encephalos, ἐγκέφαλος brain; ataxia, ἀταξία, disorganisation).

It has become traditional to consider four sub-groups of encephalo-ataxia (schizophrenia), i.e., simple, hebephrenic, catatonic and paranoid. These sub-categories are now outmoded by contemporary researchers. The Moscow group led by Snezhnevsky (25) studied over 5,000 schizophrenics (encephalo-ataxics). In this report (25) the fluid, flexible, ever changing polymorphic nature of the symptomatology is emphasised. There is an unfolding of stages in the disorder leading in some to a terminal stable stage. The progression of stages occurs at different speeds with three main courses of development which, however, are not distinct as they appear to belong to one continuous process. It would be tempting to attach names to the varying patterns but this is unrewarding as over 100 different states were observed. The same workers point to the links with acute encephalonosis on the one hand and with manic-depressive disorder on the other. Thus, whether or not there is one disorder involved or a number, in the present state of our knowledge it does not seem worthwhile to sub-categorise this syndrome.

Manic-depressive psychosis is becoming a diminishing group due to the fact that many of the conditions once called cryptogenic are now seen to have a psychopathological basis and thus are included in the group, psychonosis (neurosis). It may become even more diminished in the future by the realisation that those with the more bizarre behaviour belong to the group encephalo-ataxia. Until there is further elucidation it would seem desirable to maintain this category, but to give it a more rational descriptive title. Cyclothymiosis (cyclo, κύκλος, circle; thymos, θυμός, mind) indicates the cyclical nature of the mood changes of elation and depression. Encephalolampsia (encephalos, ἐγκέφαλος, brain; lampsia λάμπω, to shine) indicates the state of elation, agitation and sensitivity. This was formerly termed mania. Encephalobaria (encephalos, ἐγκέφαλος, brain; baria, βαρέω, to weigh down) indicates the state of depression.

The conditions considered cryptogenic are placed under encephalonosis because, all the evidence considered and in the present state of knowledge, it is a reasonable hypothesis to regard them as dependent upon organic pathology. Should time reveal otherwise, the conditions can without difficulty, in whole or in part, be moved to another section of the classification. Likewise, the nomenclature can be adjusted, e.g., assuming a psychopathology for the states, then encephalo-ataxia becomes psycho-ataxia, encephalolampsia becomes psycholampsia, and encephalobaria becomes psychobaria.

Mental Retardation

Conditions giving rise to intellectual defect have always set problems in categorisation. They can be diagnosed on an aetiological basis emphasising the clinical aspect or in terms of social disability, a social evaluation. Here clearly the clinical classification must be adopted. Intellectual retardation as such is not a clinical syndrome but a sign only of dysfunctioning of brain and one sign amongst many. Intellectual defect occurs as the result of two conditions in general: (i) the primary condition due to multifactorial hereditary elements, i.e., those patients who lie at the lower end of the curve of distribution of intelligence; and (ii) those patients whose defects are secondary to brain damage due to the five groups of agents mentioned above.

A classification based on aetiology bypasses the controversy over the term best employed to cover states of mental retardation. Terms advocated include "mental handicap," "mental subnormality" (with the defect that it suggests cultural subnormality), "mental deficiency," and "mental retardation" (but slowing up or retardation is present in many conditions). The essential situation is that the brain is damaged, at any age, and amongst those showing signs of brain dysfunction are to be found some subjects who show defect of intelligence. In fact it is not the mind (*mens,* mind) that is handicapped, but the brain; those with intellectual defect may exhibit no disorder of mind.

There would seem to be no good reason for categorising conditions leading to intellectual loss in any way other than those mentioned above for all conditions of encephalonosis. This is the method followed in the classification of the American Psychiatric Association. Indeed the failure to emphasise the clinical basis of mental retardation has been a weakness in this field. There has thus resulted failure to appreciate the great contribution of the neurologist and the importance of cerebral studies.

Secondary evaluation in terms of loss of intellectual capacity is useful and can include such grades as borderline, mild, severe, profound, and very profound.

Brain damage occurring in childhood or infancy is no different from brain damage occurring in adolescence, adulthood or old age and thus *these conditions in all age groups should be considered together.*

Organic states with mental retardation can co-exist with other syndromes, e.g., psychonosis (neurosis). This is particularly so in the higher grades of mental retardation. Furthermore, states of pseudo-retardation may occur as a result of gross emotional deprivation; such conditions of pseudo-dementia should however be considered under psychonosis (neurosis).

Epilepsy

This is not a disease category but a sign, composed of a sudden discharge by cerebral cells, due to organic pathology in the cells. The psychiatric connotations of epilepsy are as follows: (i) Emotional stress may precipitate or aggravate epilepsy—in such situations epilepsy is a psychosomatic symptom indicative of a psychonosis (neurosis). (ii) An epileptic discharge focused in some areas of the brain gives rise to episodic "mental" phenomena, such as dream states, etc.—these should be classed under encephalonosis (psychosis). (iii) Following the positive discharge there is a negative phase, as originally described by Jackson (14), in which the exhaustion of cells manifests itself in confused behaviour—such a state is classified under encephalonosis (psychosis). (iv) An epileptic may react to his disability by the development of a psychonosis (neurosis)—clinical experience shows that frequently the psychonosis predates the epilepsy and has contributed to the incidence and degrees of the attacks.

Child Psychiatry

Acute and chronic encephalonosis occurs in childhood and its essential features are no different from those in any other age group. Cryptogenic encephalonosis may also occur—though cyclothymiosis' is rarely noted in childhood. States akin to encephalo-ataxia (schizophrenia) do occur. Links

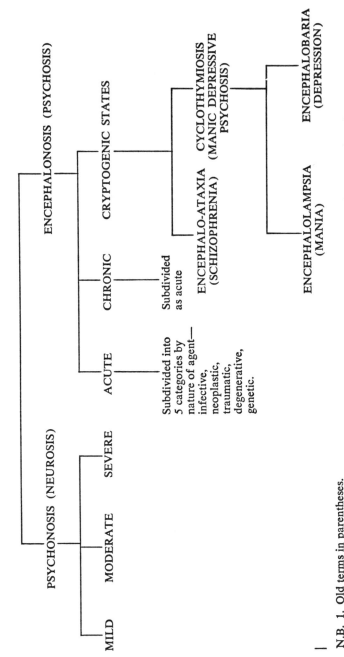

PSYCHIATRIC DISORDER

PSYCHONOSIS (NEUROSIS)

MILD   MODERATE   SEVERE

ENCEPHALONOSIS (PSYCHOSIS)

ACUTE   CHRONIC   CRYPTOGENIC STATES

Subdivided into 5 categories by nature of agent—infective, neoplastic, traumatic, degenerative, genetic.

Subdivided as acute

ENCEPHALO-ATAXIA (SCHIZOPHRENIA)

CYCLOTHYMIOSIS (MANIC DEPRESSIVE PSYCHOSIS)

ENCEPHALOLAMPSIA (MANIA)

ENCEPHALOBARIA (DEPRESSION)

N.B. 1. Old terms in parentheses.
2. Mental retardation in all age groups would normally be classified under Chronic Encephalonosis.

FIGURE 1

with adulthood are suggested by the similarity of symptomatology, the known start of adult states in early childhood—Vrono (34), Yudin (36) and Streltsova (31)—and the follow-up studies of childhood psychosis shown by some, e.g., Bennett and Klein (1), to result in a state indistinguishable from adult encephalo-ataxia. Others claim a distinct condition in childhood, pointing to a separate peak of incidence in early childhood. The matter can be resolved to the satisfaction of all by calling these early conditions encephalo-ataxic-like states.

Much confusion is caused by the use of the term "autism." At best it indicates "withdrawal with phantasy"; sometimes it is an euphemism for childhood encephalo-ataxic-like states. Under its umbrella are gathered a heterogeneous group of conditions that can include severe psychonosis (neurosis) due to emotional deprivation, aphasic states, deafness, brain damage syndromes, as well as encephalo-ataxia. The sad payment for ignoring classification by aetiology is that all these children are treated alike.

Relationship of Encephalonosis to the International Classification of Diseases (I.C.D.)

A number of categories listed in the 8th Revision, 1965, would fall under encephalonosis: Psychoses 290–299; Schizophrenia 295; Affective psychoses 296; Involutional paraphrenia 297.1; Unspecified psychotic states 309; Mental retardation 310–315.

CONCLUSION

It is suggested that psychiatric disorders be classified in two main aetiological groups: (i) *psychonosis,* dependent on psychopathology, and (ii) *encephalonosis,* dependent on organic pathology. The former, psychonosis, is subdivided into mild, moderate and severe forms. The latter, encephalonosis, is subdivided into acute, chronic and cryptogenic forms. The same classification is suggested for all age groups. Secondary evaluations are employed to a limited extent. Multiple diagnoses are possible. Figure 1 shows the categories in diagrammatic form.

For those who would wish to leave open the question of the aetiology of the cryptogenic group, an alternative classification is possible. Psychiatric disorder can be subdivided into three groups: (i) psychonosis (neurosis)— mild, moderate and severe; (ii) encephalonosis (psychosis)—acute and chronic; and (iii) cryptogenic states.

An essential requirement of a classification, it was suggested earlier, should be adaptability to new concepts of aetiology. To foretell the trends of the future is difficult. Clearly the conditions now grouped under "cryptogenic" are those most likely to call for regrouping. Some argue for a metabolic aetiology for encephalo-ataxia, in which event it would be classified under chronic encephalonosis. Some conditions of encephalolampsia (mania) may well be thought to show the psychopathology of agitation and be reclassified under psychonosis (neurosis). Conditions of encephalobaria are often being reclassified as reactive disorders and would find themselves reclassified under psychonosis (neurosis). The conditions remaining under cyclothymiosis will then be regarded as essentially organic and endogenous.

REFERENCES

1. BENNETT, S., and KLEIN, H. (1966). Childhood schizophrenia: 30 years later. *Amer. J. Psychiat.*, *122*, 1121.
2. BLEULER, E. (1911). *Dementia Praecox or the Group of Schizophrenias*. Trans. by J. Zinkin (1950). New York: International Universities Press.
3. BRIGHT, T. (1586). *A Treatise of Melancholie*. London: Vautrollier.
4. BURTON, R. (1628). *The Anatomy of Melancholy*. Everyman's Library (1964). London: Dent.
5. CULLEN, W. (1776-1784). *First Lines of the Practice of Physic*. 4 vols. Edinburgh: C. Elliott.
6. FAERGEMAN, P. (1963). *Psychogenic Psychoses*. London: Butterworths.
7. FEINSTEIN, A. R. (1967). *Clinical Judgment*. Baltimore: Williams & Wilkins.
8. FEUCHTERSLEBEN, E. F. VON (1845). *Lehrbuch der ärztlichen Seelenkunde*. Vienna: Carl Gerold.
9. HARVEY, W. (1628). *De motu cordis*. Transl. by K. J. Franklin. *The Circulation of the Blood and Other Writings*. Everyman's Library (1963). London: Dent.
10. HOCH, P., and POLATIN, P. (1949). Pseudoneurotic forms of schizophrenia. *Psychiat. Quart.*, *23*, 248.
11. HOWELLS, J. G. (1968). Family psychopathology and schizophrenia. In: Howells, J. G. (ed). *Modern Perspectives in World Psychiatry*. Edinburgh: Oliver & Boyd; New York: Brunner/Mazel.
12. HOWELLS, J. G., and OSBORN, M. L. (1970). The incidence of emotional disorder in a 17th century medical practice. *Medical History, 14*, 192.
13. HUNTER, R., and MACALPINE, I. (1964). *Three Hundred Years of Psychiatry*. London: Oxford Univ. Press.
14. JACKSON, J. H. (1958). *Selected Writings of John Hughlings Jackson*. New York: Basic Books.
15. KASANIN, J. (1933). The acute schizoaffective psychosis. *Amer. J. Psychiat.*, *90*, 97-126.
16. KRAMER, M., et al. (1969). Cross-national study of diagnosis of the mental disorders. Supplement, *Amer. J. Psychiat.*, *125*.
17. LANGFELDT, G. (1937). *The Prognosis in Schizophrenia and the Factors Influencing the Course of the Disease*. Monograph. London: Humphrey Melford.
18. LANGFELDT, G. (1969). Schizophrenia: Diagnosis and prognosis. *Behavioural Science, 14*, 173-182.
19. MENNINGER, K. (1967). *The Vital Balance*. New York: Viking Press.
20. MOREL, B. A. (1860). *Traité des Maladies Mentales*. Paris: Masson.
21. PLATTER, F. (1662). *A Golden Practice of Physick*. London: Peter Cole.
22. RAWNSLEY, K. (1966). An international diagnostic exercise. Proceedings of the

IVth World Congress of Psychiatry. *Excerpta Medica Int. Congr. Series No. 117*, p. 360.
23. RAYNER, E. W. (1966). The concept of psychosis. *Medical Proceedings, 12,* 443-449.
24. SCHNEIDER, K. (1959). *Clinical Psychopathology.* London/New York: Grune & Stratton.
25. SNEZHNEVSKY, A. V. (1968). The symptomatology, clinical forms and nosology of schizophrenia. In: Howells, J. G. (ed). *Modern Perspectives in World Psychiatry.* Edinburgh: Oliver & Boyd; New York: Brunner/Mazel.
26. STENGEL, E. (1959). Classification of mental disorders. *Bull. of World Health Organization, 21,* 601-663.
27. STENGEL, E. (1960). A comparative study of psychiatric classifications. *Proc. Roy. Soc. Med., 53,* 123-130.
28. STENGEL, E. (1967). Recent developments in classification. In: Coppen, A., and Walk, A. (eds). *Recent Developments in Schizophrenia.* Ashford: Headley Brothers Ltd.
29. STEPHENS, J. H., and ASTRUP, C. (1963). Prognosis in "process" and "non-process" schizophrenia. *Amer. J. Psychiat., 119,* 945.
30. STIERLIN, H. (1967). Bleuler's concept of schizophrenia: A confusing heritage. *Amer. J. Psychiat., 123,* 996-1001.
31. STRELTSOVA, N. (1964). *The Korsakoff Journal of Neuropathology and Psychiatry, 64,* 1.
32. STRÖMGREN, E. (1969). Uses and abuses of concepts in psychiatry. *Amer. J. Psychiat., 126,* 777-788.
33. SYDENHAM, T. (1682). Dissertatio epistolaris ad Gulielmum Cole, M. D. . . . de affectione hysterica. Quoted by Hunter, R., and Macalpine, I. (1964). *Three Hundred Years of Psychiatry.* London: Oxford Univ. Press.
34. VRONO, M. S. (1972). Schizophrenia in childhood. In: Snezhnevsky, A. V. (ed). *Schizophrenia.* Moscow: Medicina.
35. WILLIS, T. (1672). De anima brutorum. Quoted by Hunter, R., and Macalpine, I. (1964). *Three Hundred Years of Psychiatry.* London: Oxford Univ. Press.
36. YUDIN, M. (1941). Schizophrenia as a primary defect—psychosis. *Papers of the Central Psychiatric Institute, 2.*
37. ZUBIN, J. (ed.) (1961). *Field Studies in the Mental Disorders.* New York/London: Grune & Stratton.

IV

FAMILY PSYCHOPATHOLOGY— EXPERIENTIAL PSYCHOPATHOLOGY

Experiential Psychopathology

Definition

Experience is all that an organism (individual, family or society) has been subject to or undergone in life. In the organism that we meet today is found the end result of the whole of its experience until now, beneficial and harmful. In this book the view is held that all psychopathology arises from harmful experience—hence experiential psychopathology.

Experiential psychopathology regards psychopathology as having arisen from harmful experience—all the harmful events the organism has been subject to or undergone in life.

Experiences are seen in actual, real terms, as they occurred to the organism and not as assumed to occur by someone else at the time or later. Translation into any other than real terms is not required. The only truth is the event as it occurred. Events must not be fancied, manufactured, or distorted. Symbolic meanings cannot replace facts. It follows that no weight is given to schools of thought which rely on the translation and interpretation of events in the light of accumulated and stereotyping dogma. Truth cannot be limited in this way. To reveal, clarify, describe, is permissible, but to translate into other terms is distorting. Harvey (1) repeated the saying of his teacher, Fabricius, "Let all reasoning be silent when experience gainsays its conclusions."

The events to which an organism can be subject are legion. Every possible event can be met by any organism. However, so infinite are the possibilities that it would be extraordinary if any two organisms were to meet the same two sets of events. Thus an organism has to be understood against the background of its own unique experience. That is its life experience. Most organisms meet predictable common events; some meet the unusual; some meet both.

137

The possible combination of events is infinite. Thus variation is great. To expect that all combinations of circumstances can be covered by a few well described situations, even if fanciful and intriguing, serves merely to limit the truth and produce dogma. Experiential psychopathology allows a new beginning in the understanding of the disorders of psyche; it implies starting from a *tabula rasa* and relying on careful observation, deduction, and experimental verification.

Experience must not be confused with the process of learning. Learning is concerned with specific data, is deliberately acquired, formal, guided, regulated, and only a part of experience. Experience is concerned with general data, is unsought, often informal, often unregulated, not always discerned, and includes learning. Each is important. But experience would be limited if regarded only as learning.

The family moves through its experience and sends off epitomes of itself, individuals, to found new families, and both individual and family are significant organisms within another and larger organism, society. Thus we must take account of the experiential psychopathology of each, individual, family and society. Each is equally significant as a phenomenon, but in clinical practice there are operational advantages in taking the family as the functional unit.

The Basic Psychopathological Process

The psychopathological process is understood in terms of the experiential process—all the adverse events the organism has undergone in its life experience. A "process" is defined as "a continuous series of events."

The organism is either an individual, a family or society. The organism is especially vulnerable to adverse events in its early history and early damage will influence subsequent reactions to events.

The fundamental need of the organism (individual, family or society) is to function harmoniously; harmony results from conformity with the biological rules or "cosmic plan." This harmonious functioning can be disrupted by a number of agents, noxious or harmful agents, physical and psychic, acting on the fabric of the organism—either psyche or soma, or both. For its defence the organism employs a number of coping devices against the noci-vectors.

If the coping devices are only partly adequate or fail there is a resulting dysfunction, morbid process, which may or may not be appreciated by the organism. The morbid process reveals itself by indicators; if only the organism is aware of these, they are termed symptoms, but if they are apparent to others as well, they are termed signs.

The psychopathological process is an amalgam of the psychic noci-vector, the coping mechanism of the psyche, its damaged fabric and the indicators of this damage.

A purely psychically based medicine is as valueless as is a purely organically based medicine. A holistic approach is alone acceptable. Therefore the fabric of the organism must be conceived as a whole—soma and psyche, and the impact of disruptive agents considered as they apply to both. Thus we have to practice a medicine of the whole psychic and somatic entity—psychosomatiatria—and in the case of an individual, pananthropic medicine (healing of the whole man). However, the effects of physical noxious agents are so adequately covered in medical texts as not to need discussion here. The emphasis will be on the effect of psychic, rather than physical, disruptive agents. Thus, we consider the effects of psychic noci-vectors (*psychic*—from a psychic source; *noci*—harmful; *vector*—a force with direction) on the somato-psychic organisms—Individual, Family and Society.

The author believes that somatic noxious agents are responsible for encephalonosis, including encephaloataxia (schizophrenia). Thus discussion of encephalonosis is not appropriate here. However, due to the contemporary interest in family psychopathology especially in relation to encephaloataxia, this subject merits discussion and a chapter is devoted to family psychopathology and encephalonosis in the section entitled "Special Aspects of Family Psychiatry."

What follows is a résumé of experiential psychopathology, to be expanded in a companion volume.

REFERENCE

1. WHITTERIDGE, G. (1971). *William Harvey and the Circulation of the Blood.* London: Macdonald.

Psychic Noci-Vectors

General

A "vector" is a force with direction. "Noci" indicates its harmful, adverse, damaging, noxious nature. "Psychic" displays that it arises from a psychic or emotive source. The adverse effect of a psychic noci-vector on an organism is felt throughout that organism, both in its somatic and psychic parts; a psychic noxious event can as readily produce migraine as it can anxiety.

Here is an example of a powerful psychic noci-vector operating on an individual organism: After intercourse a husband says to his wife, "I did not have an orgasm because I am saving it for someone else." One might expect a marked physical and psychic hurt reaction in the wife; she could be expected to be sick, angry, tearful, miserable. A reverse vector, and a beneficial one, might be as follows: A husband sitting on a settee says to his wife, "I think I shall always sit on this settee rather than on a chair, then I can always have you close to me." The wife might be expected to glow, physically and emotionally, with pleasure.

Psychic noci-vectors can be actual or threatened. The psyche has the endowed property of anticipation and can maintain itself in a state of anxiety while anticipating stress. The psyche of the individual or the group also has the property of imagination and can thus set up internal stresses that can be damaging.

The essential nature of communication has been discussed earlier in this book. Organism A conveys a meaning to Organism B and this alters the relationship between them. The meaning conveyed may have varying degrees of acceptance by B, depending on its degree of beneficiality; it may also convey varying degrees of harmfulness. In psychopathology we are concerned with harmful communication. What has been described is the

140

simplest interaction. Normally B reciprocates and a continuous process of communication is initiated which continues for varying periods.

In the above we have considered only two psychic organisms, A and B. Interactions may be more complex. A and B may be groups of people, e.g., families interacting with families. Again, A and B may be psychic organisms within a number of organisms and a complex psychic pattern of communication occurs among all the protagonists—a transaction. In this transaction the fortunes of A, or any other psychic organism, can fluctuate from moment to moment; at one instant a number of psychic sources collectively convey pleasant meanings, at another they band together to convey hurtful meanings. The meanings may even be contradictory.

Communication, then, is a complex pattern of transactions. Benevolent communication leads to harmonious functioning in the recipient. Malevolent communication leads to malfunctioning in the recipient. This applies to any organism—individual, family, society, or group within society.

The psychic part of the organism during its experience acquires attitudes, as explained previously. *An attitude,* with its related beliefs, myths, interests and values, *is to assume an opinion* in relation to an object of thought, i.e., to endow an object with qualities. These qualities can often be graded in opposites, e.g., love at one extreme and hate at the other. It is also possible to make a scale of degree, e.g., much love, some love, neutral, some hate, much hate. These attitudes or opinions dictate the meanings conveyed to other psychic objects. At the receiving end they may be acceptable. On the other hand they may be so unacceptable as to do considerable damage; in this event they constitute psychic noci-vectors. An attitude cannot be separated from its context, e.g., in one setting an individual may feel strong hate towards one person, but convey love to another person in the same setting. The term "vector" takes account of the attitude as a force and its directive quality.

In estimating the effect of a psychic noci-vector a number of factors have to be taken into account. These will be briefly described. They are concerned with source, meaning, conveyance, dynamic qualities, vulnerability, latent period and restitution factors. The chapter will conclude with some illustrations of psychic noci-vectors.

Source

Psychic noci-vectors must come from a psychic source—individual or group psyche. An individual may be beset by forces from others within the family as individuals, or groups of individuals, and from individuals and groups within society. A family can be beset by individuals within the family, or individuals or groups of people outside the family. Society can be beset by individuals or families or groups of people within society.

As the family is the basic unit in society, it is of special importance. It is the unit within which the founders of new basic units, families, are forged. Psychic noci-vectors from the preceding families can do great damage to the functioning of the present family. Again, psychic noci-vectors in the present family can do great damage to the epitome of itself which it sends forth into the future to found new families. Within the family are the closest interactions, those that last longest, the most significant and intense, and those likely to be reinforced again and again through time. A family can produce the most benevolent of vectors and at the same time the most malevolent.

All psychic organisms possess the capacity of *imagination*. New thoughts can be generated out of the raw material of the psyche. These thoughts need not be expressed, but they can be altered according to immediate experience. There is a capacity to anticipate attack, even to exaggerate or diminish the force of probable attack, and to visualize its results. Thus people as individuals, or as groups, are prone to worry. Such thoughts can become psychic noci-vectors themselves. Thus there is attack from within—intra-psychic trauma. A possible setback is assumed to happen although it may never happen. It may be exaggerated. The event may show that it could not have happened, or was not as disastrous as expected. People "worry before it happens" or "jump their fences before they come to them." People or groups made insecure by previous experience are especially prone to anticipate stress. Thus, this state of anticipatory anxiety is to some extent manufactured. Others are in an expectant state, a state of tension, because of the anticipation of real stress.

Meaning

The effect of a communication is dependent on the meaning conveyed. The recipient interprets from the message the attitude of the other party on the point at issue. The attitude may be for or against him and vary greatly in its quality. The meaning may be open or overt, e.g., fear of being dropped or a threat of aggression; or hidden and covert, e.g., a husband becomes greatly anxious when his wife is giving birth because of the loss of his mother during his sister's birth. The recipient may even be unaware of the source of anxiety. It may be simple or subtle and in the latter event take on the character of a hint, innuendo, implication, insinuation or intimation. Again, some vectors of low threshold value may not reach the awareness of the recipient—subliminal trauma. The message cannot be separated from its context, e.g., in one situation an exclamation conveys joy and in another alarm. The same word or act may be interpreted as friendly by one person, while another person in the same setting sees it as hostile; the interpretation depends upon the meaning to that person or group and this is dependent on a host of factors such as previous experience, vulnerability, age, etc.

Meanings can be conveyed to others by the *absence* of action, e.g., not to send a birthday card to one's child may be as significant as to have done something hurtful. Again, parents may not tell their children that sex is taboo, but the absence of discussion conveys the same meaning. Dylan Thomas relates in "Under Milk Wood" how the prostitute passes the women gabbling at the village pump and how she senses their hostility "by the noise of the hush." These negative noci-vectors may escape the onlooker. What is inappropriately not said is as vital as what is said.

Some *physical* vectors, though immense in power, may have little effect on individuals or groups. Physical or material lack have no effect unless they injure the psychic worth of the person, e.g., economic status may be important because the grandparents demand it and without it the image of self suffers, or because it leads to psychic stress, e.g., poverty may mean continual personal degradation, disturbing neighbors, etc. Physical hazards may even be advantageous to the psyche; external hazards such as earthquakes, floods, forced migration, persecution, war, may have the result of bringing people together so that the quality of communication actually improves.

Psychic noci-vectors may be *contradictory,* i.e., the same psychic source may emit simultaneously two or more messages with conflicting meanings. Or the conflicting, or different, messages may come from a number of sources. The organism, as will be seen later, can cope with such contradictions up to its own capacity.

Conveyance

Psychic noci-vectors are communicated, as with any vector, through the *five senses.* The commonest avenue is through speech. Verbal symbols have meaning which is conveyed to others in this economical fashion. But non-verbal communication can be equally compelling. Sometimes a composite message is conveyed by an amalgam of the five senses, or by combined verbal and non-verbal behaviour. Very subtle messages can be conveyed in this fashion. Within a family, economy of expression takes place over time and much can be conveyed by grunts, mannerisms, affectation of speech, gesture, etc.; these meanings may not be apparent to those outside the family circle until they become attuned to them. Fortunately, most people and families talk about the same things in the same way.

Dynamic Qualities

A noci-vector can have varying degrees of *strength* or intensity. Effect depends on a number of factors, but given a certain degree of vulnerability or sensitivity in the recipient, the greater the strength of the vector, the greater the effect. The use of strength is sometimes calculated by the sender so as to produce a wanted degree of effect. Often the vector is not under control and no calculation made of the probable effect, indeed there may be surprise at the effect created.

Communications may occur once or be *repeated* a number of times. The latter probably brings a considerable accumulation of effect. Once a vulnerability has been established, repetition of the same psychic noci-vector brings increasing damage; repetition even after the gap of years can still bring a response.

The *number* of psychic noci-vectors must be taken into account. There is probably a limit to the number of sources to which an organism can pay simultaneous attention; knowledge about this is least exact with respect to families and social groups. It seems that an individual can only pay attention to five or six other people at one time. Groups over about seven in number begin to fragment—this happens also to large families. Thus, an individual can be traumatized by up to seven noxious agents but beyond that number he has difficulty in conceptualising individuals as individuals. Another related limiting factor is that of span of attention; it is difficult to pay attention for long periods of time without reaching a point of exhaustion.

The programme of attack and reaction may pass through a *sequence*. It may escalate to the point of exhaustion on either side, or until another factor intervenes. A husband reacts to being ignored by aggression; the wife reacts to aggression by withdrawal; wife is upset and ignores husband; he becomes hostile; wife withdraws; husband's hostility increases and wife withdraws further; as the situation escalates, a point is reached when wife looks like a rejected, deprived child; a new factor now appears—the husband identifies himself with this deprived child, the child he was long ago; his hostility turns to tenderness and the vicious circle is broken.

The psychic noci-vector may operate over a short or long period of *time*. Time is an element that has tended to be underestimated. In the past much attention has been given in psychopathology to the nuclear incident—one devastating incident at one moment in time. Significance has to be given not only to the acute stress, but also to a long-drawn-out sustained stress. To the former there is a considerable, but not complete, capacity to adjust; all the adjustment mechanisms are urgently brought into action. But for the latter the capacity to adjust is much less, for the threshold of coping may not be reached, and the adjustment may not take place. Time, therefore, is a significant factor and the experience may be stamped into the psychic organism, making eradication difficult.

To pinpoint the *moment* in time when a psychic noci-vector was operating may be of great value in diagnosis for it may supply a clue as to the nature of the psychic noci-vector, e.g., abdominal pain at breakfast on each school morning, and never at weekends or in the holiday period, implies a relationship between school and the abdominal pain. The more obvious the indicator, usually the easier it is to make the association.

Vulnerability

Vulnerability is general or specific. Some situations would cause trauma to most people—e.g., a new, unfamiliar situation. It can also be specific due to a number of reasons. There may be a constitutional weakness, e.g., of intelligence, that might make understanding difficult. Again, the sender of the message may have special significance to the recipient and this would make the latter vulnerable. Or, the recipient may have developed over time a susceptibility to that type of stress; in the case of a family member this may be dependent on experience in his preceding family, which not only subjected him to that experience but did not allow the appropriate coping mechanism to develop. Time may have reinforced a vulnerability. For example, a child's lack of social confidence springs from the family's inability to encourage him in his first social situations; the family then encourages him to avoid social situations; it reinforces his anxiety over the years; thus lack of social confidence is maintained and he is now vulnerable to the stress of social exposure.

Age of the recipient is a factor that influences the effect of a psychic noci-vector because it influences the capacity to give meaning.

A young child has a brief memory span; it is not clear how much can be retained in the first few months. This may be a biological protection to see the child through the trauma of birth. Later, as the cerebral centres develop, the capacity for memory increases. Thus after about the age of two the sensitivity to psychic noci-vectors increases. There is evidence that early memories can have far-reaching effect on behaviour, e.g., aversions to types of food laid down in the early years last a lifetime. Early experiences that dictate early reactions may influence later behaviour because, at an early age, they are the raw material of behaviour for that person. However, the young are also protected, especially in the early months. A child's intelligence grows only with the years and a child does not develop the capacity for abstract thinking until about eight to ten years; thus the more subtle attacks on him may not have meaning. The child has the quality of "innocence" too, i.e., he can react in an open unbiased way, if allowed to do so, as he has yet no inbuilt prejudices. It is a calamitous mistake to assume that the child's mind behaves and reacts like the adult's mind. This is an important area, capable of elucidation by careful experiment; it is no longer necessary to rely on speculation in this field, which has benefited greatly from the work of developmental psychologists.

In the senium, again, the results of age may need to be taken into account; the memory span decreases, intelligence wanes and abstract thinking becomes more difficult. Recent events, in particular, are quickly forgotten. But the sway of inbuilt prejudices is great.

Latent Period

A psychic noci-vector may appear to have had no effect because there is a *latent* period between the action and its result. This may be due to a number of reasons: (i) There is a state of shock—it can be seen in bereavement, for instance. (ii) The event may call for immediate action and thus attention is given to this and there is no time to work out the meaning of the event. Later, when the emergency is over, the meaning of the event becomes apparent and its effect shows itself. (iii) When the effect is somatic, it may take the organ concerned time to show evident signs of damage, e.g., a woman quarrels with the neighbour, but the swelling in her neck, due to the reaction of her thyroid gland, is only apparent many days later. Thus, the connection between the stress and its effect may be lost. To be able to tie the indicators of stress to an event is of great value diagnostically.

Restitution Factors

Psychic noci-vectors may be counteracted by chance *restitution factors*. For instance, a foreman becomes antagonistic to a man at his work. The man reacts by anxiety, yet he cannot take the obvious step of finding alternative employment. His anxiety increases. He becomes ill. He loses his job because of his absences. He now has to take another job and does so with marked improvement in himself. Thus chance operates to counteract noci-vectors. Examples of restitution factors include—marriage to a compatible partner, death of hurtful parents, loss of harmful husband, a new teacher, change of neighbours, a pleasant playmate, etc. One of the aims of vector therapy is to systematise the deployment of restitution factors, which are then not left to chance.

Illustrations

Some psychic noci-vectors may be *shared* by a number of people—there are hazards common to all—e.g., failure to have children; undertaking a pioneer role with consequent colleague and social antagonism; children leaving home with consequent adjustments; death of a spouse or child or relative; denial of intercourse because of physical defects; separation due to war service; relating own experiences as a child to the nurturing of one's own children; illegitimate births; loneliness of old age; hospitalization of spouse or child; problems of accepting new developmental roles; cultural clashes, etc. All these are common hazards, and ability to cope does not appear to be due so much to the strength of the stress as to having developed a right attitude in the past—usually in the preceding family. A sign of good psychic health is the capacity to adjust to life's inevitable hazards.

A few of an infinite number of examples of psychic harmful interactions would be:

Intra-psychic	Guilt at illegitimate birth of a child; fear of pregnancy.
Spouse-spouse	Retirement of and therefore prolonged contact with a disliked spouse; intervention of a third party in marriage; disparagement by spouse.
Parent-child	Rejection and lack of love; blame for any lack of achievement; depreciation of child's worth.
Sibling-sibling	Birth of an unwanted rival; rivalry for parental affection.
Group conflict	Mother and sisters accept a new child; father and brothers reject it.
Family-society	Employer using his position to make sexual advances; working under a father who is antagonistic; angry teacher; teasing by schoolmates; critical neighbour.

Attitudes are conveyed in ordinary but often devastating phrases, such as: "Don't do that"; "Go to bed, for heaven's sake"; "Take that"; "You were wrong there"; "You won't go to heaven"; "God doesn't like that"; "If you don't do this, then . . ."; "You don't like me"; "I hate you"; "At one time you were so good"; "You are 100% selfish"; "Keep quiet or else"; "If you do that, you will upset your mother"; "Don't ask any questions, but do as you are told"; to a plump girl—"You must be attending slimming classes"; to any middle-aged woman—"Your children must be quite grown up"; to anyone—"It is all your fault"; to a wife—"Other people's homes are tidy"; "You are ugly"; "I won't have a child by you"; to a husband—"I once had a smart husband"; "Everyone gets promotion but you"; "You behave like your mother"; "Go to hell;" "Don't touch me."

Coping Devices

When the organism, individual or family, is under attack from psychic noci-vectors, it has to meet the attack and, if possible, contend successfully with it and defend the integrity of the "idea of self." Thus it has to cope by the use of a *number of devices* or expedients to meet or attenuate the effect of the attacking agent and repair its damage. Coping involves defence, adaptation, and reparation. It is the price the organism has to pay to preserve its integrity.

The coping devices may be completely or only partly successful. If partly successful, then the organism is left with a handicap. This may be general or focal, i.e., sensitivity to any stress or to one stress only, e.g., social intercourse.

Just as the psychic noci-vectors are acquired through experience, usually within the preceding family, so too are the coping devices. The child imitates, consciously or automatically, the devices adopted by his fellow family members of any age. Sometimes by chance he comes across a device that for him, in a particular circumstance, appears to work. This will be his special device until experience causes an adjustment or change. He may use it even at times when its employment is inappropriate. Thus some of the coping devices are employed in common by many people. Others are particular to a person, stamped on him by previous experience, and become his "stock in trade." The same applies to a family or to any larger group.

To contend with the opposition, the whole functioning of the organism may be called to action. This will include the endowment as well as the acquired aspects of the psyche. Not only does a coping device need an apparatus for its execution, but it consists of an attitude and is associated with a feeling tone or mood; mood is especially evident in the more acute and automatic reactions, e.g., aggression.

The acquired aspect of the psyche can react by use of either *automatic* or *directed* devices. The advantage of the automatic devices is that they are

149

immediate and overwhelming. But they may be ill-directed, inappropriate, and diffuse. The automatic devices are primitive, e.g., anger and flight. The directed devices are slower, more acute, and sometimes highly sophisticated, e.g., sarcasm and carefully-thought-out acts. Animals are more dependent on automatic response and homo sapiens, on directed response.

In an acute attack, the organism may be forced to react by shock—the centres of defence become exhausted. This passive state has the advantage that the organism cannot grasp any further significance in the attack and thus its influence is reduced. Exhaustion of attention is an important merciful defence mechanism of the organism. It is likely to be reached earliest in acute trauma. In sustained trauma the threshold of exhaustion is seldom reached, hence the powerful effect of long-drawn-out stress.

The attack may be directed at one aspect only of the self and thus only a local defence is required, e.g., an attack on the person's social status. The attack may also be directed at a number of aspects or on the whole self, e.g., the statement "I hate you."

A study of the ways by which well-adjusted people react to attack will expose devices that can be employed in therapy, e.g., forgetting is a fundamental biological coping device; yet at times in therapy we make forgetting impossible by repeated recollection of previous mishaps. Constructive phantasy, hope, is another healing device.

The use of a particular coping device may be dictated by the situation. The appropriate devices must be employed in a given situation and this may limit the choice or dictate the employment of one device, e.g., faced with a deaf-mute, a non-verbal response is essential.

The nature of the attacking agent may determine the most appropriate response; its source, the meaning conveyed, the senses used for conveyance, its dynamic qualities (strength, number, repetition, sequence), whether acute or chronic, short or sustained, the vulnerability of the organism to that trauma, and age are all elements which determine the response to stress. A source within one's own psyche has to be handled differently from an external source. Normally the defence involves the same senses as those used by the attacking agent, but not always. Usually, the more acute and severe the trauma, the more severe and automatic the defensive response. A sustained attack calls for a sustained defence. A repetitive attack calls for a discontinuous response—with the possibility of learning the most effective response in between attacks. A number of noci-vectors may have to be met by the psyche with an equal number of defensive vectors to match them.

In a well-balanced organism, the coping devices are usually controlled, well directed, and, usually, successful. The less-balanced organism has so many weaknesses that its response may be ill-judged. Excess of anxiety leads to inattention, dithering, indecision, and even to a misunderstanding of the nature of the attack. A balanced organism may suffer considerable attack and be able to respond appropriately. For example, a loved person is lost (almost like losing a part of the self). At first there may be a stunned response with apparently little reaction; this is followed by maximum grief; this fades as reparation sets in—forgetting plays a part and there is a realistic reappraisal of the situation and a deployment of its assets. In the unbalanced, guilt, anxiety, hostility, may be superimposed on grief.

In children, the coping devices, especially the directed, tend to be simple. They get more complex with age. They are crude in simple folk and sophisticated and subtle in the intelligent, e.g., the latter may believe it is better to have an adverse decision than no decision—at least it allows of a trial operation.

Psychic noci-vectors may be contradictory. The same psychic source may emit simultaneously two or more messages having conflicting or different meanings. Or the conflicting or different messages may come from a number of sources. This can cause bewilderment in the recipient, but not madness. This occurrence is so frequent in day-to-day life that organisms quickly develop obvious ways of coping with it. Given a number of different or contradictory messages, the recipient can:

1. Ignore them all, claim they show lack of agreement in the senders, and use them as an argument for following his own policy.

2. Behave according to the resultant of the forces bearing on him; his behaviour may please all his assailants or none.

3. Select the one message that most appeals.

4. Select the message that is most compelling or strongest.

5. Do nothing.

Coping involves establishing attitudes which are strongly held, these are attempts to adapt and they may clash with the attitudes of others and therefore be destructive and maintain the opposition of others. Such attitudes are difficult to change, as they are considered essential by the self as coping devices. They are easier to dissipate if the coping becomes unnecessary, i.e., the threat is diminished and security increased. *Hence in therapy it is essential to produce security, or coping devices against insecurity must continue to operate.*

Examples of Coping Devices

The whole organism can be brought into action in any attack and one or many of the devices below brought into action. The devices can be divided into those that are *primitive* and automatic, and those that are *directed*.

Primitive

There are three groups:

1. Those involving aggression, such as verbal hostility (abuse, swearing, sarcasm, cynicism, etc.) or non-verbal (ignoring, depriving, punishing, tantrum, physical harm, homicide).

2. Withdrawal in verbal terms (silence) or non-verbal (to move away, to hide, to contrive not to be noticed, apathy, sleep, suicide).

3. Anxiety—to be in an anticipatory state. The alarm mechanisms are kept on the alert—sometimes for a lifetime. Anxiety can be displaced on to objects, themselves harmless, which are associated by chance with the fear situation—thus phobias are created.

Directed

Any apparatus of the organism may be implicated:

Perception—Any of the sensations from the five senses may be exaggerated or dulled, e.g., an inability to hear. In a state of heightened tension, meanings may be misconstrued and harmless objects regarded as the subjects of suspicion, leading to paranoid states. There may be partial or complete denial of meanings.

Memory—The normal machinery of forgetting is a healthy defence against stress and always comes into play in time. It may operate inappropriately and too early. In the process of remembering, events and meanings may be projected on to the wrong person.

Realistic Thought—Healthy reactions include apology, understanding, toleration, relating to previous experience, forgiving, diversion, avoidance and insightful rationalisation to find effective answers, rationalisation in humour.

Unrealistic Thought—Lying, attention-seeking and hysterical behaviour, attention-seeking by regression or illness, selfishness, meanness, overprotection arising from fear or guilt.

Phantasy—Daydreams, overcompensation leading to boasting, snobbery, etc., identification.

Behaviour—Overactivity (illusion of action), obsessions and compulsions (an attempt to control and predict events so that they can be anticipated), conformity, perfectionism, hypermorality, and artificial aids such as rhythmic activity, (thumbsucking), chewing gum, drugs, alcohol, excessive sexual activity.

Physical—The whole of the organic apparatus also responds protectively. Its responses may lead to psychosomatic illness—not to be confused with hysterical behaviour. In the former there is no contrived illness; it is an inevitable result of psychic trauma. In hysterical states there is a simulation of illness because of the overwhelming need of the organism to cope. Illness is a common method of avoidance and widely employed.

Damage to the Organism

General

Like all elements in the cosmos, human organisms—individual, family and society—are controlled by the formulas governing the universe; they are part of the "cosmic design." One of these formulas is the need to function harmoniously. The cosmos, the universe as an ordered whole, remains imperfect and therefore the possibility of dysfunction is still an essential ingredient of it. Evolution strives to reduce dysfunction. Our developing awareness of psychic matters and our striving for psychic self-improvement are parts of this movement onwards. As the universe evolved, man developed the capacity to evaluate life experience and change it, to produce harmony. Therefore, man is driven on by a need to be harmonious and this in action is creative. This creative capacity is part of the cosmic endowment. The origin of this process, its rules and its regulation is a mystery.

Evolution affects both physical and psychic matters. Each has equal worth in the universe and, furthermore, the physical and psychic are linked. For this last reason there is value in considering psychic matters in known physical terms, as long as it is appreciated that each has in addition qualities of its own—even if at opposite ends of an elemental spectrum. Just as a caress can lead to a pleasurable physical sensation, so psychic communication can lead to a pleasurable feeling. Psychic messages are needed to satisfy the intra-psychic processes of behaviour. In the cerebrum there is a sensitive highest level functional area that can function harmoniously or unharmoniously. It seeks pleasure and harmony. It has a capacity to want this, i.e., given an equal choice of harmony or disharmony it will select the former. Possibly there is a regulator or governor, imposed by the developing plan of the universe, that works towards harmony.

The organism moves through time directed by its place in the cosmic

154

plan; the motivation of the organism is beyond its control, it dances to the tune set for it in the pattern of things. The organism has a capacity to understand and react to situations but this capacity is the result of previous events and is thus, again, controlled by the cosmic plan.

Homeostasis, maintaining the constancy of the internal environment, is one factor in good functioning—as it is in its other sense, maintaining the balance between internal and external environments. Homeostasis, in both its meanings, is not as fundamental as the need for harmonious functioning, but it is an indication of good functioning.

The organism has an endowment of a physical and psychical apparatus, e.g., an apparatus that allows it to think, an apparatus which has a number of properties that can be developed to an optimum capacity, i.e., a determined degree of intelligence for a particular thought apparatus. The human fabric, somatic and psychic, is complex and composed of multiple, different, but linked elements. Experience acts on this endowment. Experience can be beneficial or harmful, good or adverse. As the result of experience the organism accumulates added characteristics. ("Properties" denotes the endowed entities, "characteristics" denotes the acquired entities.) If the experience is beneficial, the organism manifests indications of good functioning; if adverse, it displays indications of malfunctioning. Usually, in its imperfect state, it shows indications of both.

The fabric of the organism, be it individual, family or society, is the area on which the psychic noci-vectors operate, its most vulnerable part being its acquired characteristics. Within the fabric is found the morbid process —either organic or psychic pathology. In both the organic and psychic areas there are not only changes due to the noxious agent, but also changes due to attempts to cope with the agent, when coping devices come into play. Thus what is seen in the fabric following damage is due both to the damage caused by the noxious agent itself and to the attempt to cope with the agent; there may be great elaboration of the coping devices.

The organism is always under day-to-day fluctuating trauma, which can be neutralized, or can leave behind small blemishes, e.g., cat phobia, like a bunion, is an inconvenience, but not a threat to the basic integrity of the fabric. Even so, the weakness can flare up, e.g., if a person makes a living by looking after cats, it would be a liability, or a bunion is a serious liability to a runner. Again, if a person with cat phobia married a woman who is fond of cats the strain on the relationship might be severe.

There are degrees of disability; few people are completely well and unblemished, e.g., at any time a twinge of indigestion under psychic trauma may become a stomach ulcer, perforate, and so threaten life.

Discussion will now be centred on the damaged fabric, as it affects the simplest organism, the *individual,* then the special aspects of family and society will be discussed.

The Individual

The organism consists of a somato-psychic apparatus. This is made up of its endowment and its acquired part. The organism is subdivided into a number of systems, each of which is served by an apparatus with properties and capacities. Here we are concerned with the psychic system, the organic substratum of the brain and the other systems that serve it. The cerebrum has a number of sections with apparatus, properties and capacity; some are associated with feeling tones or moods. The general aim of the organism is laid down by the "cosmic plan" of which it is a small part.

The organic brain makes psychic functioning possible. Sensations become percepts in its reception areas by consulting previous experience held in its memory areas. Percepts can pass to the thought areas and creative and original ideas can be formulated by manipulation of new material and old material stored in the memory. Action is initiated through the motor areas. This endowed machinery can be damaged. Intoxicants can disorganise it. (So in the author's belief can the agent responsible for encephaloataxia, where the agent strikes at the endowed machinery of thought.) The "higher" properties of thought, imagination and creativity, transcend local areas and require the activity of a number of areas. The ultimate awareness of activity in a feeling tone is termed a mood; some moods are direct and easy to interpret, but others are mixed, complex, and difficult to describe.

The endowment interacts with the environment and through experience develops a number of acquired characteristics, e.g., attitudes (including a central "idea of self"), character, temperament, knowledge, etc. It is this acquired part of the organism which is predominantly damaged by adverse psychic experience.

Some attitudes are complex in that they are composites of a number of basic attitudes. One blends with another to form a composite attitude and this then blends with another basic or composite attitude to form yet another. The basic English vocabulary is of about 1,000 words, only some of which are verbs. The number of basic attitudes that can be covered by these words are few, but they are still sufficient to describe adequately the fundamental attitudes. Blending of attitudes leads to the use of more elaborate words. Exact words must be distinguished from those used merely to hide attitudes; anxiety is a great coiner of abstruse words, as they make the best smokescreen. Basic attitudes are the raw material of society and the product of experience over time; these attitudes are available to families and individuals. We must differentiate an attitude from mood, e.g., to be aggressive towards someone and the mood of feeling angry. The damaged "idea of self" may set up wrong attitudes in an attempt to cope. These may aggravate the situation by provoking the attacker to strike again.

The "idea of self" is acquired over time due to the interaction of the endowed psyche with the environment. This interaction produces the acquired aspect of the psyche. It is this "idea of self," built up layer by layer in its many aspects through experience over time, which is attacked by opposing attitudes. The "idea of self" is a summation of attitudes—ideas, beliefs, interests, values, conscience, character. It is complex and has many elements, all of which can be damaged. Some elements are fundamental and important, e.g., notion of self worth. Some are less important, e.g., the notion that one has very good hearing. Any aspect or the whole can be attacked and damaged.

People are hugely concerned to meet "nice" people. A "nice" person is he or she who does not antagonise the "idea of self," or, better still, actively supports it by praise, encouragement, appreciation, etc. "To be liked" is very important to people. A great deal of effort in social intercourse goes into establishing whether others are "nice" or "nasty," for or against one, a support or a threat. A clash of attitudes leads to dislike and antagonism. Appreciation comes from others and thus there is a need for companionship, "belonging" and acceptance.

In a damaging interaction, the sequence of events is as follows:

psychic noci-vector ⟶ awareness of attack (sometimes) ⟶ insecurity ⟶ attempts at coping ⟶ if failure to cope ⟶ damage. The changes produced by this total process—psychic noci-vector, damage, and coping—are what the subject notices in himself—symptoms, and what an observer can perceive—signs; these changes are termed indicators and include both signs and symptoms.

Why is there a need to attack? Attack is dictated by a clash between the attitudes held by the protagonist and attitudes believed or known to be held by the antagonist. Disagreement is often mutual. The incompatibility may be very basic and hidden behind superimposed and secondary disagreements. The basic clashing attitudes can be strongly held and have been created by lengthy exposure to experience in the past. The more basic attitudes are created within the family—usually the preceding families.

The epitomes of the preceding families come into the present family with strongly held attitudes (sometimes amounting to strong needs—"I need to be loved," "I need to be protected").

Attitudes are expressed in the present family and may clash with those of the spouse, if he has equally strongly held but opposing attitudes. Children too, in the present family, soon come to adopt strong attitudes, e.g., "I need mother to love me." But if father holds the view, "I need all my wife's attention, as my mother gave me none," then there is an inevitable clash between father and child. Some of the attitudes are carried down the generations (we have yet to work out all the rules that govern this).

The attack may be aimed at one aspect or the whole of the "idea of self" of the antagonist. The one aspect is selected because:

1. It is the attitude of the "idea of self" of the antagonist which aggravates the protagonist most.

2. Attitudes of the "idea of self" known to be weaknesses may be selected because of their vulnerability.

The attack arouses insecurity and attempts to cope. The attempts to cope will meet with complete, varying, or no success, depending on circumstances. If the attack is acute, the coping will be assisted by the automatic arousal of mood, e.g., anger or fear. A more insidious attack is less likely to arouse mood. The response may be automatic at the behest of mood. The advantage of this primitive response is that it is automatic, quick, and massive. It also has dangers in not being guided by forethought. Sometimes to interpret the aroused mood may be difficult as a number of conflicting moods may be aroused or they may be mixed and complex. A young woman finds herself unexpectedly pregnant and she may experience a number of moods: "I have done wrong"—guilt; "He imposed this on me"—anger; "Can I manage?"—anxiety. Thus, she may well say, "I don't know what I feel." Due to previous experience, people differ in the capacity for arousal of mood, which may vary from excessive arousal to lack of it. More often, thought takes over and directs the coping efforts, of which there are many. If the possibility of further attack persists, then the psyche remains in a state of expectant fear—anxiety.

Damage may be completely repaired, partially repaired, or permanent—unless contrary experiences eradicate it (a sudden loss of confidence may be repaired almost at once by sustained praise and encouragement by an ally).

If there is a failure in coping, then there will be damage to an aspect or aspects or the whole "idea of self," e.g.: (i) Depreciation of the value of self, "I am unworthy," leaves a mood of depression (which can be mixed with other moods, e.g., anger or anxiety at the same time). (ii) The thought that the self is to blame arouses a mood of guilt. (iii) That the "idea of self" is utterly worthless, "I cannot live with myself," leads to the action of self-destruction, either by a negative act of not protecting the self, or by positive destruction of self (suicide can go hand in hand with other attitudes—to be a martyr, to arouse attention, to punish others).

The counterpart of damage to one aspect of the "idea of self" in the organic part of the person would be damage to one organ. The counterpart of damage to the whole "idea of self" in the organic part of the person would be damage to the whole body. Death of the body is the counterpart of complete loss of the "idea of self"; they coincide. Damage to the "idea of self" is the essence of psychonosis, i.e., damage to the acquired part of the psyche primarily (in encephalonosis, including encephaloataxia, damage is to the cerebral apparatus of psyche—i.e., the endowed part).

Aspects of the "idea of self" may be vulnerable to special stimuli. These vulnerable areas have been produced in the past. There may be no awareness of them. They may not be adversely stimulated for long periods of time. Children are very susceptible to damage. This may handicap them in basic functions for the rest of their lives, e.g., abilities to express love to another, to have intercourse with a spouse, to parent children, to relate to people, etc., i.e., from damage and from coping have arisen attitudes which hamper these basic functions.

Severe emotional trauma leads to damage which is at once manifest in a number of ways: (i) The damage may be severe enough to allow the use of the words "shock" or "stupor." (ii) The coping mechanisms must come to the fore and this negates more constructive efforts in our activities. (iii) There is the experience of an unpleasant mood, e.g., anguish, anxiety, depression, guilt. (iv) Organic functions and apparatus may also dysfunction. (v) The "idea of self" suffers damage.

Long-drawn-out engagements may produce an escalation of coping and damage. The engagements may only cease after exhaustion on one or both sides. The coping devices, physical and psychic, tire, thought tires of producing more countering arguments, the centres of mood are completely discharged, and the damage done demands a respite.

The physical response of the body is automatic, although it may be influenced by previous experience. Some responses are coping devices—the action of brain centres, the autonomic nervous system and the hormonal pattern as a reaction to aggression and fear—to help fight or to aid flight. Primitive mechanisms prepare the person for either. With both there is an accompanying mood. Secondary ill effects can develop from using this machinery excessively. These ill effects may be local. The local response may be determined by a weakness in a particular system, which has been produced by previous psychic experience involving it, or by organic weakness, e.g., an existing arthritis gets worse. A local response may also carry the full weight of an idea, i.e., cerebral mechanisms may dictate a small lesion at a particular highly meaningful point, for example, blush associated with shame. In addition to the acute reactions, chronic stimulation over a long time can also have its physical counterpart—no psychic condition is free from a reflection in the physical sphere.

So close is the tie between the acquired and the endowed physical apparatus of psyche, the cerebrum and the nervous system, that damage to the acquired part is reflected in bodily change also. A depressed person shows physical changes—pale skin, lifeless facies, flaccid limbs, constipation and slow pulse (unless there is concomitant anxiety). Acute fear may cause perforation of the stomach, or the hair to turn white or voiding of urine. The physical change in a person may belie his insistence that he has no problems. *Again, we see the need to practise a medicine of the whole man and to assess the physical condition of a psychonotic sufferer.*

Here is an example of a traumatic exchange. The analysis of a brief statement by a daughter concerning a quarrel with her father a few minutes before displays how, on both sides, the attack is directed at the "idea of self" (both father and daughter are present in the interview):

Therapist: What happened in the last hour then?

Daughter: He was being 100% selfish. Driving along, he wouldn't let me open the window. He had the heating full on and I was suffocating and I was very tired. He swore at me and called me a yob and God knows what, because I wanted the window open.

Father's attack on daughter during quarrel:

He would not open window   —i.e., would not listen as she is unimportant—attacks her notion within her "idea of self" that she ought to be loved by father.

He kept the heating on   —i.e., he is overbearing—he attacks her notion of adulthood within her "idea of self."

He swore at her   —i.e., he debases her—attacks her notion of adequacy and self respect within her "idea of self."

He calls her a yob   —i.e., he makes her feel inferior—attacks her notion of self respect within her "idea of self."

Summary: He is aggressive, both verbally and non-verbally. His mood is of anger.

Daughter's attack on father during interview:

He was selfish	—i.e., attack on the altruistic notions within his "idea of self."
He would not let me open the window	—i.e., he is unreasonable—attacks his notions of a responsible adult within his "idea of self."
He had the heating full on	—i.e., again unreasonable, as above.
He swore at me	—i.e., he uses bad language—attacks his notion of fairmindedness and rational notions within his "idea of self."
He called me a yob	—i.e., he is unfatherly—attacks his notion of fair play towards adolescents within his "idea of self."

Summary: She retaliates after the event, she is verbally aggressive and hostile. Her mood is of anger. She conveys attack in two ways: (i) directly, and (ii) in statements of fact which carry an implication of criticism.

Conclusion: Father attacks her during quarrel. She attacks him during interview. Both are aggressive and hostile and hurl hurtful attitudes at the other aimed at damaging the acquired "idea of self" of the other. The mood of both is anger.

The present exchange points also to the basic attitudes from which they spring. He dislikes her as a rival for the mother's affection. She fears him because of his continual attacks on her. At this moment she is stung into attack and hopes that in the presence of the therapist father is less likely to retaliate.

The Family

The fabric of the family must be briefly described before consideration is given to its damage, additional to that of the individual, by the psychic noci-vectors.

The family is a somato-psychic entity derived from somato-psychic fragments of preceding family entities. The endowed organic part consists of its individual members together with its collective possessions. Its endowed psychic part includes a cerebral apparatus in a number of individuals, which, collectively, allows of rapid communication amongst its members. Meanings are conveyed, percepts are formed, memory is consulted, thoughts are conceived, and fresh ideas flow out through the motor systems, both to other family members and to the external world. The collective apparatus has a number of feeling tones—more complete and diverse than in the individual and more often an amalgam of feelings.

The family system continually changes due to interaction within itself and interaction with the environment outside. Thus, it acquires general characteristics—knowledge, attitudes (beliefs, values, interests), character, conscience, temperament, aims, skills, role playing, control and decision-making machinery, arrangement and climate.

The family may be founded by damaged parents and further damage may continue due to internal or external psychic noci-vectors. As in the individual, the greatest damage is done to the acquired part. The basic pathological process is the same as in the individual.

The psychic noci-vectors can be aimed at any aspect of the integrated structure of the family. There is awareness of attack, insecurity is created, there is an attempt to cope and its failure leads to damage of some aspect of the family fabric. The family differs from the individual in that the structure is looser and there can be conflict, giving rise to noci-vectors, between elements in the family. *Frequently, the noci-vectors arise from clashing attitudes brought by family members from preceding families.*

The "idea of self" is built up by the family over time and is a complex summation of characteristics—ideas, beliefs, interests, values, conscience, character, temperament. Any of these can be damaged. Roles may change, the controlling and decision-making machinery may fail or weaken, integration is lost, conflict is increased and the climate becomes tense, traumatic or hostile.

The threat of attack causes insecurity—long-drawn-out insecurity produces continual anxiety and tension; the whole family, or fragments of it, await renewed attack. Strong moods are generated—of guilt, anger, and fear. Shock may be the initial reaction. Efficiency, harmony, confidence and cohesion are lost. Fragmentation may occur and finally the family may break up completely.

Not only does the psychic part of the family react, but so does the somatic. Somatic illness springs up in various parts of the whole—in individuals or dyads or sub-groups. Sometimes the whole family is affected. The expression of the somatic illness may change its locus as the dynamics change—indeed therapeutic intervention on a locus often merely moves the somatic disorder to another part of the family.

Family members involved in a pathological family process become a part of it and, as epitomes of the family, move on to produce potentially pathological families in the future.

Social Pathology

Society, like the family and individual, is a somato-psychic organism. The somatic aspect consists of all the individuals, families and groups within it together with its material possessions. The psychic endowment consists of the collective cerebral endowment of all its constituent parts together with the complex pattern of interaction between its multitudinous parts. Over time, like the family group, it has acquired an immense superstructure of attitudes, etc. It is this superstructure which is vulnerable to psychic trauma.

From the interaction of its parts—ethnic groups, political groups, families, individuals—can arise many areas of conflict producing potent psychic noci-vectors that threaten and harm it and its constituent parts. Society has yet to achieve the harmony which would fulfil the master plan devised for it. It has yet to find the correct pattern of functioning. Its parts are disharmonious and thus conflict and noxious vectors are inevitable. It has been especially unable to understand and control its psychic aspect.

Society is nearly always understood in economic, or material, or geographical terms. But the underlying psychic implications go unevaluated. Selfishness must lead to irresponsibility, "playing the market," and economic crisis. The crisis is studied, its toll in money is compounded, but its psychic origin remains overlooked. Hurt pride leads to a desire for revenge and self-expression which in turn can lead to war. As important as the statistics of wasted finance, the number of dead, and the economic consequences is the need to evaluate the psychic origin of war.

Society's psychopathology is essentially similar to psychopathology in the family. Any facet of society can be damaged. The noxious vectors may or may not be perceived. Insecurity is created. Attempts at coping are made and if they fail there is damage to some facet of society or to the whole of it. The controlling and decision-making machinery may fail, perverse roles are created, e.g., the Inquisition, McCarthyism, etc., integration is lost, conflict increases, and the climate becomes tense, hostile, and traumatic. Continual threats provoke anxiety and tension. Strong moods are generated. Efficiency, confidence, harmony and cohesion are lost. Fragmentation leading to warring factions may be a feature. Finally, the whole society may disintegrate and perish. On a small scale, the impact of so-called "modern" or "developed" society on a different society, e.g., the Australian Aborigines, is a violent illustration of multiple, noxious, clashing vectors on a hitherto fairly harmonious society.

As in families and individuals, the somatic and material aspects of society are involved in the pathological process. The level of physical ill-health is one index of social pathology.

Naturally, the state of society is transferred to its constituent parts—its groups, families and individuals. *To understand and improve social pathology is a fundamental way of improving the state of families and individuals. Hence the importance of creating a salutiferous society.*

Associated Matters

Conflict is not damage. But it can lead to damage as trauma can arise from it. Conflict is a clash or difference between two attitudes. It can arise in a number of ways:

1. Conflict of attitudes within one person—"to steal or to be honest."
2. Conflict between two desirable alternatives.
3. Conflict between attitudes held by two persons—"I want children. You don't want children."
4. Contradictory attitudes conveyed from one person to another—"I love you. I hate you."

Guilt is especially likely to occur in people of strong moral convictions when their actions are in contradiction to those ideals. Damage is done to the moral aspect of the "idea of self." There is an attitude of "I am blameworthy, I should be ashamed" and a mood of guilt. The feeling of being wrong may be so great that it cannot be tolerated: "Such an offensive object should not live and should be destroyed." Those continually blamed in the past are very vulnerable to blame now. In pure grieving there is a feeling of loss. If there was antagonism to the dead person in the past, there may be not only grief, but also a feeling of being "to blame" and of guilt.

The description given earlier of the functioning of the psyche puts reproductive and *sexual activities* in perspective. They are major activities of the person, but far from his total, or most important activity. A mood of sexuality is a potent motivator of action, but so are thirst—and many other activities. To explain psychic disorder in terms of sexual dysfunction alone is to limit grossly the knowledge of individual activity. Furthermore, sexual malfunction often arises secondarily to other psychic damage, e.g., in a state of depression there is loss of desire to eat and also loss of desire for sexual activity. Again, frigidity may be secondary to an inability to express emotion for another person, or anxiety may make sexual performance impossible. Difficulties in sexual activity can cause consequential reactions, e.g., wife loses her mother and is disinclined to have intercourse, husband becomes irritable at her refusal and develops a gastric ulcer. To explain behaviour in terms of stereotyped sexual dogma is to grossly limit the range of human behaviour. It is also a serious error to impose adult concepts of sexuality upon children.

Security, fear and anxiety must be differentiated. In the absence of threat or stress to the self and in a state of optimum functioning and harmony, there is complete *security*. *Fear* is aroused by something which is harmful to the self. The threat is seen and the mood of fear experienced. Fear can sometimes be displaced to harmless objects. It can be exaggerated by introspection when allowed to hold the field of attention and push out ideas that would put the fear in perspective. It is a primitive response and has an attached physical apparatus. *Anxiety* is a state of anticipation of threat to the self. It is sustained. People talk of being in a state of tension. There is a continuous alerting of the associated physical apparatus. Chronic body changes may occur—loss of weight, moist skin, furrowed face, etc. Because of previous experience, some people expect stress—they are of an anxious disposition. They may react to a minimal stimulus. Such persons are at as great a disadvantage as those who are so non-sensitive to stimulation that their phlegmatic reaction puts them in danger.

Aggression is a primitive coping mechanism associated with a physical apparatus for its performance and a mood of anger in awareness. It has increasingly come under the control of thought. The physical apparatus can even be dictated to put on a sham demonstration of anger. Anger in performance or in threat is one way of contending with attack. Thus, it is prevalent in those who are insecure. It can be stimulated by childhood experiences; some families regard it as the first choice when attacked, threatened or anxious. There is an *attitude* of hostility, an *activity* of aggression and a *mood* of anger.

Anomalous conditions of the person due to untraumatic experiences must not be confused with danger, e.g., lack or excess of emotional response (cold or volatile people). A person may display such anomalies without being disharmonious or dysfunctioning, if in an environment where the anomaly is acceptable. For example, a homosexual may be healthy, balanced and happy if in an environment that accepts his way of life; in a different hostile situation, he can become psychonotic, if he is the recipient of psychic stress. A gipsy may steal, but within his own society his action is normal and healthy.

Indicators

The man in the street, like a family or society, aspires to happiness, a state of psychic and physical harmony, which has its own indicators. Some of the indicators of harmonious psychic functioning are: loving, relating, co-operating, enjoyable sexuality, balanced self regard, security, self-confidence, responsible attainable goals, well-being, productiveness within capacity, hopefulness, creativeness (the capacity for self-improvement). These are associated with physical well-being, e.g., beneficial sleep, sound digestion and elimination, ample appetite, co-ordinated muscle action, sexual satisfaction, clear skin, etc.

In pathology, the psychic noci-vectors strike the psyche of the organism, which responds by deploying its coping mechanisms, and damage to the psyche may or may not occur. This process displays itself by indicators.

An indicator can be any part of the whole process—psychic noci-vector, damage, or coping mechanism. Taking the analogy of a car with dirt in the petrol makes this clear. The dirt in the pipe, i.e., the noci-vector, may cause an irregular movement of the car, the lack of petrol leads to defective combustion and hence loss of power, i.e., damage to its functioning, and the need to press hard on the accelerator to produce more petrol is an attempt to cope. The indicators, irregular motion, loss of power and excessive use of the accelerator, are all due to different parts of the whole process. All are useful indicators of the trouble and together give the experienced motorist a clue to the nature of the disorder. Similarly a piece of shrapnel causing a body wound has a number of indicators—the hardness is due to the noxious vector, the shrapnel, the loss of sensations is due to a cut nerve, and the warmth around the wound is due to the body's inflammatory coping device. The indicators are not the process itself, they are the parts that can be assessed. They warn the individual of pathology. To a trained observer they may demonstrate the nature of the pathology. Hence the

166

need for a careful examination to identify as many indicators as possible and reach an accurate elucidation, diagnosis, of the pathology.

The organism subjected to the process, or an observer, notices a change in functioning, something different happens from the accustomed—pain, or anguish, or anxiety, or a rash, etc. The change that can be detected by the organism iself is termed a symptom. The change in the organism that can be detected by an observer is termed a sign. Damage to the psyche tends to lead to fundamental changes—grief, depression, withdrawal, guilt, anger, fears, etc. These changes in the self may be so obvious as not to escape the attention of the person. They may be very obvious also to the observer and so constitute signs. An indicator is the part of the process which is noticed—it is not more significant than the rest of the process and is not the whole of it. Indicators—signs and symptoms—are produced by the whole process and therefore all these factors which determine the choice of psychic noci-vectors, damage, or coping, determine the indicator.

The psychic noci-vector, as it influences the place and mode of attack, the damage done, and the responding coping devices, is a factor in determining the nature of the indicator.

The family's influence on choice of coping devices is great and hence it may also determine the indicator. Given a certain constellation of factors operating, conflict can be resolved only in certain definite ways. A particular form of coping, and hence a particular indicator, is inevitable in given circumstances. This leads to diverse and sometimes extreme as well as fanciful ways of coping. No other way of coping is possible.

These coping devices, and hence indicators, can be passed on from one generation to the next. A grandparent copes with his social inferiority by fastidiousness in dress; his son adopts the same coping device—and so does the grandson. In the preceding family men meet attack with aggression, the men of the presenting family adopt the same device, which is also found in the succeeding family. Thus familial communication may be confused with genetically induced traits. Faced with the same psychic noci-vector as on previous occasions, the same coping devices are quickly employed and therefore the same indicators are seen. Repetition leads to a stereotyped process and hence to stereotyped indicators.

The psychic pathological process sometimes follows a general pattern, more or less common to many families. In that case, common indicators will be apparent. At other times, the process is special and unique to a family and thus the indicators are unusual.

The indicators of psychic pathology can be either psychic or somatic. Thus an examination of psychic and somatic functioning is required to make a complete assessment of the indicators. Any bodily system can be involved in the pathological process. Indicators of dysfunction in the soma are termed psychosomatic disorders—they are many and diverse. It is rare for careful examination not to expose some psychosomatic disorders when the organism has been subjected to psychic harmful agents. The psychosomatic disorder must be differentiated from the hysterical. The first is an automatic pathological response, e.g., abdominal pain due to bowel spasm at the thought of going to school where one is bullied by a classmate. The hysterical response is a simulated attitude because the need to simulate is great, e.g., the child simulates abdominal pain, which has no related bowel spasm, so as to avoid going to school. The term "hysterical" denotes a special attitude—one of simulation. But many attitudes are adopted without simulation and are not hysterical—the real situation is that a need exists to hold firmly on to an attitude. For example, a child refuses to eat—he cannot do otherwise while caught in a deadlock with father who states, "Just eat and I will not be cross." The child states, "If you stop being cross, I will eat"—and thus cannot eat until father changes his attitude.

As in the field of organic pathology, a particular indicator may be shared by a number of different psychopathological processes. Inability to eat, for example, may arise from severe depression, from a reaction to grief (Mary Stuart's dog "pined away" and refused to eat after her beheading), from a conflict with the family when food is an issue, from concentration of interest elsewhere arising from severe anxiety and the need to be alert, or from gastric pain produced by acute anxiety. The same is true of organic pathology—dyspnoea (shortness of breath) may be seen in anaemia, in carcinoma of the lung, in pneumonia, and in cardiac failure.

When attempts are made to remove an indicator, the attempt may be successful, but the indicator is usually immediately replaced by another—the *substitution of indicators*. The process has not changed, but the therapy has produced an additional factor that pushes the process in another direction. This is very conspicuous in families when the presenting pathological member is given much assistance; he is soon replaced by another family member who has become sick.

Indicators of pathology must be differentiated from bad habits. Many attitudes are not the result of psychic noci-vectors, but are wrong attitudes inculcated in a non-stressful situation. To exploit others may be a way of life arising from that person's values, or it might be a coping mechanism indicating a pathological process. The first is of interest to sociologists, the second a matter for clinicians. This confusion leads to non-clinical procedures being advocated for clinical disorders and to armies of well-meaning citizens attempting a clinical role.

When the organism is fearful enough about its health, it will take one of its indicators as an excuse for seeking help. It may notice only this one conspicuous indicator. It may regard only that particular one as a sign of danger. It may feel it will lead to attention. This indicator is termed "the complaint," or the presenting symptom. It is crucial to appreciate that the presenting symptom is not the whole process, nor is it more significant than the rest of the indicators. There must be a global assessment to lead to adequate diagnosis. The importance of indicators is that they warn, they lead to seeking professional help, and, taken collectively, they often point the nature of the pathology to the clinician trained in reading the indicators and in systematic examination that allows of a total appraisal, leading to a discernment, diagnosis.

Indicators are not the psychopathological process and attempts to treat the indicators as if they were the process are futile. This can limit the usefulness of behaviour therapy. Similarly, a sign of a stressful process such as a rash, perhaps due to a hurtful marital situation, may be helped by an ointment but leaves untouched the process itself; it can only relieve any secondary stress caused by the rash. The process itself must be treated for effective therapy. The psychic noxious agents causing the process must stop operating or the coping devices must be strengthened, and the psychic damage must be repaired.

Indicators of morbid processes as they present in the individual, family and society will be briefly outlined.

Indicators in the Individual

Like the family and society, the individual reacts as a somato-psychic organism. Thus there are somatic as well as psychic indicators, signs and symptoms, and it is rare for this not to be the case. The somatic indicators are usually multiple and in the nature of the so-called "psychosomatic disorders." The choice of psychosomatic responses depends on a number of factors—previous trauma involving a particular organ with a reawakening of memory in relation to it; the organic mechanisms of reaction to stress may be overstimulated, with damage to a weak organ; cultural suggestion, e.g., blushing in western society is an index of shame. The selection of the site where damage develops is probably determined centrally by the brain, as the lesions do not follow a segmental distribution, which would be the case in local damage to the central nervous system.

It is usual to subdivide emotional disorder in the individual into certain clinical categories—anxiety states, obsessional states, hysterical states, etc. This practice has grave weaknesses. It pays attention to the presenting symptoms, often elevates them to the status of a disease, and limits the description of the process. The process is all-important and cannot be covered by one or many labels. Each process is made up of such a combination of circumstances as to be unique.

Either psychic or somatic symptoms may be the first to be noticed and constitute the presenting symptom. Age influences the indicators. Hostility may be manifested in an infant by temper tantrums; in a child, by lying; in an adolescent, by rebellion; and in an adult, by criminality. A person is bound by the strength and range of his endowment at a given period of development. There may be resurgence of psychonosis, and hence indicators, at nodal points in development, e.g., school entrance, puberty, marriage, childbirth, menopause, retirement, etc.

Sex gender may influence indicators, e.g., a woman tends to develop signs in the reproductive system. Gastric and duodenal ulceration is commoner in men.

Examples of indicators from 25 patients are:

Vaginismus	Bouts of drinking	Indigestion
Nightmares	Screaming fits	Moodiness
Ill temper	Tremors	Irritations of skin
Epigastric pains or	Headaches	Fainting attacks
discomfort	Numbness in the body	Violent behaviour
Chest pains	Worry	to wife
Shyness	Fear of crowds	Cancer phobia and
Backache	Pumping in stomach	other phobias
Bad temper	Giddiness	Wanting to run away
Nose bleeds	Globus hystericus	Lack of concentration
Forced pregnancy	Insomnia	Inability to go to work
Pains in the abdomen	Diarrhoea	Inability to go to
Fearfulness	Muscular pains	school
Dyspareunia	Belching	"Run down"
Frigidity	Palpitations	Cramps in the hand
Crying fits	Sweats	"Pins and needles"
Bed wetting	Loss of weight	Shortness of breath
Dyspepsia	Asthma	Loss of hair
Attacks of panic	Bouts of fever	Failing an exam
Frequent ill health,	Dysmenorrhoea	Colitis
coughs, colds	"Bad heart"	Migraine
Loss of appetite	Drug addiction	Depression

As can be seen, the above can be divided conveniently into somatic and psychic indicators. In no patient did one group, psychic or somatic, exist alone. Depression of varying degrees is a very common symptom. This was also found to be so in an investigation of symptomatology shown by patients of Dr. John Hall, Shakespeare's son-in-law (1), 300 years ago.

Indicators in the Family

The family too reacts as a whole, with both its psyche and its soma. Rarely is a disturbed family without signs of somatic disorders and indeed this may be its most conspicuous feature—and its reason for seeking help. The total range of symptomatology in a family may be great. Indicators arise from the clashing attitudes within the family or between the family and its psychic environment.

Indicators can arise anywhere in the fabric of the family—in its individuals, in its external and internal communication system, in its physical structure (even to proneness to a streptococcal infection), and in its general characteristics. Careful examination will usually reveal that indicators appear in all its dimensions, especially if the disturbance is severe. However, a family group may not manifest dysfunction equally throughout its system. One aspect of it may show disproportionate dysfunction due to the "set" of emotional events at a particular time.

Indicators are strikingly apparent in problem families, because emotionally sick families carry a high degree of psychopathogenicity. In one family, consisting of mother and two children, the following were seen:

Dimension of the Individuals:

Mother— Aggression; rage; despair; depression; panic; lying; stealing; accident-proneness; excessive smoking; alcoholism, attacks of vomiting; fainting attacks; gastric ulcer; enuresis; shaking fits.

Child 1— Tension; tearfulness; fear of the dark; nightmares; enuresis; lying.

Child 2— Irritability; depression; enuresis; lack of confidence.

Dimension of Internal Communication:

Mother/Children—Overprotectiveness; rejection; hostility; depreciation; neglect; disparagement.

Dimension of General Psychic Properties:

Two illegitimate children; low morality; shared symptom of enuresis; no aims or purpose; conflict.

Dimension of External Communication:

Isolation; truanting from school; exploitation of welfare agencies; quarrels with neighbours; poor school performance; mother unemployable.

Dimension of Physical Properties:

Poor diet; squalor; debts.

The choice of indicators is a reflection of family dysfunctioning. The individual's choice is dictated by his life experience in the family, e.g., an angry family evokes anger in a child. The choice of expression in a relationship is similarly determined, e.g., physical hostility may be taboo and verbal hostility alone possible. The material changes in the family can take place only within the limits set by its condition. Group manifestations are a family expression, e.g., sulking may be an expression of hostility in a particular family. The community interaction may determine the indicators, e.g., that fear be controlled by obsessional ritual or that sexual taboos be imposed. Again, gastric ulceration is a common indicator in Western civilisation, but not in primitive communities. Not only do present events dictate choice of indicators, but so do events from the past. Every indicator has to be understood as a manifestation of past or present family dysfunction, or as a resultant of both.

It is fundamental to the doctrine of family psychiatry that psychopathology must always be thought of as an expression of dysfunction in a whole family group. A family can show manifestations, indicators, of dysfunction at any point in its system. Thus indicators appear in the five dimensions. Almost invariably they appear in all, although this may escape notice except on the closest examination. But the family group will not show manifestations of dysfunction to the same extent through all its aspects, e.g., the second child may show more manifestations than the first, or a girl more than a boy, or the family's external relations may be more disturbed than its physical conditions.

In the *dimension of the individuals,* each family member usually shows symptomatology. Naturally, this will not be exposed if examination concentrates on one person alone and overlooks the remainder of the family. But each individual does not show psychopathology of the same kind, nor to the same degree.

In the *dimension of internal communication,* each relationship will usually show disharmony. Naturally, this will not be seen unless each relationship is examined. In practice, the mother/child relationship often comes under far greater scrutiny than the father/child relationship; the marital relationship also receives a fair degree of attention, but not always from the psychiatric service. Each relationship will not show psychopathology of the same kind, nor to the same degree.

A disturbed relationship may give rise to any indicator in the physical or psychic fields, in both individuals of the partnership, e.g., an obsession in the wife and a rash in the husband. Sometimes the symptomatology is shared by both partners, e.g., impotence in both (a psychosomatic reaction); joint depression, suicide or *folie à deux* (affective changes), or overt quarrelling. Furthermore, some indicators tend to be associated with a particular relationship, e.g., a mal-relationship between husband and wife is often responsible for premature ejaculation, dyspareunia, impotence and frigidity.

Hence, too, family patterns may dictate choice of indicators, e.g., in some families open quarrelling is forbidden and its members sulk instead. Cultural pressure may also influence choice of indicators, e.g., sexual taboos increase the incidence of sexual disharmony.

That a particular relationship comes to the attention of a referral agency may be fortuitous. Quarrels between husband and wife may evoke the attention of friends; the faulty relationship between mother and infant may be picked up by the regular surveillance of a community "mother and baby" clinic; the relationship most under stress may come to attention, e.g., a marriage, due to the intervention of a third party. That indicators of faulty relationships come to attention rather than individual indicators is equally fortuitous.

Symptomatology in the *general psychic dimension* manifests itself in a pattern common to the whole family. Families may be prone to particular types of physical disability, e.g., accident proneness, stomach disorders, or speech disturbances. They manifest affective changes as a group, e.g., panic may be the group reaction to stress. The family's pattern of behaviour is shared by all its members, e.g., exploitation of neighbours. Choice of family group symptomatology may be influenced by cultural pressure; e.g., the culture may dictate that fear be controlled by obsessional ritual.

That group disharmony rather than individual or relationship disharmony comes to the attention of a referral agency is again fortuitous. Usually this is less likely to happen, as few agencies ascertain whole family patterns of dysfunction. It is not inconceivable, however, that in time many more agencies will function as family agencies, e.g., in a number of countries the personal doctor operates more and more as a family physician.

Family dysfunction frequently manifests itself in the *dimension of physical properties,* e.g., poverty despite an adequate income; sloth resulting from apathy and disinterest; low income due to lack of application; loss of employment as a reaction to family emotional crises. Yet again it is fortuitous that adverse material circumstances are the manifestations that arouse attention in referral agencies, rather than individual, internal communication, or general disharmony. Most often these manifestations come to the attention of social agencies. But selection factors operate, as an agency may have a special function, e.g., a housing agency may ascertain sloth but overlook employment failure, or an agency may serve lower income groups only and overlook child neglect in a higher income group.

In the *dimension of external communication,* signs of dysfunction may arise at the three points of contact: individual-community interaction, e.g., stealing outside the home by a child; partnership-community interaction, e.g., parents' refusal to send a child to school; or family group-community interaction, e.g., quarrelling with the neighbours. The community influences the family by informal and formal means. Enforcement of the latter is entrusted to agencies with statutory powers, e.g., police, courts, health inspectors, child-care agencies, etc., and these, in addition to enforcement functions, may accept responsibility for ascertainment of dysfunction. Usually agencies with statutory powers are likely to observe signs of dysfunction in this dimension of family-community interaction.

Indicators in Society

Society, too, reacts as a somato-psychic entity with psychic and somatic indicators. Not only may there be high incidences of psychosomatic disorders, but also signs of psychic disruption, like social unrest, low morale, apathy, strife, war, corruption and fragmented incohesive public action. The indicators may follow a common pattern through a large population, e.g., the panic reactions common in the Middle Ages. Mass suggestion can affect the choice of indicators, e.g., the increase in drug addiction in adolescents forced by massive propaganda to display their adulthood in this fashion. There may be an interplay of family and social factors in indicator production, e.g., alcoholism may be the accepted expression in a given population, but only those in disturbed families manifest it to a severe degree.

Some indicators are termed "social" problems, e.g., high divorce rate, high suicide rate, alcoholism, drug addiction, promiscuity, child neglect, etc. Some of these are "social" only in the sense that a large number of people are involved, like tuberculosis 50 years ago. Like tuberculosis, however, the eradication of these problems involves not only large scale preventive action, but also curative procedures at individual and family level. The preventive actions must be devised and guided by knowledge acquired through curative procedures.

REFERENCE

1. HOWELLS, J. G. and OSBORN, M. L. (1970). The incidence of emotional disorder in a 17th-century medical practice. *Medical History, 14,* 2, 192–198.

V
FAMILY DIAGNOSIS

Introduction

A farmer, driving to the nearby town, thinks he discerns a red flush on his field of barley; the event provokes an urgent systematic enquiry. Is it a fact? What caused it? What is the responsible fungus? At the end of the afternoon a small plane trailing a cloud of insecticide delivers the exact remedy. So, diagnosis (dia-gnosis, through knowledge) has led to correct therapy.

Yet, in psychiatry, diagnosis is eschewed. The fashionable vogue is to plunge into therapy. It is as if in surgery, at the signal of abdominal pain, we plunged in with no knowledge of the anatomy of the abdominal organs, no understanding of their function and no systematic enquiry to discern the focus of the pain. In psychiatry, the sign of emotional anguish is enough. We plunge in.

But this behaviour is not calculated perversity. It is presumably our defence against the admission of ignorance. The anatomy of the personality has yet to be worked out, the functioning of the psyche is obscure, and the understanding of psychopathology is at a rudimentary stage. Dependent on, and ruled by, the fertile but illogical and uninformed imagination of a number of well-intentioned clinicians over the last 70 years, we hesitate to start afresh—such is the daunting influence of what has become established opinion. Better the wrong landmarks than no landmarks. But lost we are.

To help is a laudable aspiration. But to plunge into the abdomen with no prior examination and no knowledge of anatomy and physiology is not help. It is a hazardous impulse fraught with danger for the patient. In that situation, masterly inactivity and reliance on nature's own defense measures might well be more effective.

To turn to systematic enquiry is the sure road to knowledge. The resources now available make this possible. One fruitful field' for garnering knowledge is the pathological. It behoves us therefore to be systematic in the clinical field, to enquire, to understand, to build on understanding and to intervene with knowledge. Diagnosis must come before therapy, not only for the good of a particular family, but also for the future of psychiatry.

Developments in a field depend on a number of factors, but probably none so retards progress in psychiatry today as the confusions of its nosology and, linked with it, the lack of agreement on criteria for defining syndromes together with the imprecision of nomenclature. Ignorance is a matter to be overcome by time and endeavour; the lack of order in known phenomena is something to be righted now. An aetiological classification is a paramount need because accurate delineation of dysfunction leads to logical investigation, and so to the meeting of the central obligation of psychiatry— effective treatment. Thus nosology was given a separate section earlier in this book.

The following matters are discussed in this section.

The family psychiatric service accepts referred patients, individual, couple, or family. Thus the *referral* procedures must be described. From it arises the intriguing question: What dictates the referral of a particular family member at one moment in the life history of his family?

Having accepted an individual or a family, it is necessary to explore the presenting *symptomatology,* the complaint, that particular organism's subjective reason for seeking help. Investigation then moves to an assessment of all the indicators, going from a presenting individual's symptomatology to a complete assessment of all the family's indicators. These procedures allow of a diagnosis in terms of organic, psychic, or mixed syndromes.

To make a diagnosis is not to elucidate the psychopathological *process* that set up the indicators. The informant may be clear about his symptomatology and the clinician understand the nature of it, but neither has any notion of the cause of it. Thus exploration now moves to the area of the psychopathology of the disordered family. The understanding of the process leads to effective, deliberate therapy.

This section of the book ends with a discussion of *record keeping* in family diagnosis and in the Appendix is found additional information about the procedures and techniques mentioned in the section.

Referral

When the organism, the family, dysfunctions there are repercussions throughout that family. The indicators of dysfunction, symptoms and signs, come to the notice of the family or of others. The awareness of the family, or a part of it, or of an individual varies greatly. In general, paradoxically, the greater the disturbance, the less the insight and the capacity to take action. The link may not be made between the indicator and the emotional state. A physical indicator may be thought to have a physical cause. A behavioural indicator may be thought to be due to some moral deficit. Long-drawn-out states of psychopathology may be assumed to be usual. Standards may be low; what are states of ill-health are often widely regarded as being "normal," i.e., usual. The dictates of relatives, or social position, or lack of finance may make it impossible to seek assistance, hence the need for awareness and then for help from outside.

Usually the whole family is affected. Uncommonly, the whole family will appraise itself and seek assistance. More usually, an outside agency will appraise the family and persuade it to seek assistance as a family. Occasionally, a dyad in the family will seek help either on its own initiative or prompted by others. More often it is the individual who seeks help by his own efforts or encouragement from others. The conditions determining the common presentation of an individual will be discussed later.

Frequently one of the indicators becomes so noticeable to the family or others, or so painful, that it becomes "the last straw" and the final reason for taking action. As will be seen later, this presenting symptom is no more significant than other indicators; it may just be the most noticed, the most painful, the most socially acceptable, the one that offers least embarrassment to the family if discussed with others, or the one that allows an overture for help without final commitment.

Referral agencies can be conveniently divided into medical and social,

179

and the latter into statutory and voluntary bodies. Some of the main medical referral agencies are family doctors, family nurses, polyclinics, hospital departments, industrial medical officers, departments for the care of the handicapped, and school clinics. Some of the main social referral agencies are child-care agencies, workers attached to courts of law, industrial welfare officers, church workers, moral welfare workers, marriage guidance services, housing departments, school welfare officers, the Samaritans, the Salvation Army, and the police.

In some countries medical agencies with associated welfare agencies are ready to offer continuous observation and support of families in what they regard as essentially a medical problem—family psychopathology. Thus, whatever the manifestations of dysfunction, they become the main referral channel to the psychiatric service. The continuous medical coverage is given through a family doctor and the continuous welfare coverage either by a home nursing visitor with experience of physical, emotional and social problems, or by an all-purpose social worker with similar experience. These services are supported by specialist medical and social agencies. A vital condition for success is that the workers offering a continuous service should be trained to see the significance of emotional phenomena. The advantage of referral through a medical service is obvious. Family psychiatry teaches the importance of a total somato-psychic approach; much of the symptomatology is physical; continuous support to a family in all its organic and psychic aspects is invaluable.

In other countries medical agencies concern themselves with the more obviously medical problems, e.g., psychosomatic manifestations, psychonosis (neurosis) and encephalonosis (psychosis), while leaving to social agencies other conditions of social importance, e.g., alcoholism, antisocial behaviour, poor material circumstances, and child neglect. There is little doubt that these latter conditions are basically personality problems and arise from individual and family psychopathology. However, these conditions giving rise to social difficulties do come to the notice of social agencies and may then be referred to the psychiatric service. Agencies may be selective in their interests and, if so, a number are required before a complete ascertainment service is given to a family. Thus in these countries there are two main referral channels, medical and social.

Direct referrals from the family to a psychiatric service carry the advantage of speed. They carry the disadvantage of possible wrong selection of specialist service, and bypass the agencies that can give continuous support, both before and after specialist help. All requirements can be met if the psychiatric service offers direct help in an emergency, but it usually accepts families through agencies only.

In the United Kingdom, an appointment is usually sought through the family doctor or personal physician. In an emergency, a family or an individual is accepted at once and the physician responsible for the family is informed. If other agencies, medical or social, become aware of a need for referral, they liaise with the family doctor, who then initiates referral. Experience has shown this to be an indispensable method. It allows of all previous knowledge on the health of the family, physical and emotional, being available. It offers a way whereby, after help from the specialist agency, the family finds itself back with the physician responsible for its continuous care.

A request for an appointment reaches the department of family psychiatry usually by letter, or more urgently by telephone. The application for the appointment is acknowledged to the referring agency and an indication given of the likely waiting period. The application, which usually outlines the nature of the problem, is placed in a confidential file. This file is under the direct care of a psychiatrist on the staff. The waiting period for a first appointment need not be long and at the Institute of Family Psychiatry for 20 years it has remained at approximately two weeks. Why have a waiting list at all? This is essential to allow a smooth deployment of staff. The period is so brief that it causes no hurt to the patient and, if it did, is overcome by asking the referring agency to indicate if the matter is urgent. In this event, which seldom occurs, the appointment is sent at once. Occasionally, the smooth routine has to be interrupted to allow a very urgent case to be seen immediately. Each week the staff take new families from the waiting list in an agreed number, with one staff member monitoring the procedure.

The key to a brief waiting list lies in making an assessment of the number of families who can receive treatment with the available resources of a particular department. The department must decide whether it wishes to see a large number of families for brief periods at long intervals and offer superficial treatment, or to see a small number frequently in intensive and worthwhile therapy. As soon as the number seen goes beyond the resources available, treatment perforce becomes superficial and, before long, not worthwhile—thus resources are wasted; the staff are frantically trying to cope with a flood of material and are unable to add to their skills by doing worthwhile work. A realistic estimation of treatment resources, then, allows a suitable number of patients to be given worthwhile therapy. The remainder are denied it. To accumulate a long waiting list, however, is of no avail as no more patients can be seen than the resources allow.

The effect of the above method is to allow all families to go through the diagnostic procedure. A number, depending on the resources, proceed to therapy—and they proceed at once without a wasteful interval which might result in the diagnostic procedures having to be repeated. Those not accepted for therapy are referred back to the referring agency—but with an appraisal of the situation, which is supplied after a short diagnostic period. Thus the referring agency is not kept waiting long for an opinion. Those denied help by the department are able at once to be given help by the referring agency, or to be sent elsewhere; the latter happens rarely, given our present day resources.

The nature of the service given by a department of family psychiatry should in general fall into two categories: (i) A diagnostic appraisal of a family's problem with a clear-cut opinion on its nature and recommendations for management. In the United Kingdom, the referring family practitioner, for instance, is increasingly being encouraged to offer help from his own resources. Given the skilled assistance of a health visitor or a social worker, a great deal can be achieved at home level. (ii) Undertaking of management beyond the resources of the referring agency.

Intake Procedure

The appointment is fixed, the letter of invitation is sent, couched in a welcoming vein and accompanied by a brochure on the department and a prepaid postcard for reply; the postcard is received back at the department, finally confirming the appointment. That the postcard is prepaid usually guarantees its return and allows appointments not taken up to be given to others. Rapport begins to be established at this early point of contact.

The family arrives by appointment. They already understand the procedure, as it has been explained in the brochure. The building, including the waiting area, is familiar as they have seen it pictured in the brochure. They are met by the receptionist. This is the first direct staff contact—and therefore important. It sets the tone for all that is to follow. Much goes on in a waiting area. In general, especially for early visits, it is a tense period. It can be relieved by an understanding, helpful, accommodating receptionist. The decor of the waiting area should be cheerful and a compliment to those who wait. The period of tension can be abbreviated by the interviewer being prompt. Inevitably, from time to time, due to some unexpected demand, a family is forced to wait. When the interviewer meets them, it should be the subject of apology and explanation—as would be expected of a courteous host. Discourtesy, and especially unexplained lengthy waiting periods, kill rapport. The receptionist conducts the family, or dyad, or individual to the staff and introduces them. Rapport building continues and the systematic diagnostic procedures have begun.

While the receptionist is usually the first staff contact with a family, it may occasionally be preceded by another staff member—the telephonist—at some routine enquiry before attendance. Departments can fail here. For effective rapport building, the telephonist must be a person of warmth, of infinite patience, and accommodating. New telephonists respond when the importance of their position is explained to them.

Intake channels can be based on family dimensions. Signs of pathology can arise at any facet of the family group—in any of its dimensions—in the individual, in that of internal communication, in its general psychic properties, in its dimension of external communication, and in its physical properties dimension. Thus intake channels can be based on any one, or on all dimensions.

Individuals, naturally, concentrate on their own discomfort and tend to seek help themselves; agencies make use of this readiness. Thus a referral service can be based on the individual with intake channels for all age groups—child, adolescent, adult and the aged.

A referral service could also concentrate on *relationships*—e.g., the marital, parent-child, or sibling-sibling. In practice, the last two are usually associated with a children's intake channel; it may be useful to establish a marital problems intake channel to gather in marital problems, a common feature of disturbed families.

Establishing an intake channel for the *family group* is invaluable—with increasing understanding of family psychopathology this will become in time the method of choice; it must never, however, be inferred that only the group as a whole will be accepted by the service.

Intake clinics based on poor *physical circumstances* are already a feature of countries with well-developed welfare systems. In advanced countries, problem or hard-core families find their way to such clinics. If the psychopathological nature of their disability is accepted, in future they will be referred to family group intake channels.

Family-community interaction may break down at many points, engendering problems which require special clinics to cope with them, e.g., delinquency clinics, school refusal clinics, university student clinics, industrial clinics, etc.

Intake channels could also be based on clinical categories. Not only may a family show signs of disruption in any dimension, but it may also present with varying types of psychopathology—psychonosis, psychosomatic symptoms, or delinquency. Thus a service could base its intake channels on clinical categories, instead of on signs of pathology in family dimensions—or on both.

Ideally the whole family should be referred from the beginning, and thus there would be no need for channels or clinics with special functions in relation to age groups or clinical categories. Until understanding of family psychopathology is widespread, to insist that nothing less than a whole family will be accepted would lead to severe curtailment of the service. Neither agencies nor families have a high degree of understanding of family psychopathology. Indeed, in general, understanding correlates with the degree of stability. Thus the more disturbed families, those most in need of help, could be neglected if it were insisted that only those perceptive enough to come as whole families were accepted.

Whatever the family or the agency offers should initially be accepted, whether it be an individual member, the whole family, or part of it. The department of family psychiatry can then itself work to achieve the desired aim of involving the whole family.

Usually, a family psychiatric service receives an individual, the presenting member, who is the starting-off point of investigation. In areas accustomed to the traditional individual psychiatric approach, it may be necessary to remind referral agencies that the service accepts individuals of all age groups by establishing intake channels for children, adolescents, adults and the aged. These may be just "clinics on paper," for administrative convenience, and have no separate identity and facilities. In large departments it may be convenient for the intake clinics actually to exist, so that slightly different facilities can be set up for the examination of presenting patients of different age groups. Some departments may wish to establish special intake clinics for certain clinical categories of patients, either as a reminder to referral agencies or for internal convenience, e.g., for marital problems, delinquency, psychosomatic states, alcoholism, etc. Some departments will have intake clinics based both on age groups and clinical categories. Whatever the starting point, every intake clinic leads to the same final aim—involvement of the whole family.

A valuable institution is that of the *evening clinic*. Patients unable to attend regularly during the day may be able to do so in the evening. This has obvious advantages to working parents in not interfering with their work programme. Thus members of the family otherwise elusive can be brought into investigation and treatment. It is sometimes the only time when a complete family can easily attend together and is thus a popular time for family group therapy.

When a family or one of its members is referred, general data on the family are completed as in Appendix I.

The Presenting Individual Patient

The family is sick as a whole; yet it rarely presents at a psychiatric service as a complete unit. An individual may be referred as the "presenting" patient, the "propositus," the "indicating" patient, the "identified" patient, or the "manifest" patient. That an individual who is alone, such as a widow, widower, single person, divorcee, student, etc., comes alone is understandable. But what determines that a fragment of the family is sent for treatment rather than the whole? The understanding of the mechanisms concerned with the referral of one member throws light on the correct arrangement of referral agencies and the organisation of the psychiatric service. It exposes important aspects of the psychodynamics of the family. It underlines the central thesis of family psychiatry—that the family is a social unit specially meaningful for psychiatry.

Some of the mechanisms determining the referral of one member of the family will be briefly reviewed.

1. *Organisation of services.* Should the psychiatric service in an area be based on adults or children or adolescents, then only that particular age group can find its way to the service, while equally, or more, disturbed members of the family cannot be accepted by the service because they are in a different age group. Thus the shape of the service determines who comes from the family.

Referral agencies tend to have special interests and attract family members falling within their specialty. The family doctor, for instance, concerns himself with individuals with physical problems; this explains why two out of three emotionally ill patients in general practice present with psychosomatic problems (3). Furthermore, a physical complaint allows the patient to try out the doctor and at the same time hide initial embarrassment. A social agency, specialising in social and welfare problems, sends patients with those problems. Should the school be the referral channel for children, it will give special attention to problems of discipline and scholastic failure. Thus the special interests of an agency determine whom they see and refer to a psychiatric service.

2. *The agency and the symptom.* Sometimes the individual or the family tends to produce symptoms which will demand attention by a referral agency. When a medical practitioner, for instance, concentrates exclusively on physical symptoms, his patients, to gain his attention, must have physical symptomatology. Should such symptoms already be present in a family member, he will consult his doctor because of them and will become the family member ascertained. In such a situation there is pressure to produce

a physical symptom—and, if possible, one of special interest to the practitioner or the psychiatric service. For example, much attention was given some years ago by the psychiatric service to amnesia; it was held that it was possible for unconscious acts beyond the patient's control to take place in this state. Many cases of so-called amnesia were reported, but, when psychiatric opinion about responsibility in states of amnesia changed, this symptom became less fashionable.

Again, courts of law can be indifferent about psychiatric disorder, but, should someone manifest some sexual anomaly, there may be rapid referral. Their susceptibilities have been provoked.

3. *The state of the family dynamics.* This varies from moment to moment in the life history of the family, as the following clinical example illustrates: At the conclusion of a brilliant survey of the exclusive treatment of an adolescent patient, who was the son of a widow, a therapist observed that, at the end of the adolescent's treatment, the widow had become severely depressed, and was now an inmate of a mental hospital. The therapist had supported the son, the dynamics of the family had changed to the mother's disadvantage, and she had become the propositus.

Thus in families there are "seesaw" movements. The person "down" at a moment in time is likely to become the propositus.

4. *Vulnerability of a family member.* One family member may be so placed as to be specially vulnerable to stresses within the family. More than this, these family members may have constellations of personality characteristics which make them vulnerable to a particular stress. In addition, ordinal position, sex gender, or age may be important for vulnerability.

A child may be the only child, the first, second, next youngest and youngest. Since the speculations of Adler (1), much attention has been given to the significance of a child's ordinal position in the family. Generally the studies are contradictory. Although the investigations on ordinal position appear contradictory, when groups are studied, the child's ordinal position in a particular family may yet be highly significant, but understandable only in that unique set of circumstances.

The sex of a child may lead to vulnerability. In many families there may be a tendency for parents to reject one gender whilst accepting the other. Again, this may only become apparent when evaluated as part of the psychodynamics of a particular family. Sex gender may also be a factor determining the attitudes of siblings.

The age of a family member may be the cause of vulnerability. The writer has observed that in some problem families a mother may pay a child a great deal of attention for the first two years, because of her own needs for an emotional "lollipop." At the age of two or three, as the child makes demands on the mother, he is rejected and another infant sought; at an early age the child is accepted, later he is rejected. Thus he becomes vulnerable. Similarly, parents talk of difficulties in acceptance of and in relating to their offspring when they are children or adolescents. Old age is anathema to some families.

5. *Anniversary reactions.* Individuals may not fall ill with equal regularity throughout the year. There are peak periods. For example, Fowler (2) reports a higher incidence of suicide amongst the Mormons of Salt Lake City at Christmas; this is probably not unique to Salt Lake City. Not only may there be dates, seasons, months of significance to whole populations, but also to individuals. Furthermore, the individual breakdown may reflect a family's association with a particular moment in time. The significance of the time may not be apparent to an onlooker, as it has meaning only in terms of the life experience of a particular individual or family. It may relate to a great variety of stresses in the past.

6. *Family motivation.* The family may make use of an individual family member; it can punish a member by sending him for psychiatric treatment, express guilt through him, and use him in a crisis as a means for getting assistance.

The psychonotic equilibrium of the family can be broken when the adolescent's behaviour becomes unendurable to himself, the family and/or society. This creates a crisis and then an appeal for help. Suicide or a suicidal gesture by adolescents may also be a cry for help to the family, as these symptoms may be the only symptom-language understandable by their families.

Of the many motivations setting in motion family dynamics, some of the most intriguing are those causing the role of scapegoat given to a family member. The member becomes the "butt" for the family. A mother, for example, may imply to her children, "Things go wrong so much because of the feeble father you have."

7. *Communicated symptomatology.* Two or more individuals in a family may share common symptomatology to such an extent that they will be referred together to a psychiatric service. The members may be beset by a common stress, as in the case of two elderly sisters who had lived closely together for many years, and who, on hearing that their house was to be sold, walked quietly into the sea, hand in hand, and attempted to drown together. The members of a coalition may borrow symptomatology from one another by imitation or suggestion. A paranoid person can persuade another of a common enemy and draw him into his delusional system. This manifestation is common in psychonotic patients.

8. *The demand value of the symptom.* From time to time a member of a

family will manifest symptoms which are striking, call attention to themselves, or have considerable "nuisance value." Thus another family member, the family, or a community agency will seek his referral. Some examples of striking symptoms are tics, speech disorders, hysterical symptoms and skin conditions. A child with encopresis, enuresis, or awkward behaviour will quickly come to attention, while an equally disturbed, but apathetic, listless, depressed child may be overlooked.

9. *Cultural attitudes.* These, too, can play a part. In some cultures, the mother is sent as the family representative to clinics, especially with children. In Nigeria, on the other hand, fathers attend with the children. This can lead to undue importance being given to the members of the family seen at clinics. Culture can also affect the demand for a service. It is noticeable in British clinics that American visitors are more ready to make use of psychiatric facilities than the British.

10. *Referral as a sign of health.* Insight into one's own emotional state is found to be inversely proportional to the degree of the disturbance. Thus highly disturbed family members avoid, "can see no point in," or obstruct, referral to psychiatric services. Less disturbed family members, on the other hand, can "see the point" and come as the family's representatives. Paradoxically, individual psychiatry can lead to a concentration of effort on those members of the family that are least disturbed.

REFERENCES

1. ADLER, A. (1945). *Social Interest. A Challenge to Mankind.* Trans. by Linton and Vaughan. London: Faber & Faber.
2. FOWLER, H. B. (1961). Personal communication.
3. HOWELLS, J. G. (1962). Family psychiatry and the family doctor. *Practitioner, 188,* 370.

Investigation

Introduction

The general aim of investigation is to obtain a complete picture of the family's functioning and dysfunctioning, assets and liabilities described in the historical sequence of the Past, the Present and the Future.

The dysfunction of the family is apparent in indicators. One or more of these come to the attention of the family, of an individual member or of the others. When there is sufficient discomfort, relief is sought and either the family, a part of it, or an individual member seeks help. Through the referral machinery already discussed the patient is sent to the family psychiatry service.

On the first appointment, either an individual, a part of the family or the whole family presents. Thus, the investigating procedure can be discussed as it appertains to (A) a family member, or (B) more than one family member, either a part or the whole family.

There are two main steps in the investigation:

1. To elucidate the indicators, the *signs and symptoms,* and so establish a diagnosis. This will be in terms of (i) psychonosis, (ii) an organic syndrome, (iii) mixed states. Psychonosis is the prime responsibility of the family psychiatry service. Mixed states will call for collaboration with others. Organic syndromes will be referred to other specialties within the medical services.

2. To elucidate the *process* of the experiential psychopathology that led up to the psychonosis.

1. establishes the nature of the disorder.

2. establishes the cause of the disorder.

When an individual presents to the psychiatric service, and it is established that his or her disorder is psychonotic, the rest of the family is drawn into investigation as opportunity allows. Thus, it is necessary to move to the family model of investigation.

Built into the formal investigatory procedure is every device for enriching the rapport with the family. The golden road to the elucidation of the intimate, significant and meaningful psychopathology is a sustained deep rapport between the investigators and the family. To follow with precision the procedure suggested could yield, on its own, virtually no useful information. Rapport brings the procedure to life. It is at this point, rapport, that the machine can fail; it requires a warm, tolerant, understanding human relationship to touch and encourage the hurt, embarrassed chords of memory to express themselves. Rapport makes for security, security for communication, and communication for meaningful information.

A. When the Individual Presents

There are five steps:

I   Evaluation of the presenting symptom (the complaint).
II   Evaluation of the rest of the symptomatology:
    1. Individual's account of the symptomatology,
    2. Formal evaluation of the symptomatology,
    3. History of the development of the symptomatology,
    4. History of the development of the person.
III A. An examination for the signs of dysfunction in the individual: psychic, somatic.
    B. Special investigations.
IV   The diagnosis.
V   Evaluation of the *process* of individual dysfunction through interview procedures.

Step I. The complaint

This is the indicator of personal dysfunction that has reached the awareness of the individual to such a degree of notice, pain or anguish that help became imperative. As it is subjective, it is termed a symptom.

Typical complaints or presenting symptoms are:
    "I have headaches very badly now";
    "I am scared, all the time";
    "After meals, I have a severe pain in my stomach";
    "I just can't sleep at night any more";
    "I feel I want to steal things";
    "I just feel miserable."

These complaints are likely to be elicited by the psychiatrist by such phrases as, "What is it that you find wrong with yourself at the moment?" The patient is encouraged to give a full account of the nature of the complaint, its intensity, time of onset, etc.

The following points should be borne in mind in relation to the presenting symptom:

(a) The patient must be allowed and encouraged to describe his experience in his own words. It is *his* experience and it must not be distorted by suggestion from others.

(b) The complaint is not the only indicator of dysfunction in the patient. It is the one that causes him to go for help.

(c) The presenting symptom is physical in two-thirds of patients seen in general medical practice. Thus, careful diagnosis to differentiate organic from psychic syndromes is essential.

(d) To some extent, the selection of indicator may be determined by the nature of the agency he consults; e.g., he is unlikely to consult a surgeon except with pain, or a marital problem clinic with anything other than a marital problem.

(e) The presenting complaint may not be the most significant indicator. Its choice is dictated by the above factors.

(f) The presenting indicator has a high chance of being one that is operative at the time of seeking help. More significant earlier indicators may have been forgotten.

(g) In the case of a young child or infant, the parents have to speak for him.

Step II. Evaluation of the rest of the symptomatology

There are four subsidiary steps:

1. *The individual's account of the rest of the symptomatology.* Even the least co-operative or insightful patient, when prompted by such remarks as "What else do you find wrong with yourself?" will be able to add to the presenting symptoms. He may go on, "Well, not only do I have headaches, but I don't eat much nowadays, and my wife complains that I am reluctant to have intercourse with her, and I certainly feel low spirited." Thus, he has already added anorexia, frigidity and depression to his list of symptoms. Further prompting with, "And what else bothers you?" "Perhaps there is something else." "In what way do you feel different?" etc., will add to the list.

Points to note are:

(a) No one knows better than the patient where the shoe pinches if he is given time to describe his feelings. Thus, at this point, a subjective account is invaluable. The description must be in his own words, untampered by others. He is not invited to evaluate his own condition, but merely to describe it.

(b) The patient recounts his own condition in his own language. This may often be more descriptive and more accurate than technical language. Certain phrases are highly characteristic of what is felt and of how the man in the street describes his highly significant experience. He may fail to grasp technical terms used by the psychiatrist later, or find them inadequate or limiting in describing his experience. He may use such phrases as: "It's my nerves, doctor"; "I seem to have become highly strung"; "I would give anything for a night's sleep"; "You see, my spirits are so low." Such phrases would be highly indicative of a patient suffering from psychonosis in the United Kingdom. Such phrases have a connotation hallowed by time and the interchange over a long time with those who have suffered similar experiences.

(c) In the case of a young child or infant the account is obtained from the parents.

2. *Formal systematic elucidation of the symptomatology.* The patient has described his dysfunctioning as well as he can in his own language. The psychiatrist now pursues further symptomatology by covering the field of symptomatology himself in a systematic fashion. It is commenced by such a phrase as "I would now like to ask you a number of questions." This usually elicits much more information.

It should be noted that:

(a) The area covered must include every aspect of organic as well as psychic dysfunctioning.

(b) In the organic field every system of the body must be covered.

(c) There are a number of charts of symptomatology available. The one developed at the Institute of Family Psychiatry is found in Appendix II.

(d) In the case of an infant or young child the account is sought from the parents.

3. *History of the development of the symptomatology.* By now, the symptomatology of the complaint, the expansion on symptomatology by the patient and the systematic enquiry by the psychiatrist can be collated into one list. The further question now is, "How has this complex of dysfunctions developed through time?"

Useful questions are "How long have you felt like this?"; "When did you first feel like this?"; "Is it true to say that you have *never* felt like this before that time?"; "What started it off?"; "What makes it worse?"; "What makes it better?"; "Has it been like this all the time?".

It should be noted that:

(a) The disorder may date back a long time, even to childhood. Some factor has caused the patient to complain now or he is a lifelong attender at psychiatric and medical clinics.

(b) The disorder may be a recent phenomenon.

(c) Its start may be vague, or sharply clear. In the former case there is a probability that it arises out of a long-standing disharmony of environment. In the latter, the precipitating trauma may be concrete and easily ascertained; on the other hand it may be different because the patient may have strong motivation for ignoring the precipitating factor.

(d) The disorder may run a fluctuating course which may make a highly significant pattern. The adult patient may feel relaxed at weekends, but suffer during the weekdays, suggesting trauma at work; a child may be worse during holiday periods at home from boarding school, suggesting trauma in the family.

(e) Persistent questioning may show that the disorder started further back than the date first given.

(f) There may be a gap between the operation of the noxious agent and the onset of symptoms because: (i) the whole person may be so caught up in coping with an incident, e.g., a crash involving death of a relative, that it is only later that its significance can be evaluated; or (ii) the pathology in the organ may take time to increase to the point where it is noticeable, e.g., a violent quarrel with father may antedate by some days the skin rash which is getting out of hand in the hot weather.

(g) In the case of the infant and young child the account is obtained from the parents.

4. *History of the development of the person.* This is a systematic enquiry into the general life experience of that person and ends with an evaluation of his non-pathological personality as the result of that experience. From this final study the individual's assets emerge.

Please note that:

(a) The evaluation of the life experience can be covered by a framework such as that described in Appendix III.

(b) The description of the present personality comes next and covers all except the evaluation of the disorder which has been previously described. It can be based on the description of the psyche given earlier in this book and summarised in Appendix IV.

(c) In the case of a child or infant the account is obtained from the parents.

It will be noted that Step II has involved the use of Appendices III and IV.

Step III:A. Formal examination of the individual for signs of psychopathology

Until now the description of the disorder has been dependent on material supplied by the patient, i.e., the patient's indicators are termed *symptoms*. Now the psychiatrist undertakes a systematic examination to discern the *signs* of dysfunction; these are gathered independently of the patient.

It should be noted that:

(a) The examination must embrace the somatic and psychic systems.

(b) The somatic signs can be indicative of (i) pathology in any system; and (ii) pathology in the encephalon—these are often termed "mental" signs.

(c) The signs of psychic dysfunction are often termed "emotional" signs.

(d) Thus, a complete examination will elucidate signs of (i) general somatic pathology; (ii) signs of cerebral pathology; and (iii) signs of psychopathology.

(e) A suitable chart of examination for (d-ii) and (d-iii) will be found in Appendix V.

(f) The value of the examination will be enhanced by meticulous care and by long experience. There is an art of examination born of experience, ingenuity, rapport, and inventiveness.

Step III:B. Special investigations

The investigations undertaken in Step III:A are supplemented by special investigations. They are not usually undertaken as a routine, but arise out of the need to supplement the data garnered to date. The appropriate special investigations are suggested by the findings to date.

Points to note are:

(a) Special investigations include examination for somatic and psychic pathology.

(b) Special physical investigations will include radiological, biochemical, electroencephalographic, pathological techniques, etc.

(c) Special psychic investigations will include a large number of psychometric techniques including those to assess ability, interest, aptitudes, character, etc. Most value comes from these investigations if the psychologist receives an adequate brief from the psychiatrist. Not to enumerate the areas of inquiry is as valueless as sending a patient to the radiologist with the request, "Please X-ray this patient."

(d) Play diagnosis will be essential in the case of a child unable to discuss his life situation in an interview. There are two steps here:

(i) Play observation. The observer is trained to give an accurate systematic account of the child himself in a play situation. It calls for careful training of the observer.

(ii) Play diagnosis. Here techniques are employed to evaluate the child's experience within his own family and society, but especially within his own family.

It is much easier to undertake operation (i) or hastily move on to so-called therapy than to attempt the more difficult, but more useful, stage (ii). There has been a full-time two-year course in these procedures at the Institute of Family Psychiatry for 20 years.

(e) It may be necessary to admit the patient of any age group to in-patient care for observation or special investigation.

Step IV. The diagnosis (the discernment)

The indicators, signs and symptoms, gathered to date are grouped together in a meaningful way to form a syndrome. In addition to the indicators, the fabric and the noxious agent are taken into account in a full diagnosis. It is supplemented by a background picture of the development and present status of the personality to which it applies.

Points to note include:

(a) The diagnosis may indicate an organic syndrome.

(i) This organic syndrome may be based on pathology of the encephalon, i.e., "mental" disorder which includes acute (e.g., delirium) and chronic (e.g., dementia) encephalonosis and which, according to the views of this author, also includes cryptogenic encephalonosis (i.e., what has included conditions hitherto termed schizophrenia and manic-depressive psychosis).

(ii) The organic sydrome may be based upon a body system other than the encephalon.

(iii) Although the primary pathology is physical, there may be a secondary psychonosis as a reaction to physical handicap, i.e., somato-psychic disorder.

(b) The diagnosis may indicate psychonosis. It is usually accompanied by secondary physical pathology (termed psychosomatic disorder).

(c) The differential diagnosis between the above conditions is made on the evaluation of the nature of the indicators. Psychic or emotional indicators denote a psychonosis but will usually be accompanied also by physical indicators (psychosomatic disorder). So-called "mental" indicators denote pathology of the encephalon. Purely physical indicators typical of dysfunction in a particular body system indicate a primary physical syndrome; if there are accompanying emotional indicators then these may be due to an accompanying psychonosis, or be a psychic reaction to the physical disability.

(d) The diagnosis may indicate a mixed state of a number of primary and secondary syndromes of physical and psychic states, e.g., a psychonosis in a person suffering also from cancer of the bowel, which has sent off satellite carcinoma to the brain, and secondary anxiety precipitated in the patient by the attitude of the family. Here, there are a primary psychic syndrome, a primary organic disorder (the cancer of the bowel), a cerebral disorder (with "mental" symptoms and signs due to the carcinoma of the brain), and a secondary or reactive psychic disorder due to the family attitude. Mixed states call for a high degree of acumen and extensive experience on the part of the clinician.

It is these complex mixed states that separate out the ordinary from the great practitioners. The first duty of a specialist physician is to give an opinion; its value will depend upon his expertise as a diagnostician. In medicine a respected "opinion" has always been valued more highly than a therapist who, following well-trodden paths, may exert skill only at a technical level.

The diversity of mixed states can be judged from the list of possible conditions below:

(i) Somatic condition only.

(ii) Predominantly somatic disorder with associated psychiatric state reactive to the somatic (somato-psychic state).

(iii) Primarily somatic condition with coincidental psychonosis.

(iv) Primarily psychiatric condition with coincidental somatic state.

(v) Predominantly psychiatric condition including associated somatic symptoms, i.e., psychosomatic state.

(vi) Psychiatric condition only.

(ii), (iii), (iv) and (v) are mixed states.

It should be noted that in (iii), (iv), (v) and (vi) above a person with a psychonotic personality or illness is liable to the following physical conditions:

(1) Psychosomatic symptoms due to the psychic state.

(2) Hysterical symptoms—simulated physical conditions responding to the psychic problem.

(3) More chronic ill-health due to worsening of psychosomatic symptoms or aggravation of existing physical conditions.

(4) More hypochondriasis, i.e., existing physical states are found more difficult to bear.

(e) Psychonosis is not diagnosed by the absence of physical indicators, but by positive indicators of psychopathology.

(f) There is no value in the traditional labels of anxiety states, obsessional states, reactive depression, neurasthenia, etc. They should be discarded. At the Institute of Family Psychiatry they were discarded 20 years ago with great benefit. Such inadequate labels arose because examination was often cursory and the patient was labelled by his presenting symptom, which was assumed to be his only symptom, and thus it was elevated into a disease category. Psychonosis is *never* monosymptomatic, as the whole personality dysfunctions. However, additional symptoms and signs will only emerge after careful history-taking. The indicators change with time, a person anxious today (anxiety neurosis), may seek more help next week by an attention-seeking symptom (hysterical state) and failing to secure help may soon after become depressed (reactive depression). On each occasion, the patient is labelled by his presenting or most obvious symptom and the other symptoms are ignored. A detailed diagnosis should list all the manifest symptoms and signs of the syndrome at that time—when psychonosis will be seen to be polysymptomatic.

(g) It is useful to describe the time element in the course of the psychonosis, thus—acute, chronic, recurrent, episodic, etc.

(h) It is useful to indicate the degree of the psychonosis. This is impressionistic, but when carried out by an experienced clinician it has value in giving a measure of the general magnitude of the psychopathology, e.g., mild, moderate, or severe degree of psychonosis.

(i) The diagnosis can indicate the general nature of the basic personality of the patient.

(j) It may be useful to mention the psychic noci-vectors if known.

(k) For record purposes the diagnosis can be brief, e.g., "acute, severe psychonosis in middle life in an intelligent woman of previously sound personality, precipitated by desertion by husband."

A longer diagnostic formulation can give a more detailed account of the indicators of pathology, e.g., to the above could be added, "She manifests apathy, anxiety, depression, insomnia, nightmares, irritability, suicidal tendencies, pruritus, amenorrhoea, and colitis."

(l) The diagnosis may at this point be:

> (i) Unclear. In this event, further investigations may be required or "masterly inactivity" to await the development of significant indicators.

(ii) Provisional. It can be a useful evaluation, but tempered by the knowledge that it lacks complete evidence.

(iii) Final.

(m) At this point the psychiatric service may have completed its task. The referring agency may have asked for a diagnostic opinion only. Thus, the individual is referred back to that agency.

(n) At this point the patient will often require an opinion on his condition couched in terms suitable to his understanding and with the maximum explanation consistent with his interests.

Step V. To elucidate the psychopathological process

The aim here is to answer the following questions: What are the psychic noci-vectors and from what disharmonious attitudes did they arise? On what psychic fabric were they acting? What dysfunction did they lead to that produced the indicators that were observed? What caused the person to be referred with his presenting symptom?

Points to note are:

(a) To elucidate the indicators is not the same operation as to elucidate the psychopathology.

(b) The understanding of the psychopathology should be based on knowledge of experiential psychopathology as outlined earlier.

(c) The life history of the patient should be explored in all its aspects both in his present family and in his preceding family.

(d) Usually, this exploration immediately reveals how handicapping it is not to have either the present family, preceding family, or both participating in the investigation. Thus, other family members may be drawn into investigation over time.

(e) Most of the work with individuals is undertaken initially in individual interviews. It may be permissible to involve the individual in dyadic or family interviews to improve knowledge of the individual, i.e., at that point in time estimation of the dyad or family itself is either unnecessary or impossible.

(f) Not only what is said and done by the individual must be given due weight, but also what is not said and done.

(g) Diagnostic interviews to elucidate the nature of psychopathology must not be confused with therapeutic interviews. They are aimed at discovering events and not changing them; a therapeutic technique, to be termed therapy, must demonstrate that (i) there has been a change; and (ii) that this change is beneficial—some changes can do harm.

It is possible, however, for small beneficial changes to spring from diagnostic interviews and thus for early therapy and diagnosis to run parallel. However, the two procedures should not be confused. Much of what is termed therapy proves to be diagnosis; if the two are separated it will be clear what little therapy is taking place and extra effort will be made to be more effective.

(h) There is no value in obtaining more information than is necessary to understand the patient's disorder and to serve as a basis for therapy. Valuable, scarce facilities are wasted in an endless search for irrelevant minutiae of information. Fac,_ with therapeutic decisions, the plea is often: "We need more information" (as yet we don't know how many of great-grandmother's teeth survived to old age!)—a blatant rationalization to avoid the hazards of decision-making.

Occasionally insufficient psychopathology emerges to explain the symptomatology. This is usually due to insufficient rapport. Extra causes may be: the individual has learned to be evasive, due to previous unskilful diagnosis; conditions are not conducive to confidential discussion; the technique is faulty; enough time is not available; the basic psychic noci-vectors are particularly hurtful and embarrassing; or interpretation is being undertaken according to some dogma rather than experiential psychopathology.

(i) Understanding the process includes assessment of the psychic noci-vectors, their origin, the clash of attitudes, the choice and nature of the symptoms, the coping devices and the psychic damage.

(j) Diagnostic interviews have many of the features of a therapeutic interview, but they can also have some differences. In diagnosis, especially in the first four steps, it is permissible to be more directive, with discrimination. It has been fashionable in some quarters to impress on all the importance of "listening." To listen alone is not enough. The whole field has to be explored and therefore there must be guidance in every direction. He who sits and says nothing will elicit little. He who guides and then sits back to give the floor to the patient learns much. Experience teaches the art of optimum direction—some of which can be non-verbal. Expectancy, interest, praise and encouragement by the psychiatrist are great motivators of patients. Rapport is the greatest revealer.

(k) Individual diagnostic interviews normally last for 50 minutes, with 5 minutes to read the notes to date and five minutes to add to the record.

(l) The number of hours spent on diagnosis will depend on: (i) the urgency of the matter; (ii) the complexity of the disorder; (iii) the facilities available. Thus the time spent may range between one hour a week for three weeks to one hour a week for six months.

(m) *Children* call for special procedures. As this book is concerned with principles, detail cannot be given here. However, some comments are deserved:

  (i) There is no merit in roundabout play techniques if the child is willing to discuss his life situation in an interview.

 (ii) Time must be spent to build up rapport.

(iii) Questions must be simple.

 (iv) Indirect techniques are best, e.g., asking for an account of events such as a birthday, first day at school, last Sunday at home, etc.; the account can then be evaluated by the interviewer rather than by the child.

  (v) A child may react against the idea of admitting his faults and thus, instead of using a standard "good" or "bad," one can employ two standards of "good," e.g., "You have a nice mother. How would you make her even nicer?" or, "How would you make your school even better?"

 (vi) A child's experience is naturally limited and he can only offer an opinion in tune with his experience. To ask a child, grossly ill-treated at home and who has never been away from his family, whether he would like to live elsewhere will always elicit the answer "No" as he will naturally cling to the only family he knows. A child who has lived elsewhere may be remarkably frank and accurate in his opinion —thus, "As a matter of fact I much prefer to live with Granny" or even, "Why don't you send me back to Granny?"

(vii) A child may reveal his dissatisfactions concerning the present in his hopes for the future—thus a question such as, "If anything you wanted could happen to you, what would you want?" may be very revealing—"I think I would like to manage on my own without women when I am a man" or "Never to go to school."

(viii) Children can also be asked to make lists in order of priority —thus, "If you had to go on a long journey in a car, who would you have to sit next to you. And who next, and who after her?" etc.

 (ix) A child is not hurt primarily by phantasy, he is hurt by events. Phantasy may reveal the hurts as he may seek solutions or compensation in his phantasy. But he does not want just preoccupation with his phantasy; he wants change in the hurtful life events that they portray.

  (x) Elucidation of phantasy is not as direct a technique as a recall of real life events by the child. Speculation about bad witches may be highly inaccurate as against a child's explosive "I hate my mother." Fairy castles can't be changed; families can. Child psychiatry has suffered much from a preoccupation with phantasy and its disinterest with facts.

(n) Having eludicated the psychopathology, the work of the psychiatric service may have been accomplished. The referral agency may have asked only for: (i) an opinion on diagnosis; (ii) an opinion on the nature of the psychopathological process in the individual. Thus, this may be a point at which referral back to the referring agency is possible.

(o) The investigation now moves to the rest of the family. They may be added one at a time or may be willing to come immediately as a family group. In the case of a single person, the family that requires involvement may be his or her preceding family.

Occasionally, the rest of the family, preceding or present, due to a variety of circumstances, can only be dealt with through the presenting family member.

B. When the Family Presents

The same procedure applies if two or more members of the family present instead of the whole family.

There are five steps:

I   Evaluation of the presenting symptom (the complaint).
II   Evaluation of the rest of the symptomatology:
      1. Family's account of the symptomatology,
      2. Formal evaluation of the symptomatology,
      3. History of the development of the symptomatology,
      4. History of the development of the family.
III A. Examination for the signs of family dysfunction:
      psychic, somatic.
   B. Special family investigations.
IV   The diagnosis.
V   Evaluation of the process of family dysfunction through interview procedures.

Step I. The complaint

This is the indicator of family dysfunction that has reached the awareness of the family (or part of the family) to a degree of notice, pain, or anguish when help becomes imperative; as it is subjective, it is a symptom.

Typical complaints or presenting symptoms are:

"We just row all the time";

"Our family is breaking up";

"Something is continually going wrong";

"We are on our own and no one wants to know us";

"People succeed, we don't";

"If I am not ill, then someone else in the family is";

"Does anyone have as many accidents as we do?"

These complaints are likely to be elicited by the psychiatrist by such phrases as "What is it that you find wrong with the family at the moment?"

The following points should be borne in mind in relation to the presenting symptom:

(a) It is not the only indicator of dysfunction in the family. It is the one that caused the family to come for help.

(b) The presenting symptom may be psychic or organic. More usually it will be psychic, as symptoms of physical ill-health are often intepreted by the family in the conventional sense of belonging to an individual.

(c) The selection of a presenting symptom may be influenced by the agency referring the family to the psychiatric service, e.g., work failure ascertained by the industrial medical service.

(d) The presenting complaint may not be the most significant indicator; it is the one which, for a variety of reasons, is paramount at that moment.

(e) The presenting indicator has a high chance of being the one that is operative at the time of seeking help. More significant indicators may have been forgotten.

(f) Families have symptomatology stamped on them by the preceding families. Thus, there may be a history of presenting symptoms over a number of generations, e.g., feeding problems, depression, delinquency, aggression, etc.

(g) The family often has a spokesman who may, or may not, be presenting a consensus opinion.

Step II. Evaluation of the rest of the symptomatology

There are four subsidiary steps:—

1. *The family's account of the rest of the symptomatology.* The family may need to be prompted by such remarks as "What else is wrong with the family?" so that further symptomatology can emerge. A family member may go on, "You see, it isn't only that we all quarrel, but Jimmy (a son) and I are depressed, my husband and I don't share the same bedroom any more, and our daughter never comes to see us. My husband is under the

doctor's care with his heart." Thus, to the presenting symptom have been added a number of others—depression in two family members, marital discord, psychosomatic symptoms (frigidity in husband and wife, angina in father), parent-daughter discord. Further prompting is usually necessary with such remarks as, "And are there other things wrong?" "In what way would you like to be better than you are at the moment?"

Points to note are:

(a) No one knows better than the family the extent of its own dysfunction. Thus, a subjective account is invaluable. The family describes, the psychiatrist evaluates.

(b) The family should be encouraged to give its account in its own language. Technical jargon which it may have picked up may not exactly describe what it experiences and so limits the account.

(c) Tactful prompting will encourage all the family members, including the children, to add to the family account. Discussion will go on until a consensus is reached; in this fashion the symptoms may be given more detail and thus flavour, extent and conditions of operation emerge.

2. *Formal systematic elucidation or symptomatology.* The family has described its dysfunction as well as it can in its own language. The psychiatrist now pursues further symptomatology by covering the field himself in a systematic fashion. This provides more information.

Points to note are:

(a) The area covered must include every aspect of somatic as well as psychic dysfunction of the family.

(b) It is useful to follow a chart of family symptomatology, such as the one found in Appendix VI, which, of course, will embrace a chart of individual symptomatology for each individual family member (Appendix II).

(c) Symptomatology will be found in each of the dimensions of the family. Disturbed families are disturbed as a whole.

3. *History of the development of the family disorder.* By now the symptomatology of the complaint, the expansion on the symptomatology by the family, and the systematic enquiry by the psychiatrist can be collated into one list. The further question is how this complex of family dysfunction developed through time.

Useful questions are: "How long has the family been like this?"; "When did you feel the trouble began?"; "Have you ever been a happy family?"; "What brought the change?"; "When is the family happiest?"; "When is the family most miserable?"

Points to note are:

(a) The history should start from the moment of first contact between husband and wife, i.e., the first contact between the two preceding families as represented by their respective epitomes.

(b) The dysfunction may date from the onset of contact between husband and wife, or may have emerged at any point subsequently.

(c) There may be nodal points in the life of the family of especial significance, e.g., marriage of the parents, birth of the first child, birth of any of the subsequent children, change of occupation or location, death of relatives, advent of a third party, the last child leaving home, marriage of one of the children, retirement, etc.

(d) The start of dysfunction may be vague or sharply clear. In the former case, it is probable that it arises out of mounting disequilibrium produced by the interaction of the preceding families in their representation in the parents, their epitomes. In the latter, the precipitating trauma may be concrete and easily ascertained, e.g., it may date to the time when the family returned to live close to a preceding family.

(e) The family disorder may run a fluctuating course whose pattern is significant, e.g., the family is harmonious as long as the only child is not at home, or during holiday periods there is harmony as the family is away from a preceding family.

(f) Persistent questioning may reveal that the disorder started further back than the date first given. Not infrequently, it dates right back to courtship.

4. *History of the development of the family.* This is a systematic enquiry into the life experience of the family and ends with an evaluation of the non-pathological aspect of the family psyche as it is today, as the result of their life experience. From this latter study the assets of the family emerge, and they are of great value in management.

Points to note are:

(a) The evaluation of the life experience of the family can be covered by a framework such as that described in Appendix VII. It starts at courtship and ends at the present.

(b) The examination in (a) can include, under Dimension of the Individuals, a history of each individual's experience in his preceding family (Appendix III) and his personality structure now (Appendix IV). It should be noted that the evaluation of the children in the family under Dimension of the Individuals is an account of their experience in the present family (Appendices III and IV).

(c) The description of the present state of the family covers all except the evaluation of dysfunction, already dealt with. It can be based upon the description of the family psyche given earlier in this book and summarised in Appendix VIII.

Step III:A. Formal examination of the family for signs of psychopathology.

Until now the description of the family disorder has been dependent on material supplied by the family, i.e., it has been concerned with *symptoms*. Now, the psychiatrist undertakes a systematic examination of the family to discern the *signs* of dysfunction; they come from an objective examination from outside.

Points to note are:

(a) The examination must embrace the physical as well as the psychic aspects of the family.

(b) Each dimension of the family will be covered in this examination—including signs in the Dimension of the Individuals, as outlined in Appendix V.

(c) The examination may extend over a long period of time. At first the material coming from the family may be false, as the family is not behaving naturally, or because the observer is not yet attuned to its mode of behaviour. As times goes by and rapport develops, the family behaves naturally. Thus, early assessments are amended as time goes by until the picture is a settled one.

(d) A suitable chart of examination is found in Appendix IX.

(e) The value of the examination will be enhanced by meticulous care and by long experience. There is an art of examination born of experience, rapport and ingenuity. Trainees must spend many hours analysing video tapes on set schedules and discussing the analysis with experienced supervisors. After some time the evaluation of material will become automatic and accurate.

Step III:B. Special family investigations.

The investigations undertaken in Step III:A are supplemented by special investigations. They are not undertaken as a routine, but arise out of the need to supplement the data garnered to date.

Points to note are:

(a) Special investigations include the examination of somatic and psychic pathology.

(b) Special physical investigations will include radiological, biochemical, electroencephalographic, pathological techniques, etc.

(c) Special psychic investigations will include a large number of psychometric techniques. Among these is the Family Relations Indicator, which has been found of great value at the Institute of Family Psychiatry. Further particulars are found in Appendix X.

(d) In the Dimension of the Individuals in the family it may be necessary to employ play techniques in the case of children. See Step III:B earlier for the investigation of the individual.

(e) It may be necessary to admit the whole family into in-patient care for observation. Usually, admission for investigation is for a short period. Indicators for admission include: (i) urgency and the need for quick intensive evaluation; (ii) geographical factors—attendance on a regular basis as an out-patient may be impossible due to distance; and (iii) a difficult elaborate investigation involving a number of special investigations.

Step IV. Family diagnosis (the discernment).

The indicators, signs and symptoms, gathered to date are grouped together in a meaningful way to form a syndrome. In addition to the indicators, the fabric of the family and the various psychic noci-vectors are taken into account in a full diagnosis. This is supplemented by a background picture of the development and present status of the family to which it applies.

Points to note include:

(a) The diagnosis may indicate a disturbance in the physical dimensions of the family. This may involve a part or the whole family. Included in the category of physical disorder it may be found that there is an' acute or chronic encephalonosis, e.g., Huntingdon's chorea, or one of the cryptogenic encephalonoses, such as encephaloataxia. There may be a secondary psychonosis as a reaction to a physical handicap.

(b) Most frequently, the diagnosis is that of psychonosis of the family. It is often accompanied by secondary physical pathology, i.e., family psychosomatic disorder.

(c) The diagnosis may indicate a mixed state of primary and secondary physical and psychic states, e.g., a family suffers from hereditary ataxia with secondary psychonosis, resulting from its difficulties of employment, and in addition father's affectional involvement with a voluntary helper has precipitated an acute psychonosis reflected in dysfunction and indicators throughout the family. Thus, there are a primary physical syndrome (hereditary ataxia), a primary psychic syndrome (acute psychonosis), and a secondary psychonosis (reactive to employment problems).

Mixed states call for careful prolonged examination, acumen of a high order, and great experience. Many disturbed families may not respond to prolonged help of great magnitude because wrong assessment of the family makes it impossible to meet the need with accuracy.

(d) Psychonosis of the family is not diagnosed by the absence of physical indicators, but by the presence of psychic indicators.

(e) There is no value in labelling families by any of the traditional clinical labels, e.g., anxious families, delinquent families, etc. In this undesirable practice, as in the individual field, families are labelled by the presenting syndrome. Symptoms are fleeting. Furthermore, psychonosis of the family is never monosymptomatic; the family is described in each of its dimensions and often displays a number of symptoms in each dimension. A detailed diagnosis can list all the manifest signs and symptoms in each of the dimensions.

(f) It is useful to describe the time element in the course of the psychonosis, thus—acute, chronic, recurrent, episodic, etc.

(g) It is useful to indicate the degree of the psychonosis. This is impressionistic, but has value to an experienced clinician in giving a measure of the general magnitude of the psychopathology, e.g., mild, moderate, or severe degree of psychonosis.

(h) The diagnosis can indicate the general nature of the state of the family in its premorbid state.

(i) It may be useful to mention the noxious agents if known at this stage.

(j) For some record purposes the diagnosis can be brief, e.g., "acute, moderate psychonosis in a family showing a mild degree of psychonosis from its inception and precipitated by interaction with the extended family." A larger diagnostic formulation can give detailed account of indicators of pathology under each of the dimensions, e.g., the following indicators of psychopathology were evident:

    (i) The individuals (symptomatology can be added in each case):
        Marked degree of psychonosis in *father*
        Moderate degree of psychonosis in *mother*
        Moderate degree of psychonosis in *son*
        Severe degree of psychonosis in *daughter*
    (ii) Internal interaction:
        Father-Mother relationship   —negative hostile relationship
        Father-Children relationship — marked mutual antipathy to daughter and somewhat less to son
        Mother-Children relationship— grossly overprotective to both with rejection of daughter, and hostility of children towards mother
    (iii) General: Father isolated by rest of family members; fragmentation of family imminent.
    (iv) External interaction: Failure at employment with impending bankruptcy; school failure of daughter; delinquency of son; isolation of family.

    (v) Physical: Feeding difficulties in daughter; enuresis in son; gastric ulceration in father; frigidity in mother.

(k) The family diagnosis at this point may be:

    (i) Unclear. Thus further investigations are required.

    (ii) Provisional.

    (iii) Final.

(1) At this point the psychiatric service may have completed its task. The referring agency may have asked for a diagnostic formulation only. Thus, the family is referred back to the agency with the formulation.

(m) At this point the family will usually ask for an opinion on its condition and this should be in terms couched to allow understanding and given with the maximum of explanation consistent with its interests. There is a tendency for clinicians to underestimate the intellectual grasp of the family and its capacity to tolerate and understand what is said to it.

Step V. To elucidate the psychopathological process in the family

The aim here is to ask the question, "What psychic noci-vectors arising from what disharmonious attitudes springing from the past and the present led to the family dysfunction which produced the indicator observed causing the family to attend with its complaint?"

Points to note are:

(a) To elucidate the indicators is not the same operation as to elucidate the family psychopathology.

(b) The understanding of the psychopathology should be based upon knowledge of experiential psychopathology as outlined earlier.

(c) The explanation should extend back from the present family to the preceding families.

The way to the understanding of the dysfunctioning of the present family invariably lies with the understanding of the preceding families of the parents and the interaction of these families through their representatives in the present. The importance of this last sentence cannot be overemphasised. Thus, in a full investigation preceding families may require formal evaluation in the manner described here.

(d) It may be of value to draw the preceding families into the investigation either alone as families, or with the present family. Thus, a family interview may consist of: (i) the present family; (ii) the present family and one preceding family; (iii) the present family and the two preceding families; (iv) collateral related families in addition to (iii).

(e) It may be of value to draw the succeeding families into the investigation, either alone or with the present family. Thus, a family interview may consist of the present family with one or more succeeding families.

(f) A family is the meaningful functioning group at that moment. Thus, it may include lodgers, relatives, servants, etc.

(g) Most work will be undertaken in family group interviews. However, there may be times when it should be supplemented by individual or dyadic interviews. Need for an individual interview may arise if: (i) there is a marked degree of psychopathology in a family member; (ii) an individual can at that moment share the information only with the interviewer and not with the family. Equally, dyadic interviews may be required, either because of an especially pathological interaction or because the couple cannot share the same information with the rest of the family at that time. Individual or dyadic interviews may have to be undertaken with children and some of the features of an interview with children have been covered under Step III:B of the individual investigation.

(h) Family diagnosis must not be confused with family therapy. Family diagnosis is concerned with describing and understanding family events and not with changing them. Much of what is termed family therapy proves to be family diagnosis, i.e., no change is effected for the better. If the two procedures are kept separate, therapy will be more effective in that it will be apparent whether or not change is taking place. It is possible for therapy to run parallel with diagnosis, but the distinct nature of the two operations must always be kept in mind. If therapy is the aim, it is a useful practice for the therapist to ask himself, "What change for the better have I produced in the last (number) of interviews—and what proof have I that the interview effected the change rather than extra-interview events?" It can be a salutary exercise.

(i) There is no value in obtaining more information than is necessary to understand the psychopathology of the family. Valuable, scarce, highly expensive facilities are wasted in uncovering irrelevant minutiae of information. Only experience teaches what is relevant. It is easy to meander on seeking endless information; this is a comfortable exercise which only hides the inability to use the information to the advantage of the family—the only justification for the exercise.

(j) Family diagnostic interviews have many of the ingredients of family therapy interviews, thus prolonged discussion of the family interview will be left for the section on family therapy.

There are, however, some differences. It is permissible to be more directive in diagnosis. To listen and leave matters to the direction of the family is not enough. The whole family field, present and preceding, has to be explored and therefore there must be guidance. Sometimes the same area has to be reworked for greater clarification. Experience teaches the art of optimum direction. Rapport with the family is the great revealer.

(k) Family diagnostic interviews normally last for at least two hours.

This is necessary as there are more people requiring to talk than in an individual interview. For a dyadic interview at least 1½ hours should be allowed.

(l) There are times when a whole day can be employed with advantage for a family interview. This is required if: (i) a point of crisis has been reached; (ii) urgent work is necessary; (iii) geographical difficulties make it impossible to work in any other way. There should, of course, be rest breaks during interviews lasting 1½–2 hours.

(m) The number of interviews required will depend largely on the complexity of the problem. Thus, diagnostic interviews at weekly intervals may extend from three weeks to six months.

(n) Not only what is said or done must be given due insight, but also what is not said or done by the family.

(o) Occasionally the psychopathological process which emerges is not sufficient to explain the symptomatology. This may arise because rapport is inadequate—much the commonest cause—or the technique is inefficient; enough time has not been spent; the interview conditions are unsuitable for confidential discussion; the basic psychic noxious agents are particularly stressful or embarrassing; the family has learnt to evade by previous unskilful attention; or distortion by interpretation is in terms of some dogma rather than in terms of experential psychopathology.

(p) Having elucidated the psychopathological process, the work of the family psychiatric service may be over. The referring agency may have asked only for: (i) a family diagnosis; (ii) elucidation of the psychopathological process. Thus, at this point the family can be referred back to the agency.

(q) At the completion of family therapy, it is sometimes useful to go through a formal evaluation as here, so that the present state of the family can be compared with its state before therapy.

Case illustration

A brief illustration of the application of the above diagnostic procedures will be found in "Family Psychiatry and the Aged" in the section on "Special Aspects of Family Psychiatry" later in this book.

Recording Information

Information comes largely from two sources:

1. The patient, either individual, dyad, or family. Interview procedures are supplemented by questionnaires, charts, reports of special investigations, etc. This latter extra information is placed in the appropriate part of the case file to be described later, or in a special miscellaneous file.

2. The referring or other agency. This may be spontaneously offered and be very valuable, e.g., the letter from a family doctor, who has known the family for a long time, perhaps over more than one generation, can contain invaluable information. Furthermore, the family psychiatry department may request information from other agencies—hospital, social worker agencies, schools, industry, etc. This information also is fed into the case file at the appropriate place or into the special miscellaneous file.

Two types of records are kept. Firstly, that of professional workers' own day-to-day notes. Some of this information may have to be withheld from the second file, uncommonly, for confidential reasons explained later. Secondly, a master file made up of reports from all the clinical workers on that individual or family. This is continually added to as time goes on. The added material is placed in the appropriate section of the master file.

Records are of two types: (i) for day-to-day purposes; and (ii) for research and teaching purposes; in this latter event the permission of the individual or family should be obtained in writing.

For the first purpose there is no useful point in accumulating more records than can be digested in day-to-day work. Sometimes, the very volume of the records can be a handicap in the family's management. Furthermore, the records must have relevance. The art of a fine clinician is to know what is appropriate and to find and record it with economy of effort. As a general rule, it can be said that the less able and less decisive a clinician, the more voluminous his records; collecting more and more data puts off the evil day of decision making. Thus, in day-to-day work, records must be brief and personal records must be in longhand. The key to relevancy and brevity will be seen in a moment.

For the second purpose (research and teaching), the greater the detail the better. Here, sound and video records come into their own. These are of little value in day-to-day work. One hour of sound tape calls for seven to ten hours of typing and more than an hour to read the record. Who can afford to double the time of an interview in order to read the full acount of the previous interview? If really thorough, the physician might read all the previous records before an interview, and become, as time goes on, a reader rather than a therapist. However, for research and teaching this is essential. Material should be: (i) recorded on sound or video tape; (ii) transcribed; and (iii) gone through sentence by sentence and each relevant item extracted and put in its appropriate niche in the family profile. If necessary, the family profile can be coded and each sentence or paragraph given its appropriate code number and placed where appropriate in the family profile. For teaching this is not only invaluable, but indispensable. There is no surer proof of the value of experiential psychopathology than to perform this meticulous but fascinating task. Every trainee must go through this exercise on one family. And then on another family. And on another. So the flow of experiential psychopathology will be ingrained in his soul. Interpretive psychiatry will be forgotten because the march of events have their own logic that answers all questions. Psychotherapy should not be attempted by anyone who has not undertaken this exercise. To know and then to treat is the proper sequence. It will now become clear why day-to-day psychiatry can be briefer. From the knowledge of families gained in this fashion, it is possible quickly to discern the relevant. Furthermore, the profile of the family is written in the mind of the interviewer and, as the material emerges, it is quickly and neatly collated under its proper heading.

Note-taking during the interview is strongly contra-indicated. However, the family will agree to, and even be helped by, the interviewer having before him a brief profile of the family.

Individual Case Notes

These include:

1. General particulars.

2. A family diagram of the present and preceding family as relevant. This is not detailed, but allows for easy orientation to the basic structure of the family (Appendix I).

3. Evaluation of complaint.

4. Individual's account of the symptomatology.

5. Formal evaluation of symptomatology (Appendix II).

6. The history of the development of symptomatology.

7. History of the development of the person and his present personality (Appendices III and IV).

8. Examination for signs of dysfunction (Appendix V).

9. Reports of special investigations.

10. The diagnostic formulation.

11. Reports of interviewer after discerning the psychopathological process. The material is listed under the appropriate section of the appropriate dimension of the present, preceding or succeeding family—either in a brief day-to-day schema or a more elaborate record for research and teaching.

12. Miscellaneous additional material—agency reports, letters, drawings, etc.

13. Summaries at regular intervals of progress to date.

14. Card index and item sheet for recording material of unusual interest.

15. Follow up reports after closure.

Family Case Notes

These include:

1. General particulars of the family.

2. Brief diagram of the presenting family and of preceding families if appropriate. This is not detailed, but serves for quick reference.

3. Evaluation of complaint.

4. The family's account of the symptomatology.

5. The formal elucidation of symptomatology (Appendix VI).

6. The history of development of the family disorder.

7. History of the development of the family (Appendices VII and VIII).

8. Examination for signs of family dysfunction (Appendix IX).

9. Reports of special investigations—including F.R.I. (Appendix X) and in-patient observation.

10. The diagnostic formulation.

11. Reports of interviewer after discerning the psychopathological process—listed under appropriate section of appropriate dimension of the present, preceding or succeeding family.

12. Miscellaneous additional material—agency reports, letters, drawings, etc.

13. Summaries at regular intervals.

14. Card index and item sheet—for unusual material.

15. Follow up report after closure.

Conventional Symbols

There are a number of conventional symbols often employed when representing the family in diagrammatical form. Thus:

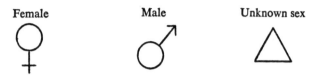

Marriage is indicated by two vertical lines below the Female and Male and joined by a horizontal line. Thus:

Living together, without legal marriage, is indicated by broken lines. Thus:

Children are shown by vertical lines below the horizontal line of the marriage. Older children to the left and younger to the right. The sex of each child is shown as above. Thus:

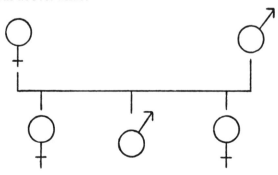

Children from unions outside marriage are shown thus:

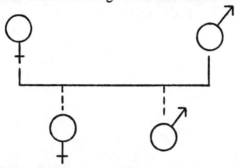

Twins, linked children, are shown as follows, with S indicating similar twins, DS indicating dissimilar twins. Thus:

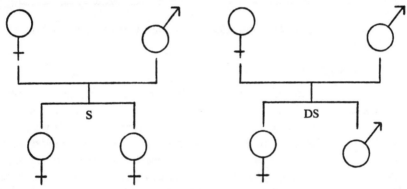

Further details can be given if necessary—such as dates of birth (b.), death (d.), marriage (m.), separation (sep.), and divorce (div.), e.g.:

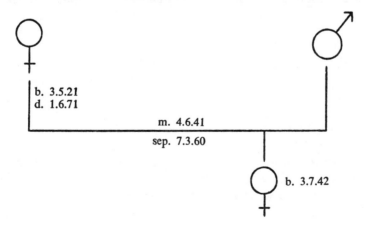

The order of marriages can be indicated by horizontal lines, the highest being the earlier, e.g., male married twice is thus:

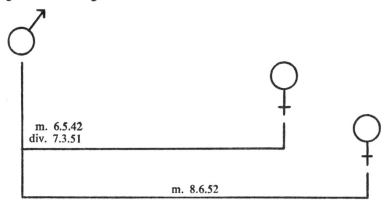

m. 6.5.42
div. 7.3.51

m. 8.6.52

Overelaboration probably impedes rather than helps understanding.

Confidentiality

Breach of confidence is usually a final blow to rapport, and without rapport we cannot profit. A person's experience belongs to him. He lends pieces of it to us, like he would his goods, for a good reason—so that we have the means to help him. In the trading between him and the clinician, seeking help with his disorder is the only business. He lends his experience for this one purpose alone and, after its completion, he expects to receive it back. To give his goods to others without his explicit wish is dishonest. He interprets from such a failure that he deals with someone who cannot be trusted. Without trust there can be no rapport and without rapport we are unable to help. In psychiatry, the more hurtful, embarrassing experiences, those most difficult to give, are the most necessary to reveal. Thus, rapport and its attendant, confidentiality, take on great importance.

Confidentiality between professionals and patients is essentially the same as between any people. The golden rule is not to transfer information to any third party without the knowledge and consent of the patient. Patience and rapport may bring greater security in the patient, who then allows transfer of information to a third or more parties. Explanation that shows that the help of the third party is essential to his clinical problem may encourage agreement, or he may decline the help in preference to retaining his information. The choice is his. It may encourage him if he understands that the third party is bound by the same principles.

Professional workers have their own ethical codes. In the case of administrative staff who have access to records it is important to instruct them regarding confidentiality. In some services, new administrators are invited to sign an undertaking that they have read a warning notice on confidentiality. Records should be destroyed when they are of no further use. At all times patients should understand that no written record will be kept if he desires it so.

Appendices

A number of points should be borne in mind in using the following procedures:

1. The key to the place of a particular procedure is found in the text of the chapter on investigation.

2. A particular procedure is used in full or in part as is appropriate. Irrelevant information merely confuses the picture.

3. Any procedure that can be completed by the patient, or the family, or non-clinical personnel, helps to save clinical time. Some procedures, however, are valuable only when used by a clinician.

4. Some procedures aim to help obtain a picture of psychopathology. But these procedures are not concerned with obtaining a picture of the whole process of psychopathology. They supply a framework on which can be placed the material of the psychopathological process as it emerges in the interviews.

5. Procedure I is concerned with General Data.

6. Procedures II-V are concerned with the Individual.

7. Procedures VI-X are concerned with the Family.

APPENDIX I

GENERAL DATA

(N.B. A similar data sheet can be completed
for Preceding or Succeeding Families)

1. *Names of clinical workers*: PSY.   *Case No.*

                                     PSYCHOL.

                                     S.W.

                                     Child Therapist

                                     OTHER

2. *Name,* if individual :

   Name, if dyad   :

   Name, if family   :

3. *Address* of individual, dyad, family :

4. *Telephone no.* of individual, dyad, family :

5. *Referred by*:

6. *Family composition* (If individual is single put under "others" or place
                      in his preceding family if it is attending)

Family Members Christian Name	*Age*	*Date of birth*	*Date of death*	*Date of separation or divorce*	*Nature of school or occupation*
Husband					
Wife					
Child 1					
Child 2					
Child 3					
Others: 1					
2					
3					

7. *Brief Diagram of Presenting Family* (If patient is an individual, give his present or preceding family as applicable)

e.g.

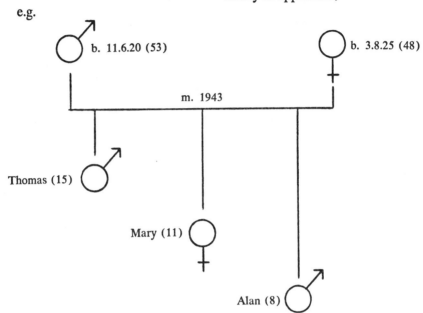

b. 11.6.20 (53)

b. 3.8.25 (48)

m. 1943

Thomas (15)

Mary (11)

Alan (8)

APPENDIX II

SYSTEMATIC ELUCIDATION OF SYMPTOMATOLOGY OF PSYCHONOSIS IN THE INDIVIDUAL

©

J. G. Howells

Introduction

Points to note are:

1. When the patient has exhausted, with prompting, his account of the presenting symptom (complaint), further appropriate questions are asked in a systematic form to elucidate the remainder of the symptomatology.

2. This is the patient's *subjective* account.

3. The symptomatology falls into two main groups: physical and psychic. This allows of a holistic assessment of the functioning of the individual. *Only by covering the whole field will the polysymptomatic nature of the psychonosis be apparent.*

4. The physical group has an important and large sub-group concerned with the elucidation of symptomatology denoting cerebral dysfunction (encephalonosis).

5. Whenever possible, the patient should describe, and have recorded, his answers in his own words. This makes for a more realistic account, unbiased by the psychiatrist. Elaboration with examples can be sought. (The examiner's comments and evaluations can be put in brackets.)

6. Seek facts with accurate knowledge of place, time, mode of onset, previous diagnosis and treatment.

7. While all the area should be covered it is only necessary to record positive data.

8. The chart is suitable for all age groups. But the area covered can be adjusted somewhat for each age group. In the case of *children* much of the information is sought from parents.

9. Much can be gleaned about the basic personality of the individual family member from his behaviour at the interview. This information is useful for inclusion later in the chart on basic personality structure (Appendix IV).

10. During this procedure *signs* will emerge about the individual's condition. This information is included later in the chart of examination for signs of psychonosis (Appendix V).

11. Trainees need prolonged training in history taking so that after time the pattern of questioning is retained by the mind and can be followed automatically and yet accurately.

221

A. SOMATIC DYSFUNCTION

A:I. GENERAL SYSTEMS

1. General.
    Appearance: Acquired defects or disfigurements; whether demeanour appropriate to that sex gender.
2. The Alimentary System.
    Appetite : Pain : Nausea : Vomiting : Dysphagia
    Indigestion : Constipation : Diarrhoea : Encopresis.
3. The Urinary System.
    Colouration of urine : Dysuria : Frequency : Urgency
    Hesitation : Enuresis : Wetting by day : Polyuria :
    Obstructed flow.
4. The Genital System.
    Menses—regularity, dysmenorrhoea, amenorrhoea, premenstrual tension.
    Sexual intercourse—frequency, satisfaction, dyspareunia, vaginismus, frigidity, premature ejaculation.
    State of sexual development—masturbation, homosexuality, polygamous heterosexuality, monogamous heterosexuality.
5. The Muscular System.
    Restlessness : Involuntary movements : Gait :
    Grimacing : Left or right handedness : Clumsiness.
    In children—thumbsucking, rocking, head rolling, head banging, hair pulling, nail biting, etc.
6. The Skin.
    Sweating : Rash.
7. The Circulatory System.
    Dyspnoea : Palpitation : Fainting : Flushing :
    Anginal Pain.
8. The Respiratory System.
    Cough : Dyspnoea : Pain.
9. Endocrine and Metabolic.
    Excessive gain or loss of weight : Energy
10. The Skeletal System.
    Backache : Pain and swelling of joints.
11. The Peripheral Nervous System (excluding central which is covered in detail in A:II.)
    Sensations of pain, warmth, cold, etc. : Movements :
    Muscle wasting : Muscle tone : Paralysis.

A:II. CENTRAL NERVOUS SYSTEM (CEREBRUM)

Consciousness	—	Concentration : Withdrawal : Headaches : Epilepsy.
Special senses	—	Sight : Hearing : Taste : Smell.
Speech	—	Absence : Poverty : Speed : Incoherence : Dramatisation : Form : Content : Stammer : Circumlocution : Appropriateness.
Sleep	—	Insomnia : Nightmares : Early waking : Restlessness.
Perception	—	Aphasia : Hallucinations : Delusions.
Orientation	—	In time and space.
Memory	—	Immediate recall : Recent and past events.
Affect	—	Flattening : Incongruity.
Thought	—	Incoherence : Circumlocution : Irrelevancy : Perseveration : Concreteness : Flight of ideas.
Judgement and rationality	—	Especially about own condition.
Intelligence	—	Vocabulary : General information : General ability.

N.B. Information about some of the above elements may only be obtainable from a relative.

B. PSYCHIC DYSFUNCTION

Items 1–6 indicate diminishing emotionality; items 7–10 indicate increasing emotionality.

The areas in which these items manifest themselves are: home, school, work, neighbourhood.

1. Anxiety.
   Tense : Worried : Anxious : Fearful (specify) :
   Timid : Anguished : Sensitive : Indecisive :
   Highly strung : Panicky.
2. Withdrawal.
   Unable to concentrate : Shy : Solitary : Day dreaming :
   Sulking.
3. Depression.
   Apathetic : Miserable : Weepy : Pessimistic :
   Despairing : Sad : Suicidal : Self-injurious.
4. Self depreciation.
   Unworthy : Self-blaming : Lacking in self-confidence :
   Submissive : Inferior : Guilty.
5. Rigidity.
   Compulsive : Obsessional : Hypermoral : Perfectionist.
6. Loss of body image.
   Depersonalization : Loss of interest in appearance :
   Unreality.
7. Hostility.
   Irritable : Tempers : Angry : Violent : Destructive :
   Sullen : Awkward : Overcritical : Uncooperative :
   Disobedient : Stubborn : Excitable : Antisocial hostility
   —lying, stealing, immorality, addiction, truanting, staying out late,
   running away.
8. Euphoria.
   Excited : Elated.
9. Suspicion.
   Paranoid : Envious : Jealous.
10. Attention seeking.
    Showing off : Boasting : Flamboyance.

APPENDIX III

PREVIOUS HISTORY OF THE INDIVIDUAL

©
J. G. Howells

Introduction

Points to note are:

1. An adult person is normally born into his preceding family. Having grown up in this family, he ultimately joins his present family. Therefore we must usually follow the history through two families.

2. If a single adult, unless he is living informally within a family now, his history will be concerned largely with his preceding family.

3. The history of a child or adolescent is followed within the present family only.

4. The accounts of a number of family members add up to an account of the individual dimension within the history of the family.

5. This history does not contain the detail of psychopathology. *It is a framework for orientating the investigator.*

6. Accurate dates and particulars should be given.

Historical Development of the Individual

Nationality

Religion

Birth — Wanted or unwanted : Legitimate, illegitimate, adopted : Parents' ages at birth : Natural or assisted : Birth damage.

Early development — Dates of crawling, standing, walking, first words, first sentences : Early difficulties with feeding, sleeping, behaviour.

Social — Friends.

School — Names of schools at various ages: Progress achieved : Behaviour.

Recreations — Games, hobbies, interests.

Work — List of occupations at various ages : Reasons for changes : Work satisfaction : Military service : Retirement.

University — Age : Courses : Achievement.

Sex development — Date of early interest : Historical account of relations with same and opposite sex : Sex incidents and traumas : Sex education.

Courtship — Length and quality of courtship.

Marriage — Pre-marital harmony : Sex history : Attitude of preceding families : Factors leading up to it : Forced or natural : Divorce and remarriage.

Health — Family history : List of illnesses and accidents from birth to date : Hospital admissions : Menstruation—date of onset, regularity, discomfort, premenstrual tension, etc. : Menopause.

APPENDIX IV

THE INDIVIDUAL'S PRE-MORBID STATE

©
J. G. Howells

Introduction

Points to note are:

1. As the individual moves through time, from conception to the moment we meet him, he has acquired many characteristics from experience. This is the end result of experience acting on his somatic-psychic endowment. This end result is collectively termed his "personality."

2. The individual's physical state is not covered here.

3. The aim is to acquire a picture of how the personality conforms to the expected pattern and in what ways it deviates from it.

4. From the "personality" may spring attitudes which may clash with attitudes held by others close to him.

5. Psychopathology is not included here.

A. PHYSICAL STATE
(not covered here)

B. PSYCHIC STATE

Questions are asked to elucidate the following.
These are answered: (i) by the patient himself;
(ii) by the examiner as the result of
acquaintance with him over time;
(iii) from special tests.

1. Attitudes, which include:
    (a) beliefs and prejudices
    (b) values
    (c) ambitions and aims
    (d) interests.
2. Character—his predominant values.
3. Conscience—his predominant values which, if not acted upon,
    precipitate self-blame.
4. Temperament—his predominant moods, positive and negative.
5. Knowledge—his general level of enlightenment on:
    (a) general matters
    (b) special subjects relevant to his way of life.
6. Skills, aptitudes, vocation.
7. Role playing—his predominant roles in the family, e.g., views on
    parenting, marital role, etc.
    —his predominant roles in society.
Psychologists have effective techniques for elucidating the above in detail
if required.

APPENDIX V

EXAMINATION OF THE INDIVIDUAL FOR SIGNS OF PSYCHONOSIS

©

J. G. Howells

Introduction

Points to note are:

1. This procedure is concerned with an *objective* assessment in a systematic form to elucidate signs of psychonosis. It also helps to differentiate between psychonosis, encephalonosis, and other organic states.

2. A full examination is in two parts:

    A. Examination for signs of physical dysfunction.

    B. Examination for signs of psychic dysfunction.

The first part is fully covered in texts of somatic medicine and will be briefly covered here (A:I); one portion of it survives here in a full examination of the cerebrum (A:II). The second part is given in full as is appropriate in a text on psychic medicine (B).

3. Wherever possible, the patient should describe, and have recorded, his answers in his own words. This makes for a more realistic account, unbiased by the examiner (the psychiatrist's remarks can be put in brackets.)

4. During the examination, much can be gleaned about the basic personality of the patient. This can be used in Appendix IV.

5. The procedure is suitable for all age groups but can be modified for a particular age group.

6. The reception of the *child* is designed to make the visit a pleasure, i.e., friendly attitude of receptionist, the interesting and attractive waiting room, and a separate waiting garden for children. Rapport is established between the child and the receptionist, who is then able to introduce the child to the psychiatrist.

The psychiatrist forms a friendly relationship with the child; in achieving this, the most important ingredient is a genuine personal interest in the child. The young child should be introduced to play material and be given a free choice of such material at the initial interview. The mental examination should be made on the basis of the play situation, or the interview in the case of older children.

No pressure is ever used to separate child from parent, and a child so wishing can return to a parent immediately.

7. Trainees need prolonged experience of the examination procedure so that after time, it becomes "second nature," is retained by the mind, and can be followed quickly and automatically.

229

A. SOMATIC SIGNS

A:I. GENERAL SOMATIC SYSTEMS (See texts in somatic medicine
     for detail)
     Examination to include:
  1. General Physical Appearance—Dress, posture, facial expression, tics,
      grimacing, looks sick or well, demeanour, restlessness.
  2. The Alimentary System
  3. The Urinary System
  4. The Genital System
  5. The Muscular System
  6. The Skin
  7. The Circulatory System
  8. The Respiratory System
  9. Endocrine and Metabolic System
 10. The Skeletal System
 11. The Peripheral Nervous System
     Special investigations.

A:II. NERVOUS SYSTEM (Cerebrum)

Consciousness   —   Concentration (See Test 1 below) :
                          Withdrawal : Headaches : Epilepsy.

Special senses   —   Sight : Hearing : Taste : Smell.

Speech   —   Absence : Poverty : Speed :
                          Incoherence : Dramatisation : Form :
                          Content : Stammer :
                          Circumlocution : Appropriateness.
                          (Record any unusual pieces.)

Sleep   —   Insomnia : Nightmares : Early waking :
                          Restlessness (ward observation).

Perception   —   Aphasia : Hallucinations—auditory, visual
                          (See Test 2 below), olfactory, tactile :
                          Delusions (persecution, influence, unreality).

Orientation   —   In time and space (See Test 3 below).

Memory   —   Immediate recall (See Test 4 below) :
                          Recent and past events (See Test 5 below).

Affect   —   Flattening : Incongruity.

Thought   —   Incoherence : Circumlocution :
                          Irrelevancy : Perseveration :
                          Concreteness (See Test 6 below) : Flight
                          of ideas.

Judgement and
  rationality   —   Especially about own condition.

Intelligence   —   Vocabulary : General information (See
                          Test 7 below) : General ability.

N.B.   (i)   Information about some of the above elements may only be
              obtainable from a relative.

     (ii)   Special tests may be required for sight, hearing, aphasia,
              intelligence.

   (iii)   The following are tests that can be used quickly in the
              interview situation.

1. *Concentration test*

The patient is asked to subtract 7 from 100 and to continue subtracting. An impression is soon obtained of his capacity to concentrate.

2. *Hallucination enquiry*

Ask such questions as:
    Are there any unusual experiences in your thoughts recently?
    Do your thoughts ever speak to you?
    Do you ever feel possessed or influenced by other people?

3. *Orientation enquiry*

Ask such questions as:
    Where are you now?
    What is my name?
    Where do you live?
    What is the date?
    Which day of the week is it?

4. *Retention test*

Give the patient the following numbers to repeat after you. Normally 7 digits can be retained. If he fails on one list try on another to check on the first response.

694	532
2786	8352
57846	48732
934287	925746
7149368	7928475
83925174	64153962
317492568	529841637

5. *Test on memory of past*

Ask such questions as:
    What is your date of birth?
    Where were you born?
    What are the names of your brothers and sisters?
    What are the names of your children?
    What was the name of the school you went to?
    Where did you live as a child?

6. *Test of concrete thinking—proverbs test*

Tendency to think concretely rather than abstractly can be brought out by asking:

What is meant by "A rolling stone gathers no moss?"
What is meant by "A bird in the hand is worth two in the bush?"
What is meant by "A stitch in time saves nine?"
What is meant by "All work and no play makes Jack a dull boy?"

7. *Test of general information*

Ask questions such as:

Please name the King (President).
Please name the Prime Minister (Secretary of State).
Please name the capitals of France, United Kingdom, United States of America, U.S.S.R., etc.
Please name three large seaports in this country.

B. PSYCHIC DYSFUNCTION

Items 1–6 indicate diminishing emotionality; items 7–10 indicate increasing emotionality.

The areas in which these items manifest themselves are: home, school, work, neighbourhood.

The examiner's evaluations are gathered from first-hand contact with the patient in the interview situation.

1. Anxiety.
   Tense   :   Worried   :   Anxious   :   Fearful (specify)   :
   Timid   :   Anguished   :   Sensitive   :   Indecisive   :
   Highly strung   :   Panicky.
2. Withdrawal.
   Unable to concentrate   :   Shy   :   Solitary   :   Day dreaming   :
   Sulking.
3. Depression.
   Apathetic   :   Miserable   :   Weepy   :   Pessimistic   :
   Despairing   :   Sad   :   Suicidal   :   Self injurious.
4. Self depreciation.
   Unworthy   :   Self-blaming   :   Lacking in self confidence   :
   Submissive   :   Inferior   :   Guilty.
5. Rigidity.
   Compulsive   :   Obsessional   :   Hypermoral   :   Perfectionist.
6. Loss of body image.
   Depersonalization   :   Loss of interest in appearance   :
   Unreality.
7. Hostility.
   Irritable   :   Tempers   :   Angry   :   Violent   :   Destructive   :
   Sullen   :   Awkward   :   Overcritical   :   Uncooperative   :
   Disobedient   :   Stubborn   :   Excitable   :   Antisocial hostility
   —lying, stealing, immorality, addiction, truanting, staying out late, running away.
8. Euphoria.
   Excited   :   Elated.
9. Suspicion.
   Paranoid   :   Envious   :   Jealous.
10. Attention seeking.
   Showing off   :   Boasting   :   Flamboyance.

APPENDIX VI

SYSTEMATIC ELUCIDATION OF FAMILY PSYCHOPATHOLOGY

©

J. G. Howells

Introduction

Points to note are:

1. The individual may be explored first, then the investigation moves to the family. Or the family may present as a whole from the start.

2. When the family has exhausted its account of the presenting symptoms, further appropriate questions are asked in a systematic form to elucidate the remainder of the symptomatology.

3. This is the family's *subjective* account.

4. The symptomatology falls into two main groups: psychic and physical.

5. Whenever possible, the family should describe, and have recorded, its answers in its own words. Elaboration with examples can be sought. (The examiner's evaluation and comments can be put in brackets in the record.)

6. In reporting facts, there should be accurate knowledge of place, time, and mode of onset.

7. Whilst all the area should be covered it is necessary to record positive data only.

8. Much may also be gleaned at the interview about the basic personality of the family (for Appendix VIII) and signs of psychopathology (for Appendix IX).

9. Trainees need prolonged training in history-taking, so that after time the pattern of questioning is retained by the mind and can be followed quickly and automatically.

A. PSYCHIC DYSFUNCTION

Defects in any of the following areas:

1. Dimension of the Individuals (as Appendix II)

2. Dimension of Internal Communication

Father ⟷ Mother		Quality of relationship
Mother ⟷ Child		+ or −
Father ⟷ Child		
Sibling ⟷ Sibling		
Coalition ⟷ Coalition		

3. Dimension of General Psychic Properties
    i. Attitudes—beliefs and myths, values, interests, aims.
    ii. Character—predominant values.
    iii. Conscience.
    iv. Temperament of family (1–10 as under individual)—anxiety : withdrawal : depression : self-depreciation : rigidity : loss of body image : hostility : euphoria : suspicion : attention-seeking : mixed states.
    v. Skills, aptitudes.
    vi. Knowledge.
    vii. Defects of leadership and decision-making.
    viii. Defects of role playing, e.g., loss of interest in parenting ⟶ child neglect.
    ix. Defects of arrangement and cohesion.
    x. Conflict.
    xi. Autonomy of the person.
    xii. Daily pattern.
    xiii. Climate.
    xiv. Efficiency in achieving aims.

4. Dimension of External Communication

Family ⟷ Extended family		
Family ⟷ Friends		Quality of relationship
Family ⟷ Work		+ or −
Family ⟷ School		
Family ⟷ Social—e.g., isolation from community, antisocial acts, delinquency, alcoholism, drug addiction.		

B. SOMATIC AND MATERIAL DYSFUNCTION
(Dimension of Physical Properties)

1. General physical health of the family

2. General ill-health in any of the physical systems and symptoms shared by the family, e.g., multiple psychosomatic disorder, accident proneness, sexual difficulties, feeding problems, speech, etc.

3. Disturbance of material state.
   i. Primary or secondary poverty.
   ii. Sloth.
   iii. Inadequate diet.
   iv. Inadequate clothing.
   v. Inadequate education.
   vi. Inadequate transport.
   vii. Inadequate recreation.
   viii. Loss of status.

APPENDIX VII

PREVIOUS HISTORY OF THE FAMILY

©
J. G. Howells

Introduction

Points to note are:

1. The presenting family's history starts at courtship.

2. Each of the two founders of the family represent preceding families. An account of each must be recorded in our history.

3. The family at each stage is recorded under its five dimensions (as in Appendix VIII).

4. A detailed history of the presenting family and preceding families would record its history in its seven phases.

5. Information on each family, present and preceding, under its five dimensions follows the pattern of Appendix VIII.

6. The history on this chart does not record psychopathology; it is a framework on which psychopathology can be placed later.

The history of the family is divided into two sections:

A. HISTORY OF PRESENTING FAMILY
B. HISTORY OF PRECEDING FAMILY

A. PRESENTING   I PRIOR FAMILY (courtship to present—in
FAMILY (P.F.)   five dimensions)
                     II IMMEDIATE FAMILY (now—in five di-
                                    mensions)
                    III CONTINUING FAMILY (from now on-
                                    wards)

N.B. Especially in a brief history, the above can be amalgamated into
     one account

B. PRECEDING PARENT FAMILIES

HUSBAND'S PRECEDING   *WIFE'S PRECEDING FAMILY*
FAMILY
(1) Dimension of Individuals   (1) Dimension of Individuals
(2) Dimension of Internal   (2) Dimension of Internal
       Communication   Communication
(3) Dimension of General Psychic   (3) Dimension of General Psychic
       Properties   Properties
(4) Dimension of External   (4) Dimension of External
       Communication   Communication
(5) Dimension of Physical   (5) Dimension of Physical
       Properties   Properties

A. and B. are now shown together with all the dimensions included:

A. PRESENTING FAMILY
in its three periods as follows

I   PRIOR PRESENT (from courtship to now)
    (1) Dimension of Individuals
    (2) Dimension of Internal Communication
    (3) Dimension of General Psychic Properties
    (4) Dimension of External Communication
    (5) Dimension of Physical Properties

II   IMMEDIATE (at presentation)
    (1) Dimension of Individuals
    (2) Dimension of Internal Communication
    (3) Dimension of General Psychic Properties
    (4) Dimension of External Communication
    (5) Dimension of Physical Properties

III   CONTINUING (during our contact)
    (1) Dimension of Individuals
    (2) Dimension of Internal Communication
    (3) Dimension of General Psychic Properties
    (4) Dimension of External Communication
    (5) Dimension of Physical Properties

B. PARENTS' PRECEDING FAMILIES

HUSBAND'S FAMILY
(1) Dimension of Individuals
(2) Dimension of Internal Communication
(3) Dimension of General Psychic Properties
(4) Dimension of External Communication
(5) Dimension of Physical Properties

WIFE'S FAMILY
(1) Dimension of Individuals
(2) Dimension of Internal Communication
(3) Dimension of General Psychic Properties
(4) Dimension of External Communication
(5) Dimension of Physical Properties

If a very detailed account of the history of the family is required then the history of each preceding family, in its five dimensions, is shown divided into seven phases:

(1) Courtship
(2) Early marriage
(3) Expansion
(4) Consolidation
(5) Contraction
(6) Final partnership
(7) Disappearance.

APPENDIX VIII

THE FAMILY'S PRE-MORBID PSYCHIC STATE

J. G. Howells

Introduction

Points to note are:

1. As the family moves through time from courtship to the present, due to experience, it acquires many characteristics. This end result is collectively termed its "personality."

2. Its "personality" has a somatic and psychic part. The psychic part is subdivided into four dimensions. The physical part is assessed for its health and material aspects. Thus, there are the usual five dimensions.

3. Incorporated in the presenting family are attitudes due to the preceding families.

4. The aim is to obtain a picture of how this family conforms to the expected pattern of family behaviour and in what way it deviates.

The family is studied under five dimensions as follows:

1. Dimension of Individuals (as in Appendix IV for each person)

2. Dimension of Internal Communication (F.R.I. can assist here—see Appendix X)

			Qualities include:
Quality of Father	⟷	Mother	
Mother	⟷	Child	Friendly —hostile
Father	⟷	Child	Kind —harsh
Sibling	⟷	Sibling	Helpful —obstructive
Coalition	⟷	Coalition	Passionate —frigid
			Praising —jealous.

242

3. Dimension of General Psychic Properties

    i. Attitudes—beliefs and myths, values, interests, ambitions.
    ii. Character—predominant values.
    iii. Conscience.
    iv. Temperament—predominant moods (anxiety, withdrawal, depression, self-depreciation, rigidity, loss of body image, hostility, euphoria, suspicion, attention-seeking).
        Mixed states.
    v. Skills, aptitudes.
    vi. Knowledge.
    vii. Control—leadership, decision-making.
    viii. Role playing.
    ix. Cohesion and arrangement.
    x. Conflict.
    xi. Autonomy of the person.
    xii. Daily pattern.
    xiii. Climate.
    xiv. Efficiency.

4. Dimension of External Communication

Quality of Family ⟷ Relatives	Qualities include:
Family ⟷ Work	Friendly —hostile
Family ⟷ School	Kind —harsh
Family ⟷ Friends	Helpful —obstructive
Family ⟷ Society	Passionate—frigid
	Praising —jealous.

5. Dimension of Physical Properties

    A. Health

    B. Material—Race, social class, economic class, size, sex distribution, type of structure (nuclear, extended, anomolous), religion, district, housing, diet, clothing, transport, income, recreation, academic.

APPENDIX IX

CHART OF SIGNS OF FAMILY PSYCHOPATHOLOGY

©
J. G. Howells

Introduction

Points to note are:

1. This procedure is concerned with an *objective* assessment in a systematic form to elucidate signs of family psychonosis.

2. A full examination elucidates:

A. Signs of psychic dysfunction.

B. Signs of physical dysfunction (these are covered in texts on somatic medicine and will be only briefly covered here).

3. Whenever possible, the family should describe and have recorded its answers to questions in its own words. (Psychiatrist's remarks can be in brackets.)

4. Much can be gleaned about the family's basic state during examination, and this is recorded in Appendix VIII.

A. FAMILY'S PSYCHIC DYSFUNCTION

Defects in any of the following areas:
1. Dimension of the Individuals (covered in Appendix V).
2. Dimension of Internal Communication (F.R.I. can assist here—see Appendix X).

Father ⟷ Mother	Quality on 5 rating scale:	
Father ⟷ Child	$++, +, 0, -, --$	
Mother ⟷ Child	Qualities include:	
Sibling ⟷ Sibling	Friendly	—hostile
Coalition ⟷ Coalition	Kind	—harsh
	Helpful	—obstructive
	Passionate	—frigid
	Praising	—jealous

3. Dimension of General Psychic Properties
   i. Attitudes—beliefs and myths, values, interests, ambitions.
   ii. Character—predominant values.
   iii. Conscience.
   iv. Temperament—predominant moods (anxiety, withdrawal, depression, self-depreciation, rigidity, loss of body image, hostility, euphoria, suspicion, attention-seeking).
   Mixed states.
   v. Skills, aptitudes.
   vi. Knowledge.
   vii. Control—leadership, decision-making.
   viii. Role playing.
   ix. Cohesion and arrangement.
   x. Conflict.
   xi. Autonomy of the person.
   xii. Daily pattern.
   xiii. Climate.
   xiv. Efficiency.
4. Dimension of External Communication

Family ⟷ Extended family	Quality of 5 rating scale:	
Family ⟷ Friends	$++, +, 0, -, --$	
Family ⟷ School	Qualities include:	
Family ⟷ Work	Friendly	—hostile
Family ⟷ Society—isolation,	Kind	—harsh
antisocial acts,	Helpful	—obstructive
delinquency,	Passionate	—frigid
alcoholism, etc.	Praising	—jealous.

B. FAMILY'S PHYSICAL DISORDER
(Dimension of Physical Properties)

1. General state of health of the family and shared symptoms. Examinations, including special examinations, of its state of health as required.

2. Its material state. Questions to elucidate:
    i. Primary or secondary poverty.
    ii. Sloth.
    iii. Inadequate diet.
    iv. Inadequate clothing.
    v. Inadequate education.
    vi. Inadequate transport.
    vii. Inadequate recreation.
    viii. Loss of status.

THE FAMILY RELATIONS INDICATOR

A projective technique for assessing
Intra-family relationships

by

John G. Howells and John R. Lickorish

Description

The Family Relations Indicator (1, 2, 3) was a direct result of a change
in clinical emphasis from an individual-centred to a family-centred approach
to psychic problems. When work on the Indicator began in 1956, there
were several picture tests for use with young children. But none of them
gave an adequate coverage of family relationships, several were firmly
based on psychoanalytical concepts, and none covered all age groups. The
F.R.I. was therefore an empirical answer to a practical need.

Pictures taken from books and magazines were not very promising, so it
was decided to start from the beginning with a series of specially drawn
pictures. This enabled the authors to specify the type of scene and the
general configuration of the figures in the pictures. Drawing solely upon
the authors' experience, it was possible to cover the main inter-personal
relationships in the "nuclear family" by using six basic scenes. 1. A parental
group, with or without children. 2. Father and child. 3. Mother and child.
4. Child alone. 5. A sibling group. 6. A group containing a baby.

Later, it became clear from experience that, if only six pictures were
used, little information would be obtained. Children unable "to tell a story"
about the picture would be reduced to making perhaps only two or three
statements about it. Also "the warming-up period" might extend over the
first half of the series and, in effect, only three pictures might be effective
stimuli. It was decided therefore to produce three versions of each basic
scene, and in the second edition of the Indicator there are four parallel
versions of each picture. By having several versions of each scene it is
hoped to obtain more information, to counteract the effect of any
"warming-up" period, and to allow for the fact that some pictures would
probably have greater stimulus values than others. The complete set consists of 24 cards, i.e., six basic scenes replicated four times.

The pictures were drawn in cartoon-style. Dramatic postures and facial
expressions were avoided as far as possible and a minimum amount of

ONE OF THE CARDS OF THE F.R.I.
EXPLORING FATHER-DAUGHTER INTERACTION

background was included—just enough to suggest an interior or exterior setting.

Theoretical Basis

The theoretical basis of the F.R.I. is derived from the general theory of perception and in particular, from a theory of inter-personal perception. We start with the assumption that if S is presented with an *ambiguous stimulus* he tries to make sense of it. The response that S makes to the stimulus is influenced by a multitude of factors, as numerous experimental investigations have demonstrated. These factors may, however, be grouped into three categories:

1. The past experience of S.
2. The embeddedness of the stimulus.
3. S's present needs, wishes, defences, attitudes and so on.

The aim of the F.R.I. is to elicit information about the way in which S perceives his family and his relationship to it, at the present time.

In this context the word *perceive* is regarded as a compound of *sensation + meaning*. That is, any sensory impression is "interpreted" and given some sort of *meaning* by the experiencing S.

It is further assumed that S will usually interpret the stimulus-pictures in terms of his own family relationships, as he perceives them.

If he does so, he will be drawing upon his own past experience as it is reflected in his current attitudes, which of course influence his perceptions. However, his current needs and expectations may run counter to past experience. The pressure of phantasy or wishful thinking may result in replies which describe what *he would like* his family to be like, rather than how he actually perceives it at the present time.

The Family Relations Indicator is probably more appropriate to an *interview-centred* approach to the investigation of psycho-social problems, than it is to a *test-centred* approach. Indeed, it was a deliberate policy to refrain from calling it a "test."

Some Informal Uses

It has already been suggested that the F.R.I. lends itself to use in an interview-oriented rather than a test-oriented investigation. It may therefore be used simply to structure an interview with either parent or child, instead of presenting it formally and making a full analysis of the protocols.

A selection from the series of cards may be used in an informal manner if the investigator wishes to draw S's attention to some particular aspect of the family.

Ss, who find it difficult to talk in a simple face-to-face situation, sometimes find it easier if they have something to talk about. If they are presented with one or more cards from the F.R.I. series, they may find it less embarrassing to discuss their problems.

It is possible to divide the whole set into two balanced halves, so that only 10 or 12 cards are presented during one session.

Responses on the cards of any family member can be used as a stimulus during a family group interview. Furthermore, one or more cards can be produced and each family member's response to it presented to the whole family; revealing discussion can thus be stimulated on the similarities or disagreements in the responses.

Advantages of the F.R.I.

1. It is theoretically related to normal psychology and not to any particular "school" of psychopathology.

2. It is concerned with what the subject says, without any attempt at "interpreting" his responses.

3. It is aimed specifically at inter-personal relationships within the family.

4. It is in line with current views on inter-personal perception.

5. It may be used formally or informally.

6. So far as the quantitative output of information is concerned it is divisible into two equivalent halves.

REFERENCES

1. HOWELLS, J. G., and LICKORISH, J. R. (1963). The Family Relations Indicator. *Brit. J. educ. Psychol., 33,* 286–296.
2. HOWELLS, J. G., and LICKORISH, J. R. (1967). *The Family Relations Indicator.* Revised and enlarged edition. Edinburgh: Oliver & Boyd; (1971) Florence: Organizzazioni Speciali; (1972) Munich & Basel: Reinhardt; (1974) New York: Brunner/Mazel.
3. HOWELLS, J. G., and LICKORISH, J. R. (1969). A projective technique for assessing family relationships. *J. clin. Psychol., 25,* 3.

VI
FAMILY THERAPY

Introduction

General

The term "family therapy" means treatment of the family by any procedure that helps to restore health to the family. The term "family therapy" has sometimes been misused and employed in a wider sense to cover a family approach, or in a narrow usage to cover one treatment technique, family group therapy.

Psychonosis is a preventable disorder; severe states of psychonosis are difficult to cure; moderate states of psychonosis can be modified.

Thus, the greatest hope for the eradication of psychonosis and the improvement in the standard of emotional health lies in the promotion of emotional health rather than in direct procedures of cure. However, the two roads to health are parallel and complementary. From the curative field comes knowledge that can be applied on a wider scale in health promotion; curative measures offer a research area. At the same time, curative procedures make a small, but useful, contribution to improving the standard of emotional health.

The greatest bar to progress in therapy is not lack of personnel, or services, or efforts, small though these are; the main bar to progress is ignorance. The emotional and mental health services should not be judged by their therapeutic success; this is small. Their importance is that they exist. Because they exist they are a rallying point for the afflicted and the problem is exposed. Furthermore, they are a rallying point for a large number of dedicated and interested workers, who some day will collectively find the answer to psychonosis. Unfortunately, they are also the rallying point for an even greater number of workers who seek palliation of their own problems through working with others in a similar state; to select

253

healthy workers, the product of healthy families, is one of the greatest organisational problems facing all the professions in this field.

Ignorance is the true bar to progress. The field is complex. Research is difficult because of the many variables. The work is highly emotive and lends itself to misconception and wishful thinking. Many workers are dedicated, but their grasp of scientific principles is rudimentary. Thus, vague notions of a quality that can be termed mystical offer great appeal; the appraiser, aware of his own ignorance, assumes that the mystic has greater knowledge and that his own lack of ability prevents him seeing the truth. Thus, he assumes the truth to be there, when in fact he is faced with intellectualised wishful thinking.

Ignorance is prominent in psychopathology, a vital but most difficult area. Only understanding of the pathological process can lead to rational therapy. But, here, ignorance is at its greatest. Explanation has been invented rather than sought in carefully planned investigation. Invention has relied heavily upon thinking by analogy. Analogous phenomena are assumed to have all the same characteristics of the phenomena with which they are compared. Thus, picturesque illustrations are assumed to have causal links; links made so readily in the illustrations are assumed to apply in the life situations with which they are compared. In addition there has been a denial of known data, e.g., about the capacity of a child's memory, the child's developmental steps, and in particular his sexual development. That such obvious misinformation is allowed to go uncorrected soon makes it clear that heavy personal emotional bias is at work. For example, it is stated that children are brought up by mothers, when simple observation shows that they are brought up in a group—and yet uni-object relation therapy is sacrosanct. Psychopathologies do not tally with reality, or with experience. Such is the ignorance of psychopathology that it is not surprising that therapy is largely ineffective. With irrationality dominating the principles on which it is based, therapy must be ineffective. Cults have replaced responsible investigation. The way into the cult has often been through sickness. The patient becomes the therapist. Later still the therapist becomes the teacher. The blind and weak lead the weak and blind. The cult wards off attack by defences built on a dogma that cannot be understood, and thus cannot be attacked, by the uninitiated.

Emphasis has been given above to the understanding of psychopathology. It is important also to emphasise the importance of diagnosis. One must understand before one can treat effectively. Similarly, if one does not differentiate between diagnosis and therapy much of what happens in the process of diagnosis is assumed to be therapy. Almost all the films on "family therapy" (i.e., family group therapy) are, on careful evaluation, nothing more than diagnostic exercises. The family and the "therapist" (in truth a diagnostician) learn a great deal about the history and psychic tribulations of the family. But nothing changes. Revelation is not therapy. Insight is not enough. Let me illustrate: An account is given in one publication of about 50 "therapeutic" sessions involving a mother and son. In the last session, the mother is able to reveal that the pregnancy which resulted in the birth of her son was the cause of her unhappy marriage. She hates the husband and his son and rejects both. The cause of the son's vivid adolescent misdemeanours is now clear. The therapy is now assumed to have come to an end; revelation has been made. But the mother does not thereby stop hating. Nor does the damage done to her son over the last 15 years urgently repair itself. All that we witnessed was an encounter which allowed rapport to develop very slowly (a sympathetic friend would have reached this stage as quickly) to the point when the woman could reveal to a therapist something she already knew. The sharing of knowledge is a prelude to therapy, but it is not itself therapy.

One of the major lessons of diagnosis is to reveal the way in which somatic pathology runs parallel with psychic pathology. It is rare for psychonosis in an individual or in a family not to show itself in some somatic pathology. Only global examination exposes how common is this link between somatic and psychic pathology, and often the severe, and life threatening, nature of the somatic pathology. Diagnosis establishes the case for somatic and psychic therapy to run together.

Diagnosis must be accepted as a separate, if sometimes parallel, exercise from therapy, otherwise we shall not appreciate what little therapy takes place. It is matters such as this which lie behind the comment of an honest and particularly experienced therapist, both as psychoanalyst and family therapist. He was told by a prominent family sociologist, "I feel the need for the therapist to explain himself, what he did, how, when, and why, with a particular family." Nathan Ackerman comments, "Again and again, I try to do this but I am never sure that I succeed."

Would the populace be worse off if there were no psychotherapy? A protagonist might say that surely effort must stand for something. But the massive blood-letting perpetrated in the past in somatic medicine was also effort; it was based on wrong ideas of pathology and did much harm to those it was trying to help. We cannot contemplate the therapeutic scene in psychiatry today with equanimity. More harm than good in therapy may easily be the order of things. Psychotherapy is practised on a wide scale, with great enthusiasm, in many guises, by almost anyone. It is often insufficiently realised that bad practice is worse than no practice. No surgery is infinitely to be preferred to bad surgery. No one, least of all the patient, would accept a situation where an enthusiastic first aid worker was allowed to practice major surgery. But surgery of the psyche based on bizarre rationale is everyone's practice. Inactivity at least allows the organism's natural defence mechanisms to have their sway. Intervention may prevent this, e.g., loss in divorce, like loss by death, goes through a number of natural stages ending in resolution, helped by forgetting, which is the main defence mechanism; but misplaced "psychotherapy," by analysing the breakdown in detail over many months, merely succeeds in preventing the natural process of forgetting from playing its therapeutic part.

To prove that a procedure is therapeutic, it has to be established: (i) that a change has taken place; and (ii) that the change is for the better (it could be for the worse).

Too often we are content to delve to the point of understanding events and then we hope that "something will happen." The change must be shown to be constructive and be fashioned to this end.

But not all is lost. Some practitioners of psychotherapy, the better trained, proceeding with caution, recognise the limits of knowledge, and practice within these limits. Furthermore, some practitioners have the precious gift of a harmonious personality; this exercises itself to the patient's benefit, whatever the dogma held.

Psychotherapy is in a parlous state. The road to retrenchment is clear. We must return to the data of life, the facts of reality, to life experience as it is. If we can study, dissect, understand the life experience, we can learn how to reverse the psychopathological process. Therapy can then have a proven rationale and a predictable course. Already much progress has been made, data are available and, fortunately, the way to ameliorate through health promotion is already open.

The Task of Family Therapy

Psychopathology, discussed in detail earlier, will be briefly outlined here so as to define the adverse experiential process and make it possible to draw general conclusions about the reversal of its effects, i.e., the benexperiential process.

The adverse experiential process

It is easier to understand the psychopathology of the family, and the means of its improvement, by looking at the historical development of the "collective group psyche" of the present family. Each family is the product of two previous families, the preceding families of each marriage partner.

Each marriage partner has been habituated to act in the way he or she does by the dictates of his or her family. Thus each carries his own imprint* of life in the preceding family into the present family. Harmony results from the capacity of the two families, as represented by their members, to integrate. A clash produces disharmony.

The adverse experiential process starts in the preceding family of the adult members of the present family. Psychic noci-vectors adverse to a particular family member arise in his preceding family; these noxious agents can arise from one, several or all his fellow family members in that family. In later years they may be supplemented by adverse experiences outside the family. Psychic noci-vectors can operate in one overwhelming experience in time, but, much more commonly, they operate over a sustained period of time. This adverse experience may make the person sensitive to one or many psychic noci-vectors; he may be so vulnerable as to be in a permanent state of anxiety—always "on guard." The psychic noci-vectors create weaknesses in the psyche; the essential damage is done to the "idea of self." To cope with the adverse experience, the self adopts the coping devices that are possible in those circumstances. Later in life, with similar threats, the same coping devices are employed and the attitudes engendered by these coping devices may cause more trauma and thus damage by clashing with the attitudes of others. The most immediate, sensitive, and powerful clashes are likely to occur in the family where he is a founder member, husband or wife. The indicators of dysfunction in the past or in the present arise from this adverse experiential process in his preceding family; they are not the process itself.

As part of his imprint, each person carries: (i) a way of life with attitudes capable, or not capable, of adjusting to the way of life of a partner; (ii) a degree of psychonosis, dictated by past damaging experiences, largely in the preceding family, with damage to the psyche, especially to the "idea of self"; (iii) sensitivity to *general* psychic noci-vectors because of past experiences, largely in the preceding family; (iv) sensitivity to *particular* psychic noci-vectors because of past experiences, largely in the preceding family; (v) a tendency to react to psychic noci-vectors by the development of coping devices, which are often dictated by the set of circumstances in the preceding family—these devices are likely to operate in the present when faced by psychic noci-vectors; (vi) indicators of dysfunction used in the past which may be imitated in the present.

The individual, the epitome of his preceding family, moves through time, his formative years having been spent mostly in his preceding family. As

---

* The term "imprint" is used not in a special ethological sense but in its ordinary usage of "stamp" or "mark."

he advances he gathers new experiences, some of which will clash with the attitudes he has already acquired and will create more stress and damage; on the other hand, he may meet ameliorating situations. At each stage, what he has gathered from the past interacts with his immediate situation. Thus, he reaches the present and he is what a lengthy experience has made him. Depending on the climate in which he finds himself, he is either again in a stressful environment, or in an ameliorating situation. If the latter, he probably will not seek the help of the psychiatric services.

The imprint in the life of an adult family member may be reinforced or changed by continuing interaction with his preceding family. In therapy this reinforcement or change may be encouraged or discouraged. It is relevant to mention that improvements, sometimes dramatic, occur spontaneously as the result of the demise of a member of the preceding family. The change, beneficial or damaging, may wrongly be credited to coincidental therapy.

The liabilities brought to the present family by an adult member may be overt or covert, either to the member who brings them or to the other family members. To add to the problems of assessment by each other, standards of conduct will be judged by the family imprint of each, and these standards may deviate not only from the average standards in the community, but also from those of the other family members.

The imprint produces needs which may or may not be satisfied by the imprint of the partner, e.g., an individual, because of experience in the preceding family, may react by hostility if ignored. The partner's imprint may be able to deploy assets and allow him or her to contain this. Thus harmony results. An inability to contain brings disharmony. The great advantage of family therapy over individual therapy is the possibility of enlisting not only the aid of assets possessed by the therapist, but also the aid of the assets of the family members themselves. Harmony may be possible by building coping devices to the imprint deficiencies of the other. These new coping devices are possible if the antagonist's family imprint allows of it, e.g., to withdraw when hurt and refuse retaliation. Circumvention is a mechanism insufficiently exploited in therapy. An example of circumvention would be accepting a deficiency in a partner, and planning the way of life of the present family in such a way that the deficiency has little or no opportunity for expression. Therapy must employ all these natural procedures in a systematic fashion—deploying assets, building new coping devices and circumventing deficiencies. Success will largely depend, given the best of all therapists, upon the qualities of the imprints facing one another; there are occasions when they allow of no resolution.

While the imprints from the preceding family are of basic importance, it must not be ignored that the present family is also developing a course which is superimposing an imprint on the fused imprints of the marriage partners. Again, children of the marriage are in the process of imprinting in the present. The collective group psyche, at first composed of two fused imprints, expands as it embraces the children and all the new experiences it meets. The past impressions of the parents, however, are always paramount, even if hidden, simply because they result from a long-lasting experience in the preceding families during sensitive formative years. A family group composed of adult members imprinted with gross deficiencies does not necessarily collapse. The deficiencies may be complementary, e.g., an excessive need to be mothered in one partner may satisfy an excessive need to mother by the other partner. Again, deficiencies in an adult family member may produce marital clash, but not be inconsistent with excellent parenting; indeed, occasionally, a parent may "wall off" himself or herself with the children in an enclave that protects them from the onslaught of the family imprint of the other partner.

The benexperiential process

From the above account, and more detail in the section on psychopathology, a number of conclusions can be drawn which have implications for the reversal of the pathological process in therapy:

1. The pathological process seen now is often the result of adverse experience in the past. It can only be undone by a reverse active process— a beneficial experience which undoes the pathological process and establishes harmony. It must be active, and positive. Merely abolishing present stress is not enough. Similarly, in the physical field a deformity produced by excessive pressure on a limb in childhood, for instance, is not corrected by merely removing the pressure years later. Positive active corrective procedures have to be initiated. In general, therapeutic procedures have to emphasise the opposite of the pathological.

2. Damage caused by an adverse experiential process in the past can be aggravated by continuing trauma in the present; sometimes the adverse process is set up by present trauma alone.

The individual may be vulnerable now to the same psychic noci-vectors to which he was habituated in the past. To influence psychic noci-vectors in the present is easier than to reverse the effects of psychic noci-vectors in the past.

Psychic noci-vectors in the past have usually ceased to function; thus attention has to be directed, not at them, but at the damage that ensued. However, knowledge of past damaging vectors may help to plan an ameliorating beneficial process in the present. To know, for instance, that a negative psychic noci-vector, the absence of touch in the past, is the basis of frigidity now, may allow the necessary positive agent to be activated. This principle is employed in benexperiential psychotherapy and in vector therapy. A psychic noci-vector can be affected by: (i) reducing its strength; (ii) changing its direction; (iii) reducing the time over which it operates; (iv) changing its quality; (v) opposing it by a contrary vector.

Some present psychic noci-vectors are active in the imagination. A person has the capacity to dwell on a trauma in his thoughts. It can thus dominate perception, and do so to such an extent that it is not possible to give the trauma its correct evaluation, as nothing in perception is available to compare with it. Thus a person has a feeling that his thoughts are out of hand, he cannot break the vicious circle, and cannot see his problems in perspective. Strong measures may be required, including forced thinking, to break the vicious circle and bring perspective.

3. There is value in dealing with the sources of adverse experiential process in the preceding family by bringing them together with the presenting family member in therapy. This is easier with adolescents and young adults, but occasionally is possible with older adults. Should this prove impossible, the same situation must be dealt with in the absence of the preceding family—a more difficult task.

4. To re-experience previous traumatic situations is not necessarily beneficial; it may reinforce the effects of the previous trauma. It could be especially so if the preceding family is brought into the re-experience. To be therapeutic, the re-experience must be constructive and within the capacity of the individual and his therapist to make it so, whether it takes place with the preceding family or in its absence.

5. The effects of an adverse process are recorded in the memory apparatus; change must be directed at changing the memories laid down in it. The approach is through the same sensations which produced the memory, i.e., auditory, visual, motor, olfactory, gustatory, etc., or a perceptual experience which is an amalgam of some or all of these sensations.

6. An adverse process has usually operated over a period of time. The reverse ameliorating process must also operate over a period of time. Rarely does pathology arise in a nuclear incident; rarely will catharsis relieve damage. In therapy, time is important and this will play its part whether the benexperiential process is achieved by psychotherapy or vector therapy. In psychotherapy it will operate with general procedures as well as with specific procedures.

7. Not all the damage done in the past creates difficulties in the present family situation or, in the case of a single person, in the present individual

situation. Therefore, focal or partial amelioration may be employed, directed at the damage that creates difficulties in the present situation only. A partial task is clearly less time-consuming than a complete task and may bring an adequate functional result. The complete repair of a severely damaged person may be a massive undertaking.

8. There are *levels* from which a disturbing process can arise and can be changed:

    (i) In the preceding family—previous trauma.

    (ii) In the present and preceding families—present trauma acting on previous damage.

    (iii) In the present family—present trauma only.

    (iv) In the present and succeeding family—present stress acting on the children, who will form the succeeding family.

Therapy at level (i) is the most difficult. At levels (iii) and (iv) it may be possible to deal with the present situation so that the process does not pass to the succeeding families or, if it does, reaches them in an attenuated form. *Herein lies the best opportunity for the eventual production of emotional health in society. Should therapy never operate at levels (i) and (ii) it would only deny the possibility of relief to the present generation of sufferers. If measures at level (iv) could be certain of success, they would by themselves guarantee a steady permanent improvement in the standard of emotional health of society.*

9. The essential part of the psyche to be damaged is the "idea of self." To support and reconstruct the "idea of self" is central to any benexperiential therapy.

10. To know the nature of the psychopathological process can lead to precise therapeutic measures. Without this knowledge only general blanket measures can be, and often are, employed. These general therapeutic measures, the G factor, may help, but not as quickly or effectively as more specific measures.

11. Positive vectors are just as powerful as negative vectors. Love is as powerful as hate.

Positive vectors should be employed in therapy. These include praise, appreciation, encouragement, kindness, affection, respect, a sense of belonging, hope, security, worthiness (the opposite of guilt).

It is known that negative vectors do damage according to their power, repetition, and the length of time over which they operate. Equally, the effects of positive vectors used in therapy gain by their power and vividness, repetition, and by being allowed to operate over a lengthy period of time. Whenever possible, they should be precisely directed. However, even in a general blanket form they can be valuable.

In an imprecise non-directed form these positive elements in therapy are often present. They constitute a general factor, G factor. This factor is therapeutic, but not precise. Therapy should be directed and be more than the chance operation of the G factor. Therapy is often no more than this, and sometimes less, if, for instance, the therapist suffers from an unsatisfactory personality.

12. Trauma produces insecurity and the need for defence. Therefore, therapy must not involve the threat of trauma and must produce security. The insecure cannot reveal the intimate situations that lie at the core of the damage to the "idea of self." Precise evaluation of damage is the start of effective therapy. Attitudes change more readily when they are not necessary for the defence of self. If insecure, the organism will cling to old attitudes. The family "on guard" cannot build new and better coping devices. This applies in reparative measures within or outside the interview.

13. In pathology, the indicators are what the name implies—signs of the process of dysfunction. The process cannot be changed by changing the indicators; if the process remains the same and the indicators are changed, they will be replaced by a new set that are possible in the new circumstances. The process itself must be changed and only then will the indicators disappear. Thus, symptomatic relief is not enough and is desirable only to ameliorate the secondary effects of the symptoms.

14. The damage did not occur in an interview situation. It does not necessarily need to be ameliorated in an interview situation; the right marriage partner, for instance, may achieve more than a therapist. Thus, though therapy can employ interview measures such as psychotherapy, it can use also extra-interview measures, such as vector therapy. Both may be necessary and are complementary.

15. Attitudes from the past which clash in the present can arise from: (i) mechanisms for coping with trauma in the past, e.g., withdrawal; (ii) different living habits, e.g., different ideas of role of father. (ii) tends to alter more easily than (i), as habits are not based on the need to defend the self.

16. There is a limit to the effectiveness of therapy. Some adverse experiential processes may have been so severe and damaging that their effects can only be ameliorated by very prolonged and powerful measures, if at all. To spend valuable resources on only a few people may bring minimal relief to society. Constant attention must be given to deploying resources where they can be most effective, e.g., the young respond more easily than the aged. Vector therapy and the salutiferous society bring the best value. We must practice the art of the possible.

17. To contend with *present trauma* from noci-vectors, the therapist must assist the patient to use new, healthy, efficient coping devices, e.g.:

    (i) Putting the trauma in true perspective by applying standards and judgements and not exaggerating its power.

    (ii) Making realistic targets, thereby reducing the risks of trauma.

    (iii) Avoiding trauma that it is unnecessary to face.

    (iv) Side-stepping the trauma by a variety of techniques.

    (v) Deploying assets, e.g., using past success to compete with present failure ("Look, you are good because you can do that").

    (vi) Deploying support elsewhere, e.g., use of husband to share a potentially hurtful situation.

    (vii) Supporting, e.g., "We, you and I, will make a plan for coping with the situation."

    (viii) Forgetting, e.g., refusing to make a traumatic matter the topic of conversation.

All these, and more, are devices in *directed* therapy—not leaving possible improvement to the chance of the G factor.

N.B. ALL THIS IS CONCERNED WITH REAL LIFE EXPERIENCE. NO INTERPRETATION IS NECESSARY. NO FALSE AND FANTASTIC PICTURES ARE CREATED. ALL IS TRUE TO LIFE. THIS IS OF THE ESSENCE OF BENEXPERIENTIAL THERAPY.

18. To relieve past trauma, it is best, as has been said earlier, to bring the preceding family into therapy. Attitudes are exposed, guilt is relieved, the "idea of self" is improved. The patient is older and does not need to accept the omnipotence of parents. But there is a limit to effectiveness. It is not possible to make a family love when it does not; but it is possible to minimise the effect of the trauma this produces. Any result can sometimes be reinforced by limiting contact between the present family member and his preceding family, while mobilising help from his present family.

But the past may need management in the absence of the preceding family. The following steps are necessary:

    (i) The damaging noci-vectors in the past and the ensuing damage must be revealed.

    (ii) The effects of the noci-vectors in the past must now be met by the opposite quality, e.g., if a man is sensitive to being ignored he must now be given the opposite—attention.

    (iii) The present family must stop reinforcing the power of damaging vectors, e.g., it must also cease to ignore and give attention instead.

(iv) Any assets in the present family must be deployed to help a vulnerable family member. Usually, success will depend on the health of the family, but even a psychonotic family may have some assets that by chance fit the situation, e.g., a husband is incapable of taking the initiative in sexual intercourse; the wife changes roles and takes the lead in sexual intercourse.

(v) Situations can be relived in the interview situation with a therapist who represents not past figures but a positive person—the best of emotional influences. Positive vectors are generated in strength, over time, and with repetition.

The above can and does happen in daily life, but haphazardly without discernment. The aim of therapy is to practice it in a directed and precise fashion.

N.B. ALL THE ABOVE IS REAL LIFE EXPERIENCE. THERE IS NO INTERPRETATION. THERE IS NO FANCIFUL INVENTION. IT IS THE STUFF OF LIFE.

19. The therapist must not only use the G factor, but also apply *directed activity*—all the techniques described for the management of present and past trauma. The capacity to undertake this precise directed activity distinguishes the trained therapist from others. His skill springs from the following attributes:

(i) He is trained in ascertained psychopathology in a sure and systematic fashion.

(ii) He is knowledgeable about the nature, variety, and form of psychic noci-vectors.

(iii) He has great knowledge of the unusual.

(iv) He can make balanced judgements.

(v) He has great capacity to produce security through relationship.

(vi) He is knowledgeable of his field.

(vii) He is a positive person in his own right, and not just a figure on which other values are projected.

(viii) Long exposure in a medical training to the anguish and pain of many and varied forms of serious illness will have inculcated, in the right person, the response of caring in an immediate fashion.

20. The preceding adverse experiential process will usually have taken

place in the preceding family. Occasionally the family will be anomalous and have the features of a large group. In this case, this is the group that is the significant contributor from the past. Again, the present family group may be anomalous, but of no less significance.

Conclusion

The major aim of therapy is clear from our knowledge of experiential psychopathology. The adults come into the present family after suffering an adverse experience in their own preceding families. This adverse experience must be reversed in both parents to effect a harmonious family climate, so that its epitomes, going forth to succeeding families, will make a healthy psychic contribution to those families. The adverse process can be ameliorated by three main approaches: (i) Benexperiential Psychotherapy; (ii) Vector Therapy; and (iii) the creation of a Salutiferous Society. The three approaches are complementary and should be used together. Each will be discussed in turn.

In this book we are concerned with the general principles of therapy; details will be supplied in a companion volume.

Benexperiential Psychotherapy

General

Psychotherapy is the treatment of the psyche, individual or group, by any means. A psychotherapist is the person in immediate direction of the treatment.

In benexperiential psychotherapy, treatment consists of the use of a new beneficial experience. The advantageous experience is the therapy. Psychonosis, in an individual or in a family, is the result of malexperience, adverse experience in the past, adverse experience in the present, or the interaction of both. In contrast to the adverse psychonotic process, benexperiential psychotherapy utilises an experience which is to the advantage of, favourable to, the individual or family psyche—hence "benexperiential" therapy.

The general aim of benexperiential therapy, as in all forms of family therapy, is to produce a harmoniously functioning family in the situation within which it lives. What is harmonious in one situation may not be so in another. The standards in relation to "harmony" depend on what is regarded as harmonious or healthy at the present time in a given culture; today's "healthy" family may well be regarded as "unhealthy" by future standards, or in other cultures.

All programmes of benexperiential therapy must make a flexible use of all the types of treatment available. All the types to be mentioned shortly can be used together. The type predominant at a particular moment is the one that best meets a particular situation. This flexibility extends also to the simultaneous, or successive, employment of vector therapy. Benexperiential psychotherapy and vector therapy (also an experiential therapy) are complementary.

One of the lessons of family diagnosis, as well as of family psychotherapy, is the realization that psychic events precipitate organic pathology. That

266

psychotherapy aims at offering psychic help should not be allowed to overlook the need to offer somatic help. Psychotherapy and somatic therapy should go hand in hand. Naturally, our interest here is in psychotherapy.

Many defences are offered against revealing ignorance about psychotherapy. In discussion one may be met by the question, "What do *you* do?" which allows the questioner to avoid offering his techniques for scrutiny. Other defences evoke the use of a flood of vague, ambiguous intellectualisations which bemuse, befog, or overawe the listener. Yet another escapes to the select circles and the dogma of certain schools of psychopathology. Yet another meets any information with "I do all that." Here reliance is made on a simple exposition of the principles of benexperiential psychotherapy—revealing some knowledge and some deficiencies. The latter will be made good in time.

Types of Benexperiential Therapy

The best diameter to take is that of the period in time from which psychopathology arises. This could be: (A) at the level of the preceding family; (B) at the level of the present family; (C) at the level of the succeeding family.

In each type, the therapy is linked with the time at which the events occurred, past (antecedental), present (actual), or future (anticipatory).

ANTECEDENTAL THERAPY

Therapy concerned with the resolution of events that occurred in the past. These are antecedental events, hence "antecedental" therapy.

ACTUALITY THERAPY

Therapy concerned with the resolution of events in the present. These are present events, actual, hence "actuality" therapy.

ANTICIPATORY THERAPY

Therapy concerned with the resolution of events that could occur in the future. These are anticipated events, hence "anticipatory" therapy.

(A) ANTECEDENTAL THERAPY

Therapy turns around resolution in the adult family members of the present family attitudes springing from the preceding families. Therapy is conducted with the preceding family or in its absence, by discussion concerning it.

The aim can be:

1. *Complete resolution.* A state of complete emotional health is restored to at least one partner of the presenting family. An example is:

> A wife presents with depression. Examination exposes many other symptoms, both organic and psychic. Exploration reveals a difficult marital situation which has come to a head recently. It has been precipitated by a change in family circumstances, whereby it had been agreed that husband should emigrate in order to obtain a higher standard of living. The attitudes at work were—husband's inadequacy, husband's anger, husband's sensitivity to being ignored, wife's ambition, wife's withdrawal. Briefly, the sequence of events was—wife's ambition demands a higher standard of living; husband agrees to emigrate; his inadequacy is appalled at the risk he is taking and in his insecurity he becomes angry; husband's anger makes wife withdraw; her withdrawal, because of his sensitivity to being ignored, makes him more insecure and angrier; the situation escalates, until she collapses with psychonosis in which depression is a marked feature.
>
> The attitudes at work here spring from their respective families. Husband is the product of a family where the mother left the father because of his belligerence and so the patient was thrown into the care of this angry father. His father's anger frightened him and yet this was better than his father's ignoring of him in preference to his older brother. From this situation came inadequacy, his sensitivity to being ignored, his anger as a coping device.
>
> His wife came from a family where the father ran off with the maid and subsequently married her. He lost his fortune. He became alcoholic. Standards of living fell. Quarrels were acute between husband and wife. The little girl coped by withdrawing and thus not being involved. Her father was kind to her and she identified with his aspirations. From this situation came her ambition to retrieve the family fortune and to withdraw from anger.
>
> Each marriage partner represents his or her past and the weaknesses of each have to be played out in the present family. Further exploration revealed more handicaps, as well as assets, in both.
>
> Therapy began by resolving the present immediate situation provoked by the decision to emigrate. This restored harmony to the standard of the pre-breakdown level. Stopping at this point would have left therapy at the level of dealing with the trauma in the present.

Therapy could have gone a stage further; by dealing with the elements causing disharmony in the marriage, what is termed "focal resolution" (below) would have been achieved. In this case it was decided to go beyond this and to deal with all the unsatisfactory elements in both marriage partners arising from the preceding families. The aim was an ambitious one. Both were to receive a substantial guarantee against breakdown in most situations. Both were to be "made whole." Technique is to be discussed later.

It is important to emphasise that even the wealthiest of communities and the best provided are only occasionally able to undertake this time-consuming enterprise which is so expensive of resources.

2. *Focal resolution.* Here the purpose is to effect a resolution in only one, two, or several elements coming from the preceding family and causing disruption in the present family or in the life of any one individual. An example is:

A wife presents with frigidity of one year's standing. In addition she is depressed, she has anorexia, insomnia, amenorrhoea, etc. Furthermore, her husband is irritable, lacks concentration and his standard of work has deteriorated to the point where he has been warned that he may lose his position. Psychonosis in the children can be surmised from the boy's enuresis and the girl's asthma, starting in the last year.

Sequence of events becomes clear only with the exploration of the preceding families. In mother's family she was the only child of an agitated, hypochondriacal, rejecting mother, and a kind but withdrawing father. Faced by rebellion in adolescence by her daughter, mother used two weapons against her—feigning illness and making her feel to blame for it. These would always precipitate anger and depression in her daughter. Father came from a family with considerable emotional assets.

The immediate situation turns around a quarrel between the maternal grandparents. Grandfather threatens to give up his job and this threatens his wife's standard of living. Maternal grandmother develops ulcerative colitis. She turns to daughter for help and daughter reacts as she did in adolescence to her mother's illness—she becomes depressed. She loses appetite for life, food and sex. Husband, not understanding, reacts to her rejection of him. Marital tension and mother's state leads to disturbance in the children.

Here, the resolution turns around two elements—guilt and sensitivity to mother's illness. Grandparents are seen together, the quarrel is resolved. The ulcerative colitis clears up in maternal grandmother. Mother has no maternal grandmother illness to react to and her depression immediately clears up. Sexual intercourse is restored. Father responds. The whole family climate improves.

To guarantee against future breakdown, mother and grandparents meet to resolve mother's feeling of guilt springing from use of illness by maternal grandmother. Parents of the present family, and then the whole family, meet to discuss the process that led to the impact on their relationship together and with the children. Vector therapy is now possible—they ask advice as to whether the position is advanced by their moving to another town. This is advised, subject to discussion with grandparents, as it will reduce and formalise contact. Grandparents can tolerate the move, but want assurance about contact from time to time with grandchildren.

Here, the therapy is limited—only some elements coming from the past are resolved. The parents are not "made whole," but the elements from the past that disharmonise family functioning are eradicated. You will note the flexible employment of therapeutic platforms—individual interviews with mother; dyadic interviews with maternal grandparents; family group interviews involving mother and her preceding family; dyadic interviews with parents; family group interviews with present family; vector therapy.

The above illustration involves a family. Occasionally, focal therapy is a matter for an individual alone. An illustration is:

In the course of family group interview, it emerged that the father had a disturbing secret never before discussed with anyone other than his wife. This was that he found it impossible to urinate if someone else was within hearing. This defect was of no concern to the family, but it was highly inconvenient to him. He asked for help. Exploration in individual interviews revealed that as a young child he had a very irritable, aggressive and hated governess. She would sit him on the pot in front of her chair and from behind coerce and demand that he pass water. He found great difficulty in doing so and the same difficulty has continued whenever anyone is within earshot. At school he contrived to get round it by asking to be released from the classroom during lessons, so that the toilets would be empty of other children.

Here, the focal therapy is continued with an individual alone.

It follows from the above examples that any of the following interviews can be employed—individual, dyadic and family group as circumstances determine. In addition, multiple family or general group therapy may be indicated. Furthermore, any of the above can go hand in hand with vector therapy.

It can be seen that A (2) above is a much more manageable operation than A(1).

(B) ACTUALITY THERAPY

At this level concern is primarily with happenings in the present family. Therapy is concerned with handling psychic trauma arising within and without the family in the present.

Psychic noci-vectors may arise in the global family transaction, in a relationship between two family members, and from outside the family. The present psychic noci-vectors act on a sensitivity coming from the past.

A few illustrations are given:

> A mother presents with depression, the onset of which can be dated exactly. Her daughter has married into a much higher social set. Her patronising attitude distresses mother. The depression dates to the minute when her daughter telephoned that she had "arranged" a Christmas vacation for her mother and father.
>
> A child finds himself bullied at school or unfairly accused of some misdemeanour.
>
> A third party intervenes in a marital relationship.
>
> A mother finds herself in an employment where she is aware of pilfering by a fellow employee and is caught between loyalty to management or to fellow employee.
>
> A father is all set to be ordained in the Church and then unexpectedly finds that he has received homosexual attention from a number of men, begins to suspect the nature of his own sexuality, has grave doubts about his suitability for ordination and develops a psychonosis with acute anxiety.

Treatment at this level restores the family or individual to its pre-trauma standard. In some families this standard of health is very high and they were reacting to a massive or uncommon trauma. Other families have varying degrees of psychonosis resulting from the past. The management of present trauma does not of course change this pre-trauma standard.

The above may be practised in conjunction with therapy of the preceding family, e.g., in the last example above, father's oversensitivity to homo-sexuality may be due to misplaced ideas of sexuality in his preceding family and this may require resolution.

The above can also go on in conjunction with vector therapy to be discussed later.

(C) ANTICIPATORY THERAPY

Here, the intention is to concentrate special attention on guaranteeing the health of the children who will be the participants in, and founders of, succeeding families. Children, as they represent the future and are more amenable to change, should always be given help. However, there may be times when therapy may be possible only at their level; e.g., the parental problems may be intractable, or intractable with the facilities available, or the parents may be unco-operative. Thus, for a variety of reasons, a situation has been reached when one must "cut one's losses" and treat where one can.

An illustration is as follows:

> A woman loses her husband in World War II. In her loneliness she marries a man a great deal older than herself. She quickly realises her mistake. Her elderly husband anticipates her possible desertion and makes her pregnant. She stays "for the sake of the child," but rejects the child at birth—indeed she propels him out at the first uterine contraction with consequent cerebral haemorrhage in the newborn child and resulting limb paralysis. Following birth she rejects her handicapped child, who presents as a highly psychonotic spastic child at the age of three. The family situation for a variety of reasons proved to be intractable. Father was unco-operative. Mother had no interest in the child. The child required urgent and considerable help, which was given in terms of individual therapy for him, general supportive interviews for mother, leading to vector therapy at the earliest opportunity, whereby the interviews with mother made it possible for her to accept that the child be brought up in a foster home.

In the next illustration the family is investigated as a whole, but therapy again concentrates on the child who represents a succeeding family of the future.

> A man attempts suicide. An inadequate man, he married a balanced, kindly woman. He began to profit from her care. Then she

became pregnant, in response to which he developed an urticaria and was ill in various ways for most of the pregnancy. He displayed no interest in the child other than intense jealousy. Christmas came and with it the maternal grandparents to bring gifts for the baby. Husband locked himself in the kitchen and when he eventually emerged two days later, demanded that the baby should be given away. She refused. He attempted suicide. He is adamant—she must now choose the baby or him. Interviews with both separately, then together, support her in making the only decision possible—she must keep her baby and is well able to look after him on her own. (Supportive help for mother and advice on remarriage will still be helpful, if resources allow it. Therapy at level A(1) for father is desirable—if resources allow it). The future in terms of the child has the highest claim.

Work at this level can go on in conjunction with work at the two previous levels and in conjunction with vector therapy. It may be useful to emphasise again that treatment at this level, if always effective, could guarantee the health of succeeding families and thus of society in the future. Clearly, this can only arise by a steady improvement over a number of generations as therapeutic efficiency and resources increase. The work will be speeded up by using extra-interview procedures in vector therapy.

Yet again it may be necessary to emphasise that what is possible may not be dictated by the tractability of the situation, but rather by the resources available. It is unlikely that the highly skilled resources required to operate at level A(1) for all will ever be forthcoming; by that time work at level (C) will have made them unnecessary. To have, as in the present situation, ill-trained people handling the resources available is not only ineffective, but dangerous.

SUPPLEMENTARY THERAPIES

1. *Indicator Therapy.* From time to time an indicator, a sign or symptom, of psychonosis, will itself be sufficiently life-threatening, inconvenient, painful or giving rise to such serious secondary issues as to require management or therapy in its own right. This can happen to an indicator of a psychonosis arising at any of the levels mentioned above. The indicator may be somatic or psychic.

In the case of a somatic indicator, measures can range from an hypnotic drug to relieve crippling insomnia to emergency major surgery for a perforated gastric ulcer.

The following illustrates a psychic indicator requiring help in its own right because of its social repercussions:

> An adolescent boy presents with a propensity to steal women's clothing from washing lines in his neighbourhood. With these he masturbates while conjuring up images of the desirable young woman to whom the clothing belongs. Soon he is caught in a police trap. The court seeks help in his management. The indicator of his disturbed behaviour, the stealing of clothing, has serious social and personal secondary effects—it promotes shame and guilt, and may affect adult sexual behaviour.
>
> Exploration reveals that there is a severe father/son conflict. Father deplores most of the customary behaviour of an adolescent. The son's behaviour is a coping device inevitable in this family situation. His father, because of an anomalous upbringing by a maiden aunt, deplores any sexual expression in adolescence. His mother on the other hand is a passionate, warm, outgoing person. The mother implies the need for strong heterosexual expression, the father makes it impossible. Thus, the boy is forced to resort to strong covert behaviour.
>
> While there are other manifestations of disturbance, the presenting indicator of itself warrants attention because of the secondary effects. Thus a family interview is employed to relieve the son's shame and guilt. Both therapist and mother emphasise again and again the inevitability of the son's behaviour in the circumstances. Time, repetition, and insistence achieve the goal. Normal sexual expression is desirable. After a number of interviews, the therapist and the co-therapist, the mother, slowly and gently bring father to a position of security and relatedness where he can allow his son a dispensation—he can behave as other adolescents do and bring girlfriends home. No further sexual misdemeanours occur. The son still has other disturbing behaviour arising out of the father/son relationship, e.g., insomnia, a rash, panic attacks, lack of confidence. Having dealt with the damaging indicator, the father/son conflict is largely resolved through vector therapy—the son pursues his education away from home—a situation also of advantage to his newly gained freedom to behave in a normal fashion in heterosexual activity. Indicator therapy has been followed by therapy at levels (B) and (C) above. Lack of resources may, however, limit the management at any stage.

Occasionally indicator therapy can be achieved through behaviour therapy based on learning theory. While sometimes valuable, its limitations can be seen in the example above. To put the boy through a procedure that would prevent him stealing women's clothing, e.g., by aversion therapy, while useful in avoiding the social repercussions, would still have left him with his sexual frustration, and the disturbed behaviour arising out of the negative and destructive father/son relationship. Aversion therapy does not resolve the psychopathological process. But there are times when it can help in indicator therapy—even if, as sometimes happens, there is a substitution of indicators; the new indicator may be more tolerable than the old.

2. *General Supportive Therapy.* All persons and all families respond to encouragement, support, hope, praise, affection, interest and comradeship.

This may be all that can be offered in a particular situation and often in the past it has been the only ingredient of therapy, referred to earlier as the G factor. In all the measures mentioned to date, it is an essential and valuable component and, when the resources are denied, it may be the only measure possible.

Attention will now turn to further aspects of therapy. The *therapist* is considered first; this is followed by consideration of the *organisation of therapy;* and finally consideration is given to some *elements in technique.*

The Therapist

Selection

The blacksmith had this to say in Ronald Blythe's *Akenfield* (1)—"I always look at the parents before I take an apprentice. If you know the home, you already know the son." Family meets family—this is the essence of the encounter in benexperiential psychotherapy, not an individual therapist meeting the family. The therapist is the epitome of his own family. Thus, the meeting is between his family and the family under treatment. Selection of therapist then means selection of the therapist's family.

The therapist's preceding family is the area for exploration when consideration is being given to choosing a trainee therapist. Success in his own family will go a long way to guaranteeing success with families in treatment. Great care must be given to this task. A therapist requires an exceptionally harmonious personality; it is this which is going to make it possible to stand up to the strain of contact with very disturbed people, coping with persons with varying problems, giving security when it is required, withstanding hostility, offering toleration, charity and affection. All these qualities can be provided only by the product of an exceptionally harmonious family.

It is sometimes thought that training will overcome deficiencies of personality. It never does. Even new methods of therapy will not guarantee success by a therapist with severe personal deficiencies; the old therapies have been markedly unsuccessful both in training and in clinical work. Furthermore, it is far better for available training resources to be concerned with inculcating expertise in those of sound basic personality. It is sometimes argued that to have undergone a number of breakdowns adds insight into the process. This notion does not stand up to examination. Persons predisposed to breakdowns have suffered through the trying home situations that have denied them those qualities essential to help others. Of these qualities one of the most essential is the capacity to give emotionally; this is the very quality lacking in the emotionally ill.

Selection of therapists should turn around careful evaluation of preceding family climate followed by an apprenticeship to a master in psychotherapy. These in turn should be married to experience—experience of the world as it is. Therapists should ideally have been cast in many economic roles, roughed it around the world, had class, education, religion, cultural and other biases rubbed off in the hard school of life.

Success in psychotherapy depends upon: (i) the experience of a harmonious family; (ii) on having been exposed to a broad life experience; (iii) training under a master craftsman in psychotherapy.

In this chapter it is better to aspire to describing the ideal therapist; in practice we may have to settle for less.

Personality

In the therapist one looks for qualities such as toleration, with the capacity to understand and be charitable to a wide range of human failings; the ability to be unbiased and unprovoked by the less beautiful aspects of life; a capacity not to blame or moralise. The therapist must be friendly, kindly, understanding. He must be able to make warm relationships with a great variety of people. Indeed, the greater his adjustment, the wider his spectrum of affectivity.

Chairman and convenor

The therapist has the task not only of convening the meeting, but also in general terms of directing its efforts. After all, the family has come for therapy, not for a pleasant afternoon's discussion of contemporary social events. Thus, his presence or his words must continually remind the family group of the task on hand. He must be sensitive to the topics that the family needs to discuss and, furthermore, can discuss at that moment. Sometimes, the family has not as yet the capacity to tolerate a topic. He must give everyone in the family the right to speak and to do so in security.

Catalyst and releaser

Expectation, and sometimes silence, provokes the family towards a discussion of events which are embarrassing, hurtful or painful to them, matters which they would wish to avoid. He instigates an exchange where necessary. On the other hand, he teaches the family members that an interchange can take place without aggression, hostility and fury. He himself indicates and teaches that rational discussion can bring the resolution of problems. Above everything, he is expectant; his non-verbal behaviour conveys a deep and sustained interest in his patients.

Community representative

The healthy therapist brings with him the values and the opinions of the community; a man of the world, he sees life as it is and accepts the best of it. The family may not conform to the attitudes and principles in the community outside, but can acquire these from the therapist. Explanation may sometimes be called for. The therapist inculcates an attitude by example rather than by direct teaching. It behoves the therapist to have adequate community values of his own and be secure enough to recognise and discard outdated values.

Conciliator

The attitude of the therapist is always that of conciliator, when faced with hostility or aggression of one family member to another. His aim is to create a climate where constructive work can proceed. He is not a judge, but a conciliator. He should avoid taking sides. Indeed, he has loyalty to all the members of the family and this will be tested time and time again. He must truly be a benevolent, security-giving figure to every member of the family.

Protector

No one within the family group should, if possible, be hurt through the family discussion. Thus, to some extent, the therapist is a protector. This is particularly true in relation to the younger or weaker members of the family. In the eyes of the therapist, everyone is equal, everyone deserves support, everyone has equal rights. His loyalty is to the family group and thus to all.

Diluter

Even if he does nothing else, the therapist, by bringing a healthy attitude into the family group, quantitatively dilutes the psychopathology of the group. The only effective argument for having more than one therapist is that the dilution process is even greater. However, as will be seen, this can have disadvantages.

Absolver

Embarrassing, belittling, hurtful attitudes and experiences are exposed within the family discussion. The toleration of the therapist removes the sting from all these experiences; in particular, guilt is relieved.

Revealer

The therapist reveals and clarifies. He does not interpret (translate) into other terms. The only valid term is life experience, factual and unadorned. Revelation must not occur too soon or be used to hurt. It must never be more than can be endured—and the capacity for this depends on the degree of security. Benevolence creates increasing security and increasing endurance. Naturally, revelation itself does not produce change, but is a prelude to change.

Attitudes

The therapist's main task is to reveal to the family its collective group psyche based on the family imprints from the past. This is analysis only. Reconstruction must follow. Thus, as will be discussed later, he then has to mobilise the assets within and without the family to overcome its liabilities. He needs to build new healthy coping devices and he needs to find ways to circumvent deficiencies produced by the preceding families. Handicapped family members have usually experienced unhappy family relationships in the past. Now they are in touch with a benevolent family figure. This figure, however, exercises no power. Indeed, one of the lessons he has to teach the family is not to use force, power or authority. He aims to create a situation of security wherein the family can reveal itself, work towards resolution and thus change.

Craftsman

A therapist is a craftsman, a trained expert. A therapist should not appear to be a god, it is said, and should therefore admit weaknesses—it makes him human. Patients do not expect their therapists to be gods, but they do expect them to be craftsmen. To admit having weaknesses, of any considerable degree, is the negation of expertise. Affection can be expressed without the admission of weaknesses. This attitude of apparent honesty relieves the therapist of feelings of guilt at inadequate performance; an even more honest attitude would be to admit the need to change vocation. The therapist is fundamentally an expert and a craftsman, who uses the warmth given him by his family as an affective and effective tool in his task.

A figure in his own right

Therapists are not necessarily parent figures. Though in child development literature prime place is given to mother, in therapeutic literature father often comes into his own as an all-powerful, supportive father figure. But this is a distortion of events. Father, mother, uncles, aunts, brokers, butchers, jockeys—all can have personal qualities of the highest emotional quality. Indeed many jockeys are also fathers. What people crave for at all times from others is an affectionate relationship. This is more important than its sources, even if the latter are the parents. Love is more important than parenting. Parenting may or may not supply it. Others may or may not. Thus a therapist is not just a parent figure—he can be a figure in his own right. A therapist is not a good mother or father figure, but a good therapist.

Security-inducing figure

A number of therapists fail because they are constantly at war with the family under therapy; there is a need to outwit, manipulate, score off, feel omnipotent towards, or crush with hostility. At best this is bad technique, at worst this reflects the therapist's experience in his preceding family. Consider the following extract from the literature:

> As Dr. X suddenly flipped from his *mimicking* involvement with the family to being *sarcastic,* you had the feeling that the family was suddenly being *cut apart.* I think it is necessary at times *to hurt* in order to get at the pathology, in the same way that you can't get at the appendix unless you go through the skin and belly. And then he got

sneaky, as a master *manipulator,* and the rest of the film, to me, could be lumped in this area. (Author's italics)

Here, we have mimicking, sarcasm, to cut apart, hurt, being sneaky, manipulation. This is not therapy but war—and of a dirty variety. The analogy with surgery is unfortunate; great surgeons are renowned for the minimum of trauma, effortless technique and absence of drama. The above is not analogous to surgery but to butchery. Confrontation is at its height in films and public performances of therapy. The insecure therapist needs to exert himself, there is much blood about, the drama is great—but the family bleeds. And the audience, all would-be therapists, identify with the powerful therapist and soon the family has ceased to be as it is. It is a thing apart, responding to different roles, with different feelings, a savage dangerous thing. But it is not really different. Its members are as we are. They are us.

Hostility brings insecurity and the need to defend—even by force. Thus it maintains the unhealthy coping devices. Security is an essential precursor of change.

Therapist/patient interaction

The essential confrontation is between the family of the therapist and the family under treatment (and their preceding families) or preceding family of the individual patient. Both father and mother in their preceding families and children in the present family have undergone a holistic experience—an interaction between them and their whole family. This is not just an interaction between child and father or child and mother. (In the literature on child psychiatry, because mother comes to clinics with the child, there is an emphasis on the mother/child relationship. In literature on what is termed "transference," as the therapist is often a male, there is emphasis on the father/child relationship. Both are artefacts.)

The therapist also represents a family, complex and multidimensional, a family of the best kind. He is the amalgam of a superb G factor plus special skills. He is himself. Patients are not in touch with a phantom of their own making, but with a real person. They react to the therapist as the life experience to date, especially in their families, has taught them.

The way they interact with the therapist is personal to them and their experience and speaks of it. Thus it is helpful in diagnosis. But this is diagnosis and not therapy. It is not correct to interpret (i.e., translate); one should reveal. Any knowledge from the interaction reveals the preceding family; no interpretation is required, but simply the revelation of facts about the preceding family.

The best therapist will be aware of some weaknesses in himself—real ones from his family—and will make allowances on this account. The patient is not interested in this. To expect help from a patient is ridiculous. The therapist must go elsewhere for any help, or in the event of marked weaknesses, seek other work than therapy. In the past, the analysis of "counter transference" has been a substitute for a sound therapist.

"Transference" and counter transference" are a part of the interaction between patients and therapist. To claim that they are the whole, the major part, the more important part, of the interaction gravely limits the interaction and its potential.

Diagnosis is not therapy. The therapeutic element depends not on the analysis of the communication, but the capacity through the communication to give a new constructive experience, i.e., a benexperiential therapy. This is not achieved through an interaction with a projected image imposed by the patient on the therapist, but by an interaction with a real person— the therapist. The ideal therapist has an easy time—much of the time he automatically does and says the right thing.

Non-verbal communication

The greater part of the communication between therapist and patient occurs at a non-verbal level—an intensely affective level. Eyes, face, posture, gesture and movement convey interest, encouragement, praise, confidence, security, toleration and the expectation of change. It has the added advantage of being time-saving. Time-consuming verbal communication alone is almost exclusive to the insecure family group.

Effective therapy takes place in tranquility, peace and orderliness. Drama is for the ineffective.

Organisation of Benexperiential Psychotherapy

Here, the discussion will be concerned with the interview termed "family group therapy." This is the basic interview in family psychiatry. Nevertheless, other types of interviews will be employed from time to time. Work should be flexible. The appropriate interview procedure is employed according to the dictates of the situation at a particular moment in time. Flexibility is the keynote. Circumstances may sometimes dictate that only a particular interview procedure is possible, but one aspires to the most appropriate at a particular time in a particular situation.

Types of interviews

These are:
(i) Individual interviews.
(ii) Dyadic interviews involving any two people and the therapist.
(iii) Family group interviews involving the whole family (this may sometimes be a partial family group).
(iv) Multiple family groups—the present family may get together with related families, such as preceding, collateral or succeeding families.
The group may consist of a number of unrelated families.
(v) General groups—these consist of members of unrelated families and have many variants, depending on gender, vocation, type of problem, etc.

Comparison of Family Group Therapy with Individual Therapy

Family group therapy has some features in common with individual therapy. But in family group therapy the number of relationships is greater, the therapist is part of a web of communication and he addresses himself to the "collective psyche" of the family. The great advantage of family group therapy is that in the group there is a built-in corrective to misinformation by an individual by the sifting and re-evaluation of the others. Furthermore, it is possible to deploy assets not only in the therapist, but also in the family itself.

Comparison between Family Group Therapy and General Group Therapy

General group therapy treats together a number of individuals from unrelated families. Groups may be male, female or mixed. They may meet formally for intensive therapy, or informally in a club setting. One or more therapists may be employed, and the clinical material is interpreted according to the school of thought of the therapists. The aim is to bring profit to each *individual* in the group.

The family group has a strong identity which reaches from the Past and extends into the Future. It existed as a group before therapy, and will go on after it. It is a heterogenic group of both sexes and of all age groups. It is subject to strong influences from the extended family group. Its members have learnt rigid patterns of behaviour and communication, in relation to one another. Each member of the family has strong meaning for the others. Powerful emotions can be aroused in it, for good or evil. The strength and cohesiveness of a family group often become strikingly apparent when it is attacked from outside. The aim of therapy is to change the *collective psyche* of the family.

Flexibility in therapy

It must be emphasized that family group therapy is but one procedure of benexperiential psychotherapy, which in turn is only one part of family therapy. The use of family group therapy alone seriously limits the treatment of the family. Benexperiential psychotherapy, vector therapy and preventive psychiatry are complementary, and the most effective family therapy employs all these procedures simultaneously.

The therapeutic needs at a given moment can be met by a flexible approach ready to utilise whatever is appropriate. Thus, individual and family group psychotherapeutic procedures may be employed together, or family group therapy and vector therapy, or family group therapy and dyadic therapy, etc. Whenever possible, the whole family must be involved in the treatment process; this does not mean just for family group therapy alone, but applies to all the therapies appropriate to the task at that time.

Treatment may have to proceed with an individual, or with only a part of the family; this may be so because of inability to involve the whole family or because of the dictates of the treatment situation at that moment. But if only a part of a family is under treatment, the rest of the family is not overlooked, and the aim does not change; to adjust the whole family is still the target.

With the consent of the family group, family members can see the therapist alone, but with the understanding that, whenever possible, material relevant to family life must be reintroduced to the group. The therapist applies no pressure; he concentrates on producing security which makes revelation possible to the rest of the family. The therapist, of course, does not allow himself to be used against the family, or to show special favour to any one member. Whenever misunderstanding threatens, it pays to subject the situation to the scrutiny of family discussion; capacity to understand is often greater than imagined. There is no doubt that an experienced family therapist is more comfortable in family therapy than in individual or dyadic therapy, where there is always anxiety lest unseen family members are not taken into account.

The following illustrates the need to be flexible in family group therapy and to allow fragmentation when required:

A father, mother and daughter meet together for family group therapy. At one moment father becomes silent, anxious and restless; the group makes no progress. The father then asks that he be allowed to see the therapist alone. When he does so, he relates that some time ago he had an involvement with a third person. He ends by wondering whether this information should be imparted to the family group.

Discussion may show that two plans should be considered: (i) that the material imparted is of no significance to the rest of the family or (ii) that it is of significance to the wife, who, the patient feels, may suspect the situation. He asks for a meeting between the therapist, the wife and himself, as he feels that the matter needs resolution. Husband, wife and therapist meet—dyadic therapy. Again the couple wonders whether the information should be imparted to the family group. They decide that the event has no significance for the adolescent daughter, and they do not wish to introduce the material to the group. Or they may decide that the daughter may already suspect this relationship, is worried about it, and the matter should be divulged. Thus, the therapist, mother and daughter meet to discuss the situation. Thereafter, family group therapy continues.

Selection of families

Few units are so well staffed as to be able to apply family group therapy to all their families. Thus, selection becomes necessary. In general, units deploy their facilities to give optimum value to the community. Therefore the families selected are those with a degree of disturbance likely to respond, in a reasonable period of time, to the treatment offered by the facilities available. Families with young children have a degree of priority. They have young parents; young parents have not been emotionally ill as long as older people, and thus respond more readily to treatment. The younger the children when treatment is established, the more they profit. The number of children in the family is a factor in selection; the greater their number, the greater the benefit that will accrue to society by improving their emotional health. In all families, whatever the degree of disturbance, efforts should always be made to bring relief to the children, the young generation and the generators of new families; we must invest in the future.

To make priorities when so many require help is a trying matter. But if the number under therapy exceed the resources of a particular institution the standard of therapy can deteriorate to the point that no one receives effective therapy. When allowance has been made for administration, staff contact, meetings (and excessive conferencing is a sign of inexperience and inefficiency), reports, course attendance, teaching and investigation, a possible therapeutic weekly period of 40 hours can easily become 20 hours. This means that ten families receive two hours from a therapist if seen weekly, or 20 families if seen fortnightly—less contact than this is not valuable. Thus, interview therapy is exceedingly expensive of time and money. A clinic with five therapists might have 400 families referred to it, but be able to offer therapy to 100 families for two hours a fortnight or 50 families for two hours a week. If a clinic is wasteful enough to use two co-therapists, the number of families receiving treatment would drop to 50 families if seen fortnightly, or 25 families if seen weekly. Thus, selection of families is imperative.

It is still a matter for amazement that some clinics aspire to give all patients a complete form of psychotherapy; they end up in a scramble to cope that means superficial, wasteful therapy.

Normally, the best deployment of facilities involves selecting a few families for complete antecedental psychotherapy, a larger number for focal antecedental psychotherapy, and the largest number for actuality psychotherapy and vector therapy. Vector therapy has revolutionized the effective use of time and is usually the procedure that gives the best rewards for the time and resources available. However, the lengthier methods continually unearth new knowledge and techniques that can then be applied to the shorter methods.

Some "hard core" or "problem" families in small number are invaluable as teaching media for trainees. Thus a few should be in the treatment programme. Some help is given and the reward for this in understanding the mechanics of family life is enormous.

Senior staff members of an institution should constantly remind staff of the cost of time. Endless discussion and counterdiscussion, often purposeless, can go on. The greater the time spent on this, usually the less effective the therapists. It is a measure of the need to question whether the right staff members have been selected. Naturally, some time must be spent on structured, fruitful staff communication.

Home or clinic setting

Family therapy usually takes place in an out-patient clinic. Few clinics offer a service in the family's home. It is held by some that therapy in the clinic is a less artificial situation than therapy in the home, where it creates embarrassment to the family by provoking the interest of the neighbours, and where distractions are many. Therapists feel safer in their own clinic setting and claim that it offers a controlled environment, which makes diagnosis easier. Others claim that the home, as the family's natural setting, is more revealing, that it is easier to collect family members together there, and that it offers less distractions than a clinic. Probably the main determining factor in choice of setting is the time factor; it saves therapeutic time to bring the family to the clinic and this time is always at a premium. The family doctor, family nurse and family social worker, on the other hand, may find the home to be the best platform.

Home versus clinic setting is not a key factor in therapy. Given the right therapist, the all-important communication can ensue in any setting.

The clinic setting

The family group usually meets in the clinic setting. They can meet informally in a comfortable circle of chairs, or seated round a table. All members of the family of any age group, including infancy, are present. Less than one-and-a-half hours is unlikely to be worthwhile, and more than two-and-a-half hours is likely to be exhausting. About two hours is the average period for a group meeting. Family groups should, if possible, meet once a week and no less frequently than once a fortnight. There are times when a longer meeting with rest pauses may be indicated—even for a whole day. These longer sessions are useful for dealing with a crisis, or when the family has reached a point where it feels able to resolve a particularly difficult situation. This is a modification of the multiple impact therapy developed by the Galveston, Texas, group of workers; they brought a family into a residential setting for a once-and-for-all therapy with a stay of two to three days.

The room should be restful and quiet. Lighting should allow easy visibility, while being subdued and not harsh or revealing. All the chairs should be of equal height and size; the therapist claims no privilege. There should be playing material and reading material for the children. All need access to a toilet. A profitable arrangement can be to plan evening sessions for families unable to get together during the day.

Size of group

In family group therapy, concern should be with individuals who have emotional significance as a group. This, most commonly, is the nuclear family. But a blood tie is of secondary importance to an emotional tie. The family group in therapy should consist of those who are involved together in an emotionally significant way. Thus, the functional rather than the legal or physical group is important. For example, in a particular sct of circumstances a lodger may be a more important father figure than a husband; a nanny may be a more important mother figure than the natural mother. Thus, added to the nuclear family, there may be grandparents, siblings, relatives, neighbours, friends, acquaintances, servants, etc. Always, the approach should be flexible—in the course of therapy the group may need to shrink or expand.

Confidentiality

This applies at two points. Firstly, retaining information in the family group and, secondly, dealing with confidence as it concerns one family member within the group.

Families need to be assured that information will be kept confidential. Information must be assumed to belong to the person who gives it. It is imparted because only in so doing can the help needed be received. If it is communicated to others outside the family by the therapist, it must be with the clear understanding and permission of the family or the particular family member. Thus any recordings or notes must be made with their agreement and the anonymity of the family must be protected when they are used outside the immediate therapeutic situation, e.g., in teaching and writing. To fail means poor communication and ineffective therapy.

Within the family group, an individual may have information he wishes to impart to the therapist only. Similar "special information" relationships develop naturally within the family. The need for this is respected. While a particular family member's right to communicate alone with the therapist must be maintained, its handicapping effect on therapy must be pointed out. With increasing confidence, more and more information is thrown into the common pool by the family members. Especially in early interviews, the family group cannot produce complete security and thus complete communication. To force it beyond what the relationship in the group can stand creates greater insecurity and impedes progress.

Recording information

Given the agreement of the family, the interview can be recorded by sound or video tape. As a means of expediting day-to-day therapy, recording on tape and video has a limited part to play. Seldom does a therapist have time to consult a two-hour tape before engaging on another session. If this were done as a routine the number of families helped by a team of five therapists in one year and seen once fortnightly could shrink by half to 50 families! However, there are times when a family will profit from having a previous session played to it on tape and discussing it. More usually, the part played covers some especially significant part of the interview. Thus, any of its tapes should be accessible to a family, but the playback used with discrimination, e.g., a family member may not yet be secure enough to stand the revelation that in an interview he gives himself away so clearly. Again, one family member may use a section of tape to score off another member. Therapy aims to teach that such hostility is unnecessary.

The great value of recording interviews is in research and teaching, and not in routine therapy.

Communication

The prime channel of communication within the family group is speech. However, much more occurs which has meaning to the family. The seating arrangements can reflect divisions and coalitions in the family. Posture and gesture may convey what is felt and perhaps what an individual might wish to do, or how he would like to be regarded, his aspirations, and his defences. At first the therapist may find it difficult to understand both the verbal and the non-verbal communications, as families have idiosyncracies. He must, with time, become attuned to the language of that family. The role of non-verbal communication has already been stressed as a major part of the skills of the therapist.

One or multiple therapists

Another matter of organisation is that concerning the choice of one therapist or several. Usually, economy dictates the choice of one only. At first, therapists new to the field have difficulty in shifting loyalty from one person to a group. Yet, all have had experience of such a loyalty within their own families; such a shift is possible once the group idea is grasped and habit given time to work. Having a number of therapists carries the danger of each forming an attachment to an individual family member and setting up rivalries. On the other hand, if more therapists are introduced there is more dilution of family disturbance. It has been argued that a number of therapists are collectively wiser and more skilled. But an experienced individual therapist should have the skill to manage alone. The greatest problem in having multiple therapists, and the final argument for one therapist, is maintaining adequate communication between a group of therapists; one therapist is usually of one mind, and comes from one preceding family.

Much profit comes in teaching from bringing a trainee into a family interview if this is tolerable to the family. Skills can be maintained by therapists playing video tapes of their therapy to colleagues for comment.

Preceding families

When a family has a member with psychopathology springing from a preceding family, then that preceding family should always be involved if it is accessible. It is much easier to resolve difficulties in the past if the past can be made present. Resolving the past through the imprint of the past life in the individual is more difficult. The preceding family is seen with its family member from the present family or jointly with the present family— depending on what is required. Even two preceding families or collateral families may be included. This latter is a form of multiple family therapy.

Prognosis

The effectiveness of family group therapy is dependent on a number of factors: (i) The less the degree of family disturbance, the more rewarding, of course, is the therapy—with our present knowledge, even the best therapists may have difficulty in resolving a severe degree of family emotional disorders. (ii) Problems of the Present resolve very satisfactorily— problems with deep roots in the Past are resistant. (iii) In general, the younger the family members, the more effective the therapy. (iv) Recent acute situations resolve more easily than long-standing, chronic situations.

Even in the most resistant families, family group therapy can be a valuable technique in conjunction with vector therapy; insight can develop to the point when the family can accept adjustment which will change the pattern of intra- and extra-family dynamics in its favour.

Equally good results can be obtained with all clinical categories, including the psychonotic, the psychopath, the alcoholic and the delinquent. In the writer's experience, family group therapy is not a profitable procedure for "process" schizophrenia.

What constitutes resolution will depend on the target set. Targets could be:

1. Relief of the presenting symptom in the presenting family member.
2. Resolution of psychonosis in the presenting family member.
3. Resolution of psychonosis in all family members to make the family harmonious in present circumstances.
4. Resolution to the point when the contribution of this family to the foundation of succeeding families will be healthy.

5. Complete resolution of psychonosis throughout the family to guarantee harmony under all ordinary circumstances.

Clearly (1) is much easier to achieve than (5), which is only occasionally attempted.

A routine follow-up contact with the family can reinforce previous procedures, offer continuing support, and may, with the detachment of time, allow a realistic appraisal of the extent and techniques of clinical effort. If investigation and diagnostic procedures are carefully followed, the family indicators will have been carefully recorded before therapy. Following therapy, the family can be reassessed as to the state of its indicators and a comparison made with its pre-therapy phase.

There are few good follow-up studies of family group therapy. Problems of evaluation, which are considerable in individual psychotherapy, are even greater in family psychotherapy. Often family group therapy amounts to an evaluation of family dynamics without any clear benefit to the family, analysis without reconstruction. Allowance must also be made for the fact that factors change by time alone; chance may change the pattern of adverse vectors to their advantage and the longer the therapy (and thus, time) the more likely this is to happen.

However, careful research could show that family group therapy is not only the most potent form of therapy, but also has, in most situations, a clear advantage over individual therapy.

Individual interviews

There are a number of indications for the use of individual interviews.

1. An individual person is the referred patient and the rest of the family refuse to co-operate.

2. The referred patient is a single person and it is not immediately possible to involve the preceding family.

3. The referred patient is an individual with a problem that does not involve the rest of the family—but later it may be necessary to involve the preceding family.

4. The referred patient does not see at first that the present family is involved.

5. Having started with a family or dyadic interview, a family member requests an individual interview for clarification of what appears to him to be a personal problem.

6. One family member may alone show psychonosis of a severe degree. To cope with his experience in his preceding family, individual interviews

run alongside the family group therapy. This may be a prelude to involving his preceding family.

It is not necessary to elaborate on the procedure of an individual interview here, as its main features are similar to those of family group therapy. Usually, interviews last 50 to 60 minutes but may be usefully prolonged at significant points in the therapy. The individual may be of any age group— child, adolescent, middle aged or of old age.

It may be useful to briefly outline the steps in the therapy of children.

In the Institute of Family Psychiatry, a child psychotherapist undertakes the investigation and treatment of the child patient in collaboration with the family's psychiatrist. Together psychiatrist and child therapist outline the project for a particular child.

The first aim is usually to establish rapport by the use of much play material. Thereafter, systematic observation of the child takes place in the play situation; this gives a base line for comparison later on.

Play diagnosis follows. The aim here is to encourage the child to reveal his problems as he knows them and also to express what he knows about himself and his relationships within the family, the school and the neighbourhood. A young child can only communicate through play; an older child may spontaneously verbalize to the therapist. The play medium appropriate to the child's age, sex and inclination is supplied. It is usual to corroborate information obtained through one medium by that disclosed by another. There is a systematic evaluation of the child's family life.

Play therapy is the final technique and is employed for one of the following reasons: (i) to support the child while the parents are receiving treatment; (ii) to support the child when the family environment cannot be changed, or when he cannot be separated from it; (iii) to help to separate the child from his family, either for short or lengthy periods; (iv) to make a lasting change in the child's personality. The relationship between therapist and child is the most potent therapeutic medium. Within the safety of this relationship, the child expresses his fears, guilt, hate, and, sharing these with the therapist, is encouraged to healthier reactions.

Child psychotherapy is at its most effective when undertaken as a part of family therapy.

Adolescents are particularly sensitive to such matters as being regarded as adults, confidentiality, and the relationship between the therapist and their parents. It is often wise to commence therapy with the adolescent in individual interviews. When rapport is established the advisability of a family group interview is discussed. He will need reassurance that any matter that has passed between therapist and adolescent can be kept confidential as long as he wishes. The aim and organisation of the family group interview is also the subject of preparation.

Dyadic interviews

A dyadic interview is an interview that includes any dyad in the family—these can vary greatly, but the commonest are those that include the marital couple, parent and child, or two siblings.

Indications for a dyadic interview include:

1. The referred patient may be a couple and it may be necessary to start with them before including the rest of the family as they do not see that the rest of the family is implicated.

2. They may alone be available. They may have no children or immediate relatives.

3. Other family members may refuse to co-operate.

4. At a given moment in family group therapy a particular relationship may require special attention.

5. A dyad may have a problem that does not include the other family members.

Sometimes before embarking on dyadic interviews it is wise to see each person individually. The right moment to bring them together can be gauged after preparation. Again when the situation requires it, they can receive individual interviews and this is made clear to them in the preparation. The bringing together must not be over-hasty. Some interviews may be too traumatic—one or the other member may not be ready for harsh revelations, rapport may suffer or he may move out of therapy. Family members sometimes cope with one another by being secretive, withholding information or saying little. These coping mechanisms must not be pushed aside until both partners are secure enough to deal with the consequences.

Multiple family therapy

Here, a number of families come together for therapy. Multiple family therapy is of two types:

1. The families are related, e.g., starting with the present family, either a preceding family or collateral or succeeding families are brought in. They can be immensely valuable in either benexperiential psychotherapy or in vector therapy. The clan has assets and resources, and these can come into play. Naturally, the process is not undertaken without the understanding and preparation of the presenting family.

2. Unrelated families. These are less useful. Each family has its unique historical background and a psychonosis arising out of it. These preceding families are not available and the crucial past situations cannot be dealt with. Each family is anxious to receive help for its own problems.

Such groups are most useful when discussing general problems of living which are of common interest. It has been argued that disturbed families can help one another. In general, disturbed families, like disturbed individuals, are not effective therapeutic agents. The other families are particularly prone to pick up the unhealthy reactions. Such families are not very understanding, and less so than a well selected and trained therapist. Normally, families profit from contact with healthy families. There would be more profit in mixing healthy and unhealthy families—with a preponderance of healthy ones. But healthy families usually see no good reason for being used in this way. It should be remembered that the larger the group, the more diluted it is. Furthermore, the larger the group, the less often can one member of it talk in a given period of time. As in all groups, there is an optimum size for useful communication. The group should probably not exceed seven persons.

General group therapy

These groups include a number of people from different families. They are organised in various ways:
1. By age—groups of children, or adolescents, middle aged, aged.
2. By sex—groups of men or women.
3. Mixed sex groups.
4. Economic, social or religious groups.
5. Groups, all of whom have common syndromes, e.g., agoraphobia, asthma, fetishism, etc.

Activities can be very varied—some groups revolve round discussion, or dancing, teaching, art, etc. Some groups have a number of activities and take on the features of a club. All are of value in a supportive way.

The most useful groups are those in which a number of healthy people are able to exert a precise effect on a small number of sick people. Naturally, the younger the patients the more rapid the change. Thus groups are especially useful for infants (day nurseries, play groups, children's clubs, adolescent's clubs, etc.). Here we impinge on vector therapy, to be discussed later.

Even larger groups are useful (i) for their supportive effect, (ii) for discussion of general problems of living, and (iii) as a means of diagnosing and having access to vulnerable people.

However, they are not a very potent therapeutic milieu for advanced ill-health because:

1. Each member of the group has a different preceding family unique to him.

2. Attitudes from the past interfere with the present family, who cannot be dealt with as that family is not there—nor its preceding family.

3. Each member is an epitome of its own family and each strives for expression.

4. The amount of collective psychopathology is great, but there is no common interest in dealing with it.

At this point we also touch on group relations in in-patient care, and this will be discussed under vector therapy.

Elements of Technique in Benexperiential Therapy

In the discussion that follows it is assumed that the standard interview is the family interview; most of the information would also apply to other types of interviews.

Major principles.

Insight. To confront is a hostile exercise. To reveal is untraumatic. Revelation is tolerable in the security of a sound relationship with a therapist. Insight implies the understanding of the significance of psychic events as they relate to that person or family. It leads to an awareness of the psychic noci-vectors that led to the damage to the "idea of self" in the past, the vulnerabilities there were produced, and the coping devices employed. It allows awareness of the attitudes set up by this process in the past which clash with the attitudes of others today. It allows awareness of the psychic noci-vectors operating today on vulnerabilities produced by the past.

Insight is only a prelude to therapy.

Psychic noci-vectors now. The psychic noci-vectors or vectors must be identified. They may be operating on a sound personality or on a vulnerable personality, which, on removal of the vectors, can only return to its pretraumatic state.

The following procedures, alone or together, are employed against the noci-vectors:

1. Resolve the conflict of attitudes from which the vector comes. Thus the quality of the vector can change.

2. Reduce the power of the vector. Frequently, preoccupation with it

allows it to dominate thought and appear more threatening than it actually is. Thus putting it in perspective will reduce its power.

3. Reduce the time over which the vector works.

4. Arouse assets in the individual to measure up to it. Self-confidence allows of healthy coping.

5. Share the experience with the patient and allow other constructive people to do the same.

6. If it is not essential to his interests to meet it, allow the patient to side-step the vector without loss of face.

7. Counter the vector with opposing vectors of greater strength, repeated, and of long duration.

Damage to "idea of self" in the past. The damage is repaired by putting the self through a benevolent new experience. This is a process. A process is a "continuous series of events," e.g., guilt, with its damaging feeling of unworthiness, having been exposed, is countered. The security of the relationship with the therapist or others and the reduction in damage allow maladaptive coping devices to be put aside and be replaced by new healthy devices—usually imitated from the therapist or others. Special attention should be given to the more powerful coping devices listed previously. Insight allows identification of previous damaging vectors; to use benevolent vectors of reverse but greater power than the damaging vectors is central to success.

It is crucial to understand that a process requires time over which to operate. The greater the damage and the longer it has been operative, the longer the period of therapeutic time required. Intensity of therapeutic process can reduce this period.

The greater the damage, the greater the number of unsatisfactory elements in self, and the greater is the therapeutic effort required.

It is fundamental to understand that the therapeutic process need not take place exclusively in the interview situation. The following are possible:

1. An exclusive interview process. This is necessary for very damaged people and calls for frequent interviews over a long time.

2. Guidance by therapist and use of others, especially the family, as allies in therapy.

3. Vector therapy, guided by the therapist. Benevolent influences in the family and outside are utilised to repair the damage to self; they can also be used to counter any psychic noci-vectors in the present.

The importance of the process and the use of extra-interview therapists can be shown by two brief illustrations, one from ethology and one from clinical practice.

Harlow (2) and his colleagues have been conducting for many years a series of intriguing experiments with monkeys. This work passed through a number of phases and has now reached the ultimate in interest. The sequence of events was as follows:

A number of young neurotic monkeys were produced by deprivation situations. Some grew up and the females were mated. They became neurotic mothers and rejected their infants. So severe was the deprivation of the infants left with their mothers, that they had to be rescued. The workers now sought some means of treating these second-generation disturbed infants. They tried behaviour therapy in vain. They tried the care of adult monkeys—but these punished the infants and there was no success. Then they paired a disturbed monkey with a younger healthy monkey. The older monkey did not threaten the younger, nor did the younger impose rules on the older. The relationship prospered and in six months there was a marked improvement in the older monkey. The workers concluded that the young monkey was effective, even though it had never read about psychotherapy!

Here is a therapeutic process at work—and effective. To understand this process is to know the full nature of therapy. We now know a great deal and can hasten and enrich this process. But, even without full knowledge of its nature, the right process can still work.

Mr. X is an angry man. His father was an angry man. His father made him very insecure and damaged his "idea of self." His father ignored him and he is very sensitive to being ignored. It makes him angry—this is the device he adopted from his father as a means of coping. Mr. X is quickly angry—not only with men but with women, his wife, his son, his daughter, his friends. Ignore him and he is angry, and it matters little who ignores him. He feels "little inside," unworthy, despised. Mr. X has help. His preceding family is not available. A strong secure relationship allows him to talk without shame or fear of his early deprivations. But that alone does not make him less angry. The relationship passes into its constructive phase. In a long, intense companionship he is given attention, his assets are realistically emphasised, his self-appreciation improves, and his most sensitive vector, being ignored, is negated by attention.

Others are encouraged to enmesh him in the same pro-Mr. X experience —i.e., benexperiential therapy. Thus therapy was shortened by the use of the extra-interview therapists.

Fallacies

It may be useful to outline some of the major shortcomings of some methods of therapy used at present:

1. *Listening* is not enough. There has been a tendency to regard the therapist's role as being a passive one of listening. This is far from the case. In the diagnostic formal phase there must be active questioning with much participation by the interviewer. In the elucidation of psychopathology the role is less active, but direction is required to cover the whole area and active clarification of data may be required. As we have seen, the therapist has a highly active role in therapy, even if non-verbal; guidance, experiential process work and decision making are essential parts of his role.

2. *Decision making* is an essential part of therapy. It is held that the therapist must never make decisions or even be involved in the decision-making process. This at worst is a deliberate avoidance of responsibility, at best it is bad technique. In surgery such a situation would be unacceptable. Take a moment of decision in psychiatry, e.g., the decision by marriage partners to seek a divorce. This requires involvement. The formula is not "I will make the decision for you," but rather, "We will explore the situation together and my skill will clarify the issues for you better than you can do on your own. In the light of this, you and I will be able to arrive at conclusions. If you and I disagree, I shall make my view clear to you and you have a right to follow the course you wish without my concurrence as to its wisdom, but still with my support. If we agree, you will be able to carry on with my concurrence." Support is never withheld, there is no upset at advice not followed, blame and guilt are not part of the transaction, and for the patients to change their mind later is a possibility. But the therapist does not shirk being involved in decision making. Skill cannot develop in situations where there is avoidance of responsibility.

3. *Diagnosis* must precede therapy and not be confused with it. To garner information, to develop insight are elements of diagnosis. But diagnosis and information collecting must proceed to the point of relevance only. To avoid decision making, it is easy to slip into a situation where it can be said "but we have too little information." This puts off the evil day of decision making. It is not usually relevant to know the colour of the maternal great grandmother's hair before coming to a conclusion as to whether William should live with his father or his mother.

4. *Insight* is not enough. To explore a situation and reveal why a trauma was suffered is not of itself therapeutic. Insight is a prelude to the constructive phase which of itself is therapeutic. To be aware that one's finger hurts because it has turned septic does not of itself open the abscess, but it is an

essential prelude to effective therapy. In psychotherapy, the constructive phase is much more difficult and hence there is a tendency to be content with insight.

5. In decision making, the family or individual has no greater *wisdom* than the therapist; if the latter is competent, he should have considerably more wisdom than the patient. To shirk responsibility it is easy, when convenient, to say, "The patient knows best and can make the decision." But it is the patient's confusion that has brought him looking for help. Psychopathology is a complex field for the most experienced; the patient is usually lost in it and the more disturbed he is, the greater his confusion.

The warming-up period

In every course of therapy, there is an initial phase of warming-up which may extend from a few minutes to several interviews. This is inevitable, as the therapist and the family have to get to know one another. The family has to go through a period of convincing itself that it can allow the therapist to join the family, that it can trust him, have confidence in him, and confide in him as an equal partner. To some extent every interview starts with a warming-up period. The therapist must be sensitive to the need for a warming-up period.

Explanation

It is valuable, at the start of therapy, to explain to the family the expected organisation in general terms. It is possible also to explain to them in outline the rationale of therapy, as stated above. Furthermore, it is wise to point out some of the rules under which the family is meeting; for instance, that every member of the family has equal voice, whether it be child or grandparent. Not all these working rules will be acceptable at first. Again, the family will go through a testing-out period, but the attitude of the therapist continually reminds the family of the working rules.

The facts and no interpretation

Interpretation in family group therapy is in a sense a contradiction in terms. The only truth is the truth of an event within the life experience of a particular family member or a particular family itself. The event does not need interpretation, it is a fact. Thus, a therapist enslaved by interpretation theory will be less effective. It is only the family who know the facts at first.

It can be educative to hear three experts discussing information conveyed by a patient. They can radically disagree amongst themselves, biased by their personal experiences and their school of interpretive psychopathology, but the only true meaning of the information is that given by the fourth person, the patient himself. Broadly, people's experiences follow the same pattern, but the significance of events is unique to each person. Stereotyped interpretations have little significance. The therapist must constantly be on guard against assuming that other people's life experiences are like his own and have to be interpreted in the same context.

The greatest errors are made because of dogma—situations and words are distorted to fit in with the creed. Let me illustrate. A therapist is helping a husband and wife with their marital problems. Discussion turns to sex and they reveal a most unsatisfactory situation in the physical act which has steadily deteriorated since the start of the marriage. The therapist, by his canons, traces everything back to sexual disharmony. Yet data are produced to show that both partners have had satisfactory sex relationships before marriage, succeeded early in marriage and do now on the rare occasions when they are happy together. The partners insist that their problem is one of personal incompatibility. The therapist insists it is sexual incompatability. They seek help for their relationship as they are convinced, and know, that given harmony the sexual intercourse would be satisfactory. But they are offered advice for the sexual disharmony alone.

Some regard objects and even words as having special significance and always to be rigidly interpreted in a particular way, e.g., one therapist equates "dog" with "prostitute." Any mention of a dog carries this hidden meaning. For some people in special circumstances this might be so, but for a large number of people a dog is a dog. The term "gas" by the same therapist is equated with the anus and hides anal eroticism. The word "piece" is equated with an "attractive woman," whenever it is mentioned.

We can see how remote from reality the explanations become when we study this brief extract from an interview:

> Father picks at his nails. Therapist observes this and calls attention to it. At this point son, in defending his father, is critical of his mother as the mother has said this is a disgusting habit. Therapist then makes the remark to son, "What kind of piece would you like to pick out of your mother?"

The therapist claims he made this remark to bring out son's erotic interest in his mother, i.e., mother is a "piece." But he is arguing from analogy, and very approximately at that, and giving special meanings to words. It is father who picks at his nails and not son, even if we accept that to pick at one's nails is hostility. But it is son who is hostile and he is not "picking."

Hostility and picking are given to the son when hostility alone belongs to him. The therapist in his mind then links picking with a "piece"; piece is equated with "attractive woman" (when it could just be a piece of nail or anything). But the word "piece" was first used by the therapist and might reflect his views, but hardly those of the son. Then it is further assumed that the son has an erotic interest in the mother, even though he did not use the term. This is sheer fanciful invention decreed by dogma and takes us away from the facts. The true meaning is simpler and more direct; the son wishes to support his father against the hostility of the mother and the therapist, who has made a partnership with her.

Again, take statements based on preconceived ideas such as: "The child is in love with its mother. This is why he is hostile to his father." But he may love both. Or: "This child (of three) always wants to go to the parents' bedroom in the mornings. He wants his father out of his mother's bed, so that he can have intercourse with his mother." An interpretation is put upon a situation which is not proven; many other explanations are possible. Furthermore, as ideas are based on sexual pathology alone, adult notions are transferred to the child. Situations are made to fit fixed ideas. Chance associations are given casual significance. This distorts the truth.

Patients, individuals and families, do not always find it easy to grasp the significance of events. They are not psychopathologists. They more readily see the significance of a chain of material, rather than of emotional, events. They wish to forget what is hurtful, embarrassing and damaging to the "idea of self." Thus, they must be led to the truth and the truth lies in real events. To misinterpret adds to their difficulties. (But they can come to believe the misinterpretation.) The exercise is only necessary and justifiable if it can lead to what they want—help. Thus, it is necessary to point out, explain, clarify, underline, reveal—but not to distort.

The therapist, equally, may not know. He has not the capacity to know simply by wanting to. He is dependent on data. He must have facts and the facts must be real. The facts are concerned with the people he helps. The therapist may, by his greater knowledge of similar situations, arrive at the truth before the family. He should guide them to the truth—by revelation, clarification, explanation and sometimes by repetition. Explanation must be in words they can understand. If a family comes to the truth in terms of a dogma, then it is likely that the therapist is imposing foreign notions upon them.

There is a time and a way of making a revelation. It should add to security and not take away from it. It should not be a confrontation or a display of hostility. It should be so judged that the family can cope with it, without upset, and it should be used constructively. A statement can be attenuated and pitched at a level which is acceptable at that time. There has to be a delicacy about these things based upon experience of life and a need not to hurt others. Damage can easily be done—a brutal statement to a lady that she is getting old, however true, is unconstructive.

But truth never emerges without rapport; the darker the secret, the deeper the rapport needs to be, and rapport makes for security.

Degree of insight

Insight is the understanding by the family of the mechanisms of the emotions. The greater the disturbance in the family, the less the insight. The developing understanding of the significance of emotional events takes longer with a more disturbed family, but time spent on insight is essential. Understanding, however, is not therapy. It is discernment, diagnosis. Having seen the course of events, it is essential to re-experience and to reconstruct.

Intelligence has no correlation with insight. Dull, undisturbed people can have remarkable insight. Very intelligent, highly disturbed people may have no insight. Intelligence can help or retard interviews; insight has great relevance to the speed of progress.

Silence

The family has to learn that silence on the part of the therapist is an invitation to talk. The easiest interview for the family is when the therapist does all the talking, but this interview is the least worthwhile. The greater the security of the family, the more silent their therapist can be; the greater the skill of the therapist, the more silent also will he be. The therapist moves to non-verbal communication, significant and time-saving. Silence is the biggest and yet gentlest pressure that the therapist can put upon the family to get it to work. However, the family may need to be silent from time to time. During this silent period it is working in contemplation; afterwards may come a true move forward in the family's affairs.

Interruption

The aim should always be to interrupt as little as possible; interruptions result in a break, an artificial break, in the flow of the family's thinking; the wrong comment or question may cause it to go off on a line of thought of less significance, or may give it an opportunity to avoid discussing something which is relevant. Direct questions very rarely bring profitable results.

Far better to ask indirect questions, which will inevitably lead to the area being discussed. For example, it is of little value asking an individual, "How did you get on with your mother as a child?" It would be much more profitable to suggest topics which will inevitably throw light on the relationship between mother and daughter.

The above does not contradict the need to guide. The therapist can pick up cues from what has been said and lead the family to an area requiring exploration. Sensitive areas may be avoided or skirted at first. The therapist makes a note of these and guides the family back to them on a later occasion. This may need several excursions. As rapport and security improve, so the sensitive, but highly significant areas, are dealt with.

Allies in the family

The most disturbed of families has assets. These are of two kinds: (i) Disturbed family members have elements of their personalities that are beneficial to other disturbed members. (ii) A family may have a comparatively healthy member who, given new cues and insight, can have a beneficial effect—even when there is no formal therapy. A therapist must evaluate the assets of the family and use them to the full. Thus family members can be allies in therapy.

Avoidance

Families are naturally uncomfortable when embarrassing, hurtful material springs up. Thus, there will be not only avoidance of such topics, but invention of apparently good reasons for not discussing them. They miss interviews, are late so as to allow little time for discussion, keep silent, raise superficial, irrelevant topics, attack the therapist for his inadequacy, etc. This behaviour is based upon insecurity. Avoidance is hanging on to old coping devices. These are moments for particular patience and tolerance. Even more effective than discussion of this behaviour is to raise topics that will deepen the rapport. As this improves the avoidance melts away.

Family swings

During the course of therapy, the mood of various family members will change; as one improves, another deteriorates, and so forth. These swings are to be expected in the course of therapy. Indeed the mood of the whole family in normal circumstances is a variable entity.

Danger to the family

Management of severe, acute situations in the present or re-enactment of material from the past naturally provokes acute symptomatology. The therapist has a responsibility to control matters in such a way that the risk is reduced to what is reasonable. Family members prone to being epileptic (10% of the population) may have epileptic attacks; others may become accident prone; ulcers perforate; cerebral thrombosis and coronary thrombosis are a possibility; suicidal attempts are made. A careful eye must be kept on the somatic and emotional health of the whole family. Danger must not rise above a manageable limit. Irrelevant, but highly traumatic events, e.g., war experiences, are sometimes best circumvented and left encapsulated in their coping defences. It is not effective therapy irreparably to harm or kill the family—or have the family kill others.

Acting to real trauma and not the object of the stress

Some of the trauma in the present is evoked by trauma in the past, e.g., a husband's attitude reminds the patient of mother or father. But the patient reacts to the image of father or mother only if the husband's behaviour is like that of the father or the mother. The behaviour is the stimulus and not the conveyor of it. Thus, a man who behaves aggressively provokes a bigger response in a person sensitive to aggression than does a man who looks like the patient's aggressive father, but who is not aggressive.

Levels of discussion

The family moves through certain levels of experience in the course of therapy. At first, its concern is with superficial matters of the moment, then it moves to transactions in the present family, then it moves back to its experiences from its early days as a family and, lastly, it moves to the preceding families. The most fundamental therapy takes place at the last level.

Family events

Much profit comes from getting a family to describe actual instances in its own immediate life experience and, as time goes on, in its past life experiences. This is description without interpretation. In this way, a far more factual picture is obtained of real family events and its reactions to them. Subsequently the therapist and the family together can give significance to the events.

Closure

Therapy ceases when the aim outlined at the start has been achieved. Usually there is a weaning-off period which may last for either a few minutes or several hours of therapy, depending upon the family, its needs, and its degree of disturbance and thus of dependence.

Somatic therapy

This must go hand in hand with psychic therapy.

The individual or family reacts as a whole to psychic noci-vectors—thus the soma is affected. Rarely does psychonosis in an individual or family present without somatic complaints which may be severe and life-threatening.

Somatic therapy will be required for:

1. The somatic disorders produced by the psychonosis. Any system in the body may be affected. Examples would be: migraine, ulcerative colitis, thyrotoxicosis, gastric ulceration, asthma, coronary thrombosis, cerebral thrombosis, etc. Furthermore, existing somatic disorders, e.g., multiple sclerosis, epilepsy, will be aggravated by psychonosis. Psychonotics, especially the elderly, eat badly and therefore dietary and vitamin deficiencies may need correction. There may be anaemia for the same reasons.

2. Iatrogenic disorders. These are conditions precipitated by therapy, and can include any of the above.

3. Symptomatic relief. Tranquilizers reduce tension, anti-depressants make depression more tolerable, sedatives and hypnotics guarantee a night's sleep, etc. All these medications carry with them emotional elements— hope, a gift from the therapist, encouragement of something done, suggestive value, and a bridge with the therapist. Drugs must nonetheless be used with caution. In some patients, as they fear any drug medication, they may have a deleterious effect. Also drugs may produce toxic states in some patients and confuse diagnosis.

Features of Benexperiential Psychotherapy

It may be useful to tabulate some of the main features:

1. Benexperiential psychotherapy utilises an experience·which is favourable to the individual or family psyche.

2. It is based upon experiential psychopathology.

3. The "idea of self" is the essential target of therapy.

4. The diagnostic procedure is separated from the therapeutic process.

5. Interpretation is not employed. The experience is all. Thus there is no dogma.

6. The process of re-experience is central to therapy either within or without the interview.

7. Confrontation is not employed; security is encouraged.

8. Decisions are made.

9. It is complementary to vector therapy.

10. Being experiential, it opens therapy to the scrutiny of research procedures.

REFERENCES

1. BLYTHE, R. (1969). *Akenfield*. Harmondsworth: Allen Lane. The Penguin Press.
2. SUOMI, S. J., HARLOW, H. F., and McKINNEY, W. T., JR. (1972). Monkey psychiatrists. *Amer. J. Psychiat., 128*, 927-932.

Vector Therapy

Psychonosis is a preventable condition; it is difficult to cure.

Some of the measures discussed under benexperiential family psycho-therapy are effective in some conditions. However, should none of these measures apply, psychonosis could still be eradicated in a number of generations. This could be achieved by the widespread application of vector therapy, supported by a movement towards the salutiferous society, to be discussed later.

Psychotherapy is a difficult art. Good results are not easy to obtain. Even in situations when psychotherapy is effective, the lack of resources limits its value. Results are difficult to assess; methodologically satisfactory surveys are seldom encouraging. In the present state of knowledge it is understand-able that precision should be lacking.

Yet the prestige of psychotherapy is high. Patients need emotional con-tact, relish hope, and are even less able than clinical workers to evaluate results. The appeal of psychotherapy to the therapist is high, as it represents direct personal help to the patient. When an investment is large enough there is an unacknowledged conspiracy of uncritical acceptance. Resources which would be more effective in vector therapy are wastefully deployed in psychotherapeutic quests. Psychotherapy has its place, but not the right to its present manpower.

Benexperiential family psychotherapy is largely concerned with the pre-ceding family, vector therapy is largely concerned with the present and suc-ceeding families. It allows a beneficial process, benexperiential therapy, to be deployed outside the interview.

Vector Therapy Defined

Constant efforts to produce harmony in the intra-psychic life of the indi-vidual by re-alignments within it have been made for the last 70 years. The emotional force brought to bear has been that of the therapist. But family psychiatry, selecting the family as the unit, exposes the individual as being in the field of forces within the family, which in turn is in the wider field of forces of society. Within these fields there are potent emotional forces, continually bearing, for good or ill, on individuals and on families. These forces, if positive, can be deployed in therapy, but have to be counterbalanced, or removed should they be negative.

Restitution factors operate by chance to change the lives of people to their advantage. For example, a young woman, comfortable but emotionally hard pressed at home, is forced to seek employment due to the illness of her father. What at first seems a misfortune proves to be the reverse. She finds herself, by good fortune, working with employers who, deprived of a daughter of their own, virtually become her substitute parents and compensate for her trying home conditions. She lives for the first time. Many instances could be given of the beneficial changes in circumstances of people—due to marriage, death of relatives, changes in school, changes in employment, movement of relatives, divorce, etc.

In the above example, advantageous circumstances came about due to chance; the aim of vector therapy is to arrange the changes by design in an organised fashion.

Vector therapy is of course a part of benexperiential therapy, as the change of forces produces a new beneficial experience and corrects a disadvantageous one. But it takes place outside the interview, although it may be guided by the therapist.

A vector denotes a quantity which has direction. Force, including emotional force, is a quantity with direction and therefore can be represented by a vector. *Vector therapy readjusts the pattern of the emotional forces within the life space to bring improvement to the individual or family within the life space.*

Vector therapy can involve:

1. A change in the *magnitude* of the emotional force, e.g., father's aggression may be diminished.

2. A change in the *direction* of the emotional forces with no change in its magnitude, e.g., father abuses mother instead of child.

3. A change in the *length of time* during which the emotional force operates, e.g., father works away from home, spends less time at home and his aggression has less duration.

4. A change in the *quality* of the emotional force when one force replaces another, e.g., father is kind to his son instead of being aggressive.

To effect these changes, the source of the emotional force may have to move, e.g., by father going out to work; or the object of the force may have to move, e.g., the child going to boarding school to avoid father's aggression.

An individual moving in time through his life space encounters emotional influences that help to make him an integrated healthy person, but in varying degrees he may meet adverse emotional influences that make for disintegration and ill-health. In either event, account has to be taken of the quality of the influence, its force, its direction and the time during which it operates.

Faced with a disintegrated individual, reintegration is possible by mobilising a set of influences in the present that may still nullify the effects of the previous adverse influence. This can be done (i) by the mobilisation of intense, precise, beneficial emotional influences in the interview situation as well as outside it, under the direct control of a therapist, i.e., by psychotherapy; or (ii) by mobilising less intense emotional influences of a general nature known to be beneficial over a long period of time outside the interview, i.e., by vector therapy. Thus, for example, a child disintegrated by being deprived of the right kind of care, instead of being subjected to psychotherapy, is placed in a foster home selected for its ability to provide the right care. In the latter case, reintegration comes from a new set of beneficial vectors able to act over a long period of time.

Naturally, psychotherapy and vector therapy can be employed at the same time on the same family; they are complementary. Indeed, the process of deploying beneficial experience in psychotherapy in the interview by the therapist can be enhanced by the therapist using allies in the family or outside the family who work on the same formula. In this event the therapist directs both activities, intra-interview psychotherapy and extra-interview vector therapy, and the two lines of approach can be a powerful combination. Vector therapy can also be very effective on its own; the family interviews reveal the nature of the psychopathology, which is resolved by vector therapy alone outside the interview. In vector therapy the therapist does not use his own personality in the experiential process, but still directs the therapy, either alone or with the help of colleagues.

Again, a therapist may direct vector therapy to help the whole or part of a family and use focal psychotherapy to help one family member. This simple abbreviated case history will illustrate.

> The presenting family member is a three-year-old child in status asthmaticus; he is the youngest of four children. The parents are wealthy. Mother has helped her husband build up a large business During this period the three older children have been brought up by a nanny. When the fourth child comes along the business is well-estab lished and mother feels she will change roles and mother this child.

But she is irritable, domineering, forceful. The infant reacts by stubbornness. Conflict develops. Mother is exasperated by her lack of success and drives on. The child's tears turn to sobs and sobs to asthma and, ultimately, to status asthmaticus. He lashes out, refuses to eat and wakes the house with his night terrors. He is seriously ill. The family doctor asks for analysis of the family situation and appeals for urgent help as the child could die.

The above situation is exposed. Help could be offered in two forms: (i) The therapist could employ his personality to gain a picture of mother's weaknesses, based on her life in her preceding family, and then resolve them by focal antecedental psychotherapy. In time she could become a better, if not ideal, mother. (ii) The adverse vectors from mother could be replaced by more beneficent vectors—from, say, a substitute mother.

The urgency of the child's problem dictates the second approach. He cannot wait for his mother to become a better mother after a programme extending three to six years. He could die in the meantime and, in any event, his personality would suffer great damage. Thus, vector therapy is the first choice. A number of interviews, gently and without blame or guilt, bring mother to the point that it is acceptable to change roles back to the original pattern; she returns to the business and a carefully selected nanny takes over the care of the child. The response is dramatic; the status asthmaticus disappears, the child gains weight and sleeps at night. Mother takes the credit for a love that allows her to deny herself the immediate gratification of mothering for the sake of the child. But at the times when they are together she reports "he is fun now."

Now I come to my final point. Using vector therapy as above still does not preclude the use of psychotherapy. This mother had the time, and as it happens the necessary means, to seek some resolution of her basic attitudes through focal antecedental psychotherapy—but at no disadvantage to the urgent needs of the child. Thus vector therapy here helped the family and the child's succeeding family, while psychotherapy helped one family member, the mother, and of course the family indirectly.

Vector therapy is concerned with emotional forces which must spring from a personal source and which are directed at a personal object. It may be useful to list the personal sources of emotional influences which play upon an individual family member and which have to be repatterned through vector therapy.

1. Influences from within the individual.

2. Influences springing from outside the individual and within the family, as follows: (i) from one individual; (ii) from family members who may form a coalition with common features, such as the female members of the family together, or the parents together, or the paternal or maternal relatives together, or the children; (iii) from the family group as a whole.

3. Influences outside the individual and family and within the community, as follows: (i) individuals in the community (these may be enumerated as relatives, friends, neighbours, schoolmates and teachers, workmates and casual acquaintances); (ii) collective community influences.

4. Influences from outside the individual, family and community and within the culture. Cultural pressure exerts powerful control over the major values. Communication media like newspapers, radio, television and national organisations convey these values to people at large.

Principles for the Application of Vector Therapy.

To be effective, a number of general considerations have to be borne in mind when practising vector therapy.

The extent of the family's co-operation depends on the degree of *rapport* achieved by the therapist. This rapport calls for effort and time; the greater its depth the greater the readjustment of forces that can be tolerated by the family.

This is not a matter that can be hastened. Nor will the rapport achieved necessarily be utilised at once. A relationship built up over the years may unexpectedly bear fruit. For example, a family could not tolerate one of their children going to boarding school because the mother had herself been through an unhappy experience in a badly run boarding school. Suddenly, she became aware of a niece who had been greatly helped by such an experience. Facts rather than words convinced the mother. She returned to the therapist and the arrangement for the child's boarding school education was made. But she was able to return only because she knew that there would be no blame and the return would be a happy reunion.

An individual and his family must co-operate with *insight*. Insight springs from understanding. This may be induced by individual, dyadic or family group sessions. The family must see its own predicament and work to define the procedures that will help itself.

Coercion is foreign to vector therapy. It is abundantly clear that families who do not understand why a change is necessary will ultimately frustrate one's efforts. Within a positive relationship the attitude to the patient is— We have a problem. We need a solution. What is possible? Why is such a step helpful? People have good reasons for avoiding actions that can help them. For instance, they may fear the consequences of the steps proposed —their own or the preceding families' experience may have been unhappy in this respect. The fear may be ill-based, irrational and even absurd, but it exists. As it exists, it has to be brought out into the open and facts brought forward to demolish it. Again, guilt is a powerful frustrator of activity. A simple proposal to a highly rejected mother that her daughter be brought up in a foster home is an admission of her failure. Guilt must be assuaged. This is only possible if the proposed change is presented in a constructive fashion. Not, "You are a failure." But, "You have been caught in an unfortunate experience and no one is to blame; you have tried to meet the situation; you need more help; you are willing to accept the assistance to help your child; you are prepared, if need be, to sacrifice the care of the child for the good of the child; you are an admirable mother." Such an approach is only possible if the professional worker believes there is no reason for guilt and blame and can accept that people are the victims of events and not the makers of events.

While insight is necessary, it is still essential for the professional worker to be able to come to conclusions on the available data and offer advice. It is a policy of cowardice to avoid giving advice in order to avoid responsibility. "The patient knows best" is not a tenable situation, unless the worker is ignorant, ill-trained, and unsuitable. It is no more reasonable than for a surgeon to say, "You have a brain tumor, think about it, and tell me if you want it out." The patient will argue, "But how can I weigh up the pathology of a tumour, assess the importance of its site, guess at the possible difficulties of an operation, evaluate the risks of operation as against no operation?" In these circumstances he will ask, "What do you advise, doctor, and tell me the risks?" The advice may be, "You will die if you don't have it out and I advise you do" or, "You will live longer if the operation, which carries a 5% mortality rate, is successful. I advise an operation" or, "Whether we operate or not the chances are the same. What are you most comfortable with?" Advice is definite, while the final decision is left to the patient, but the patient's decision is strongly influenced by the advice given by a trusted adviser and only in extraordinary circumstances is it overruled. In psychonotic situations, too, experts can reach a point when advice can be positively offered. When it is withheld, it is oftener because of avoidance of responsibility rather than ignorance.

There must be a *reliable diagnosis* of the pattern of the emotional forces within a particular family. By using family group diagnosis, supplemented by individual methods of investigation, it should be possible to achieve an accurate picture of the family situation. Unless this picture is accurate, the forces will be incorrectly adjusted and a poor therapeutic result obtained.

This can be demonstrated by a simple illustration which exposes two family situations that appear alike but are in fact different.

> In family A we have four family members: father, mother, paternal grandmother and a grandchild. Father is well adjusted and, almost by definition, so is his mother. The wife is highly maladjusted and brings up her child in a powerful negative relationship. Naturally, the child becomes disturbed. One simple change in this pattern of forces is to send mother out to work, and let the paternal grandmother bring up the child in a positive relationship. The child responds.
>
> In family B we had the same four members, but here the wife is well adjusted. Father and his mother are grossly maladjusted. The dominant grandmother insists on bringing up the child in a negative relationship. The child becomes disturbed. Hence, to resolve the situation, grandmother must go out to work. Mother brings up the child in a positive relationship and the child responds.
>
> Hence, the need for accurate diagnosis. The two situations appear to be the same but are not. What is appropriate action in A is not so in B.

Again, the manipulation of forces is concerned with changing the emotional rather than the material events within the family. *Emotional prescriptions* are required for emotional ills. Experience with highly disturbed families shows that they are unhappy, often despite excellent material conditions. Families of high economic standing are not immune from unhappiness. Again, a sharp improvement in living conditions does not bring happiness with it; people often look back with nostalgia to the happy days of struggle. A material change can help if it changes the pattern of emotional forces, e.g., a move to a better neighbourhood can bring beneficial change if it takes the family away from a nagging, domineering, destructive mother-in-law. Equally, it can be an unhappy change, despite material gain, if it brings the family closer to such a person.

The above is demonstrated by the following:

> An adolescent boy suffered a severe head injury which left him with epilepsy, complete loss of vision in the right eye, about half his vision in the left eye, loss of smell and taste, and damage to his pituitary fossa that led to diabetes insipidus with its consequent massive increase in weight. However, when it came to assessing personality the parents said that there had been such an improvement here that they felt on balance, the accident had been a fortunate event! Before the accident he had been awkward, difficult, disinterested and

they had been toying with the idea of seeking psychiatric help. It might have been tempting to have supposed that the cerebral injury had been responsible for the change. But the mother was quite clear about the reasons. She said, "You see, I know my boy needed more attention. I could never give it to him because his father was jealous. In hospital he got what he needed and I was so pleased." Then, "You see, my husband was a lonely man. He was jealous of my boy and they got on very badly. That's why my boy was so awkward. Then, when this happened, my husband began to go to hospital to have a game of draughts with my boy. They became mates. Now that he is home they are like brothers. Mind you, I get less of my husband's time now, but it's worth it for my boy. My boy is so much easier now. He's a much nicer boy."

In some instances, vector therapy may need to go *hand in hand* with some variant of benexperiential psychotherapy. For example, in family A where the father-daughter hostility is reduced by daughter being brought up by a loving maternal grandmother, with frequent visits from her mother, psychotherapy is not required, as the well-adjusted mother can maintain a satisfactory marital relationship. Indeed it improves when the daughter leaves the home. In family B the situation is not dissimilar. The hostile father makes the daughters' care away from home essential for the sake of the succeeding family. But left behind is an equally unsatisfactory husband-wife relationship. This worsens when daughter leaves, as she has been the scapegoat and taken some of the sting out of the marital relationship. In family B, the marital relationship must be resolved—either by benexperiential psychotherapy or by vector therapy. The departure of the daughter has allowed her to be helped and exposed the basic damaging father-mother relationship, which can now be dealt with as a much less complex situation than if all three family members were together.

Change induces insecurity which must be combated by the therapist's continual emotional *support*. Change is not possible without security—this is a major lesson of psychopathology. Insecurity means the need for old coping mechanisms to operate; the defences are up. Thus, the vector therapist must maintain a secure milieu throughout the operation, which in a badly affected family may go on for years.

Also, just as damage to the personality is produced by negative influences working over a period of time, so it becomes necessary in reparative work to allow *time* for the positive influences to bring results. For instance, a child does not immediately respond to a happy foster home, but goes through a number of stages. For a few days to two weeks there is a "honeymoon period," all is new, strange and different and the child is on its best be-

haviour and so is the home. The child then reverts to its customary behaviour and stage two begins. Over the next nine months or so there is a
steady improvement if the foster home is well adjusted. Stage three begins—
the new changed behaviour is consolidated over time. Thus we must allow
time for change and consolidation.

Furthermore, therapy should not concentrate on any one member of the
family, but should aim at helping the *whole family*. The maximum benefit
comes from the utilisation of services for all family members at the same
time—a total front programme. But, as childhood is the period of maximum
personality development, it is obvious that special attention, if not priority,
will be given in vector therapy to the early age groups.

Exact assessment of family dynamics is now a reality. A worker, using
interview techniques, can aim at targets different from psychotherapy—
effecting rapport with the family, developing insight in the family, prompting
the family to action causing change in their favour in the field of forces, and
deploying those family agencies which can help to produce and sustain the
changes. Liaison between a family psychiatry service and community agencies becomes all important.

At times *separation* of family members—one member or part of the
family from the rest—may be necessary. Partial separation may be required,
e.g., day foster care, day hospital care, day employment for mothers, etc.
Sometimes semi-permanent or permanent separation may be essential, e.g.,
foster care, boarding school care, adoption, etc. At its most skilful, the
separation policy may allow a family to fragment and subsequently for new
and better families to be made from the fragments. This subject has been
the victim of the gravest of misunderstandings which has brought cruel
consequences to children and a major hampering of vector therapy and thus
of the preventative opportunities.

The importance of well-considered separation is such that a chapter is
devoted to "The Evil of No Separation" in the section of the book on
"Special Aspects of Family Psychiatry."

Resources for Vector Therapy

Organised facilities to support Vector Therapy

It will be clear that many of the facilities required for undertaking this
work with families are at present not available in the community and new
services will have to be planned. Community health services are, by and
large, designed to help the physically ill, the psychotic, the retarded, but not
the emotionally ill.

In the past, too, services have tended to be ineffective for a number of reasons. It was insufficiently realised that a "social problem" was invariably a personal problem that would respond to emotional help only and not to material help. Furthermore, measures for the analysis of family dynamics were crude; thus help was applied in the dark. To add to the difficulties, facilities were inadequate. The social worker, through vector therapy, is the main agent of change and now has a promising approach.

Facilities must supply treatment in emotional terms to satisfy an emotional need. It is fundamental to vector therapy that facilities compensate for, or improve, bad personal relationships. The most important therapeutic agent available in the community is a relationship with a well-adjusted individual. Thus it is necessary to mobilise those who are emotionally healthy at the points where they can be of maximum assistance to the unhealthy. The strong must help the weak. At some of these vantage points are found such people as nannies, home help workers, day foster mothers, staffs of day nurseries, staffs of residential nurseries, house parents in children's homes, staffs of special institutions for the deprived and maladjusted, workers for the handicapped, teachers, welfare workers, doctors, nurses, the helping professions generally, and executives of all walks of life. To bring the right people to the right place may necessitate a re-allocation of rewards and prestige.

Much advantage comes from one all-purpose family worker being responsible for the day-to-day continuous support of families. But such a diversity of special facilities can be used to the best advantage only if the specialist workers are available to support the all-purpose family worker. The all-purpose worker must have experience of physical and emotional ill-health, as these conditions are indivisible. Specialist personnel will include health and social workers.

Facilities must exist for children, adolescents, adults and the aged, for all social groups, for all religious denominations, and for the single and the married. Facilities must give seven-days-a-week cover.

A large number of facilities are required to make possible the re-patterning of the psychic noci-vectors bearing within and without the families. Some re-patterning requires *no external facilities*. For example, a child presents at a children's intake clinic in a state of severe and acute psychonosis. Investigation reveals a traumatic mother-child relationship. The father is a sad eye-witness of the deterioration in his child. He is a well-adjusted, caring person who, however, believes that the upbringing of his child is a matter for mother. Sorry, but uninvolved, he spends his time helping community agencies to help others. A number of sessions with father, stamping in him a true concept of the role of father, can transform the situation. The wife joins the discussion and soon accepts help offered by her husband.

He takes on the main parenting role. The wife in this case becomes the secondary parent. Father shifts from activity in the community to activity in the home. There is a dramatic improvement in the child as the benevolent relationship with father replaces the destructive relationship with mother. No public money has been expended except on half a dozen interviews. The parents do not change (though mother could still have benexperiential psychotherapy) but the difference to the child and, therefore, a future family is immense.

By the use of vector therapy and family interviews major changes can be made in the emotional climate of families, even in the absence of family psychotherapy. Three examples will be given, none of which are dependent on either psychotherapy or community resources. By chance, mother is the principal agent in each instance; it could equally be father. The main changes are the reorganisation of the pattern of vectors and roles within the family.

> The first example concerns a family where mother's pregnancy immediately precipitated a severe depression in father. After a difficult pregnancy in which father avoided any discussion of the baby, the child was born. The father had no interest in him and contrived to take his wife from the child whenever possible. The mother arranged for the child to live with loving foster parents nearby. She visited regularly with much enjoyment. A position was reached when father could just tolerate the child at home, and the child returned to live with his parents. After a number of years the mother realised that, due to the antagonism of father to the child, the child was developing signs of disturbance, some of which annoyed her husband. She sought help.
>
> The whole family is seen and the above situation revealed. Mother, now with insight, becomes the vector therapist. By the use of relatives, boarding school and the child's playmates, she so reconstructs the child's life that he and father rarely meet, with immense improvement in the child. The usual triangular situation below is replaced by the horizontal deployment of forces:

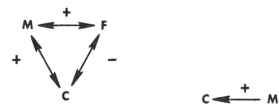

The above is reminiscent of the family situation in our second example. A child was referred to the children's intake clinic for encopresis. After one visit, the mother wrote that the child was so much improved that further attendance was not required. A follow-up visit some months later revealed how this came about. The mother explained that the one visit had confirmed what she had always believed to be correct: her sullen, hostile husband was responsible for her child's state; her child was perpetually anxious. Thus, she reconstructed the life of the family to the child's advantage. Father was encouraged to work at night, thus cutting down contact with the child. The boy had a close playmate who lived nearby. This child's father was especially happy with children. Mother arranged for the child always to be in the other home when her husband was awake at home. The child's tension and consequent encopresis cleared up. The mother had become a vector therapist who had re-patterned the alignment of forces in her child's life and in the life of the family.

The third example concerns a higher income group family where there was intense antagonism between father and his two daughters; "They cannot live together," the mother said. The family came for family diagnosis due to drug addiction in the eldest daughter. Father was hostile, belligerent and alcoholic. Mother was depressed and anxious. The younger daughter was cold, withdrawn and depressed. Exploration revealed the basic situation. Father came from a depressed background in which he had been "kept down, pushed into the ground" by a dominant mother, who believed in harsh discipline for children. The wife came from a happy family, where a relaxed relationship with children was the order of the day. The father needed this loving woman's attention. This she could give. But he demanded all her attention, and became violent and then alcoholic if denied it. Alone, the parents flourished due to mother's capacity for loving. Together with the children, "life was hell." The mother-father relationship was satisfactory, the mother-daughters, excellent, the father-daughters, appalling. With insight developed over a number of weeks, the family now repatterned their lives—a triangular pattern of forces was replaced by a horizontal arrangement. Mother and father lived together, happily. The daughters moved to a flat nearby. Mother visited regularly. The daughters visited father at specified times for short periods—these he could manage.

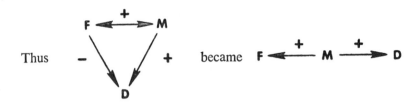

Thus ... became ...

To effect a change of emotional forces, a *large number of facilities* are called upon, even in just one family. For example, in one family the following facilities were employed:

1. Duration of contact between a violent father and his son was reduced by father becoming a night worker.

2. More beneficial male influence came from encouraging the boy to spend time with his uncle, the mother's well-adjusted, pleasant brother.

3. The family moved nearer the well-adjusted maternal grandparents and away from the interfering, dominating paternal grandparents, bringing much relief and support to the mother and allowing the boy to spend time with the maternal grandparents—again to his advantage.

4. The boy reacted badly to a strict school teacher, thus a change of school, bringing a more benevolent teacher, was effected.

5. Father mismanaged his men at work, and they retaliated. He was given a job of equal status, but not involving employee management, with benefit to himself, the factory and his family. At the same time, father received psychotherapy at late afternoon appointments.

Psychotherapy and vector therapy are complementary.

As has been said, many changes can be made in the pattern of the vectors without using *community resources*. Frequently these resources are required. They have to be planned for every age group in the family. They can involve no separation of a member from the family, partial separation, or complete separation. The accompanying table indicates some, and only some, of the resources. These can be regarded as samples. Once the principle is accepted, many other resources will come to mind.

Of the age groups, childhood is the most important, as children are more likely to change in their formative years. They also represent the future. Infants are the most important age group of all. Right decisions made early in the life of a child will be to his benefit throughout his life. Yet there is a reluctance to make decisions in the early years, especially if they involve separation.

Yet sometimes crucial decisions have to be made even before the arrival of a child, early in pregnancy. Most children are a joy to a mother, but in particular circumstances a child may be unacceptable and destined to be unwanted and unloved. A woman, by terminating a repugnant pregnancy, can wait for the auspicious moment when she can give birth to a loved, wanted and welcome child.

When an unwanted child is to be born, there should be no forcing of the issue about his care and no decisions based on rigid rules. Each case is unique. The mother's true feelings should be allowed to emerge and a decision made in terms of care by the mother (or the often forgotten father), or by foster parents until the mother's situation resolves itself (it should not be deferred over long). Caution should be exercised in giving the care of illegitimate children to grandparents. Frequently (but not always) the grandparents are responsible for the young mother's emotional state that led to the illegitimate pregnancy; they have already proved themselves not to be the best home for a child. These early decisions are crucial and have far-reaching consequences for the child and the health of families in the future.

It can be seen that even if children find themselves in highly disturbing homes (at least 10% of the population), their emotional health can still be guaranteed. The home may be changeable without removal of the child, if some of the resources listed are brought into play; e.g., the right nanny can transform the life of the child, a wrong one can wreck it. The United Kingdom, and Winston Churchill, owe much not to his mother, a distant figure, or his father, whom he is said to have met for only an hour in his whole

I	II	III
Care at Home	*Day Care Away from Home*	*Permanent or Semi-Permanent Care Away from Home*
AGE 0-5		
(a) Relatives for substitute parenting	(a) Day foster care in foster homes and special day nurseries	(a) Foster homes
(b) Home Help Service (substitute parenting)	(b) Selected child minders	(b) Adoption
(c) Selected nanny (substitute parenting)	(c) Nursery schools and classes for emotionally disturbed infants	(c) Care by voluntary bodies
(d) Sitter-in service (substitute parenting)	(d) Therapeutic play centres	(d) Convalescent homes for children and/or parents
(e) Home visiting ("good neighbour service")		
(f) Playmate supportive figures (soft toys)		

I *Care at Home*	II *Day Care Away from Home*	III *Permanent or Semi-Permanent Care Away from Home*

AGE 5-17

I	II	III
(a) Relatives for substitute parenting	(a) Day infant, junior or secondary schools for maladjusted children	(a) Foster homes
(b) Home Help Service (substitute parenting)	(b) Evening, week-end and holiday adventure playgrounds and clubs	(b) Adoption
(c) Selected nanny (substitute parenting)	(c) Special care in ordinary schools, e.g., remedial classes	(c) Boarding foster homes for the school child
(d) Home visiting ("good neighbour" policy)	(d) Day hospitals	(d) Hostels for maladjusted children
	(e) Change of day school or class within a school	(e) Boarding schools for maladjusted children
	(f) For adolescents, groups for education in family life	(f) Selected boarding foster homes and hostels for adolescents in employment
		(g) Care by voluntary bodies
		(h) Convalescent homes for parents and/or children
		(i) "After-care" hostels
		(j) Planned holidays
		(k) In-patient units

AGE 17-60

I	II	III
(a) Home Help Service (supportive)	(a) Sheltered employment	(a) Selected boarding homes
(b) Sitter-in service (respite)	(b) Selected firms	(b) Hostels for maladjusted adults in employment
(c) Support by general practitioner, home nurse and social workers	(c) Day hospital care	(c) "After-care" hostels
(d) "Good neighbour" policy	(d) Evening, week-end and holiday clubs	(d) Convalescent homes
(e) Adult therapeutic groups	(e) Social centres	(e) Night hospital
(f) Selected part-time work for mothers	(f) Change of work	(f) In-patient units
(g) Family Planning Service		(g) Divorce
(h) Emergency advisory service		(h) Work away from home
		(i) Night work

I *Care at Home*	II *Day Care Away from Home*	III *Permanent or Semi-Permanent Care Away from Home*
AGE 60+		
(a) Home Help Service	(a) Clubs for the aged	(a) Houses with separate rooms for elderly parents
(b) Supportive work by all agencies	(b) Day hospital care	(b) Independent flats
(c) "Good neighbour" policy		(c) Supervised flats
(d) Therapeutic groups for the aged		(d) Hostels with flatlets and warden
(e) Emergency advisory service		(e) Hostels
		(f) Convalescent homes
		(g) Holiday Homes

life, but to his caring nanny, Mrs. Everest, the old lady who appears so vividly in his only novel, *Savrola,* as his comfort and help. Given a home of moderate pathology, some of the day-care procedures can be employed. When separation is necessary, some of the listed resources come into play.

One of the stumbling blocks in the substitute care of the young is to assume that natural parents provide better qualities of parenting or caring than others. Many parents are excellent, most display a degree of failure, some fail very badly, a few are deliberately destructive. Equally, substitute parents, most of whom are already parents of their own children, will display the same degrees of capacity—excellent, a degree of incapacity, severe degree of incapacity, positive hostility. But inherent in vector therapy is the notion that only positive vectors are employed in its practice. Therefore, the substitute parents are selected. They are selected for excellence. Thus one improves on the mischance that came the way of the disturbed children. This is illustrated by the following example.

A mother is referred with depression. She gives a life-long history of psychonosis resulting from gross depression in her own home. In adolescence, she found herself pregnant by a man whom she refused to marry, whom she despised and from whom she ran away. She had the child and found herself with no interest in him. He was placed for a short period in a foster home in the hope that she would take to the child when the feeding problems were improved. The child was returned to her. She found herself unable to feed him on the breast despite the pressure of the nurse. The child's health deteriorated again and a lengthy hospital admission followed. He was returned to his young mother. She struggled on with him and then decided to have him adopted. Her own mother objected, as in her eyes this was improper (after all, she had struggled on with an unwanted daughter and this daughter should repay this by looking after her own son.) She placed the child in a day nursery and matters were somewhat easier, and so she battled on.

However, the child soon became unmanageable. She sought help and he was taken on for child psychotherapy. There was a temporary improvement, but no real change. She lost hope—she had sought expert help but there was no change. She became depressed and was herself referred for help. In a few interviews the above story emerged. She is frank about her distaste for this child of a man she despises. Two policies are possible: (i) Psychotherapy for mother, to change her personality so that she can love this child—a massive task needing resources for a number of years. Can the child wait a number of years? Will she then be better as a mother than a willing adoptive mother? For *this* child she is less adequate than an adoptive mother and, indeed, does not regard the child as her own. (ii) Accept that she will never feel that this child is hers. Arrange for a loving adoptive home for the child at once. Relieve stress on the mother. She may yet meet a man she can admire and love and whose child she can accept. The second alternative is clearly the measure of choice.

Due allowance must be made for chance restitution factors in childhood or later. Allowance must also be made for the few people fortunate enough to have had the advantage of psychotherapy—and to have benefited from it.

It has already been said that the most valuable therapeutic force is a relationship with an emotionally healthy person. How does one select such people to man the day nurseries, day foster homes, special schools, hostels for disturbed children, in-patient units and the helping professions? The principle, and it is paramount, is that the individual is not selected, *his family is selected*. Emotionally healthy persons, epitomes of healthy, warm, well-adjusted families, are those few people who can have the toleration, capacity, resources, width of reaction, charity, and kindness to make significant changes in the emotionally sick. Thus the families of the applicants are screened. This of course must be done with great care; families may appear less inadequate than they are. In this way the strong are truly deployed to help the weak.

Some of the resources require brief further comment.

It must be accepted that there are families where mothering and fathering, i.e., parenting, is inadequate, whilst the community stands by passively watching a disturbed infant grow up. The community, however, can act by changing the pattern of emotional influences playing on the child. It can apply the practice of *day foster care,* which is the planned separation of child from unsatisfactory parents for as long as possible during the day to supply the child with satisfactory substitute parents. Once it is accepted that separation need not lead to deprivation, it can be seen that this can be an important practice in preventive psychiatry. Carefully selected foster parents accept children boarded to them for the greater part of the day. For the same purpose, it is possible for these infants and young children to attend well-staffed nurseries. This procedure is only possible if the utmost care is given to the selection of staff, chosen for their ability to give the children positive parenting, understanding, and receptive care. In other words, the child receives in the nursery or in the foster home, through the day foster care programme, those ingredients necessary for his emotional health, missing within the home situation. A change of emotional forces has been brought about. Here is a good example of day foster care happening by chance:

A young mother sought an opinion from the children's intake clinic. Her problem was as follows: The product of a highly disturbed family, she was blessed with a loving supportive husband. Her marriage was sound and the happiest episode of her life. But she had a three-year-old son, with whom she battled all day long; tears, temper, punishment were the order of the day. The husband picked up the pieces in the evening. One day, on leaving the beach, the child refused to put his coat on. He was in the midst of a temper tantrum when a middle-aged women who was passing by stopped and came over; in a few minutes he was playing happily with her. The younger mother told the older of her problem. They came to an understanding; after breakfast the child would be taken to the older woman who would care for him during the day, and he would be collected from her home before father's return in the evening. The arrangement worked wonderfully. Father came home to a relaxed mother and child. But fate intervened in the form of the patient's mother-in-law; she was abashed that her daughter-in-law did not care for the child herself. The young mother asked: "Who is right, my mother-in-law or I?" She was congratulated on her perception; she had organised day foster care on the principle of vector therapy.

In an older age group, an example of a useful procedure is that of the special *therapeutic club*. Usually, disturbed children or adolescents are excluded from child or youth clubs. They are regarded as too disruptive to the club as a whole. It is felt that average or healthy children suffer by having this disruptive element among them. Thus, disturbed children have no option but to remain outside in their unhappiness, or to get into more trouble. These therapeutic clubs accept such disturbed children. It is an essential criterion of membership that the child be emotionally disturbed or antisocial. A healthy child cannot be admitted to such a club. Once accepted, the club supplies positive, emotional parental care. This it does through careful selection of staff able to supply the necessary nurturing. A high ratio of staff to children is required. The children are stimulated to interesting project work, in the course of which they come into contact with adults able to supply them with the understanding and warmth which they require. Sometimes a group relationship is not possible; then the group has to fragment so that one individual can be dealt with alone. The same type of club can be extended not only for the evening, but also for weekends and through the long holiday periods. The adverse parental influence is replaced by a beneficial substitute influence; again a change of forces has been effected.

This type of club could be organised under the provisions of "Intermediate Treatment" for delinquent children, as suggested in the United Kingdom (Intermediate Treatment. H.M.S.O., London, 1972). The key is not the activity itself, but the marshalling of warm, positive adults in a close constructive personal relationship with the delinquents.

Therapeutic play groups are a useful resource. The play group movement is spreading like wildfire in the United Kingdom despite the anti-separation philosophy of many authorities. In one town with a population of about 100,000 there are over 50 official play groups. Experts are often wrong, and to disregard expert opinion that fails to work in practice is a healthy reaction. These play groups can be formally organised to allow specially selected warm, sound parent figures to give substitute care to children.

Informal groups are also possible. Hence nurses and social workers can bring small groups of about five mothers together. Each looks after all the children for one morning a week. Thus the children are guaranteed the company of each other and the undivided attention of an adult every morning. These groups should not contain more than one, or at the most two, disturbed mothers; the healthy mothers can only contend with this proportion.

Divorce and remarriage is perhaps the most extensive operation met with clinically. Some families need to fragment when the degree of incompatability is such that it cannot be remedied. Not every family situation is modifiable and, if it were, the resources for its modification are still not available. The absence of resources cannot be overlooked; it is fatuous to assume that somehow, somewhere they will be found. There are not enough resources to go around, and there will not be for decades yet. This is a fact of life. In the meantime, families need relief. Divorce is one relief, sometimes followed by—and here they need help—remarriage to a more compatible partner. It is a bad and sad principle for parents to keep together "for the sake of the children." In most, but not all, circumstances this adage will guarantee a deformed childhood for the children. Far more valuable for them is to be brought up within an advantageous pattern of forces in a remarriage.

At divorce, children are often given to the custody of the mother. Legislation in many countries is biased in favour of the mother. However unsuitable she is, the children are left to her untender care. Courts should have the advice of expert opinion in allocating the children to the parent best able to care for them. When remarriage is pending, this should be taken into account. More liberal divorce laws will take much of the bitterness out of divorce actions, allow more collaboration in making arrangements and more willingness to give consideration to the requirements of the children. So will the quality of families improve.

Most mothers profit from going out to *work;* they are better mothers for it. The more disturbed and failing the mother, the greater the need for her to work. It is a daunting, destroying business to be battered all day long by the children. Much is heard of the negative influence of the mother on the child, but little about the traumatic effect of the child on the mother. The mother's self-confidence is not encouraged by acknowledging her own failure. Respite is required. Thus the two parties are helped. The children receive the compensation of the care of a day foster mother or day nursery; the mother, the satisfaction of succeeding at work and the company of fellow employees.

Substitute care away from home can be arranged in *boarding establishments* of various kinds—hostels, boarding schools, special boarding schools. These must be selected for their capacity to give substitute parenting for a particular child. Hostels give home care, and the children go out to school; they have the advantage of giving care throughout the year. Special boarding schools give home care and education under one roof; they may tend to specialise in the latter. They have the disadvantage of giving care within the school terms only. They then may need to be supplemented by camps, foster homes, etc., during holiday periods.

Day hospitals are for those children, adolescents, adults and the aged beyond the facilities of the resources mentioned but able to live at home during the night. They should not only give occupation or recreation, but also be governed by the principles of benexperiential therapy.

Benexperiential in-patient units

The structure of these is discussed under "Organisation" later. They are of many forms, catering for all age groups from infancy to old age, dyads, and family groups.

One principle applies to all—the therapy is through a *process* of re-experience by carefully selected staff. Unlike the therapeutic community, the crucial relationship is patient-staff and not patient-patient. The handicapped cannot give to the handicapped. The patient does not go through a formal course of therapy. He goes through an informal *process of re-experience*. The staff need not have the sophistication of book-happy, academic therapists. They need the positive, constructive, love-producing experience of a happy preceding family. The patient is bathed in a pattern of communication from staff that supplies a mature, secure, formative, encouraging, re-experiencing milieu. Some day we may guide this process with precision, distil it to its essential ingredients and supply these in strength. We do not need to wait on that day. Benexperiential process is available now.

Not only do patients, individuals or families, gain from removal from the psychic noci-vectors outside, but they profit from the beneficial vectors within. A patient's stay is governed by his requirements; the greater the degree of psychonosis the greater the length of stay. The more chronic the psychonosis the longer the stay. The damaging effects of wrong experiential processes cannot be undone in an instant; the re-experiential processes need time over which to operate.

The optimum size of an in-patient group is that of a family of patients and staff of about seven in number. All in-patient units for psychonotics should be organised on the benexperiential process principle. When the staff is in doubt about an action to be taken they should ask themselves, "What would we do in our own families?" If they come from the right kind of family the action will be correct. Following discharge, the patients should not return to the process which produced the damage that made in-patient care necessary. This pre-admission situation should be resolved or by-passed.

With the hospitalised patient, whether accompanied by his family or not, no evaluation is made or procedure undertaken without relating it to the context of his family. This does not mean that the individual must always remain in contact with his family. His and their particular need may be for him to escape from it. But this manipulation will be undertaken more effectively if evaluated in terms of the total family situation. It leads to a flexible use of hospital facilities—sometimes for an individual, a dyad, a part, or the whole of the family. The admission procedures involve a family evaluation, as do the ward regime and discharge procedures. The out-patient and in-patient management should be a continuous whole. Members of the family are not mere "visitors," they are participants in the clinical process. Thus, a family may join a member who is a hospital in-patient for therapy at stated intervals.

Indications for the admission of the whole family are:

(i) Inaccessibility of the family due to distance.
(ii) Separation for therapeutic reasons from another family with whom they are sharing accommodation.
(iii) Crisis.
(iv) Family diagnosis.
(v) Research.

A Salutiferous Society

The third approach to experiential family therapy calls for consideration of the concept of a salutiferous, health-promoting society (1). In the long term this is the most effective help to society, the family and the individual.

The family is the basic organism in society. As a constituent of society it contributes to society. Equally, society contributes to it. Each family relates to all the other families that make up the psychic environment outside itself. It benefits from the influence of the environment outside itself; it can equally suffer. The more health-promoting, salutiferous, is society, the more will its families benefit.

Thus it is essential to examine society for its health-promoting potential. Should the functioning be inveterate, set and permanent, this would be a wasteful exercise. Its malignant permanence would have to be accepted. Fortunately, society, like the family and the individuals, is endowed with the capacity to change. Its infinite pattern of functioning can be restyled; herein is society's capacity for health. In the final hierarchy of phenomena, the pneumococcus is as significant as a person. In some circumstances, it might even have greater importance than a person. In our set of circumstances, the pattern has to be moulded against the pneumococcus and in favour of man. Man has the capacity to develop awareness to the point when he can, within the limits allowed him, reshape the pattern of functioning to his advantage. Hitherto, his predominant endeavour has been concentrated on adjusting his material environment. With this task largely accomplished in developed countries, there should now be resources to re-pattern the psychic sphere of living.

The author sees society as a vast field of forces in which elements are loosely defined—culture, community, neighbourhood, family, individual; essentially each element has equal significance. The emotional forces within the life space produce degrees of well-being or harm and they can be repatterned to promote either. Understanding of this potential for change in either direction allows the conscious selection of patterns of emotional forces toward bringing well-being to society and to the elements within it. Thus, through generations, a reshaping of the emotional stratum of society has great opportunities for society's emotional self-improvement.

Much thought and print has been expended in attempting to define health. It is easier to feel it than to define it. Its correlates are easy to delimit and describe—emotional and physical well-being, the capacity to adjust to life's stresses, the ability to cooperate with others, unselfish actions born of security, efficiency, and productivity. All these indicate harmonious functioning in the individual—what he feels is the comfortable state of "being well."

Most definitions of health are in terms of the individual; it may be more realistic to attempt it in terms of society, which ultimately dictates the state of its elements, families and individuals within it. It might be thought that society is sick only in the sense that it contains a number of sick people. It is more correct to say that society itself is sick and therefore must contain a number of sick individuals. At the moment, forces within society are arranged in a pattern that provokes emotional ill-health, which flows from one generation to the next. Society carries within it the capacity for health because its fields of force carry the potential for rearrangement. This fact makes clinical endeavour worth while. Health and "normal" behaviour of course must not be confused. The normal, usual, statistically average state of emotional functioning in society is far from "health." With each succeeding generation it is hoped that the emotional norm will increasingly approximate to health—a state of affairs being achieved slowly and with difficulty in the field of physical health.

The clinician's endeavour is the production of health. In family psychiatry the goal is a healthy family, with, of course, healthy individuals, a task always limited by the fact that social ill-health pulls the family towards conformity to its norms. Over the generations, small gains in the rearrangement of the vectors will have a cumulative effect on society. Gains can be made at individual, family and social levels, and the process is indivisible. For the present, the family is the vantage point. Progress can be made only at the speed with which knowledge develops. But clinical effort carries the prospect of new insight; research and clinical work go hand in hand.

It is one of the central themes of this book that discernment must come before change, diagnosis before therapy. So it is with any effort to make society health-promoting, or salutiferous. It is necessary to know what is required for healthy human functioning—be it individual, familial or social. The lessons of health often emerge from a study of ill-health. Thus, the first step is a massive assessment of dysfunctioning in society. It can operate at three levels: (i) what accounts for the dysfunctioning in society as an organism (where do its harmful leaders, movements, collective aggressive acts, etc., spring from); (ii) what accounts for the contribution of society to the dysfunctioning of the family (what harmful values, habits, restrictions, etc., does it impose on the family); and (iii) what accounts for the involvement of society in the dysfunctioning of the individual (what harmful psychic noci-vectors spring from its institutions—schools, industry, neighbourhoods, etc.).

Central to any evaluation is to establish standards. Paradoxically, standards of health often emerge only after an examination of ill-health. The absence of ill-health is easier to ascertain than the presence of health. Over time, sometimes as the result of trial and error, the pattern of optimum functioning for a salutiferous society will emerge. A further complication is added by the fact that what is optimum functioning at one moment in history is not optimum functioning at another. Fortunately, change takes place in collective human functioning at such a slow rate that this is unlikely to be a serious complication. It might be supposed that change in society takes place very rapidly today. But this would only be true of material change; the level of general psychic well-being in the most materially developed of societies is often not only very low, but lower than in materially poorly endowed societies.

It may be useful to contrast briefly what is being said about the creation of a salutiferous society with what is termed "social psychiatry." This latter has been the subject of much confusion, especially concerning such aspects as "therapeutic communities," "therapeutic milieu," "community psychiatry," etc. The first two are concerned with the climate of psychiatric institutions, a humanising movement that allows of more patient involvement, greater freedom, and a constructive group feeling; they are a reaction to the rigid institutionalisation of the last two hundred years, and only partly ameliorated, here and there, by the efforts of Pinel, Chiarugi, Conolly, and Tuke in the 19th century. Community psychiatry has affinity with social psychiatry and the terms are often used synonymously. It is a movement that wishes society to take a larger share of the care of the mentally ill, who, according to it, should remain in the community. Thus, it emphasises the need for day hospitals, hostels, etc., to keep patients in the community rather than in hospitals and the need for "after care" agencies to facilitate their discharge from hospitals. All the above are elements, but only a few, within a health-promoting society, a salutiferous society. The salutiferous society is concerned not only with the management of the identified ill, but much more with identifying influences that encourage dysfunctioning, and then re-patterning social living so that the level of emotional, and not "mental," functioning improves. It has to do not only with the management of the alcoholic, for instance, but with all the adverse practices in society that set up the particular combination of psychic noci-vectors that precipitate alcoholism.

The salutiferous society has affinity with the preventive movement in the physical field that has made such a significant contribution to the improvement in the standard of physical health. It is more useful to talk of the promotion of health, than the prevention of ill-health. It is easier to persuade a person to win a race than to persuade him not to lose it. Hence, health promotion and the term "salutiferous." The salutiferous society could be said to embrace both psychic and physical health; here it will be employed as it relates to the former. Indeed the two are indivisible, as change for the better in one encourages an improvement in the other. In preventive organic medicine there has been a systematic analysis of those elements in life which are antagonistic to physical health. The tubercle bacillus was isolated, it was shown to have a bovine form, the bovine form was transferred by the milk of affected cows to children and hence bovine tuberculosis that was responsible for such deformities in children in the past. The understanding of this process led to large-scale preventive procedures largely by promoting the health of cows. (As in physical medicine, so in psychic medicine, the understanding of pathology is the key to health promotion.) It will be noticed that curative and health-promoting medicine go hand in hand. Clinical work led ultimately to the isolation of the tubercle bacillus; preventive measures then took over. Curative medicine is both a palliative and a research endeavour. Similarly, there is no contradiction between curative and preventive psychic medicine. They complement each other. Psychic medicine has its palliative and research functions and leads to large-scale health promotion efforts.

Satisfaction of material needs to a large degree, together with the recognition of emotional phenomena, makes it now within our grasp to enter this new phase of social action. A perceptible improvement may be all that can be achieved by community action in one generation, but this will have a cumulative effect over the generations. Individuals are most susceptible to emotional influences in their early, formative years, and special attention should be paid to this fact when planning community measures. Thus the psychiatric service for children has a duty to make its findings on the emotional life of the child known to those agencies able to effect improvements in community living.

To conclude, the concept of the salutiferous (health-promoting) community is based on the idea that the whole emotional stratum of society should promote healthy emotional living. The family should lie in a field of forces conducive to its well-being. Thus, following an examination of the field of forces, a re-patterning of the forces takes place, which will encourage optimum conditions for emotional health. The programme calls for an examination of every aspect of social functioning, its standards, roles, institutions, organisation and aims. Every one of its multitudinous facets should be examined to assess its value in promoting emotional health. Those which are conducive to health should be retained; those that are antagonistic to health should be changed. The concentration is not on a sick person, the patient, but on the emotional self-improvement of the whole society. Over the generations, increasing self-improvement will result in a salutiferous society that supplies optimum conditions for emotional health in itself and its elements—culture, community, neighbourhood, family and individual.

Towards a Salutiferous Society

It is outside the scope of a book devoted to principles, to explore every avenue of social functioning. Thousands of instances from hundreds of areas would be necessary to approach a complete account. A few areas, and a few elements within them, will be taken for the purposes of illustration.

Values

Much harm comes to people from a common tendency in society to be critical of others to the point that they feel worthless, culpable and guilty. Some social institutions, for instance some religious movements, mistakenly regard this as a pathway to salvation. Underlying this widespread failing is a feeling of inferiority—others are blamed, cut down to size, so that the critics can feel superior. The widespread employment of this mechanism leads to immense unhappiness. Its removal would be a positive step towards happiness. It is clearly insufficient to expect that awareness alone will alter this practice. But it is a first step. The underlying inferiority also needs management.

Again, force and coercion, despite centuries of historical lessons pointing to the value of the reverse, are employed as instruments of social policy on an international, national and local level. "Force from force will ever flow," in the words of Shelley, is a truth. Force evokes insecurity, inferiority, bitterness, hostility and a determination to react, if possible, with greater severity. Even if there appears no alternative to force, an avowal to use as little as is necessary to accomplish the task would be a valuable contribution. Just as force is a step backwards in interview psychotherapy, so it is in social action.

Competition has the virtue of encouraging creativity, effort and achievement. But it must be balanced by the right motives and be aimed at the common good. There is an optimum degree of competition which, if exceeded, becomes destructive to others and the individual, family or community. In education, children are frequently encouraged to be in severe academic competition with one another. Some obtain an excessive idea of their prowess. Some lose hope forever. At the same time an attitude of selfishness is inculcated which makes for sharp antagonism to others in many walks of life at a later date and fosters a disinclination to co-operate. An excess of the competitive spirit is destructive.

Legislation

Laws are ultimately created by the regulators of society, leaders, or by public opinion, to put into practice what is thought to be right for the common good. But some of the precepts on which legislation is based are themselves harmful. Whether or not the examples given below are correct is immaterial. The lesson to be drawn from them is that legislation should be evaluated for its emotional effects on society.

Divorce is sometimes regarded as an attack on the family and thus it is made difficult. It is thought that excessive divorce could kill the family. Yet a high divorce rates does not mean fewer families. Men and women are strongly attracted to each other and, following divorce, often come together in new unions. Should these new unions be satisfactory, they will not terminate, but will produce well-adjusted epitomes who will go forth and found stable succeeding families. We should endeavour to steer the divorced partners towards healthier unions. Again, it is supposed that highly incompatible partners should stay together "for the sake of the children." But this practice is an attack on the family. It must create such a climate of disharmony that it produces disturbed children, who will in time found unstable succeeding families with a tendency to break up.

There has been much discussion in recent years on the advantages or otherwise of extending the control of childbirth into the first three months of pregnancy by allowing termination of pregnancy on the request of the mother. Some of the discussion (2) has turned around the philosophical issue of when the foetus can be regarded as a human entity; religious and legal bodies can hold vividly differing viewpoints, from the opinion that conception is the moment when life starts, to the opinion that an intrauterine age of 36 weeks indicates viability and independent existence. Even the Roman Catholic Church, in its long history, has found this decision of great complexity and, in the mid-19th century, changed its definition to its present attitude. But to the woman such discussions are irrelevant. To her the moment of psychological acceptance that she has a child is the crucial moment. Some develop an image based on willing acceptance at conception, to most it comes with "quickening" at about the 16th week, to others at birth—and for some acceptance is never achieved. The latter do not wish to nourish and produce an unwanted entity. Nor is it desirable to society that they should do so. Unwanted children are at risk emotionally. Thus it could be argued that to extend birth control into the first three months of pregnancy is highly desirable in that the mother has a last chance of preventing the birth of an unwanted child. The control of conception is now, but only now, universally regarded as desirable. Indeed the controversy over termination has suddenly underlined the value of birth control. But those who now oppose termination previously opposed the use of the "pill" and, before that, of contraception in general. This faces us with another subject for close study in a salutiferous society: What determines rigidity of attitudes? Those rigid in one direction are invariably so in another.

The subject of divorce leads to a consideration of another aspect of legislation. This is the tendency in law in many countries to give preferential consideration to the mother. The unique value of parenting by mother has been emphasised as an element in the extraordinary doctrine of psychoanalysis. In divorce proceedings in some, but not all, countries custody of the child is invariably given to the mother. Often this is correct. But each situation should be carefully evaluated and, in some circumstances, the child, and hence his succeeding family, would benefit from custody by his more loving father.

Authority

A society requires control and regulation. The regulation should arise as a willing acceptance by people that its laws are apposite and in the public interest. A basis of public support makes law enforcement much easier. Nevertheless, a machinery is necessary for law enforcement and this is usually placed in the hands of the police. The police can be regarded as friends and allies, but all too often they are regarded as a threat and as enemies. Thus there can be hostility between the public and its servants. The attitude of the police in these circumstances is crucial. Unnecessary force and belligerence lead to hostility and fear in return. Guns are met by guns. The greater the public hostility, the more insecure the police and the harsher their actions in self defence. From this confrontation come insecurity, fear and damage to a large number of people—no less to the police. Yet the right partnership can easily be developed. And it can start in childhood. By incidental help over small matters, children can grow up firmly convinced of the value of police as friends. This can be enhanced by the police being actively involved in positive welfare programmes.

Societies need a machinery for massive collective action, they need a government. The control of this machine means wielding massive power. The machinery should be so constructed that its power is always at the behest of the people, or delegated to those under the public's control. Those who wish for personal power naturally regard governmental machinery as a ready access to power. The misuse of power can deploy the whole of national organisation into a pattern of stress for its people. Probably no country has yet achieved an ideal prescription for the control of the collective national power.

The control of power can be the subject of early experience. Most children attend an institution, the school, where power has to be exercised. A number of people have rights—parents, headteachers, teachers and pupils. The school is far more than just a platform for the acquisition of knowledge. It is a slice of life. Thus, the way in which power, leadership, group relations, regulation, beliefs and logic are dealt with makes an indelible impression on children. The functioning of our schools and their advantageous or disadvantageous contribution to a salutiferous society is worthy of study.

Organisation

Some methods of organisation lead themselves to personal satisfaction, others to inferiority, disillusionment and the misuse of power. The inflexible use of the pyramidal structure is such a method. Essential in some situations, it is destructive in others. The pyramid consists of workers at the periphery with a hierarchy of power, usually termed "administration," above. This is highly damaging in any situation in which the focal point is at the periphery and where the aim of the organisation is to give maximum service at the periphery. This is especially true of the helping professions. In them, there should be satisfaction in personal communication and the best people should be deployed. However, the best people, whether or not they have administrative gifts, are pulled away from the periphery up the pyramid by higher rewards and a refusal to be supervised by those less adequate than themselves. However, it is possible to create just as effective a system by a horizontal organisation, i.e., rewards and power going equally to all. Those with administrative flair are encouraged to organise, but with no greater rewards, and no more prestige or status, than their colleagues. The old guild system was very effective. An apprentice, or a trainee, learnt the craft and aimed to be a master craftsman; the journeyman was awaiting a master post or falling short of the necessary skill; the master had equality with all other masters.

Mention has already been made of the deployment of the invaluable, emotionally healthy section of society. Emotionally, the healthy are the salt of the earth. They have an invaluable asset, the capacity to communicate health to others. As a part of the programme of vector therapy, they must be deployed to act as a curative force for the psychonotics. In a salutiferous society, they must be deployed at key points—nurseries, homes, schools, the helping professions; they promote health and thus raise its standard.

Groups of people have an optimum size and structure for the most effective functioning. This applies not only to small groups, but also to estates and townships. It has been shown, for instance, that to create a township of young people leads in time to heavy demands for child care, which must be supplied, and ultimately leads to an aging population that can receive no support from the young.

Practices

People are more important than parents. More important for a child than right care from a parent is right care from somebody. The right care does not necessarily depend on the person supplying it being a "parent." Yet the assumption that only parents can give the right care denies children help from many ready sources.

Again, some people, due to happy childhood experiences, have great capacity as parents. But some have none, others very little. Yet once designated as parents, persons have heaped on them complete and continuous responsibility for supplying loving care, and utter condemnation for failing in their responsibility if they are unsuccessful. We should be realistic and accept the varying capacities for parenting. Once this is accepted without blame, it becomes possible for parents lacking capacity to share responsibility with others without a feeling of failure or guilt. This in turn would make much easier the task of the helping professions and allow for the fortunate public with great parenting capacity to come helpfully forward without a feeling of competitiveness with the natural parent.

Knowledge is being slowly gained about the factors that control selection of complementary marriage partners. This can lead to a much higher prevalence of happy marriages. Basically, the more balanced people are, the greater the choice. Again, families should have a hand in selection. Happy family members choose those that conform to their families. Thus family selection in the old days was often successful. A formal test should be a deep and lengthy pre-marriage experience. Formal engagement should be replaced by trial marriage.

For a child to love a brother, sister, mother, aunt, nanny, teacher or playmate is acceptable. It is felt that a number of loving relationships are a virtue and an asset. Yet the same child, once grown up and married, must deny close loving to others outside the family circle. This is an artificial constraint, often not accepted in practice, but a widely held delusion. Again, it is supposed that the future of the family is protected by hostility, jealousy and deceit. Once families are secure, they will be able to add to their own strength and security by a pattern of loving, interlocking relationships.

Teaching

Teaching conveys facts; it does not change attitudes. Many essential functions in life are easily carried out; but there may still be a failure to do this because of underlying emotional attitudes. Mental defectives can manage intercourse; a university professor, because of attitudes that inhibit him, may be unable to do so. Educating him about the procedures of intercourse, giving him data he probably already possesses, does not overcome his emotional block. Thus there is a limit to what can be achieved by education in health matters. But where there is ignorance, education can overcome it, and it can extend the range of those people already adjusted enough to be able to make use of further data. Education is most effective with well-adjusted people, those who are already the best performers. It is less effective with the emotionally ill, those in most need of assistance.

To convey right information is a small but valuable part of a salutiferous society; many countries devise schemes for teaching mental hygiene. Slowly, knowledge is garnered about some of the nodal points in the life experience of a family—birth, sexual practices, preparation for marriage, childbirth, preparation for death, bereavement. But, notoriously, experts can be wrong. There is no greater fool than an expert fool. Because of emotional biases extraordinary errors can be made—for example, preoccupation with the breast feeding experience, instead of the infant's whole waking experience; an almost total absence of interest in fathering; unchecked hypotheses about the child's sexual life; separation being accepted as synonymous with deprivation, and the "natural home is better than any other home" philosophy; the mother-child relationship overvalued and the father-child relationship undervalued. False propaganda does harm. Much of the propaganda handed out during "mental health days" is ill-conceived. Little attention is paid to the meanings conveyed to the public. For example, the impression is often given that the mentally sick are peculiar and extraordinary. While this may attract some monetary help to these unfortunates, it also perpetuates the fear of mental illness. The terms "insanity" and "emotional disorder" are not clearly differentiated or understood by the public. Furthermore, the confusion causes the emotionally ill to be reluctant to seek help lest they be classed with such peculiar and extraordinary patients. Sometimes the emotional needs of the propagandists militate against a healthy approach.

REFERENCES

1. HOWELLS, J. G. (1963). *Family Psychiatry*. Edinburgh: Oliver & Boyd.
2. HOWELLS, J. G. (1972). Termination of Pregnancy. In: Howells, J. G. (ed.) *Modern Perspectives in Psycho-Obstetrics*. Edinburgh: Oliver & Boyd; New York: Brunner/Mazel.

VII
SPECIAL ASPECTS OF
FAMILY PSYCHIATRY

Fathering

Fathering is an element in family life as distinct as mothering. Yet legal enactions, social policy and art forms, in Western culture, although not in all cultures, neglect fathering in comparison to mothering. The neglect of fathering is at its greatest in contemporary child psychiatry and psychology. In fact the father can be a major factor in health or pathology. To restore balance this neglected aspect of family life will receive extra attention here.

Some psychoanalytical writers do not regard fathering as an element in family life as distinct as mothering. In this connection, Ackerman (1) states: "I am inclined to believe that there is no separate fathering instinct." Proponents of this point of view regard any tender, kind, solicitous care of the infant by father as "mothering." This carries the implication that such behaviour by men is not masculine—yet it is regarded as a virtue in the marriage relationship. The same view regards these qualities as borrowed from, or an imitation of, the mother and not intrinsic to the father.

Again, this viewpoint tends to emphasize the biological function of the mother in child care—that she alone bears and breast feeds the child. Furthermore, it is assumed that father is a latecomer to the child's life— arriving on the scene only when the child begins to talk and be independent. All these views can be challenged.

The author asserts that fathering is an element in family life as significant as mothering. Fathering and mothering may have many components; most are probably in common, a few may be dissimilar. There are more likenesses in mothering and fathering than there are differences. Both are the product of an intimate emotional experience with their own parents of both sexes; they must absorb components from both. Both also have much in common with relatedness elsewhere—foster parenting, adoptive parenting, marital relatedness, grandparenting, etc. A child in his tender years requires this protective relatedness from any source—normally, it is given equally

341

by father and mother, sometimes better by father or mother, and sometimes better by others. Each situation is unique.

Again, to overemphasize mother's biological role in bearing the infant is to overlook the psychological climate of conception and pregnancy. The acceptance of father by mother may be the predominant factor in leading to the acceptance of a child from him, and uniquely from him. Thereafter the parents become a pair linked in a common endeavour, in which, however, only one of them can physically bear the yet unborn child. The father's thoughts, feelings and actions influence the mother's regard for her child and thus, indirectly, the child. Striking evidence of the father's involvement is seen in the couvade syndrome (9).

The first child emerges into an already formed psychological group situation of father, mother and child. The group of a second child is a larger one, consisting of four people. The child may be introduced to the group in any order—often he meets father first, if the mother is incapacitated. Thereafter, what he receives from each member of the group is dependent on their feelings for him, their capacity for relating, and the roles given them. This is infinitely variable and unique for each family. The one thing that a father cannot do for his child is to breast feed him—although there are isolated instances of the child being soothed at his father's nipples. In the contemporary bottle-feeding society, this is not the handicap that it might appear. All else a father can do directly for his child.

When not directly participating in his care, the father still influences his child through his intimate relationship with the mother; after all, a father normally regards a child as a tangible evidence of his own union with the mother. The child is fortunate in the insurance of two parents, whereby one can compensate for the other. Father supports mother and child. Equally, mother supports father and child. The part played by a particular father, or a particular mother, is dependent on their own previous family, clan and social experiences.

After a brief discussion of fathering in the animal kingdom and in anthropology, fathering will be evaluated as it stands in contemporary society. Without diminishing the role of the mother, it is hoped that the role of the father will emerge as an essential component of family group life.

The Animal Kingdom

By selecting the appropriate facts from a mass of evidence, one can support almost any point of view. Students of child nurture have not hesitated to seek support for their hypotheses from ethology—in the study of animal life both in the artificial conditions of the laboratory and in the wild.

Again, it is mothering which is invariably the focus of study. Argument from analogy is always dangerous and never more so than here.

The main lesson to be found from the study of the care given to young animals is that nature is flexible. The need is to nurture the young so as to continue the species. Depending on the situation, nature will use a variety of means to achieve its purpose. Parenting in many forms will be employed; paternal care will often be an ingredient in this, and sometimes it will be the only care. Most important to the young is not *who* offers the care, but that care is given. The intensity of care and quality of care varies with the species—nature meets the need by means appropriate to the situation with a broad concept of parenting and a flexible utilisation of the means available. *Parenting* is more important than the parent.

Paternal care is employed by animals. Indeed, sometimes it is the only parental care, as a few examples will show.

In the stickleback, the male selects the territory for his nest and builds it. He attracts the female and persuades her to spawn in his nest. The male may receive eggs from a number of females. Their work consists only in supplying the eggs and after that is completely over. Thereafter the male fertilizes the eggs, cares for them and brings up the young. Caring for the eggs includes guarding them and "fanning" them by inducing a flow of current over them. The young are kept together in a swarm by the father, who is quick to chase and catch in his mouth those that wander.

The males of some marine catfish and other catfish found in the rivers of South America carry the eggs in their mouths until they hatch. They do not eat at all during this period. The father's interest in his duties does not wane after the young fish hatch, for he swims with them for a time and, when danger threatens, holds his mouth open so that the frightened youngsters can dash into it to safety.

Among Emperor penguins, care is predominantly by the male, as the young live in the male pouch while the female goes off in search of fish. The male phalarope bird builds the nest, is courted by the female, and after the eggs are laid, takes over the entire responsibility of incubating them. In most ostrich-like birds, the males undertake the incubation of the eggs.

Darwin's frogs of Chile use the male vocal pouch as a nest where the young are incubated and emerge as young frogs. In the midwife toad of southwest Europe, the male looks after the string of eggs and, when these are ripe, hatches them in water. The female seahorse lays her eggs in a pouch within the male, who thereafter has the care of the eggs and of the young.

Sometimes the paternal care is selective; in wild cattle, the male calves, but not the female, are looked after by the herd bull. Nature may also offer substitute paternal care. The female hornbill, for instance, is imprisoned in a tree hole and fed by the male. Should this male die, another unattached male hornbill will take over the fathering.

Especial attention must be given to the primate animals as being most closely related to man. As in man, diversity of methods of care is the striking finding and it may include care by males.

Infant care can be a group activity involving different age groups and both adult sexes. Russell's (8) commentary on hierarchies in Japanese monkey bands states that the females approve of male interest in infants and, when females with young are having their next babies, middle-rank male leaders and middle-rank sub-leaders may take charge of the one-year-olds. Baby sitting is a way of ingratiating themselves with the females.

In baboons, as Devore (2) reports, the birth of a new infant absorbs the attention of the entire troop. From the moment the birth is discovered, the mother is continuously surrounded by other baboons, who walk beside her and sit as close as possible when she rests. Juvenile and young adult males express only perfunctory interest in the infant, but older males frequently come and touch the infant. The degree of interest shown by adult males varies considerably. On several occasions the most dominant males carried young infants on their bellies, as long as 20 minutes in one instance. All the adult males of the troop are sensitive to the slightest distress cries of a young infant and will viciously attack any human who comes between an infant and the troop. Adult males, even young adult males, allow infants to crawl all over them with impunity. Jealous protection by the adult males continues unabated as the infants grow and the older infants and young juveniles increase their efforts to entice them into a play group. By the end of the tenth month the infant, who until now has depended largely upon its mother for both companionship and protection, looks to its peers for companionship and to the adult males for protection. In the description of the mother-infant relations in the baboon, Devore stresses that the relationship of the infant to the adult males is important at every stage of the infant's maturation. Devore goes on to mention additional examples of male care.

Zuckerman (11) describes what appears to be a very similar relationship in the London Zoo colony between an infant and an adult male hamadryas baboon after the death of the infant's mother. Itani (4) has described in detail a routinised form of paternal care in Japanese macaques during the birth season. Devore concludes that the evidence from baboons and Japanese macaques suggests that social bonds between adult males and infants are very strong in these terrestrial species, in striking contrast to the weak bonds between infants and adult males in more arboreal species, for example in langurs.

Perhaps the most striking example of exclusive male care is provided by the marmosets of South America (10); the male takes the young to the female for suckling, but this is the only child care allowed to her.

This brief study of infant care demonstrates the variety of methods employed in the animal kingdom for the care of the young, methods that are repeated in human societies. That care is given is more important than the method, or the individual employed. It should be noted that fathering in the animal kingdom is an entity as well defined as mothering—if the term "instinct" is employed it would apply as much to fathering as to mothering.

That there can be great variety within one order or even within one family of animals is also noted; hence the danger of generalizing within even one family. It may be that the capacity to adjust by replacing one method by another is greatest in the higher vertebrates and is put to its maximum use in homo sapiens.

Anthropology

Each culture imagines its way of child rearing and family life to be the best. An appraisal of history and of many cultures today shows how varied are family patterns and child care practices. As in the animal kingdom, nature is more concerned that the human child should have the required care than she is about the way in which the care is given; over the latter she displays variety and flexibility. Her main instrument for child nurture is a group, the family. Fathering, within the group, is not neglected, as will now be demonstrated.

Amongst the Arapesh, for instance, Mead (5) states that the father plays an equal part with the mother during pregnancy. The child is thought of as the product of father's semen and mother's blood. The child's conception is a joint endeavour, and during the early weeks of pregnancy, following the cessation of menstruation, the father "works" to produce his child by strenuous sexual activity with his wife. His involvement with mother and infant after the child's birth is so close as to earn the phrase that he is "in bed having a baby." The child's strength is also thought to be dependent on the father, who is forbidden sexual intercourse until the child can walk and is then believed strong enough to withstand the parents' sexuality again. The care of children is regarded as the task of both men and women.

Again, on the island of Manus, in the Admiralty Islands, Mead (6) reports that the father is the dominant and the tender, loving parent. After the birth of her first child, the mother lives with her family. Then she returns to her husband's house and from the first he takes a fiercely possessive interest in the child, male or female. As soon as the child can stand, the father takes the child from the mother. She is set to work, while he spends all the time left free from his fishing with the child. The child is his constant companion and at night sleeps with him (even the female child until she is seven or eight years old). The second-born gives mother a child for a few months, but, at this time, the first-born moves even closer to his father. The life of all the children is around the father, whether he be their natural or adoptive father. There is a strong personality resemblance between the adopted children and their adoptive father.

As often appertains in primitive societies, should the social economy require father and sons to work together, then father may exert a great influence on the upbringing of sons, and mothers, conversely, on the upbringing of their daughters.

Not only do anthropological studies demonstrate instances of exclusive paternal care, but they challenge, too, an over-rigid definition of the qualities required in "masculinity" and "femininity." Mead (5) quotes her experiences in New Guinea. The Arapesh ideal of a man is that he should be mild and responsive; the Arapesh ideal woman should be the same. The Mundugumer ideal is that of a violent aggressive male and female. The Tchambuli reverse what we commonly regard as masculine and feminine attitudes—their ideal woman is dominant, impersonal and managing, while the man is dependent, art-loving and unmanaging.

Social anthropology reveals the same variability and flexibility in the care of the young homo sapiens as in the animal kingdom. What is appropriate in a given situation is the means employed. The family group is paramount, and within it fathering has an important place; in a particular milieu there may even be exclusive care by the father.

Fathering in Contemporary Society

Father is largely neglected in contemporary social literature on the family in most countries, and the available literature concentrates on a few aspects of fathering only. There is support for the idea that the absence of father may have an adverse effect on the family. This carries the implication that he means something when present. The literature suggests that he plays a part in child development, but authorities disagree about its nature. Some see father as secondary in the contemporary family, while others give him a more powerful role. Some direct studies suggest that his participation is greater than expected.

The Newsons (7), for instance, found a high degree of participation by fathers in the lives of the children they observed. They found, for example, that 57% of Social Class I and II (upper professional) fathers were highly participant, 61% of Social Class III (white collar), 51% of Social Class III (skilled manual), 55% of Social Class IV and 36% of Social Class V (unskilled).

Again, Gavron (3), in a sample of middle-class parents, found 44% of the fathers would do and, in fact, did everything required for their children from playing with them to soothing them when they cried at night, from feeding them to changing their nappies. A further 21% were rated very helpful by their wives, which meant they would do most things as a matter of course, but drew the line at one or two things, usually changing nappies. Another 31% were rated by their wives as interested but not helpful. Only 4% of the wives in the entire sample rated their husbands as non-participant.

In working-class families, Gavron found, as with the middle-class families, that the degree to which the father participated in the lives of his children was quite striking, and the degree of participation was even greater than among the middle-class families. 52% of fathers were rated by their wives as doing anything and everything for their children as a matter of course. A further 27% were prepared to do most things, drawing the line as did some middle-class fathers over changing nappies, and getting up at night. Of the remaining 21%, 12% were considered "interested but not helpful" and just over half to be uninvolved in their children's lives.

Precise figures are available on the extent of fathering from the Ipswich Thousand Family Survey. Table I shows the pattern of relating by mother and father in each year of the child's life up to the age of 10 years. Some obvious conclusions emerge: (i) Father's relating amounts to an average of 12.71% of the child's relating time during 24 hours during the whole

TABLE I

PATTERN OF RELATING OVER TWENTY-FOUR HOURS
BY AGE OF CHILD (WHOLE SAMPLE)

Age of Child	% Relating Time	
	Mother	Father
1	25.84	12.10
2	26.72	12.05
3	25.99	12.97
4	25.16	13.62
5	26.85	12.25
6	21.38	12.57
7	22.50	12.85
8	20.38	13.64
9	19.04	13.02
10	19.89	11.88
AVERAGE	23.45	12.71

ten years; mother's period of relating is twice father's relating time. (ii) Father's relating time amounts to approximately the same per cent for every year including the first year of the child's first 10 years. Mother's contribution tends to decline with the years. This does not support the common contention that father is less interested in his children in the first two years.

It would be interesting to know whether the father is less interested in his children than the mother or whether he has less opportunity, by the nature of our economic system which dictates that fathers are more often at work than mothers. The latter contention is supported by the figures relating to the time of day; in the evening mother's per cent of relating time fell from 23.45% for the whole day to 19.23%, while father's contribution rose from his average for the day of 12.71% to 16.05% in the evening. Again, when the figures for the day of the week are considered, it is seen that father's per cent of the child's relating time increases from the average of 12.71% for the whole week to 18.71% on Sundays; indeed on Sundays it is only just short of mother's per cent of relating time—23.38%. We can conclude that, given the opportunity, father appears almost as interested as mother and shows no less interest in the first few years.

It is questionable whether fathering is a recent phenomenon; to a considerable extent it has always been active. However, some writers have assumed a recent increase in fathering and give a number of reasons for the change. It is argued that the small modern home brings the child closer to father; but the poorer classes have always lived in small houses. The absence of servants forces the father to help mother with the children; but most families have never had servants. That mother now tends to work forces father to help; but in many societies, women have always worked. The equality of the sexes, it is thought, may make the modern woman more independent of her husband, and thus able to demand help from him. Furthermore, she sees her role in terms not too different from his; thus, sharing of roles is more possible. Affluence in society calls for less hours of work, and father can participate more readily in family life. It should be noted that, in varying degrees at different times, these reasons have always applied in some societies.

Neglect of Father

To conclude, the neglect of father in the literature on contemporary society is striking; in most of it, it is assumed that child care is matricentric. The small amount of literature available is contradictory; research on such an important topic is small, often indirect and, in general, concerned with secondary issues. Some direct studies suggest that father participation is greater than expected. Research is rarely concerned with the nature of fathering.

Reasons for this neglect in the Western world may be several. In the Christian religion, a far more prominent place is given to Christ's mother, Mary, in His upbringing than is accorded to His father, Joseph. The Madonna and Child have been a frequent subject for the artist in the last 1,900 years; Joseph and Child are rarely depicted. Again, by tradition in the Western world, the man assumes the main role of breadwinner, while the woman has charge of home and children. This may help to explain how, where women traditionally work, the parenting is more likely to be a shared responsibility.

The reasons for the neglect of fathering in child psychiatry that may emerge from an investigation could include the following: (i) The tendency for mothers to accompany children to clinics may lead to neglect of fathers and the assumption that the mother alone is involved in the child's problem. (ii) The fact that child psychiatrists are frequently women may introduce a bias through empathy with the female parent—this is especially likely to happen if the psychiatrist's mothering capacity has been frustrated. (iii) There is sometimes a tendency for attention to focus on the intrapsychic illness of the child patient, for which his parents are assumed to have no aetiological significance, and his mother only was assumed to need guidance in the management of his illness as the operative parent. (iv) In the childhood of adults, and of child psychiatrists, there may be more subtle factors that, in the Western world, set up a preoccupation with the mother—especially the idealization of the mother. For example, preoccupation with the problems of family life is greatest in those who have suffered adverse family experiences. Thus selection factors may bring less well-adjusted individuals into the field of child care, who would assume that their anomalous backgrounds are characteristic of family life generally. There may also be selection in terms of social class; child workers may come from backgrounds where servants, and thus less participation by fathers, were common.

The Father in Clinical Work

Just as bad mothering has a capacity to cause pathology in the child, so has bad fathering. That this is largely ignored in psychiatry is apparent. The neglect seriously limits the practice of child psychiatry. The father is a significant element in the child's life from conception—he influences the child, for good or evil, (i) directly, (ii) through the mother, and (iii) as a contributor to family climate. The child's meaning to the father determines father's attitudes. Father may be a focus of stress to a child, to several children or to the whole family—but meaningful only in that particular family. Like the rest of the family, father may help to shape the symptomatology of the child faced with his stressful family situation. He may be a sick family element in need of therapy, he may conversely carry considerable potential as an ameliorating therapeutic force. Thus the father must be evaluated as an element in any clinical exploration of the family. Legal provisions have yet to give father a just place when guardianship of children is considered at divorce; the needs and rights of the unmarried father have had even less consideration. The neglect of father in any study of child care is a serious omission in the assessment of an important variable. Research should not only be directed to fathering, but also to the factors that have led to his neglect hitherto.

Conclusion

The means of child care are less important than the needs of child care. Parenting is more important than the parents. It is maintained here that in parenting, fathering is as distinct an entity as mothering. While pleading the acceptance of this truth, it must be understood that both are but two elements in the total family matrix.

REFERENCES

1. ACKERMAN, N. W. (1958). *The Psychodynamics of Family Life*. New York: Basic Books.
2. DEVORE, I. (1963). Mother-infant relations in free-ranging baboons. In: Rheingold, H. L. (ed.) *Maternal Behaviour in Mammals*. London, New York: John Wiley.
3. GAVRON, H. (1966). *The Captive Wife: Conflicts of Housebound Mothers*. London: Routledge and Kegan Paul.
4. ITANI, J. (1962). Paternal care in the wild Japanese monkey, Macaca fuscata Fuscata. *Primates, J. Primatol.*, 2, 61–93.
5. MEAD, M. (1935). *Sex and Temperament in Three Primitive Societies*. London: Routledge and Kegan Paul.
6. MEAD, M. (1962). *Growing Up in New Guinea*. London: Penguin Books.
7. NEWSON, J., and NEWSON, E. (1963). *Infant Care in an Urban Community*. London: Allen and Unwin.
8. RUSSELL, (1967). *The Listener*, 77, No. 1985.
9. TRETHOWAN, W. H. (1972). The Couvade Syndrome. In: Howells, J. G. (ed.) *Modern Perspectives in Psycho-Obstetrics*. Edinburgh: Oliver and Boyd; New York: Brunner/Mazel.
10. WENDT, H. (1965). *The Sex Life of the Animals*. London: Arthur Baker.
11. ZUCKERMAN, S. (1931). *The Social Life of Monkeys and Apes*. London: Kegan Paul, Trench, Trubner.

Families Nurture Children

Families make more families. The representative from the present family to the succeeding family is an integral part of the first family and carries its ingredients into the second and so into the future. This representative is the child. This child is nurtured in its impressionable and formative years by the whole family. It is fallacious to assume that the child is nurtured only by its mother. The part father can play has been emphasised in the previous chapter.

For a number of reasons, Western culture has tended to overlook that the child is brought up in a group situation, the family, and has given undue emphasis to one element in the group, maternal care. It is an unusual situation for an infant or child to relate to his mother alone, even in the first few days. In the nuclear family, it relates to father, mother and siblings; but nuclear families are infrequently as small as this, and in addition often have within them grandparents, parental siblings, friends, servants and the child's peers. The contribution of each member of a group to the infant is variable; mother may be paramount in giving care; less often father may have the major role—or a grandparent, a relative, or a sibling. The care given by any family members, including mother, may be constructive or destructive, depending on their personal qualities and the meaning of the child to them. To be part of a group gives the child protection; what one member of the group lacks in his care may be supplied by another; for homo sapiens, nature did not "put all its eggs in one basket."

To prove that the child is nurtured in a family group calls for a brief review of some of the relevant findings of the Ipswich Thousand Family Survey. That the concentration of care given by father and siblings is no less than that given by the mother emerges from another analysis, that of *One Boy's Day*. Both studies will be reviewed here.

351

The Ipswich Thousand Family Survey

By studying a random sample of 100 children in each year of age up to 10 years, making a total of about 1000 children for the 10 years, it was possible by time sampling to establish the percentage of relating time between the child and all other possible humans during a 24-hour period. The findings for each year for the first 10 years are to be found in Table I. It should be noted that "relating time" is greater than "actual time," as of course relating can go on with a number of people at the same time.

Relating is defined as the position of one person with respect to another and offering the possibility of communication. The investigation studied the pattern of relating as it applied to a random sample of children 0-10 years in the town of Ipswich during one year while the child is living at home. The pattern of relating is studied (i) throughout a 7-day week, (ii) for school attendance weeks and holiday weeks, (iii) for each month of the year. The 1000 families are a random sample selected from birth records.

The first and clearest conclusion that can be drawn from Table I is that the child during these impressionable first 10 years relates to a number of people—mother, father, siblings, relatives in the home, others in the home, acquaintances outside the home, peers outside the home, and others

TABLE I

PATTERN OF RELATING OVER 24 HOURS BY AGE OF CHILD
(GIVEN IN PERCENTAGES)

Age	Mother	Father	Siblings	Adult Relatives	Others	Acquaintances	Peers Out of School	Peers and Teachers	Alone	Asleep
1	25.84	12.10	12.81	6.79	0.71	2.58	1.53	0.06	0.47	37.09
2	26.72	12.05	16.26	6.19	0.02	4.10	2.54	0.04	0.39	31.67
3	25.99	12.97	20.03	6.29	0.20	2.91	2.23	0.08	0.40	28.90
4	25.16	13.62	21.27	4.54	0.46	3.61	2.63	0.74	0.39	27.57
5	26.85	12.25	19.97	5.02	0.44	4.15	1.92	0.56	0.66	28.17
6	21.38	12.57	19.32	3.82	0.21	3.06	2.81	7.84	0.55	28.44
7	22.50	12.85	17.94	4.45	0.01	3.22	2.35	7.29	0.66	28.72
8	20.38	13.64	19.27	3.18	0.18	3.42	2.68	8.39	0.47	28.39
9	19.04	13.02	18.87	2.98	0.09	3.69	2.65	10.81	0.72	28.13
10	19.89	11.88	19.58	4.60	0.00	4.12	3.78	7.92	0.84	27.39
AVERAGE	23.45	12.71	18.62	4.79	0.24	3.49	2.51	4.27	0.55	29.37

at school. It is equally clear that this fact also appertains in the first five years and also in the first year.

Most of the time is spent in the home; for the whole 10 years, 89.27% of the time (including sleeping time). In the first year this amounts to 95.34% of the 24 hours. It can be seen that the mother, father and siblings are the main relaters in the home, while adult relatives are a significant influence also.

The mother is the longest relater, amounting to 23.45% of the relating time; the siblings come next with 18.62% of the time; and father next with 12.71% of relating time. In view of the prominence given to the mother-child relationship, it is very important to note that this is considerably less in duration than that of the rest in the family, 23.45% compared with 36.36%. The mother is the longest single relater, but the rest of the family collectively have a far longer relating time. In the first year the same appertains, 25.84%, as against 32.41%. The proportion of mother relating to all relating (in and out of home) is 23.45:46.63, i.e. 1:2.

That father spent less time with his children is due not so much to his lack of interest, as to lack of opportunity, due to being the main bread-winner in the community under study; this is supported by the fact that in the evening his time approximates to that of mother, 16.05% (Table II), as against 19.23%, i.e., 83% of mother's time. This increases on Saturday (Table III), and on Sunday amounts to 80% of the time spent by mother. Father's time spent with his children was similar in all income groups with a slight increase in the higher income group and a small drop in the lower income group.

TABLE II

PATTERN OF RELATING ACCORDING TO TIME OF DAY
(IN PERCENTAGES)

Time	Mother	Father	Siblings	Adult Relatives	Others	Acquaintances	Peers Out of School	Peers and Teachers	Alone	Asleep
MORNING	28.78	14.72	23.47	2.40	0.19	0.69	0.81	1.81	1.33	25.81
DAY	31.76	15.16	25.02	7.42	0.35	6.10	4.29	8.18	0.09	1.63
EVENING	19.23	16.05	16.15	4.06	0.19	1.96	1.47	0.01	1.62	39.26
NIGHT	1.16	0.61	0.07	0.04	0.00	0.01	0.00	0.00	0.06	98.05
AVERAGE	23.45	12.71	18.62	4.79	0.24	3.49	2.51	4.27	0.55	29.37

TABLE III

PATTERN OF RELATING ACCORDING TO DAY OF THE WEEK
(GIVEN IN PERCENTAGES)

Day of Week	Mother	Father	Siblings	Adult Relatives	Others	Acquaintances	Peers Out of School	Peers and Teachers	Alone	Asleep
MONDAY	24.33	11.36	18.12	4.37	0.15	3.43	2.54	5.37	0.65	29.68
TUESDAY	23.20	9.26	17.21	4.20	0.76	3.14	2.35	7.46	0.57	31.84
WEDNESDAY	22.56	9.49	18.24	4.73	0.45	3.67	2.60	7.02	0.44	30.81
THURSDAY	23.34	11.05	17.11	5.76	0.00	4.07	2.79	5.12	0.47	30.29
FRIDAY	23.98	10.60	17.61	4.34	0.14	3.54	2.16	5.93	0.49	31.20
SATURDAY	23.36	16.78	21.36	4.37	0.02	3.81	3.22	0.02	0.49	26.56
SUNDAY	23.38	18.71	20.09	5.63	0.18	2.86	1.95	0.26	0.73	26.22
AVERAGE	23.45	12.71	18.62	4.79	0.24	3.49	2.51	4.27	0.55	29.37

An important finding that emerges from Table I is that father's relating time with his children is not significantly less in the first two years. Contemporary psychoanalytical theory maintains that father is not a significant factor in the first two years and that when contact does occur he takes on a "mothering role." The facts suggest that the father's influence is direct, as strong as in any other age group and consists of himself in a fathering role rather than any qualities borrowed from his wife.

An interesting finding was the amount of time spent relating to siblings. For the first 10 years this amounted to 18.62% of the day (Table I) and was not much less than the time spent with the mother. The significance of the influence of child upon child has been grossly underestimated in the literature on contemporary child care.

That mother, siblings and father should account for the majority of the relating time emphasises the importance of the nuclear family in child care, especially as it is by far the commonest type of family.

Concentration of care: Analysis of One Boy's Day

Relating offers the possibility of interaction with another, but does not of itself tell us how much use is made of the time for interaction. It could be argued that some members of the family circle were more active in making use of communication and therefore they would be of greater significance in having an effect upon another family member. It was possible to analyse (2) this feature of relating in an allied investigation which will now be reported. By great good fortune an American study is available which made a very exacting study of 24 hours in the life of a seven-year-old boy. So detailed are the data that it is possible to make an accurate measurement of the amount of relating time spent with his possible objects and, furthermore, to make an estimation of the amount of communication between the boy and the same objects. By comparing the second chart with the first it is possible to estimate the use made of relating time for communication and thus compare the concentration of interaction given by the relating persons.

This study—*One Boy's Day* by Barker and Wright (1)—is astounding in its detail, reporting for one day the minute-by-minute life of a boy of seven in an American town. The authors of the book offer no analysis or interpretation of their observations; they merely report the facts. However, so detailed is the study, that it has been possible for the author to determine from the facts reported (i) the number of minutes of physical contact between the child and those around him, and (ii) the active use the child made of this physical contact with others around him as a means of communication.

One waking day, consisting of 813 minutes, was chosen for observation in the life of this seven-year-old American boy in a small American midwest town; it was a weekday, Tuesday, in 1949, during the time of the year when the child was attending school. The period of waking time was 7.00 a.m. to 8.33 p.m., i.e., 813 minutes. Eight observers were chosen, seven of them well known to the boy. They each had an observational period of approximately 30 minutes and each recorded every fact and impression in a minute-by-minute diary. Everything the boy did and said was dictated into a tape recorder by the observer on the task, the boy's body movements were recorded, and attempts were made to interpret his thoughts. The tape was then played back to another person who queried any unclear passages, until a final clear script was arrived at. This was transcribed in the form of a minute-by-minute observation throughout the day. The transcription, without interpretation, was published as a book, in 1951.

After a careful analysis of *One Boy's Day* it was possible to list all the people and animals, within and without the boy's home, who had physical proximity with him on the day of the study. Having listed the living objects to whom he related, it was possible to extract from the data the exact amount spent by each object in proximity to the boy. The observers were excluded. The total relating time was then calculated. This produced a "Chart of Relating."

Further careful study of the data on the criteria below produced a "Chart of Communication," i.e., the minutes of physical relating which the boy used for communication with each object were calculated.

Furthermore, by comparing the two charts it was possible to calculate the percentage of relating time used for communication with each object, i.e., the use made of the relationship.

Relating and communicating are different entities. Relating offers the possibility of communication, but the individual may or may not make use of his opportunity. At this point it may be useful to discuss how relating and communication are defined. It should be noted that the same definitions were accepted for each person; if these definitions are limited for one person, they are also limited for another and thus comparisons between persons are valid within the criteria employed.

The term "relationship" denotes the passive standing of one person to another. A chart of relating shows to whom the boy relates and for how long. Two persons can turn this situation of relating into a communication; this describes the active process of associating between people. A chart of communication records with whom the boy was communicating and for how long.

The intensity of communicating must also be taken into account. Many meanings can be conveyed during communication, some subtle and almost indiscernible, some discernible with ease, and some blatantly obvious. In the first category might come a father who sits with his family at a meal without exchanging a word with them; yet his presence influences the family. Into the second category may come an ordinary conversation around the meal table. In the third would come a heated argument between members of a family. The analysis of the data in *One Boy's Day* could embrace safely only the second and third categories. As the first category was excluded, it is likely that more communication took place than is recorded. However, comparisons of communication between different persons can safely be made within these criteria, as the same criteria for communication were adopted for all interactions.

It can be said that the greatest use of relating time for communication was made in the case of his friends outside school (78.9%), with animals (69.7%), with neighbours (64.4%), with mother (53.6%) and father (50%). It is of some importance to note that by the criteria employed to define communication, the use made of it during the relating time was almost identical for mother and father. The results of estimating the relating time used for communication are seen in Table IV.

It could be argued that, although longer communication takes place for instance with his peers (19.8% of his waking day), the communications

TABLE IV

% USE MADE OF RELATING TIME FOR COMMUNICATING

Object	Time in minutes	% of relating time
Father	56/112	50%
Mother	82/153	53.6%
Neighbours	9/14	64.4%
Friends outside school	71/90	78.9%
Friends in school	90/299	30.1%
School teachers	44/229	19.2%
Courthouse staff and other adults	15/37	40.5%
Animals	30/43	69.7%
Alone	108/108	100%
Total use of "relating time"	505/1085	46.5% (including self communication)
Use of relating time for communicating	397/1085	36.6% (communication to others only)
Total use of "waking time"	397/813	48.8% (communication to others only)

with his parents (17% of his waking day) may be more significant for his personality development, in that they reinforce impressions that have existed between his parents and him for seven years. This would be as true for his father as for his mother and for siblings, had he had any. If the same proportions of relating and communicating had existed throughout his seven years as on this typical day, it would seem that father's influence was hardly less than that of the mother. The concentration of influence from siblings could not be measured in this study as he was the sole child in the family.

Implications

The implications of the above works, the Ipswich Thousand Family Survey and the analysis of *One Boy's Day,* are far-reaching.

In the Ipswich Thousand Family Survey, the obvious is statistically confirmed—children are nurtured by families. The child relates to a number of people. From conception onward the child is part of a group of people of much significance to one another. As an active participator in a polydynamic open system, he gains and loses from the continual transaction— depending on the quality of that transaction. He cannot be understood apart from the group and the transaction and he is destined to carry their influence on into the future.

The analysis of *One Boy's Day* shows that the use of relating time for communication within the family is the same for father and mother.

The biological advantage to the individual is obvious. Had he been condemned to a need and an ability to relate to one person alone, then, having lost that person, his life would be over. Furthermore what he may lose in one relationship he may gain in another. Defects of one parent are compensated by the other, or by a relative, a sibling, or a nanny.

The theory of the necessity of one unique object relationship, and that being his mother, is no longer tenable. A child needs his family, including his mother. In our society, due to the economic situation, mother may give more care than any other family member, but it would be a shallow experience, lacking richness, to be tied to her alone. Mothers vary in this capacity to relate to others, including children. So do other family members. But to centre child care on the whole family allows one family member to compensate for any deficiencies another may have in relating to children. A number of good relationships are better than one.

Contemporary child care theory emphasises the importance of a continuous relationship with one object, preferably the mother. This is an extraordinary distortion of the true situation. A child is brought up in a discontinuous relationship with a number of objects, or subjects. Mother holds the infant aloft, and in mid-air hands him to father for a gyration around his head and as the infant steps down to his lap, his sister plays a rat-a-tat on his toes, while the family dog licks his face. Strange anomalies in the psychopathology of the child-care experts drive the child into a caged-in, locked embrace with his mother alone. The child gains from a number of relationships rather than from a single one. All the essential ingredients of caring are to be found in fathers, aunts, uncles, grandparents, foster parents, etc. *The capacity to relate does not depend upon gender role, legal status, mental status etc., but upon the relating experiences of that person in his own preceding family.* All these people too may have demonstrated a capacity to relate. All have a capacity as nurturers. And neither nature nor child cares who is the nurturer as long as nurturing occurs. Nurturing, like any other device in nature, is a contrivance to a particular end; the end is the important thing. Hence the use of a large number of nurturing devices.

Allied to the notion of a need for a continuous relationship with one object is the theory of imprinting. The danger of thinking by analogy has never been better demonstrated. What is an appropriate and valuable mechanism in the life of a duck may be a positive disadvantage in another species. A baby elephant to oe 'aaequately protected must walk between its mother and an "aunt"; to walk in a single line would make it a ready victim to a tiger. Of thousands of possible mechanisms, nature uses those best suited to her particular purpose in a particular situation. The capacity not-to-imprint is also essential for the welfare of an infant of homo sapiens.

Psychoanalysts have gone on record to maintain that the first two years of a child's life is not a period that calls for participation by fathers. The facts deny this contention. Fathers are involved in conception, a positive and essential contribution. They share the anticipation or strain of pregnancy; increasingly they wish to share the joy of the moment of birth. They are full participants from the moment of birth and communicate as freely as mother. But not they alone. At a new birth in the family the feelings of any existing children are immediately engaged; and how can one forget the joy of grandparents?

The above studies underline the importance of siblings. They contribute a large amount of relating time—almost as great as does the mother. The child in *One Boy's Day* had no siblings, but if children relate to others in the home to the same degree as they do to peers outside (the highest concentration of care in the above investigation), then their impact on one another must be a major factor in family life. Parents claim recognition of their contribution to children; siblings are less able to ask for theirs. We cannot omit the same careful evaluation of their contribution to family life.

The founders of future families, it seems, spend the major part of their time in the family. It is strikingly apparent that the home is the predominant milieu of a child. In the first five years it amounts to 93.56% of relating time including sleep; it is less in the over fives (84.60%), and for the whole 10 years amounts to 89.18% of relating time. Thus we have to look for the aetiology of psychonosis in the heart of the family.

Conclusions

These findings have great relevance to clinical practice—the family must be the unit in management, the aetiology of psychonosis will be found there; all relationships must be evaluated; family members can change roles as child nurturers; substitute and multiple parenting are a reality; separation procedures may be employed, not just from mother, but equally from father or the family; vector therapy can employ compensatory substitute relationships; to harmonize the founder of more families offers an area where effort can bring rich rewards; the diachronic course of the family can be influenced.

The child strives to survive, but cannot be sure of it. Thus nature has supplied him with the security and help of a group—a family group, a security enhanced by its not being dependent on one person alone. His personality is flavoured and moulded by a number of interdependent individuals who form a part of a complex whole, a polydynamic system, the family group, the situation. From his family he learns the essential lessons of marriage, parenting and family life to come. His success will be his family's success, his failure theirs. Harmonious families produce more harmonious families. Sadly, disharmonious families reproduce themselves. To guarantee healthy families by existing and new techniques is the greatest challenge to contemporary psychiatry.

REFERENCES

1. BARKER, R. G., and WRIGHT, H. F. (1966). *One Boy's Day, a Specimen Record of Behaviour*. New York: Harper & Row.
2. HOWELLS, J. G. (1971). Interpersonal transactions in the day of a seven year old boy. *Acta paedopsychiat., 38*, 262–270.

Childbirth as a Family Experience

Introduction

The family is a complete organism, a unity in its own right, as real as an individual. The individual is an organised system; so too is the family. An event in any part of this organised system impinges on every part in the rest of the system; every experience within the organised system belongs to the system. Thus childbirth and its attendant pregnancy is an experience that belongs to the family as a whole.

The psychiatry of pregnancy is concerned with abnormal psychopathology produced at this nodal point in the life history of the family. It may be useful to exemplify those emotional traumata that can arise within and without the family group during its experience of pregnancy and childbirth. We then move to a consideration of the symptomatology indicative of disturbed family functioning at this period.

The obstetrician is likely to observe symptomatology in the family member under observation—the mother. However, when emotional sickness arises in pregnancy, an evaluation of the whole family will add to its understanding. Pregnancy may result in new emotional implications stressful to the family psyche.

Family Traumata Precipitated by Pregnancy

It is necessary to remember that pregnancy is part of the continuing life experience of the family, which, during this time, is not specially protected from the usual stresses of living. However, in addition to the usual stresses, others can occur due to situations provoked by the experience of pregnancy itself. Some of these situations will now be discussed. The list is not ex-

361

haustive; in a particular family may arise a unique, atypical situation not covered here.

Emotional stresses have one feature in common, they come from an emotional source—another person or group of persons. Those persons most capable of being the source of stress are usually other members of the family who are close and significant. Only after an accurate examination of the family should measures to elicit the source of stress move outside the family, and even then it is wise to consider the extended family before exploring sources further afield.

Some of the special stresses of pregnancy, many of which are associated with the family, are as follows:

1. An increase in the number of family members has significance in itself, as the whole psychodynamic situation changes each time a new member is added.

2. Spouses have to shift roles to become parents.

3. Pregnancy implies a sexual experience and in some women this revelation precipitates guilt and emotional illness.

4. The pregnancy may be unwanted, having been due to either an accident or imposition by one or other partner.

5. A mother may seek more children than is desirable because of the search for gratification through having infants.

6. Children may be sought only as a solution to marital tension or emotional illness.

7. One or the other parent may become a rival to the child.

8. Parents may be unable to accept the extra responsibility of the care of another.

9. Phobias and myths about pregnancy, many fear-producing, may be released and add to the stress of the pregnancy.

10. Children may be rejected following birth for a multiplicity of reasons, but a central feature is that the meaning of the child is unacceptable to the rejecting parent.

11. Either parent may see the extensions of others in the child, leading to acceptance or rejection of the child or flavouring their attitude to it.

12. Attitudes of grandparents may intervene to produce trauma.

13. There may be gender preference of children.

In conclusion, it must be emphasised that even when one member of the family suffers the major impact of psychic trauma, the whole family inevitably has a changed experience; it is invariably implicated in the situation that produced the trauma; the result of the traumatic situation influences the whole family; its resolution is thus a matter for the whole family.

Family Symptomatology

In addition to signs in the individuals, the stresses of pregnancy may, for instance, give rise to a faulty husband-wife relationship—symptomatology in the dimension of internal communication. Again, some families react to stress by excessive spending, which may lower their financial state—symptomatology in the dimension of physical properties. In some families stress may result in a hostile attitude towards others and even in outbursts of delinquency, i.e., symptomatology in the dimension of external communication. Lastly, the dimension of general psychic properties may be affected, e.g., a mother may use her privileged position in pregnancy to become a destructive leader within the family.

It cannot be denied, however, that obstetricians are usually in a position to detect symptomatology only in an individual. Thus, the way in which individuals may react will be briefly outlined. It must always be borne in mind that at least three people are involved, the father, the mother and the child. It may be of value to consider the symptomatology as it affects these three individuals in the three periods—the antenatal, natal and post-natal. Once symptomatology has been ascertained in one individual it behoves the clinician to understand it by reference to an exploration of the whole family. One's duty thereafter is to adjust the whole family.

Antenatal Period

The mother may and does display any psychosomatic symptoms usually met with in clinical practice. Symptoms particularly associated with pregnancy are spontaneous abortion and miscarriage, cravings and aversions, hypertension, and toxaemia and hyperemesis gravidarum. Furthermore, the mother may develop any of the whole range of mood changes which can end in severe depression and even in a suicidal attempt. Lastly, there may be changes in the mother's behaviour. This may result in an attempt to rid herself of the unwanted pregnancy through induced abortion. If unsuccessful, it may precipitate feelings of guilt due to the possibility of having damaged the foetus. Should the foetus subsequently be damaged by accident, the mother is again liable to blame herself.

The father may also display any of the symptomatology of psychosomatic disorder. A particularly vivid example of the involvement of the father is to be seen in the couvade reaction. Furthermore, he too can suffer cravings and aversions of pregnancy. He may also develop any of the symptomatology of mood changes which, again, may extend to depression and even suicide. Lastly, there may be a change in the father's behaviour. Striking examples of this are two fathers seen by the author who have always involved themselves in delinquent behaviour or criminal behaviour on each occasion that their wives have become pregnant, i.e., the switch of attention from themselves to the unborn child has resulted in a feeling of rejection and the re-awakening of hostility, their response to rejection in childhood.

Emotional stress from the mother, or indeed the family, can put the child at hazard in the uterus (3). Sontag (1) has shown that the children of anxious, neurotic mothers are smaller and more active than those of placid mothers. Again, Spelt (2) has been able to condition the child in utero to external noise. Indeed, this phenomenon was well known to Shakespeare, who referred to the hazards of the child in uterus on more than one occasion, as for instance lack of love for Richard III by his mother:

> Why, love foreswore me in my mother's womb.
> And, ...
> She did corrupt frail nature with some bribe
> To shrink mine arm up like a wither'd shrub.
> (Henry VI, Part 3, III, ii, 153–156).

Natal Period

In the mother there may be uterine inertia leading to delay in labour. The example that follows demonstrates the role of anxiety in delay.

It is well known that the reverse can occur—there may be a precipitate birth. An example of this was given earlier in the book.

Furthermore, there may be any of the signs of change of mood in the mother which can lead to acute distress. Lastly, there may be a change in behaviour which may make her agitated, awkward and hostile, or passive and withdrawn.

The father too may develop acute physical changes at the time of childbirth and, again, the couvade reaction is a most startling example. There may be any signs of change of mood. Lastly, there may be a change of behaviour.

The child, too, may suffer due to emotional stress at his birth. He may suffer from the consequences of delay in delivery or from a precipitate birth. Birth may be premature, leading to all the dangers of prematurity; these premature infants are termed "shock babies" in some localities, i.e., the result of emotional shock.

Post-natal Period

The mother may suffer any of a large number of psychosomatic symptoms. A particular example of physical involvement may be the loss of milk in the breasts. There may even be transfer of symptomatology from mother to the child. For example, a woman, who had nursed her father suffering from carcinoma of the colon and consequent constipation, became constipated on his death. At the birth of her child, she lost her constipation, but her child became constipated instead. Furthermore, there may be any of the signs of mood changes, of which the most common and evident are those of anxiety and depression. These will be demonstrated below. A central factor in postpuerperal depression is the meaning of the infant to the mother, in which again may be reflected the meaning to her husband. Lastly, there may be a change of behaviour in the mother. If this takes the form of hostility towards her infant, it may in an extreme case lead to infanticide.

Examples of postpuerperal depression are seen in the transcripts of discussions between a doctor and two patients, Mrs. P. and Mrs. M., both of whom had had physically traumatic pregnancies.

Mrs. P. suffered a forced marriage and an infant imposed on her by an unwanted husband. She tried to abort the foetus. She had a complicated pregnancy with delay in labour.

Doctor	What did you feel like afterwards?
Mrs. P.	Well, I think I was rather sort of low after it. I can remember crying a lot. When one of the neighbours came in one morning I just seemed as if I couldn't help it.
Doctor	Why did you think that you were low?
Mrs. P	Well, I suppose it was the marriage. As I say I didn't get married because I wanted to get married.
Doctor	Why did having a baby make you feel low?
Mrs. P.	Well, I suppose it was because it was a forced marriage and I didn't want him.
Doctor	You didn't want the baby?
Mrs. P.	No, I didn't.
	I was anaemic and I used to attend the clinic and they used to give me tablets, but I never took them. I suppose I just got better myself, and didn't take no more notice of it.

Mrs. M. wanted her child and husband, but his jealousy and rejection of the baby drove her to depression and thoughts of suicide.

Mrs. M.	Well, I suppose it was rather a disappointment because it was his baby as well as mine and I thought he would feel about her as I did.
Doctor	Did you find yourself rather miserable?
Mrs. M.	Yes.
Doctor	Depressed?
Mrs. M.	Yes, that's right.
Doctor	Did you feel that life wasn't really worth living?
Mrs. M.	I did after Mary was born. I really did. I felt, when I was terribly low, that if it hadn't been for the baby I'd have thrown myself in the river or something.
Doctor	Yes.
Mrs. M.	I don't suppose I ever should have done, but that's what I felt like.
Doctor	Yes. But you didn't feel any desire to take the baby with you. Did you feel antagonistic towards the baby or not?
Mrs. M.	Oh no.
Doctor	You felt the reverse?
Mrs. M.	Yes. I said to myself, well I must just carry on because I've got her.
Doctor	In effect she kept you going.
Mrs. M.	Yes. Sort of feeding her and looking after her. Of course I got more and more fond of her although I was fond of her right from the start. She got more interesting as she got older.

The father, as in the other periods of pregnancy, may develop signs of psychosomatic disorder, mood changes, or a change of behaviour.

The child also may have evident symptomatology. From the moment of birth, indeed perhaps before birth, the infant may manifest signs due to emotional trauma. There may be physical disorders, such as feeding, weaning and habit problems, and mood changes, such as apathy and dejection. Lastly, there may be behaviour problems, such as crying, restlessness and awkward behaviour. The handicapped children have their own set of special problems.

An example of a child disturbed from birth, if not before, emerges from the following brief transcript of a discussion between doctor and Mrs. P. again. It might have been expected that this unwanted child of an unwanted husband would be disturbed by the situation and it seems this was so from birth or perhaps even before.

Doctor	Did you feed the baby yourself?
Mrs. P.	Yes.
Doctor	How did he take to feeding?
Mrs. P.	Well, he was a bit of trouble at first. And he used to cry a lot during the night. He was a lot of trouble like that. When we used to take him out he shrieked. I've never heard a baby shriek like it before. I should say he was very highly strung.
Doctor	That the baby was?
Mrs. P.	Yes.
Doctor	How early or late did he start doing that. I mean was it during the first few weeks?
Mrs. P.	All the way along.
Doctor	From the very first?
Mrs. P.	Yes.
Doctor	From the first few days?
Mrs. P.	Yes.
Doctor	Would you say he was very highly strung, from the first few days?
Mrs. P.	Yes.

Family Management

Once an element in the family has shown signs of psychopathology it is then necessary to proceed to an exploration of the family dynamics. In obstetric practice it is usual to start with the mother or with the infant. Thereafter the rest of the family should be involved so as to make it possible to get a total picture of the functioning and dysfunctioning of the whole family. Problems of pregnancy cannot be regarded as exclusively concerning the mother alone. Every problem of pregnancy concerns the whole family. Its elucidation will only be possible in the light of family dynamics. Treatment should lead to a healthy family unit, which is essential to the nurturing of healthy children and, in due course, the begetting of further healthy families.

The family approach can also influence obstetric practice. Preparation for childbirth should be given not only to the mother, but to the whole family. Imagine what one would learn about grandparents' or children's attitudes from such a procedure! Children should be prepared for the next child and so reduce sibling rivalry. Fathers should be prepared for the coming child. Home confinements are popular with families and the home is the milieu of choice; childbirth is truly a family event when conducted at or near home.

Economic and social considerations may make home confinements less possible. In this event, hospital admission should be of short duration and the family invited into hospital to participate to the full. The implication of every obstetric event is clearer in terms of the family. Throughout obstetric practice, all procedures should be framed to deal with it as a family experience. Healthy families can mobilise their strength to combat any complications, and even in sick families the assets are not inconsiderable.

Conclusion

It is asserted here that childbirth and pregnancy are family experiences. The family is an organised system and any event within any part of that system affects the remainder. Childbirth is such an event affecting the whole family.

Childbirth is normally an unstressful experience. However, traumata special to pregnancy can be precipitated by it. Some of these special traumata have been outlined. Stressful pregnancy affects the whole family, which is likely to show signs of it in all its dimensions. In obstetric practice these signs may first be noticed in an individual, especially in the mother. Equally, disability in other family members may be explained by mother's pregnancy. Any disability at any point in the family should always lead to an exploration of the whole family. Treatment is only effective on a family basis. Furthermore, only in this way can one establish a stable family platform for the coming generations.

REFERENCES

1. Sontag, L. W. (1941). The significance of foetal environmental differences. *Amer. J. Obstet. Gynec., 42,* 996–1003.
2. Spelt, D. K. (1948). The conditioning of the human fetus in utero. *J. exp. Psychol., 38,* 338–346.
3. Stott, D. H. (1969). The child's hazards in utero. In: Howells, J. G. (ed.) *Modern Perspectives in International Child Psychiatry.* Edinburgh: Oliver & Boyd; New York: Brunner/Mazel.

Family Psychiatry and the Aged

Introduction

The aged, like others, are the product of families. From birth to old age the individual is the object of swaying fortunes within this small group, the family. Old age brings no lessening of the family influence and no safety from the perils of its emotional climate. Age brings change—psychological, biological, physical, neurological, and social—but it takes place within a framework, the family, that remains essentially the same.

Family psychiatry has as its central tenet that the functional unit in a clinical practice be the family rather than the individual. The family, rather than the individual, is the patient. This approach has thrown new light on the psychopathology of emotional states. The individual is seen as one element in a field of emotional forces. Any event in this transaction of forces affects every other element in the system. Each element is a part of the whole, continually responding, advantageously or disadvantageously, to the ebb and flow of the tides of family emotion. The flow of family emotion brings safety or danger, benefit or loss, health or ill-health. The individual reflects the changing nature of the forces besetting him. The individual in his early years is especially vulnerable to noxious emotional forces. Hurt here may leave permanent deficit, susceptibilities to special stresses, and a handicap that can worsen with ill fortune or improve with good fortune. The changing fortunes of time play throughout the years on any initial strengths or weaknesses. At last the individual reaches old age. But respite is not yet. To his dying day he has to contend with the still active, elemental family life.

In old age are to be found two areas of pathology: (i) that which the individual brings with him from earlier years; and (ii) that which is the product of the senium. Naturally the first must be added to, or will react with, the second.

The pathology that concerns the psychiatrist is: (i) that which springs from damage of the encephalon—encephalonosis displaying so-called "mental" symptoms (in truth organic); and (ii) that which springs from damage to the psyche—psychonosis that displays so-called "emotional" symptoms (truly psychic).

We shall see in the span of the clinical examples that follow, how encephalonosis and psychonosis react the one on the other.

In clinical practice it can also be seen how in the evaluation of pathology there has been much neglect of psychonosis. As in other age groups, psychic pathology emits from the destructive effects of noxious psychic forces or noci-vectors that come from other psychic sources—other people; these other people are, most commonly, members of the family circle.

Turning for a moment to the world of literature, we can find a number of excellent accounts that exemplify the statements above. None is more starkly clear than that of Shakespeare's description of Lear's "madness" (2) which was no madness at all. Lear displayed an advanced dementia of old age; but he was also beset by family ill fortune that established his psychonosis and the anguish arising from this killed him. I will follow Shakespeare in his account.

Lear's decaying physical powers, dementia resulting from senility, are recognised and described by Shakespeare. He says that not only can we expect the "imperfections" of Lear's "rash" personality, but in addition the "unruly waywardness" of old age.

> The best and soundest of his time hath been
> but rash; then must we look from his age to
> receive not alone the imperfections of
> long-engraffed condition, but therewithal
> the unruly waywardness that infirm and
> choleric years bring with them.
> (King Lear, I, i).

Dementia leads to loss of judgement and thus to rash decisions, such as Lear's banishment of his most affectionate daughter and by so doing placing himself in the power of his other unscrupulous children. This loss of judgement too is depicted:

> Oh, Lear, Lear, Lear!
> Beat at this gate that let thy folly in
> And thy dear judgement out!
> (King Lear, I, iv.)

One of the cardinal symptoms of dementia is the loss of memory, especially for recent events, and thus inability to recognise people. The King can take the Fool, Edgar and Kent for high justices.

Lear:	I'll see their trial first.
	Bring in their evidence.
(To Edgar):	Thou robed man of justice,
	take thy place.
(To the Fool):	And thou, his yoke-fellow of equity,
	Bench by his side.
(To Kent):	You are o' th' commission,
	Sit you too.
	(King Lear, III, vi).

Lear himself can half perceive his disability and has a feeling that he should be able to recognise those about him and remember recent events, which escape him, like blurred images from a dream.

> I fear I am not in my perfect mind.
> Methinks I should know you, and know this man;
> Yet I am doubtful; for I am mainly ignorant
> What place this is; and all the skill I have
> Remembers not these garments; nor I know not
> Where I did lodge last night.
> (King Lear, IV, vii).

Defect of memory and disorientation in time and place lead to confusion —well portrayed here by Shakespeare. Lear's thoughts become incoherent. In his agitated mind images come and go in quick succession with no link between them. He suffers from illusions, misinterpreted phenomena. He imagines himself to be recruiting men for his army and offers enlisting money (press-money); he comments on a man handling his bow as if he were employed to scare crows. Then he thinks he sees a mouse and wants to catch it with a piece of cheese. In the next instant he grabs his gauntlet and offers to fight a giant, whilst calling for the foot soldiers with their brown painted halberds (brown bills). The image of arrow returns to his mind, and he sees it flying like a bird to the centre of the target (the clout).

> There's your press-money. That fellow handles
> his bow like a crowkeeper; draw me a clother's
> yard. Look, look, a mouse! Peace, peace; this

> piece of toasted cheese will do't. There's my
> gauntlet; I'll prove it on a giant. Bring up
> the brown bills. O, well flown, bird! i' the
> clout, i' the clout—hewgh!
>   (King Lear, IV, vi).

But when the end comes it is emotion that kills him, not old age. The emotion released by the death of his beloved Cordelia overwhelms him and he raves, unable to accept this last terrible blow.

> No, no, no life!
> Why should a dog, a horse, a rat, have life,
> And thou no breath at all?
> Thou'lt come no more,
> Never, never, never, never, never!
>   (King Lear, V, iii).

When death comes for him it is a welcome release, as Kent knows when he stops Edgar's efforts to revive him.

> . . . . O, let him pass! He hates him
> That would upon the rack of this tough world
> Stretch him out longer.
>   (King Lear, V, iii).

So the old king dies, killed not by his venerable age, but by an emotion, grief.

Esquirol would have listed grief under the heading of "moral causes." In his book (1) he presents two tables, one of physical and one of "moral" causes of dementia. The highest single aetiological factor in the list of physical causes is "progress of age." An analysis of 40 cases for "moral" causes reads as follows:

Disappointed affection	5
Frights	7
Political shocks	8
Disappointed ambition	3
Want	5
Domestic Trials	12

Lear suffered them all, including "want," in his aimless wanderings. But like less exalted mortals, it was his "domestic trials," the damaging family relationships, more than any other single factor that affected him deeply enough to lead to his death (2).

This damaging family climate now requires further consideration. What are the damaging noxious vectors that arise within it, what damage results, how is this field to be explored, how can the ill-effects of family life be ameliorated?

Family Psychopathology and the Aged

Family psychiatry demonstrates how psychic noci-vectors arise from clashing attitudes within the family. Painful blows are dealt to the "idea of self" of a family member. But these clashing attitudes do not spring only from the climate of the present family. The most fundamental spring from the preceding families of the two adult family members. Each family member is an epitome of the preceding family from which he springs, carrying with him a psychic self uniquely formed by it, and with the capacity to agree or disagree with the epitomes of other family climates which it will meet in its course through time. From the preceding families come pathological attitudes, coping devices and the indicators of pathology, the symptoms. The climate of the present family depends upon the complementarity of the two preceding families.

Discussion of the family and the aged will be accompanied by a case description that will serve to illustrate many facets of psychopathology, investigation and treatment. A lady of 70 (Mrs. S.) presented at the Geriatric In-take Clinic of the Institute of Family Psychiatry, referred for a slow response to convalescence following an embolism in the chest. Her physician discerned that she was depressed and sought assistance for her. It emerged, almost at once, that the embolism had followed a quarrel with her husband in the course of which he had begun his habitual angry response to frustration by banging the table. She was admitted to hospital as an emergency because of embolism of the chest. The old lady said, "I knew something must give." Her grasp of the significance of emotional events was out of the ordinary and was accompanied by a rare understanding of their effect on her somatic state.

This case history illustrates the clashing attitudes now, their basis in the past, and the aggravating additional stresses. The major clash now:

The old lady gives a clear account of it. Long experience in the upbringing of her nine children and the many vicissitudes of their families allows her to see clearly her own situation. The last child leaves home, her husband retires, they move to a small apartment, no longer can either deny the mutual disharmony that submersion in child care and long hours of work have allowed them to ignore over the years. I quote the typescript of the interview:

.... after having a family of nine to look after, all of a sudden, my husband and I were left on our own. ...

.... all of a sudden I seemed left with my husband and everything seemed at a dead end. I was easily getting depressed.

.... I got a nose bleed .... well then I have had about three or four since I have been home. Little things gets on my nerves, and if he gets riled with me, he bangs on the table. And I say there is no need to do that. I said "We are in this room. Don't shout, I can't put up with it." When I was younger I should have shouted back perhaps. But my husband is very erratic tempered if you know what I mean.

Again:

.... If I upset him he flies up and if I say anything. I might say, "Well what have I had to look forward to this week, just sitting there looking at you and the four walls. You don't even walk out with me."

And again:

I conceal my feelings you see and they boil up inside me because I know if I say too much to him he will upset me, you see what I mean.

The old lady can see the process. She has insight. But insight does not solve problems. Insight is never enough. The danger is considerable. Her nose bleeds with stress. She has had a clot in the chest. Members of her family have died with thrombosis. She makes the links. She feels in danger when the husband bangs the table.

The past makes the present

The old lady's problem is acute now. But its roots lie in the past—and beyond into his family: a coming together; a long courtship in the days of depression; she moves away to a better job; he saves his pennies and calls for her; she has already forgotten him; but her father exerts pressure—the boy is respectable; she accepts the father's values—not her own; so the past dictates the choice of her husband; the marriage; the quick disillusionment, as his other, non-respectable, attitudes emerge; the birth of the first child is marred as the product of him; but she loves children and accepts them as a part of herself and her family and not his; the long submersion in children begins.

She speaks herself of the marriage:

.... if he had been a bad man I wouldn't have married him. It was just that I think that at the time I got married, I didn't really want to get married, if you can understand my meaning. At 21 I would have eagerly married. But by the time the six years was round I regretted it. I didn't want it and four months afterwards I was very unhappy.

.... he treated me very well. But I just didn't want him enough for anything to happen at all between us. I had a good job in London, and wanted to go back to it, you see. But I had been with him so long, that Dad said it wasn't fair me keeping him so long, and just end up like this. So I really married through Dad, if you can understand my meaning. . . .

.... I liked kiddies, but by the time I married I didn't . . . . I became pregnant right away, you see . . . . It made me miserable.

But the past goes beyond marriage—to his family. From it he gathered the attitudes she found so difficult to tolerate.

The lack of feelings:

.... When we lost a dear one in our family, my brother at 22 and my sister at 26, I really felt it for months after. Whereas my husband lost a sister in hospital and he lost a brother suddenly a few weeks ago and he just carries on the same!

And the quick temper that she fears and finds dangerous:

.... His family are rather quick tempered, very quick tempered. As a family they soon fly. He bangs on the table if something upsets him. But of course he doesn't see that when I tell him.

The quick temper again, coming from his family, and its dangers confirmed by experience:

Yes, he is very fiery. So was his mother and sister, who died with a stroke. She died in a temper, she had had a quarrel just before she died. I remember that.

The husband, if consulted—and he must be consulted—would point to the sexual frustration. She uses the age-old defence mechanism—illness. She cannot give herself to him in mutual enjoyment. The children are to be desired for themselves alone and bring her the support and interest she needs. She yields after a long siege.

I just think he comes to bed the nights he wants me. That doesn't worry him. I don't want him. I just don't want him and I told him so. I think it is my general health you see. I can't put up with it. That is telling you frankly. I can't put up with it and I go as long as I dare go and then he sort of goes up in the air a mile.

Special stresses

Old age brings its own special stresses as does any age period. As the years go by, cherished friends and relatives are lost—by death or distance. In a large family, losses are inevitable and each brings its grief and strain. The ultimate strain is to be left with a disharmonious spouse.

The treasured daughter who died of multiple sclerosis. The tension from her own family behind it. Does the old lady hint at a psychopathology of multiple sclerosis?

> .... I found within the last four years I have had rather a lot of trouble. You see, I have brought up nine children. Four years ago I lost a daughter who was very dear to me, with multiple sclerosis.
>
> The one with multiple sclerosis, her husband wasn't at all good to her. No; and the doctors at the hospital told me that it was mainly through him and his women that had brought it on.
>
> .... I think he broke her spirit really. I could see it, you see ....

Then the daughter who went far away to Australia. A very special daughter. Not weak and needing protection, but her "right hand," a support, a replica of a loved mother, a replica of her family and not that of her husband:

> She had evidently spoken about going to the others, her brothers and sisters. She hadn't mentioned it to me because I think she knew that it would upset me. You see she was the fifth child born. Therefore, she was my right hand as I told her husband when he married her at nineteen. I said, "You are taking my right hand," and she was the living image of my mother to look at at birth.

The loss is remembered to the day. No clouding of memory here. But a cerebral thrombosis that she so fears could bring a terrible toll to her cerebral functions.

> Dr.   And then, when this daughter went to Australia, when was this Mrs. S?
>
> Mrs. S.   Oh, it did cut me. It will be two years come the 27th June. This year she will have gone two years.

This daughter spares something for the old man too. For both, there is the compensation of a letter and the satisfaction that all is well.

> Well, we have got a daughter in Australia. My husband reads and all his books seem to be about Australia. She emigrated. That was

another pill for me. She had three lovely children that we adored and of course that sort of, well, she went in the June, and that is when I started going down hill. It played on my mind you see. Of course, with the other girl I said well it was God's choosing and I had to let her go. But you were going on your own accord and I may never see you again and that upset me, you know. But I am getting over that because she writes and says they are very comfortable and happy.

Then the last and youngest daughter leaves:

But the youngest daughter is in Germany. She has been there over a year. Her husband is in the Army and I am worried about her. You see, she is having a baby any day. So may be that is what has made me depressed the last few days again, if you can understand my meaning. . . .

The last loss leaves her alone with husband—the greatest stress of all.

. . . . four weddings in two years and then all of a sudden my husband and I were there alone after having so much to do. My mind was occupied all the while, you see, when I had the family.

Experiential psychopathology

It should be noted that in this account of psychopathology we have been concerned with real events. No attempts have been made to interpret in the light of any psychopathological dogma or school of symbolism. The facts speak for themselves and need no interpretation. The lives of the aged are real. A chain of real events lead to pathology. The life as experienced is what counts. This is experiential psychopathology.

Family Diagnosis

This is based on two main questions:
1. What are the indicators of dysfunction in the individual?
2. What process in the family sets up the dysfunction?

Elucidating the indicators

The steps are:
1. The investigation starts with the presenting indicator. In Mrs. S.'s case, it was the embolism in the chest.
2. Then comes a history-taking that allows the geriatric patient to reveal

any other subjective indicators of dysfunction, traditionally called the symptoms. These are organic and psychic.

Mrs. S.'s account fills in the picture, clearly reveals psychic as well as organic pathology and hints at the aetiology within the family. She recalls husband banging on the table, the somatic result, and goes on:

> ... I suppose that was what caused the terrible pain. They took me away that night. I don't remember it, only waking up in the hospital, you see, the next day. So they must have put me under sedation. Anyway, I was in terrific pain when they took me away in the ambulance ....

She has another psychosomatic indicator, her nose bleeds. She knows why, and she fears the implications.

> I said, if you hadn't have upset me, my nose wouldn't bleed, you see. Sometimes when I get upset my nose bleeds and it worried me because my father died suddenly with cerebral haemorrhage, you see, and he was younger than I am now.

Her account also soon reveals psychic indicators. She is, of course, an organism that reacts as a whole.

> ... my whole trouble is nerves. I so easily get upset.

Her terminology, perforce, is simple—"nerves" she calls her psychonosis. But she can see the link with her physical weakness and her attacks of tremor.

> ... and my nerves got me so low that I was too weak to walk even.
> ... and the least little thing upsets me and then I shake and then I can't control it ....

3. Mrs. S.'s account, revealing though it is, must be supplemented by a careful questioning based on a form designed to reveal any dysfunction in the somatic or psychic fields.

4. Lastly, Mrs. S. is examined for signs, objective to the examiner, of psychic or somatic dysfunction.

5. If necessary, the above must be supplemented by special somatic or psychic diagnostic procedures. Mrs. S's embolism would certainly call for this.

All the above has been a formal examination and now ends by formulating a diagnosis for the data collected. Briefly, in Mrs. S.'s case it could be termed "acute psychonosis presenting with embolism of the chest." This can be extended by listing all the somatic and psychic indicators. We are now in the era of somato-psychic medicine and no investigation of any patient is complete without a global assessment that includes both psychic and somatic fields.

The family process

The above tells us in what way Mrs. S. dysfunctions. But it does not tell us *why* she dysfunctions. Thus, we move now from the individual to the family. The other family members are drawn in, they meet as a group and the procedure of family group diagnosis takes place.

The first part of the investigation was directive; this part is non-directive. The material tumbles out from the family, is analysed under the framework of the 15 family dimensions, and the family encouraged to discuss neglected areas.

Mrs. S. told us a great deal which was reported under family psychopathology earlier in this chapter. But this is a one-member, slanted view of the family. Husband must also be seen, possibly alone initially and then later together with his wife. This must be done with care—a clumsy interview could result in the counterpart of table banging by husband—and this is dangerous to Mrs. S. (and perhaps to the husband also).

Once the family process is revealed, a family diagnosis is made, e.g., in the S. family a brief formulation might be: "Disharmony in the marital area of the family resulting in acute episodes of family psychonosis superimposed on a state of chronic family psychonosis, and presenting with embolism in one family member." A longer account could tell of the contribution from both preceding families (husband's and wife's families) that led to disharmony in the present family and its course through time to the present.

Family Therapy

The above term is used in the sense of treatment of the family by any procedure. Certain principles are basic:

1. The whole family, in this case Mr. and Mrs. S., must be treated.

2. The family must be treated in both somatic and psychic areas. Somatic therapy is enormously important, and in Mrs. S.'s case it was life saving. Drug therapy may be an essential part of psychic therapy also. But with care in the aged, as Mrs. S. relates:

> ... I took one (tablet) and before that had been down a half hour I was like this you see (showing a tremor of the hands). It was over

acting the nerves. They were too strong. Each time I had only got it down about a half an hour and I would be like this, the chair and bed would shake and I would have to go and lie on the bed in the next room . . . .

3. Psychic therapy can be in terms of family psychotherapy or vector therapy, or both.

Family psychotherapy can be applied in three ways:

1. *Complete antecedental psychotherapy* aimed at changing in many ways the essential disharmonious situation in the family. It involves dealing with the effects of the two preceding families (the husband's and wife's families). A number of factors may exclude this possibility: (i) It is immensely time consuming. (ii) The number of psychiatrists available for this work could only meet the needs of a few of the aged. Unskilled psychiatric help is dangerous, just as bad surgery is worse than no surgery. (iii) It may be difficult to justify expenditure of the limited resources when the span of life to run is so short and so many families with young children are denied help. (iv) Old people do not respond easily, as the process has gone on for so long.

2. *Focal antecedental psychotherapy.* Here small parts of the total situation are dealt with. Usually these are the major attitudes that cause friction in the family, e.g., Mrs. S.'s reluctance to have intercourse with Mr. S. In the aged even obvious situations are sometimes difficult to resolve, as they have been so fixed with time. Behind Mrs. S.'s reluctance to have sexual intercourse is her distaste for Mr. S. and that has the deepest of roots.

3. *Supportive psychotherapy.* This is based on the rationale that certain measures have a tonic effect on the psyche—hope, encouragement, praise, appreciation, sharing of dangers, affection, etc. This should be an essential part of any contact with the aged, even for somatic therapy alone.

Vector therapy has a different rationale. It is based on the observable fact that within and without families there is a pattern of emotional communications—of vectors. Some of these emotional interactions bring pain, anguish and destruction; some are beneficial and constructive. The aim of vector therapy is to analyse the pattern of interaction within and without the family, to bring relief to the family. Vector therapy is effective only if the evaluation of the interactions is correct. We must know before we change. Are we right in our evaluation that Mr. and Mrs. S. are disharmonious together—or does someone else intervene to create disharmony for his or her own purposes? Thus family group diagnosis is an essential preliminary. Careful work in time reveals a basic disharmony between Mr. and Mrs. S. Once the pattern of the emotional vectors is clear, the family interview is then employed to reach a degree of rapport between therapist and family which makes change possible. The family must accept its handicaps with insight, be free of guilt and able to see change as an opportunity for relief. Insight, time, patience, lack of blame are the ingredients for success. Coercion should never enter the scene.

Mr. and Mrs. S. have employed vector therapy with success for years. They have simply not met, as they have contrived things so that work has been his abiding passion and the children hers. Life has been tolerable. Time has wrecked the pattern of vector therapy—both children and work have gone. A new pattern is required, so that the marital interaction operates for as brief a time as possible. Mrs. S., as the healthier of the two (an evaluation supported by her wonderful insight), is already groping for a new pattern, as we shall see in her remarks:

Mrs. S. is passionate in her need:

> I do, I do, just now I do. I need something more than just sitting looking at my husband all the afternoons and evenings.

Mrs. S. tries. But surely we can do better than this.

> Yes, the only outing I have been having is to the hospital. I have been going to the hospital for the blood pricks, you see, and that has made an outing you see.

The welfare agencies have not seen fit to help. But at least she has not been presented an analysis! A little practical help instead . . . Mrs. S reaches for it from the good neighbours rather than the "welfare."

> I have asked Mrs. Banks from over the road to come in for a cup of tea. He says, well what did you do that for? I said, well, I want company. He said, well, why don't you go over to hers? Well, Mrs. Banks said come over any time you like you see.

The neighbour helped a bit but it is not enough. She attempts a more radical solution.

Mrs. S.   . . . Last year I went to—to work in the canteen serving the young ladies with their meals. I did that for just three or four days a week, if you understand my meaning, for three weeks. Tuesday, Wednesday, Thursday, Friday, for three consecutive weeks. But then I gave it up because he didn't like it.

Dr.   How did you enjoy those twelve days?

Mrs. S.   I was very happy when I went to work.

Dr.   And when you had those twelve days when you were working, you really enjoyed it did you?

> Mrs. S. Yes, I was much better. He said so himself. He told his brothers that I was much better. I did that to forget about my daughter and what she went through, you see . . . .

Mrs. S., weak though she is, in her dire need reaches again for the solution that helped for a brief glowing moment.

> I have thought of it again. But at the present stage that I am with my legs I can't get a little job to do like I had last year when I felt myself getting low . . . .

She tried in another way but failed:

> Mrs. S. I could easily write a book. I have always wanted to. I did start to, but when I was ill I got so low that I thought I was just going to fade, you see. So I gave it up and put it on the fire.
> Dr. Do you paint?
> Mrs. S. At school I did. I was the best painter in the school. I have painted since.

So now Mrs. S. attends the day hospital to write (about life with nine children) and to paint (she loves to paint children).

She likes the principles of vector therapy, as a long practitioner. The husband has come to see merit in it also. Life begins to glow. And like an old Druidess she puts it all down to the weather.

> Dr. . . . We can help you to have a fuller life. That is the best medicine we can give you.
> Mrs. S. I think so too. I definitely think so too. It is a beautiful day today, I think you do feel better, everyone does. Even normal people feel better when the sun shines.

Conclusion

Psychonosis, with frequent and severe somatic concomitants, is a common feature of old age, as in any other age group. The aged are not immune from family influence and the trauma that often arises in the family. History taking must embrace not only a global psychic and somatic evaluation of the individual but also of the family. Therapy must be based upon a family evaluation. Psychotherapy may sometimes be indicated. But help is usually best met by vector therapy together with somatic measures as appropriate. These last seem to be in accord with Shakespeare's management of Lear.

At first the vector therapy:

> O, sir, you are old;
> Nature in you stands on the very verge
> Of her confine. You should be rul'd and led
> By some discretion that discerns your state
> Better than you yourself.
> (King Lear, II, iv).

And then the physician prescribes one of the many "simples" (drugs) that will induce sleep and give him rest from the anguish that wears him down.

> Our foster-nurse of nature is repose,
> The which he lacks; that to provoke in him
> Are many simples operative, whose power
> Will close the eye of anguish.
> (King Lear, IV, iv).

REFERENCES

1. Esquirol, J. E. D. (1845). *Mental Maladies.* Philadelphia: Lea & Blanchard. (Reprinted in 1965 by Hafner Publishing Co., New York and London).
2. Howells, J. G., and Osborn, M. L. (1973). King Lear—A case of senile dementia. *History of Medicine, 5/2,* 30.

The Evil of No Separation

The lonely child cries. Its appeal, so strongly stamped by nature, stirs the heart. The child needs the security of empathy, of love. The appeal we feel should be, and usually is, answered by the child's parents. But what if the parents cannot respond? Help the parents to respond is the reasonable answer. But what if the parents, rarely, have no capacity to respond and cannot be given it. Some would argue that even so the quality of the natural parental care is so vital that any substitution can be damaging. The child's own home, it is argued, is better than any other home; separation of the child from parent is never justified. Another point of view maintains that more important to a child than the parent is loving care. Denied love in his own home, in an uncommon instance, it should have love elsewhere. So the controversy is born—is separation of child from parent justified?

The theme running through this presentation is that separation is not synonymous with deprivation. Once clarity emerges about these two concepts then the matter is easily resolved. Most of the confusion about "separation" and "deprivation" springs from the fact that the two words are used interchangeably, and it would seem to be essential to have a clear definition of each. "Separation" of child and parent, by common usage, means that the child is physically parted from its parents and has an existence independent of them. "Deprivation" is a term which indicates that a loss is suffered and when applied to the child it usually denotes that the child is deprived of the necessary loving care for its emotional growth. Thus *"deprivation" can occur with the parent, or apart from the parent.* "Separation," then, involves a physical loss of the parent, but not necessarily of loving care. "Deprivation," on the other hand, involves the loss of loving care, but not necessarily of parents. Thus, "separation" and "deprivation" are not synonymous terms.

Separation of a child from its parents may result in deprivation or non-

384

deprivation of loving care depending on the situation. The commonest occurrence of deprivation is with non-separation, i.e., due to stressful situations at home between parents and children; separation of children and parents may sometimes be the best way of avoiding deprivation. However, the common view is that separation is the danger and that it is responsible for mental ill-health in children.

Contemporary expert opinion, particularly psychiatric, is often thought to be rigidly opposed to child-parent separation under any circumstances. Here the extent of the misconception in contemporary practice will be reviewed. Then the history of the misconception will be outlined. Subsequently the findings of one of the few direct studies on the issue will be described. To give point to the discussion the findings of an ethological study will be presented. Finally the implication of these studies will be summarised.

A Digression

But before commencing our task, we must digress so that a related issue can be aired and clarified. This is the issue, "Is a benevolent loving bond inherent in parenthood?" Cultural history, everyday experience, and statistics support a negative reply to the above question, as we shall see.

Samuel Johnson in his *Lives of the Poets* has many insightful things to say about the relationship between the poet Savage and his mother. He could see that hate and homicidal inclinations by the mother had entered into this relationship. The poet's mother wished him hung and gave evidence against him at Bath Assizes. But he was acquitted. This was Johnson's commentary: "This was perhaps the first time that ever she discovered a sense of shame, and on this occasion the power of wit was very conspicuous; the wretch who had, without scruple, proclaimed herself an adulteress, and who had first endeavoured to starve her son, then to transport him, and afterwards to hang him, was not able to bear the representation of her own conduct, but fled from reproach, though she felt no pain from guilt, and left Bath with the utmost haste, to shelter herself among the crowds of London."

Contemporary events can again make us question whether benevolence is inherent and ever present in the mother-child relationship. *The Daily Telegraph* (17th Oct. 1972) reported: "The mother admitted a charge of the manslaughter of her son Peter. Mr. John Johnson, prosecuting, said that although she had been staying in a house only 10 minutes away, she did not return home for a week, by which time the child was dead. Mr. Johnson said that she had shown utter disregard for the child's welfare.

Peter had died from malnutrition strapped in his pram, which was uphol-
stered with flock and had no mattress. Pieces of flock were found scattered
about the pram, and Mr. Johnson said one shuddered to think of the child
scrabbling with his little hands in the pram."

From our own files at the Institute of Family Psychiatry comes an extract
from a letter of a mother to her mother-in-law, who was caring for her child
during the week. Who would change places with this child? Yet the mother's
legal right to mother her unwanted child overrides the rights of the child.
She wrote: "When I read your letter I got so vexed that if you were living
a little nearer I would come down the same day and throw a heavy lashing
on Susan's hide. . . . I will be coming up just like the devil after her,
only that I won't have his horns . . . . when you speak to her and she
stretches out her mouth give her a little bit of food for the week just for her
not to die and do not give her any cover at nights, and do not light the
heater for her to get warmth. Just drag her out of the bed in the early
mornings. Nothing more to say. Hoping to see you this weekend."

Incidents such as these question the idea that loving care is ordained in
parenting. It appears that sometimes parental feelings can be a damaging,
hostile, killing force. This is supported by observations in history, where
infanticide has at times been widely practiced, e.g., some Aboriginal
mothers of Australia liked "baby meat." Today approximately one in 20 of
homicides are directed towards children. In nearly all such deaths, the
mother is the killer. In murders of older children the proportion is two by
mothers to one by fathers. Though the mother appears to be the commonest
murderer, it does not mean that she is necessarily more hostile than the
father; she may have stronger motivations as well as more opportunities for
the act.

Day-to-day experiences and the above findings suggest that the parental
bond is positive in the majority of parents, indifferent in the case of others
and hostile in the case of a small number (this takes no account of the
children destroyed by induced abortion). These are facts of life and their
evaluation must be taken into account in making realistic decisions about
children. The author enlarges on the issues relevant to child homicide in
Remember Maria, a book based on the study of the death of a child,
Maria (11).

Widespread Misconception

In the clinical field, it has always been evident that most children who
are deprived of proper care are so deprived by being in a condition of non-
separation, living with their parents, i.e., that deprivation reflects the rela-

tionship between themselves and their parents. However, the misconception has grown that emotional ill-health in children results not through parental inadequacy, but through separation. Thus separation is assumed tò be a dangerous operation for the child, to be avoided at all costs. The child's own home is reputed to be better than any other home. To review the whole literature on this topic would be too lengthy, therefore a few sample statements are taken at random to show how widespread is this misconception.

The following reflect the view of the informed public. "How seriously and lastingly young children may suffer if separated for even a day or two from their mothers . . . . has been abundantly proved" (*The Observer*, 15th Feb. 1959). "As many parents know only too well, the effects on a small child of separation from its mother can persist for a very long time" (*The Sunday Times*, 15th Sept. 1968). "It is increasingly realised that mother-child separation may be harmful to young children even if separation lasts only for a few days" (*Pulse*, 21st Aug. 1971).

Expert opinion from respected authorities is often slanted in the same direction: "On the purely psychological side there is evidence that separation from the parent or parent substitute before the age of five may have a serious effect on the emotional growth of children and may form the basis of neurotic reactions in later life" (Ministry of Health. 1961. "The part of the family doctor in the mental health service." London.) "Bowlby's work needs to be taken seriously because of his immense contribution to medical and popular understanding of the harm done to little children by separation from their mothers, harm that is liable to lead to a permanent distortion of the personality and character" (Winnicott, D.W., 1962. *Brit. Med. J.* i, 305). "If there is a break between the mother and child in the neonatal child of about a month or more, this commences delinquency in later life" (Rendle-Short, T.J., 1969. *Medical News*, 13th June). Heading in the *Medical Tribune* (16th Oct. 1969): "Separation from Parent Results in Psychiatric Ills." Followed by: "Separation from a parent plays a major role in the aetiology of psychiatric illness," according to Dr. J. Bowlby, Director of the Tavistock Clinic's department for children and adults. "Mothers who leave their children in day nurseries and factory creches may be causing them irreparable mental damage, a Swiss doctor told the International Conference at the Royal Society of Health in Douglas, Isle of Man yesterday" (*The Daily Telegraph*, 7th Sept. 1972).

Although this viewpoint was found to be fallacious nearly 20 years ago (12), the reverse point of view has been slow to exert itself. From time to time there has been a sharp comment from a judge; e.g., jailing a miner for three years for a baby's manslaughter, the judge said: "It was a thousand pities that the child did not remain in the care of the local authority" (*The Daily Telegraph,* 19th May 1972). Again, it was reported in *The Guardian* (16th Jan. 1970) that a mother wished to place her infant in the care of the local authority, as she felt unable to care for the child. The plea was rejected because of "likely effect of parting the child from the mother." The child died. The Coroner commented, "I cannot see the point of leaving a child with its mother merely to let it die of starvation."

Dr. Mia Kellmer Pringle agrees with the judge: "A child's ties with his natural family were so over-valued that he was sometimes allowed to remain with parents who were clearly disturbed or who rejected him" (*The Daily Telegraph,* 23rd Sept. 1972). Authorities have also clashed. A letter (4) re-stated the danger of separation. It provoked a dissenting reply (2). In 1966 there was another skirmish (5, 9).

History of this Misconception

Bowlby was an early worker in the field of mother-child separation. His first study took place 25 years ago (3). The views expressed in his first paper were reinforced in his work on 44 juvenile thieves (1). In retrospect it would seem that his conclusions were capable of a different explanation, i.e., that the juveniles were damaged by experiences before and after separation; deprivation consequent on both was the damaging agent and not the separation itself. A selection factor also operated—juveniles given a happy separation experience would naturally not be sent to the Tavistock Clinic. The early work led to a large-scale statistical study (6) comparing, by questionnaire of teacher and parents, the experiences of a group of children separated by admission to a sanatorium, with a group of non-separated children. The differences between the two groups were slight. Thus none of the above studies confirmed the statement that mental ill-health in children was due to separation.

In the meantime Bowlby had performed a valuable service by reviewing the many studies on deprivation, on behalf of the World Health Organization (2); they all spoke conclusively about the damaging effects of deprivation. These findings were unexceptional. The mistake was to assume that they applied to separation.

Negative findings do not find enthusiastic support, especially when they are almost immediately modified by the investigators, with the consequence that the implications are hardly registered. So strong is the misconception that a positive statement might alone have countered it, i.e., that separation can be a positive, helpful factor in child care under certain conditions.

A direct study (12) decisively contradicted the supposed dangers of separation. This was in 1955—18 years ago. This study was concerned with the separation experiences of children under five, who were separated from either parent for any period lasting over 24 hours, and compared children who were emotionally ill with a group of children who had not attended a psychiatric clinic. The findings were that the incidence of separation in the two groups was very similar, and differences were minor. Thus it could be concluded that separation does not, in most cases, lead to mental ill-health. The findings suggested that most disturbed children suffered emotionally from being with their parents, i.e., deprivation springs most commonly from inadequate parental care—thus confirming clinical experience. Furthermore, it appeared that some children actually benefited from separation. The findings also showed that the conditions applying before, during and after the separation are more important than the fact of separation in determining whether or not there will be harmful effects. The results of the study were so emphatic in making clear that separation need not lead to deprivation, that it became possible to use separation procedures in a therapeutic way (8).

Of Monkeys and Men

There is merit in looking at this issue in detachment. An excursion into ethology provides such an opportunity and supports the findings that the damaging agent is deprivation and not separation.

Harlow's early work on the monkey is well known. Its recent extension (13) has great relevance to our discourse, as a brief sketch will show. In the first part of their work Harlow and his colleagues were able to produce neurotic infant monkeys by deprivation consequent on separation. The infants were separated from their parents and became neurotic. The workers, mistakenly, thought that this was the result of separation. However, had the monkeys been placed with foster parents following separation, the neurosis would not have appeared, i.e., separation would not have led to deprivation. It was not separation per se that did the damage, but the fact that it led to deprivation. The truth of this emerges shortly.

In the second stage of their experiments, the neurotic infants were allowed to become adults and were mated—these disturbed mothers produced neurotic infants. These infants became neurotic because they were rejected by the mother, i.e., they were not separated, but they were deprived. The deprivation did the damage. (Similarly, a battered child is not separated from its family, but is still subject to gross deprivation.) Then there was a dramatic intervention. The monkeys had to be rescued to prevent deprivation continuing to the point of death. And what was the intervention? The employment of separation! The infants were taken away from the depriving mother monkeys and placed with non-depriving adult humans. Separation was employed therapeutically to prevent deprivation and death. (Might not the battered child merit the same rescue?) The first two stages of the work confirm that separation is not synonymous with deprivation. Deprivation is the noxious agent. Deprivation can occur with non-separation to the point of death. Separation saved the life of the infants.

In the third stage of their work, Harlow and his colleagues were looking for a therapist for the disturbed neurotic infants. Behaviour therapy was tried, but was not effective. So stable, young monkeys were employed as companions to the neurotic monkeys, i.e., the depriving negative parents were replaced by positive non-depriving young monkeys. The negative forces were replaced by positive forces. This re-patterning of forces is the essence of vector therapy (10).

Implications

The above makes it clear that the damaging agent in child care is deprivation and not separation. Furthermore, in certain circumstances, separation can be employed to overcome deprivation.

Separation should, naturally, not be employed if a home is immediately modifiable. Sometimes it is not. A neglectful, highly neurotic young mother, who tries to abort her child and later to give it away, has none of the "magical" parenting bond (we saw other instances in our digression). Years of the best psychotherapy have little chance of making her into an affectionate mother, and such intensive facilities are rare. In any event, the child cannot wait for three to four years. Just to preserve the mother-child relationship, regardless of its value, the real situation has to be denied. As a fact of life, we have to accept that in a number of circumstances the intransigence of the problem, the inadequacy of the therapeutic tools and the lack of resources call for different procedures.

If separation is necessary, what are the best procedures for its management? Children should not be torn out of their families. Nor should separation techniques be employed against the wishes or without the understanding of parents, unless the situation is so desperate for the child that an immediate rescue is indicated. Parents are rarely wicked, but they are often handicapped, usually by unhappy events in their preceding families. To heap on them feelings of failure and guilt adds to the handicap. Instead, the parents, indeed the family, should meet as a group. The discussion, led by a social worker, clarifies the set of forces (10) besetting the family. It comes to common agreement about solutions. It defines the forces that need change. Patient, considerate, tolerant, insightful discussion is the most effective procedure. The bonds that produce guilt and inaction are loosened. The parent figures are strengthened by the process. They are involved in constructive procedures that permit praise because their children benefit. Much work may be required, careful preparations have to be made, but the stakes are high.

As with the monkey, permanent separation procedures are sometimes urgently called for. Every case must be judged on its merits. A septic toe may respond to protective bandage, but it may require a poultice; the toe may need to be amputated; in a small number of cases the leg may have to be amputated—a decision is called for and the decision cannot be avoided. Not to make a decision could mean death. Failure to rescue a child by separation in the social field can also mean death or serious emotional injury.

Should separation be desirable and possible, the choice of substitute care become the next difficult task. Not everyone, whether a natural or substitute parent, has the right qualities for loving care. These qualities are dependent on their own experiences as children. Thus experience shows that the most apposite aspect of the assessment of substitute parents is a careful appraisal of their family life as children. Those who have been loved enough as children prove to be responsive to children. Whilst other factors have to be considered, this seems the crucial one. We saw with Harlow's monkeys what an inadequate mother a neurotic monkey, deprived as an infant, proved to be. Fortunately, foster or adoptive parents are just as representative of sound people as are natural parents, and sounder than emotionally handicapped natural parents. A child's right to loving care rather than to natural parents should be protected. If a "no separation" policy persists, the plight of the child is considerable. A defenceless member of society, he may be denied adequate care because of the protection of the absolute right of the parents to override his requirements.

Work on separation has also highlighted the requirements of parents. While there is such a thing as the tyranny of parents, there is also the tyranny of children. Parents, and in particular, mothers, are virtually the only group in society expected to continue at their task year in and year out without a break. Overprotection of a child by a parent is harmful to both. Parents need a holiday on their own from time to time, because it helps to keep alive the marital relationship, so important to the life of the family and the well-being of the children. Children, even as infants, gain from the richness of personal experiences with other people. We need not fear separation, as long as the child in the absence of parents receives warm, benevolent, loving care. Furthermore, children who have had the good fortunate to relate to a number of people accept separation so much better when it is unexpectedly forced on them by circumstances.

Conclusions

At risk of repetition we can conclude that separation is not synonymous with deprivation. We must in certain circumstances give the child the benefit of separation from parents. This should be, whenever possible, with the willing co-operation and understanding of the parents. An afterthought that may not have escaped the reader is: "How can a misconception as damaging as this thrive for so long in the ranks of our caring professions?"

REFERENCES

1. Bowlby, J. (1946). *Forty-Four Juvenile Thieves*. London: Baillière, Tindall & Cox.
2. Bowlby, J. (1951). *Maternal care and mental health*. Monogr. No. 2. Geneva: W.H.O.
3. Bowlby, J. (1953). Some pathological processes set in train by early mother-child separation. *J. ment. Sci., 99*, 265.
4. Bowlby, J. (1958). Separation of mother and child. *Lancet, i*, 480.
5. Bowlby, J. (1966). Visiting children. *Brit. med. J., i*, 297.
6. Bowlby, J., et al. (1956). The effects of mother-child separation. *Brit. J. med. Psychol., 29*, 211.
7. Howells, J. G. (1958). Separation of mother and child. *Lancet, i*, 691.
8. Howells, J. G. (1963). Child-parent separation as a therapeutic procedure. *Amer. J. Psychiat., 119*, 922.
9. Howells, J. G. (1966). Visiting children. *Brit. med. J., i*, 676.
10. Howells, J. G. (1968). *Theory and Practice of Family Psychiatry*. Edinburgh: Oliver & Boyd; New York: Brunner/Mazel.
11. Howells, J. G. (1974). *Remember Maria*. London: Butterworths.
12. Howells, J. G., and Layng, J. (1955). Separation experiences and mental health. *Lancet, ii*, 285.
13. Suomi, S. J., Harlow, H. F., and McKinney, W. T., Jr. (1972). Monkey psychiatrists. *Amer. J. Psychiat., 128*, 927–932.

The Problem of the Problem Family

Introduction

The problem family will be given special consideration in order to expose how its material failures spring from its high degree of psychopathogenicity.

The community may explain its manifestations as being due to lack of satisfactory material conditions, despite the obvious and commonplace disillusionment of those individuals who have achieved material success and still remain unhappy. Secondly, the community tends to suppose that these conditions may indicate some degree of insanity. Statistics, however, show that only a very small section, less than 0.5% of the community, suffer from process encephalonosis, while social problems involve a far greater number of people. Thirdly, the community may suggest that these problems spring from some degree of intellectual retardation in some of its members. Careful investigation, however, shows that people at all levels of intellectual endowment are liable to suffer from these social difficulties.

The above explanations ignore the fact that these conditions spring from psychopathology, i.e., from the dysfunctioning of the emotional substratum of the family. Emotion and emotional disorder are concepts that the public finds difficult to grasp. Difficulty in grasping emotional phenomena may sometimes lead to ethical prowess being offered as a solution of emotional difficulties. "Goodness" is offered as a substitute for emotional stability. But experience shows that impeccable ethical precept and practice do not safeguard against emotional illness. There is, however, no contradiction between "goodness" and stability; these qualities are different entities that can exist together.

The thesis in the investigation to be reported is that many social difficulties are due to emotional causes—to matters of family psychopathology.

393

The Investigation

In a town of 120,000 population, 80 problem families are recognised by the official agencies. A random sample of 30 of these families was taken. The initial sample was reduced to 24 families due to three families leaving the area and another three families being reclassified as non-problem families. It was accepted that help should go hand in hand with investigation.

The criteria accepted for defining the problem family were those of the agencies in the area. This had the advantage of allowing others to establish the criteria and allowing the investigation to throw light on recognised problems in the area. It carried the disadvantage that the agencies' definition was influenced by what constituted problems in their narrow fields of operation—and within the social groups with which they were concerned. Many problem families are not ascertained by the agencies; thus in any interpretations of the findings on that sample it must be borne in mind that the sample is a selected one.

Much has been written about problem families, but, due to the immense difficulties involved, careful studies are few. To collect a representative sample involves working in a geographically limited area. Establishing good reasons for continuous visiting to such families can be very difficult. To obtain co-operation to the point where members of the family will allow intimate study can be even more difficult. Apathy, distrust and belligerence are bars to easy relationships and the keeping of appointments. Psychiatric studies call for the greatest co-operation of all and hence, no doubt, their paucity.

Workers in this study (2) have collected data in this area for 16 years. Over the last seven years, due to close co-operation with the agencies concerned, especially the family doctor, it has been possible to arrange for families in the sample to be referred to the Institute of Family Psychiatry undertaking the study. Of the 24 families in the sample, 21 have been examined, i.e., 87% of the sample. Thus 41 of 42 parents and 142 children were seen; the parent of one family died. It will be noticed that each family was taken on for a full psychiatric evaluation in the same way as other individuals and families attending the Institute of Family Psychiatry. Contact was maintained for some years in most of the sample. A special schema of examination, involving more than 500 items, was employed.

Results

Emotional disorder in individual parents. On a four-point scale of emotional disorder, the findings in 41 parents were the following: The "very severe" emotional disorder group (15 parents) embraced patients who had persistent, very obvious, severely incapacitating, multiple symptoms, and whose condition required the most intensive psychotherapy for a long period, and who would be unlikely to respond to it. The patients in the "severe" group (13 parents) required intensive psychotherapy for a long period to effect amelioration of their condition. Those patients with a "moderate" degree of emotional disorder (10 parents) also required psychotherapy, but had a good prognosis. One parent was found to be nearly stable and in two parents encephalonosis replacing emotional disorder was found.

Thus of 41 parents, 38 required psychotherapy and two were encephalonotics—a significant and overwhelmingly bad state of mental health.

The overwhelmingly bad state of mental health in these families is emphasised by comparing this study with other epidemiological studies.

In the United Kingdom, because almost the whole population is on the general practitioner's "list," it has been possible to undertake research on psychiatric morbidity in the population at large through general practice. Watts (5) reviews ten such studies and concludes that the overall psychiatric morbidity, including all conditions—psychonosis, encephalonosis and psychosomatic disorders—amounts to 30.9%. The figure given in an authoritative document by the College of General Practitioners is 30%. The incidence of psychiatric morbidity of 30.9% has to be compared with our sample (N = 41, and only one nearly stable individual) where the morbidity rate is 98%.

Shepherd and associates (4) found that the psychiatric morbidity in a sample of adults in general practice was 9% of individuals suffering from "conspicuous psychiatric disability." To this they added 5% of the sample who showed "abnormal personality traits." Thus 14% could be said to be suffering from severe observable psychiatric disability. That the figure of 14% is a reasonable one can be surmised from Berg's (1) study of families attending a child welfare clinic. Here 14.2% of parents and children were said to show "severe" psychiatric problems. This figure of 14% can be compared with the figure in our sample of 69% (N = 41, 28 classified) classified as "severely" or "very severely" disturbed. Again, an overwhelmingly bad state of mental health in our sample is exposed.

Psychiatric disorder in paired parents. On the same four-point scale of degree of emotional disorder, the position for paired parents in the 21 families (41 parents) was as follows: Five families had one parent with "very severe" emotional disorder and one parent with "severe" emotional disorder. Nine families had one parent in the "very severe" group and one parent in the "moderate" group. One family consisted of one parent in the "very severe" group and one parent who was nearly stable. Four families had two parents with "severe" emotional disorder, and two families had one member with encephalo-ataxia (schizophrenia).

No family had two parents in the "very severe" category. To have one such parent was sufficient to be responsible for the plight of the family—even with a "nearly stable" partner. Two parents in the "severe" category were sufficient to handicap the family. The families having members with encephalonosis will be discussed later.

Sex of parents differentiated. Using the same four-point scale, the position in regard to emotional disorder for 21 mothers and 20 fathers is given in Table I.

TABLE I

PSYCHIATRIC DISORDERS AMONG 41 PARENTS
ACCORDING TO SEX

Category	Mothers	Fathers
Very Severe Psychonosis	13	2
Severe Psychonosis	4	9
Moderate Psychonosis	2	8
Nearly stable	0	1
Encephalotic	2	0

Thus, for this sample of families, by the criteria adopted, mothers are seen to be significantly more pathogenic than fathers. Most agencies who ascertain problem families are concerned with child neglect. This is more likely to occur if mothers are pathogenic and thus leads to conditions which will cause ascertainment. If "alcoholism" was the concern of the agencies it is likely that families with pathogenic fathers would be predominant in the sample.

Although the results are probably significant for this sample, it is necessary to add that fathers of these families are more elusive than mothers and their briefer period of examination may have led to an underestimate of their disabilities.

Families having parents with encephalo-ataxia. The definition accepted for encephalo-ataxia (schizophrenia) was that of the endogenous, "process" type; both parents showed the characteristic thought disorder and perceptual difficulties of established encephalo-ataxia.

With such a small sample, inferences must be drawn with caution. Both affected parents were mothers; when child neglect is an important ascertaining feature, families with sick mothers are more likely to be included. In one family, encephalo-ataxia in the mother was accompanied by a husband in the "moderate" category of emotional disorder; this was the least handicapped family in the whole sample and has now been upgraded to a non-problem family. The other family, which had a husband in the "severe" category, was of much concern to the social agencies.

Intellectual retardation in parents. In Great Britain, as a general rule, individuals of an intelligence quotient below 70 are said to be "subnormal," and those below 50 are "severely subnormal."

Six parents in five families were subnormal; none was severely subnormal. One family had two subnormal members. In four families with a subnormal parent, one parent also showed a "severe" degree of emotional disorder; in one family, the two parents showed a "very severe" degree of emotional disorder. Families with subnormal parents, of whom there must be many in this town of 120,000 population, do not show the characteristic features of problem families; these features are likely to be associated with emotional disorder in the parents. That this is so is suggested by the fact that the most stable parent, the one "nearly stable" person, has the lowest I.Q.—53; he could not counterbalance the influence of his "very severely" disturbed wife.

To date the intelligence quotients of 28 of the 41 parents have been assessed. The mean I.Q. is 83.6 and the range of I.Q. from 53 to 112. A number of considerations must be borne in mind in interpreting this finding. (i) The agencies who ascertained the families have a disproportionate interest in families of the lower social groups. (ii) We have found that intelligent parents of problem families are more elusive and less willing to submit to intelligence tests. (iii) The sample of 28 parents contained 17 mothers and 11 fathers. (iv) Parents of problem families live in a disruptive atmosphere which does not allow continued education, and this tends to lead to a poorer performance on intelligence tests. (v) The emotional disorder in the parents can interfere with performance on intelligence tests. (vi) Parents of problem families are often so dishevelled as to give the appearance of being duller than they are.

It is of interest to report that of 72 children tested from these families, the mean I.Q. was 90.2 with a range of I.Q. from 59 to 119. The regression to the mean is noted. A complementary study of the intelligence of children of problem families has been reported elsewhere (3).

Summary of results. One of the main results of this investigation is to make clear the high degree of psychopathogenicity that exists in the parents of problem families. It suggests that the definition of the problem family should be widened as follows: *A problem family is a family showing among its members emotional instability of such a degree that it leads to behaviour which is socially unacceptable.*

This poses the question, "Do all families suffering from a severe degree of emotional pathogenicity always manifest social difficulties?" The answer may well be "yes." But they will only be ascertained if the agencies are equally interested in social difficulties of all types, and as they manifest themselves in all age, social and intellectual groups.

Emotional Mechanisms Leading to Material Difficulties

This investigation also clarified some of the emotional mechanisms that lead to material difficulties. The emotional basis of material problems can be illustrated by analysing the root causes of two such problems in one of the families investigated.

Firstly, this family displayed the material problem of being heavily in debt. Investigation revealed that this was due to a combination of factors of emotional significance: (i) As the mother cannot mix with strangers, she sends her children to do her shopping, which is therefore less economically carried out, with consequent wasting of finance. (ii) Fear of the dark calls for all the lights to be on in the house at night with resulting heavy electricity bills. (iii) The mother's agitated state results in continuous smoking, with more spending of money. (iv) The mother's need to expiate guilt, induced by the way she handled her favourite daughter, caused her to buy expensive presents for the child—again depleting resources. (v) As mother panics in public transport, she has to visit friends by taxi, adding more to expenditure than her income allows.

Secondly, this family lived in a state of squalor. This resulted from the mother's preoccupation with her own unresolved fears, leading to an apathy and lack of concentration that made decision and quick action impossible. Accumulated commitments posed tasks too large to tackle and therefore best ignored.

Another physical difficulty for these families is their tendency to have many children due to ineffective birth control procedures. These, in problem families, are remarkably ineffective, because they are frustrated by a variety of emotional factors: (i) Some husbands wish their wives to be continually pregnant because it is only in this way that they can control them. (ii) Some mothers wish to be perpetually pregnant for only by such means do they get emotional satisfaction from the cuddling of small infants. (iii) Disturbed people are inefficient in birth control as in other matters. (iv) There is a fatalism about these families; nothing works out in life so why bother to try? (v) One of the few solaces in the lives of these individuals is sexual pleasure, which they do not wish to deny themselves and which they do not wish to encumber by birth control machinery.

Conclusion

Problem families, it seems, show a high degree of psychopathogenicity. Their material difficulties spring from this.

Once it is accepted that the core of the matter is in the severe degree of emotional instability, it is possible to redefine the problem family as "a family showing among its members emotional instability of such a degree that it leads to behaviour which is socially harmful." Study can now embrace all income groups, and it will be seen that problem families are not found in the lower income groups only. Furthermore, observation can include more manifestations than those in which social agencies are usually interested; it will be seen that many families are in dire distress, although not manifesting those signs usually denoting social failure. A family may, for example, isolate itself, be a problem family, and yet not show the usual social signs. Again, a family may denote its pathology by a ruthless drive in one sphere of activity that may even bring social acclaim—e.g., economic success. Or again, interest in religious matters may be pursued with a rigidity which may exclude normal feeling. It follows that the solution to this highly psychopathological organism, the problem family, lies in emotional measures—hence the futility of material effort and moral stricture; emotional difficulties need their own emotional antidotes.

REFERENCES

1. BERG, I. (1965). Psychiatric problems in a child welfare clinic. *Med. Officer, 114,* 315.
2. HOWELLS, J. G. (1966). The psychopathogenesis of hard-core families. *Amer. J. Psychiat., 122,* 1159.
3. HOWELLS, J. G., and DAVIES, M. (1957). The intelligence of children in problem families. *Med. Officer, 96,* 193.
4. SHEPHERD, M., FISHER, M., STEIN, L., and KESSEL, W. I. (1959). Psychiatric morbidity in an urban group practice. *Proc. roy. Soc., 52,* 269–274.
5. WATTS, C. A. H. (1956). *Neurosis in General Practice.* Edinburgh: Royal College of Physicians, publication no. 6.

Family Psychopathology Is Not Responsible for Encephalonosis

Introduction

Encephalonosis is a disorder of the encephalon (brain) produced by the direct action of physical noxious agents. This definition does not preclude psychic agents playing a part in precipitating the action of the physical agent, e.g., acute anxiety can provoke an attack of diabetes; the biochemical change acts on the encephalon and produces confusion and coma. But the direct damaging agent on the encephalon in this example is physical. [On the other hand, in psychonosis (neurosis), psychic trauma acts directly on the acquired part of the psyche.] When the damage to the encephalon is acute, the state of acute encephalonosis or delirium is produced. When the damage to the encephalon is sustained or chronic, the condition of chronic encephalonosis (dementia) is the result.

Throughout history there has been confusion as to what constitutes insanity, madness. As the pathology of acute and chronic encephalonosis was not clear, people suffering from these conditions were often termed insane, or mad.

At one time states of delirium, termed "phrenitis" in the ancient terminologies, were confused with insanity. In the old days dietary deficiencies, as well as the action of many unsuspected poisons, were responsible for many states of supposed acute mental illness—a fact responsible for many admissions to mental hospitals, even up to recent times. Today we have no difficulty in differentiating these conditions as being an organic state precipitated by organic agents—fevers, toxins, etc. Thus acute encephalonosis is now not often labelled a state of insanity or madness.

Again, confusion could occur between chronic encephalonosis and states of insanity. Chronic damage to the brain before or soon after birth led to intellectual defect (amentia). Similarly, when damage occurred later in life,

400

there was intellectual loss (dementia). Collectively, such intellectually handicapped people where termed "fools." Shakespeare (15) could differentiate
them from the insane—"Fools are not madmen," he said. Today our knowledge of aetiology and pathology allows us to recognise those handicapped
and avoid terming them as suffering from insanity or madness.

Confusion, however, remains over one group of the encephalonoses.
This is a group without defined pathology, termed "functional psychoses" in
traditional terminology, or "cryptogenic states" in the terminology employed
here. Cryptogenic states consist of cyclothymiosis (manic-depressive psychoses) and encephalo-ataxia (schizophrenia). These conditions have existed throughout history, and were truly regarded by our predecessors as
insanity or madness. However, as the pathology was and still is not defined,
there was in the past and still is today lack of differentiation between insanity (cryptogenic encephalonoses) and other conditions—especially psychonosis (neurosis).

At various times in the past attempts have been made to differentiate
between emotional states (e.g., wrath, rage, agitation, i.e., states of psychonosis) and insanity or madness (cryptogenic encephalonoses). Cicero
(106–43 B.C.) in his Tuscular Disputations reviews nosological topics and
finds that he cannot agree that the mind is influenced by black bile only,
but rather that in many instances it is influenced by the strong power of
wrath, fear, or pain; thus he defines the nature of emotional illness (psychonosis). In the Saxon miscellany of the 14th century is to be found the
following, which defines the same entity:

> Oft do we burn in rage
> And become as if we were mad.

This puts the situation very clearly—"as if." Verdi again makes the differentiation clear. He sends his librettist a prescription for the personality of
Azucena in *Il Trovatore*. He states, "Do not make Azucena mad. Exhausted with fatigue, with sorrow, terror, and lack of sleep, she is unable to
speak rationally. Her senses are overwrought, but she is not mad." Clearly
he sees that states of great emotional illness are an exaggeration of less disturbed states, but they are qualitatively different from madness and insanity.

Insanity (cryptogenic encephalonoses) and emotional states (psychonosis) are qualitatively different. Much of the confusion turns around one
point. Insufficient emphasis is given to the fact that behaviour can be extreme without people being insane. Yet, all too often extreme behaviour is
regarded as synonymous with insanity (cryptogenic states), especially one
form, encephalo-ataxia (schizophrenia). That it is so was demonstrated by
a study reported in *Science* (14). A number of professional people simu-

lated mental illness, were accepted as sick by the clinicians, admitted to hospital and in the great majority the diagnosis of encephalo-ataxia (schizophrenia) was made. The above exposes the perfunctory nature of diagnosis and the tendency to equate any extreme behaviour with encephalo-ataxia (schizophrenia). It is also too little realised that the characteristic feature of encephalo-ataxia (schizophrenia) is not extreme behaviour—lack of behaviour and indeed unusual behaviour are the prominent features. Again, encephalo-ataxia (schizophrenia) is characterised not by excess of emotion, but by lack of it. The lack of a clear definition of encephalo-ataxia nullifies many of the studies on its nature, including the significance of family psychopathology in its aetiology.

Cryptogenic encephalonoses are very uncommon in medical practice. This will become apparent if we study the statistics on one of its forms, encephalo-ataxia (schizophrenia). Pemberton (11) found that, of patients suffering from mental illness in his general practice, 93.6% presented with psychonosis (neurosis), 6.1% with encephalonosis (psychosis). On the assumption that 30% of individuals attend a general practitioner with mental illness (3), only approximately 2% of his total patients are suffering from encephalonosis. Encephalonosis (psychosis) covers a number of conditions, including the common one of senile dementia. Only a small part of the 2% is due to encephalo-ataxia (schizophrenia). Thus the percentage of encephalo-ataxia may be as small as 0.5%. That this is so is suggested in the study by Kessell (6) who in a general practice found only three encephalo-ataxic (schizophrenic) patients.

Emotional disorder (psychonosis), then, is a far commoner condition than encephalo-ataxia (schizophrenia). Psychonosis is not a minor illness. It can have drastic and dramatic repercussions on the life of the individual and the family, and can, and does, lead to death in a significant number of people each year; in the United Kingdom 30,000 people attempt suicide every year and 5,000 succeed. Furthermore, emotional disorder is so interwoven with the matrix of the family as to be the condition reflecting most sensitively its psychopathology and responding most clearly to beneficial changes in its dynamics. As will be seen later, it is doubtful if family psychopathology plays any direct part in the aetiology of encephalo-ataxia (schizophrenia).

So as to prevent any confusion in terminology, let me restate the classification adopted here. Psychonosis (neurosis, emotional illness) is regarded as being qualitatively different from encephalonosis (psychosis). Encephalonosis, on the best evidence available, is assumed to be an organic dysfunction of the encephalon. The pathology of most conditions of encephalonosis is now defined. But one group, the cryptogenic group, has no defined pathology. One of these, encephalo-ataxia (schizophrenia), is presumed to have an organic basis, although the agent responsible has not yet been identified. Confusion arises because this condition of encephalo-ataxia (schizophrenia) is confused with states of psychonosis (neurosis). The aetiology of psychonosis (neurosis) is clearly linked with family psychopathology. On evidence given later, it is unlikely that encephalo-ataxia (schizophrenia) arises from family psychopathology. It may be strange that a family psychopathologist takes up this position, but the available facts must be allowed to speak for themselves.

The condition of acute and chronic encephalonosis (including intellectual deficiency) will be considered briefly in relation to family psychopathology. Then will follow a discussion of the cryptogenic states in relation to family psychopathology.

A. Acute Encephalonosis and Family Psychopathology

Acute encephalonosis (acute organic psychosis), covering such conditions as the delirious states, toxic states, drug intoxication, should certainly be linked *indirectly* with family psychopathology.

Alcoholism and drug addiction would serve as good examples. These conditions lead to acute organic states, and are truly comprehensible against a background of family psychopathology. Family psychopathology often goes unassessed. It is this which is responsible for the psychonosis in the individual who reaches out for a means of coping; in some cases alcoholism and addiction are the devices used. Rarely is the agony of a family life so manifest as in these conditions—should the observer care to look at the family.

However, even though psychic factors, mostly based on the family, are responsible for the addiction, the damage done to the encephalon is the direct result of toxic agents arising from the metabolism of alcohol in the body. These agents are responsible for the vivid indicators of brain dysfunction that are often seen. Equally, removal of the toxic agents immediately abolishes the indicators of brain dysfunction, but of course leaves untouched the factors leading up to the addiction.

B. Chronic Encephalonosis and Family Pathology

Chronic encephalonosis (chronic organic psychosis) is the result of action by a number of organic noxious agents—infective, traumatic, neoplastic, nutritive, and hereditary. Traditionally, the damage done in early life (amentia) has been differentiated from damage in later life (dementia).

There is no good reason for this, as has been discussed under nosology; epiloia in children and Huntington's Chorea in later life both destroy brain tissue. All these conditions lead to states of varying degrees of intellectual defect.

Family psychopathology may be *indirectly* involved in the aetiology. Cerebral thrombosis might serve as an illustration. Acute psychic trauma, especially in the aged, can precipitate a crisis in the cerebral vascular system from which cerebral thrombosis can result, and this leads to destruction of brain tissue. Repeated psychic traumata will lead to considerable damage of tissue and hence dementia.

A special word is necessary about the link between family psychopathology and amentia. It will be clearer if we differentiate three types of amentia that interest the clinician:

1. *Due to brain damage.* Here the loss of intellectual efficiency is great and leads to states previously termed idiocy and imbecility. The organic pathology is a matter for understanding by neurologists. But whether or not the patient can be managed at home rather than in an institution depends on the quality of the emotional care available in the family; this is true of all types of handicap—epilepsy, blindness, cerebral palsy, etc. The more disturbed the family, the lower its toleration of a handicapped member, who may therefore be rejected into an institution, or who may require such care in his own interests. At this point family psychopathology impinges on management.

2. *States of intellectual deficiency* when psychonosis (emotional illness) is superimposed due to family psychopathology. Here the management of the person should be that of anyone suffering from emotional illness (psychonosis). The family psychopathology may be resolved so that care at home and simple occupation are possible. Should separation from the family be desirable, then institutional care should be in terms of sound substitute family care in order to resolve the emotional disability and make occupation a possibility. Caution should be taken not to return the healthy dullard to his family, unless the family climate has improved to his advantage.

3. *States of pseudo-feeblemindedness.* Individuals of average or above average ability can appear to be dull due to a number of factors—lack of educational facilities, inability to profit from educational facilities due to a high degree of emotional illness, lack of intellectual stimulus in the home, or a deliberate simulation of intellectual deficiency (Ganser Syndrome). Here the pseudo-feeblemindedness is often an expression of family psychopathology and the whole range of family diagnosis and therapy are required to help.

C. Cryptogenic Encephalonosis and Family Psychopathology

There are two syndromes to be considered here—cyclothymiosis (manic-depressive psychosis) and encephaloataxia (schizophrenia). Because of the attention given it in the literature on the family, the second requires lengthier discussion here.

Cyclothymiosis

It is as well to mention that here, too, care should be exercised over diagnosis. Encephalolampsia (true mania) can easily be confused with emotional states of elation, excitement and agitation. Similarly, states of encephalobaria (endogenous depression) can be, and often are, confused with emotional states of reactive depression; reactive depression is overwhelmingly commoner than states of endogenous depression. It is worth saying that on careful examination so few depressions are found to be endogenous that the existence of this organic syndrome is in doubt.

The aetiological factors in cyclothymiosis are not clear; presumably the organic cerebral mechanisms of elation and depression are easily over-stimulated. It is known that some physical agents can set these mechanisms in motion. It may also be that the threshold of excitation is so low that the mechanisms are set going by a minimal emotional stimulus.

In both conditions, the capacity of the family to contend with the patient will depend upon its degree of emotional stability.

Encephalo-ataxia

The author could follow the tendency in contemporary literature of overemphasising the importance of this topic. However, he may perform a useful service by using a little space to bring the matter back to its rightful proportion.

Encephalo-ataxia (schizophrenia) constitutes a long recognized disorder with the most fascinating complex of symptoms in the whole of medicine. Yet international authorities do not agree about its definition, its incidence, or its aetiology.

That there is no agreement about its definition constitutes one of the greatest barriers to the formulation of investigations on it and to the comparison of research work going on in different countries. Traditional European psychiatry bases its definition on the descriptive work of the German psychiatrists (1, 7); the syndrome to them manifests a complex of symptoms that makes it unmistakable in most instances. In some European centres, usually with a dynamic orientation, and in the U.S.A., the definition is widened to include many patients who would not conform to the strict criteria of the German psychiatrists.

In an attempt to bring order into definition, the Norwegian psychiatrist Langfeldt (9) proposed the classification of psychoses into two types— "process" and "non-process" psychoses. "Process" psychosis covers the organic endogenous type and "non-process" psychosis covers the remainder. Stephens and Astrup (16, 17) have shown that the former, "process" psychosis, is accompanied by a poor prognosis. It would seem that "non-process" psychosis includes the graver types of emotional illness, psychonosis (neurosis), especially when it manifests well-marked abnormal behaviour.

Abnormal behaviour can arise from a number of causes—toxic, endocrine, emotional and encephalo-ataxic (schizophrenic). Unfortunately, abnormal behaviour is assumed in some quarters always to be due to encephalo-ataxic processes, despite the fact that some of the most alarming behaviour is seen in agitated emotional states. The two, encephalo-ataxia and emotional illness, should not be confused, or the definition of encephalo-ataxia will be greatly widened and embrace non-encephalo-ataxic behaviour. Overlapping symptomatology does not make two conditions identical, e.g., dyspnoea in anaemia overlaps with that in cancer of the chest, but anaemia and cancer of the chest are not two identical conditions. Similarly, that some of the symptomatology of severe emotional states, e.g., withdrawal, overlaps with the symptoms of encephalo-ataxia does not make encephalo-ataxia and emotional illness into identical conditions.

Differing definitions of encephalo-ataxia constitute one of the reasons for the disparities in estimations of the incidence of the condition. In Europe, where a definition akin to the "process" definition of Langfeldt is employed, the condition is uncommon. For example, English studies (3, 6, 11) point to the low incidence of encephalo-ataxia. In some countries the condition is diagnosed much more frequently than this. Rawnsley et al. (13) concluded that international variations in usage of terms completely vitiated comparisons between countries. Kramer et al. (8) came to similar conclusions.

Definition of the condition and thus more accurate studies of incidence would gain from the isolation of the aetiological factor or factors in this condition. Many formulations are put forward—genetic, constitutional, endocrine, neuropathological, biochemical, toxic and psychological. The latter has hitherto been confined to formulations based on individual psychopathology. It was natural that with the increasing interest in the family its psychopathology should be explored as a possible fundamental aetiological factor. However, work here may be frustrated for the same reasons that operate in the other fields—and one of the most cogent is the failure to arrive at an agreed definition of the condition. Criteria employed in its definition should be clearly stated in every case. As will be seen in a moment this rarely happens.

As many views are expressed on family psychopathology in relation to encephalo-ataxia, some common criteria for establishing the value of each view must be formulated. Many parameters of judgement could be used, but here are a few crucial ones. These are:

1. Is the condition under study indubitably encephalo-ataxia? To establish the diagnosis of encephalo-ataxia it must be possible to demonstrate all or some of the following features: thought disorder, emotional flattening, perceptual difficulties with associated hallucinations, delusions and ideas of influence.

2. Is the anomaly in family functioning definable by precise criteria?

3. Does the anomaly cause encephalo-ataxia or is it only associated with it? In other words, is a definite link established between the anomaly and encephalo-ataxia. When the anomaly is present, is encephalo-ataxia produced? When the anomaly is removed will the encephalo-ataxia improve?

4. Is this anomaly always present in the family when one of its members is encephalo-ataxic? A representative sample of encephalo-ataxics must be studied.

5. Is this anomaly present in the families of encephalo-ataxics by chance? Thus the need for controlled studies using matched groups of healthy patients, psychonotic patients, and encephalo-ataxics.

6. Does the hypothesis satisfy a feature of the illness, its onset in adolescence?

A number of anomalies in family functioning are put forward to explain the development of encephalo-ataxia in one of the family members. Space does not allow coverage here and the matter has been discussed at length elsewhere (5). A striking quality of most of the literature on this subject, with a few exceptions, is the lack of clear concepts. Experts on communication, it seems, find it difficult to communicate. Intellectualization, based on a modicum of fact, flourishes. The danger of such vagueness is that it may be interpreted as a cloak for ignorance and the formulations ignored. An even greater danger is that we may assume knowledge when there is none, and elevate the work to the status of mysticism.

The studies reviewed in the previous work (5) will be assessed in the light of the six criteria put forward earlier.

1. None of the studies reviewed puts forward a cleaf definition of encephalo-ataxia, by which the subjects under study were selected and

which would find unquestioned acceptance by psychiatrists. Visitors from Europe and the U.S.A. attending clinics in each other's areas must be impressed with the wide differences in establishing criteria for the diagnosis of encephalo-ataxia. To the writer, the careful criteria for the diagnosis of encephalo-ataxia based on European psychiatry would be met only by a fraction of the patients seen under treatment as encephalo-ataxics in family orientated centres in the United States; the remainder, though having a severe degree of pathology, appear to be severely emotionally ill but not encephalo-ataxic. Thus, should this view be substantiated, the findings of studies on these patients would be relevant to emotional illness, but not to encephalo-ataxia. It is essential to have agreement about the criteria for the diagnosis of encephalo-ataxia before findings can be compared and deductions drawn from the studies.

2. The anomalies of family functioning said to be associated with the production of encephalo-ataxia in a family member are not always a single, simple, discrete concept; sometimes they are broad, sometimes fragmented into a number of parts, and sometimes several in number. There is a general broad agreement that defects of inter-personal communication are involved. But the authorities do not agree about the precise nature of the significant anomalies of communication; the greater the number of conflicting theories, the more likely they are all to be wrong. Also, the defects of communication noted may of course result from the illness and not be the cause of it. In the main, the workers concentrate on one anomaly and take little account of many other co-existing anomalies that may be present; these co-existing anomalies might be equally significant in causing encephalo-ataxia.

3. The direct link between the anomaly of family functioning and encephalo-ataxia is not well established in any of the studies. In no instance is the anomaly experimentally produced in order to cause encephalo-ataxia. The results of treatment of the anomaly to relieve the encephalo-ataxia are not convincing.

4. Most of the workers claim that the anomaly noted is always present in the families of the encephalo-ataxics studied; some maintain it varies with the sex of the encephalo-ataxic. However, it is not demonstrated that a representative sample of encephalo-ataxics are under study.

5. The possibility that the anomalies exist by chance alone is not excluded in any of the studies by adequate controls. Should the English epidemiological studies be correct, approximately a third of the population are significantly emotionally disturbed. Should encephalo-ataxics come from a representative group of families of the population at large, then in a third of families of encephalo-ataxics family psychopathology will be found by chance alone. Furthermore, disturbed families are less likely to cope with

encephalo-ataxic members, and thus institutionalised encephalo-ataxics will be present from such families in greater numbers, i.e., a selection factor may also be operating.

It may be that the psychopathological mechanisms described in the families of encephalo-ataxics may also be found in non-encephalo-ataxic families. Emotional divorce, immaturity, inadequacy, ambivalence, projection, pseudomutuality, stereotyped roles, family schisms, family skews, parental strife, family isolation, distortion of meaning, the double bind, unloving parents, incongruent communication and mystification are elements found in non-encephalo-ataxic families. Control studies will say to what extent. Experience with problem families would suggest that all pathological mechanisms are more manifest in severely emotionally disturbed families—but do not necessarily give rise to encephalo-ataxia.

6. Why does encephalo-ataxia appear in late adolescence, although family trauma has been bearing on a sensitive organism for a number of years? Some answers are offered. No convincing answer emerges in the studies. Furthermore, a number of organic states are tied to an age of onset in adolescence.

As was mentioned in the introduction the above six questions are not exhaustive. For instance, whilst on the one hand it can be argued that the family psychopathology has causal significance for encephalo-ataxia, it can also be held that the encephalo-ataxia causes family psychopathology. It would be strange if such a severe and perplexing disorder did not have some effect on the family state; this must be specially true of childhood encephalonosis, where one sees the sad disappointment and puzzlement of a mother at the lack of response from her child. Again, it must be adequately explained why one member of the family develops encephalo-ataxia rather than another, and also why that family member develops encephalo-ataxia rather than some other clinical condition.

At this point the author should reveal his own hypothesis that provides an alternative for the explanation of the data:

1. "Process" schizophrenia is qualitatively different from "non-process" schizophrenia. The former has an organic aetiology, encephalonosis, the latter is severe emotional illness, psychonosis. In the former, "process" schizophrenia (encephalo-ataxia), the perceptual and communication difficulties of the patient arise due to dysfunction of the intracerebral organic machinery of thought and communication and not due to external events in the family.

The essential question is whether the manifest pathology is caused by events within the individual, or outside him in the family. The studies assessed here sees processes at work in the family that distort communication, perception and meaning. An equally large group of workers, e.g., McGhie and Chapman (2, 10), see distortions resulting from interference with the intracerebral organic machinery of thought and communication. Such distortions are observed in organic brain lesions, dementia, acute toxic delirious states and the model encephalonoses. Thinking in metaphor, for example, can be a defence from the intrusions of fellow family members, or result from organic perceptual difficulties.

Two other views are possible as explanations of the perceptual anomalies: firstly, that an underlying constitutional weakness in the individual is released by emotional stress emanating from the family; secondly, that an existing constitutional weakness in a family member provokes a family reaction which may be harmful, but need not necessarily be so; the important and careful study of Pollin et al. (12) on identical twins may support this view. These possibilities need further exploration.

2. In the author's view the anomalies of family psychopathology associated with encephalo-ataxia (schizophrenia) are present in healthy families, mildly psychonotic families and severely psychonotic families ("non-process" schizophrenia). The more disturbed the family the clearer are the anomalies and the greater number there are—as can be seen in studies (4) of hard-core (problem) families.

3. The anomalies of family functioning described are coincidental with encephalo-ataxia ("process" schizophrenia) and do not cause it; they are found in association with severe psychonosis (including "non-process" schizophrenia), to a lesser extent in mild psychonosis, and to some extent in healthy families. The families of encephalo-ataxics ("process" schizophrenics) approximate to the families of the population at large; the population at large has marked psychopathology in about 30% of its families and therefore this will be true of the families of encephalo-ataxics by chance alone. This explains why these anomalies are found coincidentally in the families of some encephalo-ataxics. In the families of institutionalized encephalo-ataxics, a selection factor may operate to increase the incidence of anomalies—the more disturbed families with the greater number of anomalies can tolerate handicapped members less well and therefore there is an increase of institutionalized encephalo-ataxics from these disturbed families.

To conclude, the author leans to the view that the anomalies noted by workers on family psychopathology reviewed here are found with other anomalies in the families of the emotionally ill, and by chance in the families of encephalo-ataxics. They are not significant in the aetiology of encephalo-ataxia, which is caused essentially by intracerebral organic factors. It follows that the author sees no value in the concept of the "schizophreniform" family. Although the direct agent operating in the cerebrum is organic, this does not exclude the possibility that psychic stress on the organism may precipitate the production of the noxious agent that is directly responsible for the damage. The studies, however, are not wasted. Despite their present inconclusive nature, the studies undertaken to date may be the springboard for further conclusive research. Should it even be established, according to the views of the writer, that the patients under study are not encephalo-ataxics, a great deal will have been learnt from these painstaking and ingenious studies about the psychopathology of emotionally disturbed individuals and families.

REFERENCES

1. BLEULER, R. (1911). Dementia Praecox oder Gruppe der Schizophrenein. In: Aschaffenberg, G. (ed.) *Handbuch der Psychiatrie.* Leipzig und Wien.
2. CHAPMAN, J., and McGHIE, A. (1962). A comparative study of dysfunction in schizophrenia. *J. ment. Sci., 106,* 487.
3. Council of the College of General Practitioners (1958). Working party report. *Brit. med. J., 2,* 585.
4. HOWELLS, J. G. (1966). The psychopathogenesis of hard-core families. *Amer. J. Psychiat., 122,* 1159.
5. HOWELLS, J. G. (1968). Family psychopathology and schizophrenia. In: Howells, J. G. (ed.) *Modern Perspectives in World Psychiatry.* Edinburgh: Oliver and Boyd; New York: Brunner/Mazel.
6. KESSELL, W. I. N. (1960). Psychiatric morbidity in a London general practice. *Brit. J. prev. soc. Med., 14,* 16.
7. KRAEPELIN, E. (1899). Zur Diagnose und Prognose der Dementia Praecox. *Allg. Z. Psychiat., 56,* 254.
8. KRAMER, M., et al. (1969). Cross-national study of diagnosis of the mental disorders. Supplement, *Amer. J. Psychiat., 125.*
9. LANGFELDT, G. (1937). *The Prognosis in Schizophrenia and the Factors Influencing the Course of the Disease: A Katamnestic Study, including Individual Re-examination in 1936.* London: Oxford Univ. Press.
10. McGHIE, A., and CHAPMAN, J. (1961). Disorders of attention and perception in early schizophrenia. *Brit. J. med. Psychol., 34,* 103.
11. PEMBERTON, J. (1949). Illness in general practice. *Brit. med. J., 1,* 306.
12. POLLIN, W., STABENAU, J. R., and TUPIN, J. (1965). Family studies with identical twins discordant for schizophrenia. *Psychiatry, 28,* 60.
13. RAWNSLEY, K. (1966). An international diagnostic exercise. Proceedings of the IVth World Congress of Psychiatry. *Excerpta Medica Int. Congr.,* Series No. 117, 360.
14. ROSENHAN, D. L. (experiment quoted in *Science,* January 1973).
15. SHAKESPEARE, W. *Cymbeline,* II, iii, 101.
16. STEPHENS, J. H., and ASTRUP, C. (1963). Prognosis in "process" and "non-process" schizophrenia. *Amer. J. Psychiat., 119,* 945.
17. STEPHENS, J. H., and ASTRUP, C. (1965). Treatment outcome in "process" and "non-process" schizophrenics treated by "A" and "B" types of therapists. *J. nerv. ment. Dis., 140,* 449.

VIII

THE ORGANISATION OF A FAMILY PSYCHIATRIC SERVICE

INTRODUCTION

Every psychiatric service should be a family psychiatric service, accepting the family as the unit in clinical practice. Both out-patient and in-patient psychiatric services should be based on the family as the unit. The organisation of a service in family psychiatry will now be described in the light of the author's experience at the first hospital department organised completely for family psychiatry. Starting in 1949, the department (now the Institute of Family Psychiatry) by 1957 had developed its concepts to the point when family psychiatry was the only clinical approach employed. In this department family psychiatry is not a side activity, or an experimental tool, but a day-to-day service for the full range of clinical conditions.

In family psychiatry, the family is the patient. The sick individual, of whatever age, is taken to be the index of a sick family.

Family psychiatry can be practised by psychiatrists who usually accept only the referred patients of a particular age group, whether they be the aged, adults, adolescents or children. A geriatric psychiatrist, for instance, could practise a family approach in the following three ways, but family psychiatry only in the latter two, as follows:

1. Accepting the aged as the referred family member, he then uses knowledge of the whole family as a means of helping the aged. This of course is not family psychiatry, as the old person is the unit to be harmonised and not the family itself. Circumstances may sometimes force such an approach on a practitioner, but it has clear limitations. While family dynamics are altered to the benefit of the old person who is the patient, another family member becomes sick instead, hence the focus changes but the family as a whole remains sick. Again, all too often the family dynamics revert to their original state when help is removed. Furthermore, equally

415

disturbed or even more disturbed family members can be overlooked. This is a family approach, but not family psychiatry. It is based essentially on the *individual*.

2. Accepting the old person as the referred family member, the psychiatrist thereafter gives the rest of the family equal attention in his assessments and moves to treating the family as a whole. The family itself is the focus of endeavour. The aged person initially referred, though not given any more attention than the rest of the family, is given full attention and of course benefits from the harmonising of his milieu. This is truly family psychiatry. Such a practitioner, for a number of good reasons, limits himself to an introduction to the family through a referred old person. He limits himself in no other way. This might be termed *individual and family psychiatry*.

3. A family member of any age group, or a part of the family, or, ideally, the whole family is accepted as the referred patient. This is the practice at the Institute of Family Psychiarty, The Ipswich Hospital, with its geriatric, adult, adolescent, child, marital and whole family intake channels. From whatever part of the family the approach is first made, management moves to the family as a whole. This is termed *family psychiatry*. A geriatric psychiatrist may come to practise this complete approach in a number of situations: (i) He may come together with a like thinking colleague, who usually accepts family members of other age groups, and form a joint family psychiatry service. (ii) Finding himself in a district where there are no other services, he can expand his geriatric service to embrace other age groups as referred patients. (iii) He may be fortunate in starting a psychiatric service in a new hospital, where he could fashion his service in this way from the beginning. (iv) If experimentation is welcomed in his working situation, he may initiate an experimental or pilot scheme in this approach.

Another variant is, in addition to basing a service on one age group only, to base it on one clinical condition only. Some units specialise in psychosomatic states, or delinquency, drug addiction, alcoholism, psychonosis, etc. If, having accepted the referred patient, the unit subsequently moves to taking the whole family as the patient, then this approach can truly be said to be family psychiatry.

INTAKE

Ascertainment

The aim in referral procedure is to get the patient to the right clinic in the shortest possible time.

The *attitude* of the community towards the service will tend to determine whether or not patients are readily referred. The opinions held about the service by the usual referral agencies are probably much more important in encouraging acceptance of it than the opinions of the public, which are largely fashioned by that of the agencies. An understanding family or school doctor prepares his patient for a psychiatric interview and fosters rapport between clinic and patient. Unfortunately, the problems referred to a new service are likely to be the more severe, which makes success more difficult to obtain.

The family comes as a group, as a dyad, or, more commonly, as an individual.

The *age* of the patient causes him to present more readily to some services than to others.

The infant or toddler is likely to come to the notice of the family doctor or the home nurse. One investigation (2) shows that 93.1% of children under five were seen by a family doctor during a year for the mean number of times of 2.0, and for a mean of 9.55 minutes on each occasion. Probably no other agency approaches this degree of contact. Mothers are much more willing to attend welfare centres during the first year of a child's life than they are when the child is older; about 75% of the mothers attend with children under one year, whereas only about 27% of the mothers with children between one and five do so.

When a child is of school age, the family doctor and the school health service are important sources of referral. The cases referred from the school are likely to be ascertained by the school-teacher, who acts to some degree as a parent surrogate. Additional patients come from the courts and other hospital clinics.

The adolescent at work is likely to come from the family doctor, the factory doctor or the home nurse, while adolescents still being educated may come via the school or university health service. Some adolescents may come through the courts, and others through hospital clinics.

The adult will be referred by his family practitioner, his industrial medical officer, another hospital clinic, or a social agency.

The family doctor is the doctor most in touch with the whole family, and therefore has certain advantages over all other agencies. He is usually in touch with the family for many years, has a great amount of information available about the family and its social setting, and has knowledge of the family as a whole. An urban general practitioner has analysed his case material, and finds that for 78% of his patients he is doctor to the whole family—truly a "family doctor" (4). In rural areas the percentage is probably even higher. Cammock et al. (1) have confirmed these findings.

The *type of problem* or symptom presenting in the patient will to some extent determine which agency ascertains him. The general practitioner and infant welfare clinics usually refer patients with physical and emotional symptoms, while the teacher sends problems of discipline and of failure to make progress in school work. Courts of law may send patients with behaviour disorders—in the first place for a medical report and subsequently with a recommendation for treatment.

Patients with psychosomatic problems predominate in referrals from other hospital clinics. Such people are seen at surgical as well as at medical and paediatric departments.

Class and income are a factor in determining which psychiatric agency sees the patients. It is possible for an agency to gear itself to one income group—upper, middle, or lower. Sometimes the structure of a medical service makes this inevitable. Often the most neglected social group is the upper; patients in this group are forced to buy the service which they think is good for them, but it seldom proves to be the one best suited to their needs. Thus it is useful to examine a service to estimate whether it discriminates against the rich. A high standard of decoration and furniture, pleasant reception, an efficient appointment system can encourage the attendance of upper income groups, while proving no disadvantage to other income groups.

Intake Channels

The complete family psychiatric service will have intake channels for individuals of all age groups (the aged, adults, adolescents, and children), for dyads (the most usual is for marital couples), and for the whole family. Occasionally, as already mentioned, it may accept one of these groups only, e.g., the adolescent group, and from this beginning move to involve the rest of the family. In a very large service these intake channels can become clinics which are physically separate. In most services, however, they need only exist on paper as intake channels and can be dealt with in the same premises. Thus at one moment a psychiatrist is seeing a new patient who may be a child, later, in the same premises, a whole family is seen as a new patient, and the family is perhaps followed by a marital couple. This is organisationally possible, as whole family management is the ultimate aim and therefore premises that can cater for it can manage fragments of the family. Naturally, the intake procedure varies somewhat from age group to age group.

Whole family intake channel

This is the ideal intake channel and nothing is more encouraging and purposeful than to have a whole family appear together from the beginning.

It results either from an overwhelming need in the family itself, from the family's understanding, or from good introductory work by the referring agency. The organisation should make it as easy as possible for the whole family to attend—flexibility in choice of appointments, waiting areas comfortable enough for large families, play areas for the children, and interview rooms that are adequate to accommodate a family. Occasionally, it is more convenient for a family to attend during an evening clinic, or to attend for a whole day (four sessions of about one and a half hours), or to come into residential care for intensive investigation, therapy in a crisis, or intensive therapy.

Dyadic intake channels

This is probably used most commonly by marital couples. But occasionally other couples will appear—a discordant parent and adolescent, or even two adolescents. Perhaps the most unusual in the author's experience was a married woman and her medium—which proved to be a useful combination.

Referrals through the marital problems channel usually come from the family doctor, gynaecological clinics, other hospital clinics and from marriage guidance clinics. The development of voluntary marriage guidance clinics is most worthy, but their existence highlights the inadequacy of psychiatric services. This perhaps most crucial of the family's dyadic communications should not be isolated from the management of the rest of the family. Furthermore, the skills required call for great experience and the deployment of all a clinic's facilities; this can scarcely be expected to be available from people excellent and laudable in intention, but sometimes deficient of long training and experience. No psychiatric service is complete without a marital problems intake channel.

Individual intake channels

The *aged* will usually be sent by their family practitioner, a geriatrician, another hospital department, or a social agency. They may come singly or in couples. Their problem may turn around their immediate family or conflict with the succeeding family. The incidence of emotional illness in the aged resulting from special stresses that play on them has been grossly overlooked; attention hitherto has usually focused on senile dementia or other organic states. Even these may result from emotional strain. Retirement is a nodal point in their lives, as partners who hitherto had been able to spend only short periods together are now at one another's mercy. Death of friends or relatives may be another precipitating factor. There is a high incidence of psychosomatic disorder. The close collaboration of a geriatrician is usually necessary. Naturally, the aged are frail and gain much from a hospital car service, prompt appointments, being seen on a ground floor clinic, and the support of the social-work unit. An effective family psychiatric clinic for the aged can not only do a great deal for their well-being, but also reduce the need for in-patient care. Theirs is a sadly neglected cause.

Adults come singly, in couples, or with children. The referring agency is usually a family doctor, or another hospital clinic, industrial medical officers, or the courts. They exhibit the whole range of emotional and psychosomatic disorders. At the moment, many other services, particularly in organic medicine, are coping with problems that should be the responsibility of the psychiatric service, if the facilities were available. There are a number of age periods within adulthood—early manhood from 19–24 years, the young marrieds to about 40 years, the active years from 40–55 years and the period of pre-retirement to about 65. Each has its special characteristics and special problems.

Adolescents, like the aged, tend to be a neglected age group. Recently, adolescent psychiatrists are becoming a separate group, developing special services for adolescents. This is to be welcomed as long as the involvement of the family is recognised. The adolescent clinic should move to involving the family and thus practice adolescent and family psychiatry. The adolescent clinic could be an intake channel within a department of family psychiatry. Some adolescent clinics are in association with universities, city colleges, schools, and factories.

Adolescents have special needs. Often in conflict with parents, they need to feel that, initially, they can seek help in their own right and that their confidentiality is respected. The first moment of contact may not be the best moment for moving to a family involvement. The introduction of the rest of the family must be the subject of careful discussion. Its aims should be outlined and the adolescent be fully sure of the part he is to play. Misunderstandings can wreck the confidence of an adolescent in the adults who run the services and cause him to refuse much-needed help. The clinical staff and the adolescent may readily come to understand one another on the requirements of adolescents. But the young patient may need to be cautioned that it may take his family much longer to reach the same understanding—if ever. Progress may be slow and, unless this is realised, disillusionment may set in. The adolescent is also sensitive to the way in which he is received. Conscious of striving towards adulthood, he is impatient of any suggestion of a childhood status. If there is no separate waiting room accommodation for young people, then they profit more from being in the adult waiting room rather than the children's.

Adolescence is usually taken to be a period from puberty to the age of 18 to 19. It consists of two age groups with somewhat different interests; the first ranges from puberty to the age of about 15 years, while the next group in late adolescence extends from about 15 years to 19 years. The adolescent is the scapegoat of our time—perhaps of all time. An emerging challenge to the previous generation, he is the ready butt of their abuse and misuse. He stands between childhood and adulthood—encouraged to depend on the adult, but pay the price of dependence, or pushed into adult responsibilities without adult experience. His defects are grossly exaggerated by adults who control the mass media of communication—the newspapers, television, and radio. The panic of the adults is often so great that disproportionate publicity is given to the adolescent's supposed misdeeds, and this encourages him in the very activities dreaded by the adults. These activities are often adult-made.

In fact, the adolescent population carries no higher incidence of emotional illness than any other age group. The majority pass through adolescence with no, or only fleeting, problems. They, the majority, do not make news. A minority, about one-third, require psychiatric attention, and about 10% are in great need of it. Adolescence has its compensations as well as its special difficulties; adolescents are hopeful, vigorous and idealistic. Also they are specially fortunate in being often able to escape from an intolerable family and to receive help before they plunge into the next family.

In many countries, the assets of the adolescents go unused until a national emergency, such as war, appears. Then, at an early age, responsibility may be thrust upon them. Some countries, e.g., the U.K., have now accepted that adulthood can start at 18. In many countries, the form of education is a gross disservice to the adolescents. They are forced into a dependence with inadequate finance until the age of 18 and then they are sent to university centres of education for yet more years—again in a state of dependence and inadequate income that inflames rebellion. A form of education that allowed employment and study at the same time is much to be preferred. The adolescent could earn his own money, develop true notions about work, be a responsible member of society, be free of dependence on the adult, be a more serious student, and be capable of a more realistic assessment of the training offered him. University life based on academic ghettos is obsolete. It carries more disadvantages than advantages.

The *children's* intake channel covers the age group from birth to puberty. Again it consists of a number of sub-age groups—infancy, toddler, school age. Each has its characteristics and special problems. While it would be wrong to neglect the needs of any one age group, the infant and pre-school child, because of their ability to change and as representatives of the future, are of particular importance.

The following points should be noted in a child and family psychiatry service:

1. An analysis of case material shows that the great majority of presenting individual patients are emotionally disturbed. Their emotional disturbance is a result of emotional trauma, which is produced usually within the family. Encephalonosis (psychosis) in children, whether it be organic, or functional, is rare. An analysis of a thousand cases at the children's intake channel, the Institute of Family Psychiatry, The Ipswich Hospital, showed that only 6 patients were referred for encephalonosis, i.e., 0.6%. Therefore the children's service must be primarily oriented to the clinical needs of the emotionally disturbed child—99.4% of the intake.

2. The frequency of emotional disorder in children is usually given as 1–2% of all children per year. Variations in this figure will depend upon the standard adopted by the observer. In general, it is the most awkward or attention-getting symptom that receives the earliest investigation; less obvious, but equally serious, symptoms can easily be overlooked. Furthermore, the greater the skill of the diagnostician, the more numerous the children referred.

As part of a large survey of psychiatric disorders in the population of Aarhus and its county, financed by the Ford Foundation, a small but very thorough study of psychological disorders in childhood was made on the island of Samsø (Denmark) by Lange, Mogensen and Fenger (6). They found that 15.5% of all children up to 15 years of age were in need of psychiatric care. Statisticians estimate this as equivalent to 2–3% of children needing care per year, and suggested that the figure quoted above, on which present planning is often based, may be an underestimate.

3. One of the striking results of a direct link with the home through the general practitioner is the way in which the percentage of referral of children under five will increase. By 1959, in the town of Ipswich, where the service is particularly accessible to the general practitioner, 17.5% of children attending the Institute of Family Psychiatry through the children's intake clinic were under the age of five.

4. In each age group there is a preponderance of boys over girls, especially in the groups 5–10 years. This may indicate that boys are more disturbed than girls. But it may indicate that a selection factor is operating, e.g., that disturbed boys are more prone to behaviour which attracts the attention of referral agencies. Should there be such a selection factor, it

would seem important to circumvent it, so that future mothers may receive the same help as future fathers.

5. The distribution of intelligence in emotionally disturbed children referred through the children's intake clinic to the Institute of Family Psychiatry closely followed the curve of normal distribution, the mean I.Q. of children being 97.05. Mentally subnormal children should be accepted by this service if they manifest emotional disorder.

6. With children, accessibility to the source of the disturbance, the home, is very important, and on this fact largely depends the number of children ascertained as emotionally disturbed. The aetiological importance of the family has sometimes been underestimated and undue emphasis given to the child's school life. In the important pre-school age group, of course, the school cannot be a factor. In the school-age group, it would appear that the intensity and length of contact between child and school is much less than is sometimes supposed. Usually a child of school age spends approximately one-third of his waking time at school and two-thirds of his time outside the influence of the school. It must also be remembered that the intensity of contact between child and adult is very much less at school than it is at home. At home, in a family with two children, he will have a relationship in a one-to-one ratio with an adult: at school he will be fortunate to have a relationship on a one-to-thirty ratio with a teacher. Furthermore, each year contacts made with the school-teacher will be broken, and indeed in the later years he will meet a variety of teachers, each of whom he will see for only a short time each week. Thus, aetiologically, the school would appear to be less important than the home; but, naturally, it still provides valuable opportunities for the ascertainment of ill children.

7. The age of the patient causes him to present more readily to some services than to others.

The infant or toddler is likely to come to the notice of the family doctor or the home nurse. When a child is of school age, the family doctor and the school health service are important sources of referral.

8. Certain agencies will refer patients presenting with those problems or symptoms which are of special interest to them. Psychosomatic and emotional symptoms will be referred mostly by the general practitioner and infant welfare clinics. Problems of discipline and of lack of progress in school will cause referral from teachers. Behaviour disorders will cause courts of law to refer patients for a medical report, which will often lead to treatment.

Children with psychosomatic problems predominate in referrals from other hospital clinics. Such children are seen at surgical as well as medical

and paediatric departments. For example, the general surgical department
sees patients with obscure abdominal pains; the orthopaedic department,
accident prone cases; the obstetric department, early disturbances of
mother-infant relationship. The ophthalmologist sees emotionally determined squints and headaches, and from the ear, nose and throat department come such problems as pseudo-deafness, pseudo-backwardness and
chronic rhinitis.

9. The teacher refers her problems to the school medical officer by
personal contact at school health inspections or by telephone or by letter.
Others in the educational field have opportunities of observing difficulties
in the child, for instance, the speech therapist, the educational psychologist
and the school nurse. All these agencies refer the children to the school
medical officer for referral to the psychiatrist.

The school medical officer should be regarded as being in the same
position relative to the teacher and the child as the general practitioner to
the parent and child. It is his responsibility to assess the problem, and to
exclude non-psychiatric conditions, e.g., the deaf child, the child with visual
difficulties, the subnormal child, or the child with physical difficulties. Before referral, the school medical officer can usually discuss the child with
the general practitioner. Where the school medical officer can himself manage a problem, he is encouraged to do so. When a child is referred from
school, it is important to discuss the matter with the parents to enlist their
co-operation; without this measure great difficulty may arise later.

At this point it might be worthwhile to clarify the distinction between the
school psychological service and the psychiatric service for school children
by an analogy with diabetes in the physical field. Information about a
diabetic child's behaviour at school might aid the diagnostic measures of
the school medical officer and the hospital paediatrician. Thus, an approach
is made to the teacher by the hospital social worker to gather information
to assist diagnosis. After treatment, it may be helpful to the teacher to
receive information from the school medical officer or the paediatrician on
the handling of the diabetic child at school. Thus a school visit from the
medical social worker can be of value here also. Furthermore, the child,
because of his disability, may be retarded in school work to such an extent
that the teacher may need to use special educational facilities and thus she
requires the advice of the school psychological service. There is here no
confusion of function between the school health service, the hospital paediatric service, and the school psychological service.

The situation is similar for an emotionally ill child; a link is needed
between the teacher and the psychiatric service through the social worker
in order to provide information for diagnosis. During and after treatment a

similar contact is required between the psychiatric service and the teacher in order to help her in her handling of the child. Furthermore, the child, because of his disability, may sometimes be retarded in school work to such an extent that the teacher may require the advice of the school psychological service. Again, there is no confusion between the school health service, the psychiatric service for children and the school psychological service.

10. The medical officer, usually after collaboration with the general practitioner, refers the child direct to the clinic from the infant welfare clinic. Some have advocated that child psychiatric clinics should be placed at all infant welfare clinics. Except in special circumstances, such as at a large centre or a teaching unit, it is neither necessary nor practicable. The same request could be advanced by the many hospital, local authority and general practitioner clinics. Paediatric clinics sometimes ask for the same service, while forgetting that a number of hospital departments who see children could make the same request. The real need is for adequate liaison, for advice to be offered immediately over the telephone, and for urgent cases to be seen at once.

11. Children in care are referred from the Departments of Social Service. In England, in 1972, 6.4 per thousand children were in the care of local authorities (3). Some of these children are very disturbed, and since the community is acting as a parent surrogate it has a special responsibility for them. These children should be the day-to-day responsibility of a medical officer or general practitioner, like the child in his own home; these doctors seek psychiatric help as required.

12. Juvenile Courts. Magistrates usually remand the patient for a medical report either through the Clerk of the Court or the probation service and allow the full period of three weeks.

Referrals

From time to time patients knock at the department's door and ask to be seen. This is usually because the matter is immediately urgent, because they are new to the area, or because they have alienated the sympathies of the usual sources of referral. It is a disadvantage if the referring agencies are by-passed and the patient becomes his own diagnostician. Also, the usual referring agencies lose interest and many advantages are lost.

Urgent cases, however, should be accepted as a matter of emergency and then referred back to their own doctor. Less urgent cases can be referred back to their own doctors, but should this present any difficulty the clinic can approach the doctor on their behalf. Administrative conveniences should not be allowed to come before the welfare of the patient.

The Samaritans have proved the need for an emergency service for suicidal people. This service should be in an integral part of an adequate psychiatric service. This is in no way to decry the invaluable work of dedicated and humane helpers; but the responsibility thrust upon them is enormous and deserves the help of an immediately available psychiatric emergency clinic.

A convenient practice is for each general practitioner to be supplied with a number of appointment slips, each having a space for notes. These are sent direct by post to the family psychiatric service and are placed in a confidential file until the family is seen. This file is in the charge of a psychiatric member of staff. Cases referred to a particular psychiatrist are seen by him.

The same procedure can apply to any other medical referral agency, who can be supplied with the service's referral slip. From time to time agencies will prefer to refer by letter and the same procedure applies.

Waiting List

A steady flow of cases keeps the clinical staff at optimum efficiency, and for this a waiting list is required. Urgent cases should be seen at once, fairly urgent cases within five days, and the average case within two weeks. Such arrangements call for some elasticity in administration. Waiting lists were the subject of an enquiry by the Ministry of Health, U.K., in 1958 (7).

A psychiatric service should give a rapid diagnostic service, or it will hamper the activities of other agencies. If, however, it accepts for prolonged treatment all the patients requiring it, then, with the staff usually available today, a long waiting list will soon accumulate. Selection of patients for treatment is essential, as it allows the available staff to be used to the best advantage, prevents a long waiting list accumulating and lets patients pass straight from diagnosis to treatment, a highly desirable practice. The number of patients treated must match the facilities available—or the treatment will not be worthwhile. The waiting list at the Institute of Family Psychiatry has remained at about two weeks for 23 years under this policy.

Other measures which have been found helpful in maintaining a short waiting list are: (i) the omission of routine case conferences and thus saving time; (ii) placing one administrative person in charge of the waiting list; and (iii) sending a pre-paid reply postcard with the appointment, thus almost guaranteeing that if the appointment cannot be kept, the Institute will be informed.

For first attendance, the failure rate can be as low as 6% or as high as 75%. The most significant factor in a low failure rate is a short waiting list.

Other factors are the co-operation of referring agencies and the acceptance of the service by the community.

Reception

A pleasant letter should invite the patient to attend and it can be accompanied by a brochure giving information likely to be required before attendance. Attendance should be by appointment. Patients should be received in the waiting area by a receptionist, who should be welcoming and friendly and be the hostess representing the service.

The waiting area should be comfortable and, by a suitable arrangement of chair and furniture, allow some degree of privacy. Children require activity and diversion while waiting and this can be supplied in a corner of the waiting area. Of even greater assistance to children is a waiting garden with swings, sandpit, slides, pits, etc., for their entertainment. But so popular does an outdoor waiting area become that in no time adults require a section to themselves. Suitable landscaping can make this possible.

The receptionist is a key member of staff. She manages the "shop window of the service" and supplies the first emotional contact between staff and the family. The receptionist should be pleasant, balanced, friendly, welcoming, and, given these qualities, will almost certainly be attractive. It calls for tact to start the communication process between the service and the family without causing them to unburden their problem before the appropriate moment. In the best-run institutions, appointments can run late and the reasons for it should be explained to the family or individual. At the same time, the waiting period should be cut to a minimum, otherwise the implied indifference mars the rapport making. All public institutions should arrange their reception with the same care and concern as the most considerate private institution.

It should be a rule within the institution that no child be parted from its parents if it is reluctant to agree to this. Patience leads to release of tension and ultimate co-operation. Equally, any child who has agreed to be parted from a parent should immediately be returned to him if he requests it. Again, the observance of this in time makes for improving self-confidence and co-operation with staff.

Evening clinics are popular with families, with fathers who cannot attend during the day, and with mothers who require their husbands to look after the children. They are less popular with staff.

Once a new patient has attended, it is a helpful practice to explain that, should he become acutely distressed for any reason, he has only to telephone the service and an immediate appointment or home visit will be arranged.

INVESTIGATION

Case Procedure

A clinical investigation is based upon the following principles:

1. When an individual presents on his own, the first aim is to make a diagnosis. It has to be established whether the presenting patient is sent with an emotional disorder or with some other clinical entity. A diagnosis is made from elucidating positive psychiatric findings and not from negative physical findings.

2. The second aim is to quickly reveal the true emotional condition of the patient by appraising his psychopathology, bearing in mind the dynamic continuum of the past and the present.

3. The focus of the investigation moves from the presenting person to all members of the family as soon as possible. Family psychopathology is the key area. The moment when this is possible varies from family to family.

4. Assessment must be made of the family's assets as well as of its liabilities.

5. The establishment of rapport between the clinical personnel and the family is of fundamental importance. Given rapport, the relevant information will in time be forthcoming.

6. In the case of a child presenting, one practice is as follows. The psychiatrist first sees the parents, who have both been invited to the interview. A history of the complaint is taken from the parents. The child is then seen alone by the psychiatrist and a systematic appraisal is made of him in either a play or an interview situation, depending upon his age. Preferably, the whole family, including any other siblings, should then be seen together.

Physical and neurological examination of the child, if necessary, is undertaken at this interview, or, more usually, at the subsequent one. Great care is taken to make the physical examination a pleasant and rapport-building experience for the child.

7. Adolescents should usually be seen first and contact with the rest of the family be entered into after discussion with the adolescent.

8. At the first interview with a family or individual, the following *additional information* can be available:

(a) Hospital records of all family members. They are useful in explaining previous ill-health and the reason for hospital admissions.

(b) School medical officer's records in the case of a child. When children are referred from school, the records are usually sent by the school medical officer with his referring letter. When the general practitioner refers a patient, it is possible to borrow the records from the School Health Authority.

(c) School report in the case of a child. This is usually forwarded automatically when a child is referred by the school medical officer. When a general practitioner refers a child, it can be supplied by the school on request. The school report may be supplemented later by school visits by the clinic social worker.

(d) General practitioner's report. Should a child be referred by a school doctor, the psychiatrist can ask for a letter to be sent to the general practitioner inviting information about his patient.

At the first or subsequent attendance, one or more of the following special procedures may be required:

(a) Social History. The psychiatrist outlines the initial formulation to the social worker and the policy in regard to the social history is discussed between them. Formal social histories are rarely necessary. Instead, the essential historical facts about the family can be obtained by a questionnaire completed by the family alone or with the assistance of a clinical member of staff.

(b) Psychological Procedures. The initial formulation is discussed with the clinical psychologist and the problems for assessment are defined. Without this definition the procedure is as valueless as sending a patient to a radiologist without a specific request. The family, or person, is usually seen at the first attendance. Additional appointments, if required, are arranged between the psychologist and the family.

(c) Play Diagnosis. This is not undertaken at the first interview, since the psychiatrist will already have observed the child in a play situation. The initial formulation is discussed between the psychiatrist and the child therapist, who then pursues the investigation in one or more subsequent interviews.

(d) Pathological Investigations. Urine analysis usually takes place in the psychiatric clinic. More elaborate investigations call for the services of the pathological department.

(e) Radiological Examination—if, rarely, required.

(f) Electro-Encephalographic Examination—if required.

(g) In-patient Observation.

Second and subsequent attendances. The second attendance usually takes place during the following week, when all the reports are to hand. The psychiatrist now makes his second formulation. Some cases, those seeking an opinion only, can sometimes be closed at this point and sent back to the referring agency. After this attendance, a first report is prepared for the referring doctor.

In most cases, however, further attendances are necessary in order to elucidate the psychopathology. Usually, it is felt that the investigation is not complete until a picture of the psychodynamics of the *whole family* is obtained.

Procedures include individual and dyadic interviews and family group diagnosis whereby all members of the family are interviewed together. Families accept this latter procedure remarkably easily, and the psychiatrist should never deny himself the opportunity of seeing the interplay of the family dynamics at first hand. Time must be allowed for the true pattern to emerge. The relationships of the family with the community are also readily revealed, and, in particular, relationships with the extended family.

Staff liaison. The clinical responsibility for the patient should be borne throughout by his psychiatrist. The ethical position is that a referring doctor requires an opinion on his patient by a specialist, and also requires that treatment beyond his resources be undertaken by the specialist. The psychiatrist can call on the assistance of a number of expert non-medical colleagues who, while not taking responsibility for the patient, are responsible for the work they undertake with the patient. Each professional worker is administratively responsible to the senior worker in his unit, and in turn to the clinical director of the department. But each professional clinical worker is solely responsible for his own clinical work, and in this work collaborates directly with the psychiatrist concerned with that case. Each expert worker requires such information as will enable him to carry out his work effectively.

Length of Interviews

Usually, individual interviews take 50 minutes, in addition to five minutes for consulting the records and a further five minutes at the end for writing notes. Thus 60 minutes are allowed for an individual. For a dyadic interview, 90 minutes are necessary. For a family interview, two hours is usual, but this may occasionally extend to three hours. Rarely, a family may be seen for a whole day in a modified "multiple impact therapy" technique; there must be adequate rest periods for interviewer and family. This latter procedure is useful when the family can be seen once only, or when a family has reached a nodal point in therapy, or when it has much to say, or when the family is in a crisis.

TREATMENT

1. The ideal aim is to achieve a completely harmoniously functioning family.
2. Sometimes it is unrealistic to expect such a complete result and a modified aim becomes necessary, as in any other clinical field.

3. The art of medicine must not be overlooked. Every presenting patient and every family is unique, and the constellation of factors which produced the disturbance cannot be covered by any general rule.

4. The family must show improvement, not only within the therapeutic situation, but also within the home setting.

5. Benexperiential psychotherapy may be required by one or more members of the family, or the whole family, irrespective of the person who was initially referred.

6. In our present state of knowledge of psychopathology, vector therapy is the most effective therapy.

7. Selected foster homes offer the best form of substitute home care for children.

8. There is a place for an in-patient service for the short-term investigation and short- and long-term treatment of children, adolescents, adults, the aged, and families.

9. A clinical service should not be obliged to offer all the necessary therapeutic measures to every patient. Other agencies may be able to offer some forms of help just as effectively. The family doctor is in a particularly advantageous position to offer supportive therapy. Supportive work may be undertaken by the health visitor, the social worker and the teacher. Tasks such as remedial teaching, the ascertainment of educationally backward or bright children who need special school facilities, and vocational guidance, are undertaken by the School Psychological Service.

10. At the initial formulation, a preliminary plan of therapy is made. The early process of therapy may have begun at the sending of the first appointment. The preliminary plan may need alteration as further information comes to hand. The number of family members under therapy may change, or the emphasis of the therapy alter.

In some clinics, it is usual for benexperiential psychotherapy to be the prime task of the psychiatrist, while the child psychotherapist treats the child in collaboration with him and the social worker uses case work in vector therapy.

11. Drug therapy may be an adjunct to psychotherapy and vector therapy.

Reports

General

The purpose of a report is to give all who can help a patient as much information as they need for their purpose, *after obtaining the full consent of the patient*. The basis of the work between all professional workers and the patient is the ability of the patient to communicate meaningful emotional happenings. This can occur only when the patient knows that the information imparted will not be divulged to others without his consent. At the same time he cannot be helped by other agencies unless they have enough information for their purpose. This information may be the whole, or more usually a part, of the information known to the psychiatric service. It must be passed on to other agencies with the full knowledge of the patient, so that, if he wishes, he may elect not to seek this further help. Agencies readily accept the position when it is put to them in this way, and difficulties seldom arise in practice.

Reports are usually sent after the second diagnostic attendance. Follow-up reports are sent at intervals if many attendances occur. A final report is sent to the referring doctor at the closure of the case.

Children

The report goes directly to the family doctor when a child patient has been referred by him. If a hospital department is also involved, then a copy of the report goes to the specialist concerned.

With child patients it is often essential to seek the help of the school medical officer. In this event a copy of the report is sent to him, with the consent of the family doctor and the parents, so that the school doctor can advise his education authority. Sometimes the teacher has been the instigator of the referral, and it is then desirable that her interest should be maintained and her help sought; a non-medical report is therefore sent to the teacher through the school medical officer and the director of education. This may be followed by a school visit, which is more valuable than a written report. Even if the teacher has not played any part in the referral, she may still, in some cases, be able to make a valuable contribution. No contact with a school should take place without the awareness and agreement of the parents.

When the school medical officer refers, the report on a child patient goes direct to him and he is responsible for advising the education or health authority. A copy is sent to the family doctor. Communication is established with the teacher as already described. In those cases where there is a special educational problem a report is sent to the educational psychologist so that she can arrange her specialist help and an informal contact invariably follows.

In the case of referrals from a court of justice, a medical recommendation is made direct to the court through the Clerk of the Court.

Follow-up

At the end of one year after closure, it is a useful procedure to make a "follow-up" contact through the social worker who undertook casework on that family. This practice has several objectives. Families derive comfort from the thought that contact with the psychiatric service will be renewed in a year's time; any further help that is required can be arranged. An evaluation of the help given to the family can be made; some patients are able, with the detachment of time, to give a better assessment of the way in which the service helped. Follow-up studies can also be used to study the development and natural history of emotional illness (5).

FACILITIES

Siting of Units

The disorder in the family is usually a matter of family discernment, but sometimes it is first noticed at work, in school, in courts of law, in hospital, in prison, etc. The family psychiatry service must be so placed as to be able to serve the agency of discernment. In the United Kingdom, the commonest agency to be involved in discernment is the family medical practitioner service, which sees 80% of the population per annum on at least one occasion and which has an even greater contact with the very young and the very old. In some countries, the internist or paediatrician has replaced the family general practitioner. In others, there may be no family practitioner service, but the same function is performed by local clinics or dispensaries; in yet other countries, it may be the social agencies. Other agencies may be involved with industry, school or courts.

Another important factor in siting is the organisation of a medical service. In some countries, a general medical service is expected to offer a basic psychiatric service within its normal work; this, of course, carries the enormous advantage of being able to help the physical and emotional aspects of the disturbance in one service and in people well known to them. Such a general service thus requires a supporting specialist service only for particularly puzzling diagnostic problems or for problems requiring specialised facilities. Other medical services are planned as a series of services offering specialist care. Such a service may need to be close to the public, as there is no more accessible service available.

Yet another factor turns around the nature of the facilities required by the service. Usually it requires supporting facilities in organic medicine and the availability of an in-patient service; hence the contemporary tendency to abolish the psychiatric hospital and to bring its services alongside that of the general hospital—supporting the idea of a combined physical and emotional health service, the medicine of the whole person. However, for this to be effective, the family psychiatry service and its in-patient facilities must be fully integrated and, as it were, be off the main corridor or lift shaft and not isolated in some corner of the grounds. The fullest integration takes place where each specialist service within the hospital has a family psychiatric service attached to it. Placement at a general hospital also makes the psychiatric service available to the large number of patients who present at its out-patient or in-patient service with disorders initially thought to be organic in origin.

Thus, usually a family psychiatric service will be placed at a main hospital, or in an intermediate position between home and hospital—a local polyclinic or health centre which has attached in-patient facilities. Very small local units, even with a part-time staff, tend to be expensive to run, wasteful in staff travelling time, and will not be able to supply the full range of services.

Out-Patient Facilities

The architecture should be a blend of the domestic and of the functional. This does not necessarily call for a building designed as a house; it is possible to design a hospital building so that it embodies domestic features. In internal decoration, special attention should be paid to the use of colour so that an atmosphere of warmth, welcome, and brightness is created. Colours must blend, otherwise there will be a feeling of restlessness and disharmony. Lighting in the corridors and offices should be bright, but in interview rooms the lighting should be reflected from walls or ceilings, thus creating a more subdued and relaxed atmosphere. Whenever possible—in interview, waiting and staff rooms—curtains, carpets, wooden furniture, flowers and plants should add to the general feeling of warmth and relaxation.

The department can be divided into a number of units—for administration, waiting, psychiatrists, psychologists, social workers, child therapists, research and teaching. Each of the clinical areas should have its own seminar room and unit office.

Some facilities are shared—studio and control room (in which are housed all sound and video equipment and tape storage); a clinical room for weighing, height recording, urine testing, etc.; a drug cupboard, a branch of the main hospital pharmacy; library; cafeteria; staff common room; staff cloak-rooms; and a rest room for sick staff.

The administrative area will contain accommodation for the administrative officer, secretaries, typing pool, work room for photocopying and duplicating, storage rooms, records room, room for switchboard, and a small waiting area for visitors other than patients.

The waiting area has already been described. It should contain a telephone for the use of visitors and ample cloakroom facilities.

Patients should pass from the pleasant waiting area to interview rooms large enough to accommodate a whole family comfortably. The interview rooms have normally two functions—that of an office and that of an interview room; the latter being more important than the former. It should be possible to arrange the furniture so that interviewing takes place away from the desk, for instance, round a small side table on which flowers are placed. Instantaneous recording facilities are very helpful, but call for attention to sound-proofing and ventilation. Each room should have a telephone for internal and external links.

Play rooms are usually situated on the ground floor. Each room should contain all the facilities required for child psychotherapy. In addition to individual play rooms, there should be a large room suitable for group and club activities. One room should cater for adolescent activities. Further features are a two-way screen, or closed circuit television, or video tape facilities for teaching purposes, ample storage facilities for play materials and a children's lending library. There should be an outdoor therapy area. Children, unlike adults, enjoy the bright primary colours on wall areas. These facilities can be extended to make it possible to organise a day hospital in conjunction with the therapy area.

A research unit needs rooms for the research administrator, research field staff and secretarial staff; it needs considerable storage area, and a large room for administrative work on projects. In addition, there will be laboratory space depending on the nature of the experimentation. Computer time may be hired elsewhere or equipment installed in the unit.

Teaching will be based on the unit seminar rooms, a shared auditorium, and the library. The department can build up a library of sound and video tapes for teaching purposes.

Family case notes can be kept in individual locked filing systems in each interview room, while a master file is maintained in a locked filing system in the records office. At the closure of a case, the notes are brought together in one file and remain for 12 months in a cabinet housing "temporarily closed" case notes. After 12 months they are removed to a cabinet for "closed" case notes. Should a case be reopened, the notes are broken up into unit notes and held in the locked cabinet of the professional workers concerned.

The utmost care should be taken to guard the confidential nature of case notes; it is a useful practice for each member of the administrative staff to sign, on appointment, a statement that he has read the warning notice about their confidential nature. It has been wisely recommended by a government committee in the U.K. that case notes should be destroyed after having been stored for seven years.

The work of the professional staff can be supplemented by voluntary helpers. They can function as a small group, a Circle of Friends, or, in the case of a large unit, a League of Friends. In the U.K. they are usually affiliated to the National League of Hospital Friends. Such groups can serve as useful links between the department and the voluntary charitable organisations in the community, can provide funds for material aid when this is not available from any other source, and can also initiate projects which are not recognised as coming within the purview of any statutory body. The Friends acquire funds through donations from voluntary bodies, and by organising activities of their own. Small sums of money readily available at the right moment can be invaluable to patients in urgent need.

While a hospital building must take account of the requirements of its staff, it should be remembered that its work will be greatly facilitated if it is so constructed as to aid the work with patients. The work turns around the rapport between staff and patients and everything in the building that encourages this promotes the work. A big element in this is the ability to fashion the building in such a way that the patient feels a welcomed guest.

In-Patient Accommodation

Accommodation is required in the family psychiatric field for individuals (of all age groups), dyads, and families. The provision may need to be for diagnosis and for therapy (short- or long-term).

Children: Short-term units. These are for diagnosis, short-term therapy and emergencies. They should be in small units of 8–12 beds and be administered from the out-patient family psychiatric facilities. The special means of investigation, psychometric, electro-encephalogramic, pathological, etc., should be readily available. It is estimated that 10 beds should be adequate for a population of 500,000. Practice varies as to siting. Some prefer to have separate diagnostic units, while others prefer to incorporate them within their long-term units.

Children: Long-stay units. These units admit for stabilization those children who are too disturbed for placement in hostels, foster homes, etc. The children and staff require a high degree of psychiatric support. The length of stay averages two years. They should be in units of 8–12 beds organised as a home. It is estimated that two such mixed units, for boys and girls together, would be required for a population of 500,000.

Units for encephalonotic children. These should be planned on a regional basis. The optimum size is that of the home group type of 12 beds. Facilities for investigation and research should be readily available. Long-term or permanent care is required for the majority of these patients. It is estimated that two such units would serve a population of 1,000,000 people.

Adolescents: Units for long-term care of disturbed adolescents. The aim of these units is to give intensive treatment over a period of two years or more to emotionally disturbed adolescents who are unfitted for other accommodation. Home care should be supplied in units of 8–12 beds. These should be administered by the department of family psychiatry. Sexes are not segregated. It is estimated that 25 beds per 500,000 population would be required for each of the age groups 12–15 and 15–18, making a total of 50 beds. Experience has shown that young and older adolescents have different needs. It is not necessary to have closed or locked units for highly psychopathic adolescents. The above units, when properly run, are adequate.

Adolescents: Units for encephalonotic adolescents. These should be units of 12 beds in mental hospitals alongside the same facilities for adults.

Adolescents: Night hospitals or hostels. These should be of the family type with house parents, and catering for groups of 12 adolescents. These are invaluable for adolescents who, following in-patient care, still require some skilled help whilst working locally. They should be under the supervision of the department of family psychiatry, but need not be located with it.

Young Adults: Units for long-term care, for over two years. These should be in small home units of 8–12 beds with mature staff. They cater for the university student age group, 18–24. Units are shared by both sexes. It is estimated that two units of 8–12 beds would be required for a population of 500,000. This may be an underestimate.

Young adults with encephaloataxia would be accommodated separately in long-term mental hospital accommodation.

Young Adults: Night hospitals or hostels. As for adolescents.

Adults: Diagnostic units. Can admit also young adults. Short-term care for emergency and investigation; 12 beds for a population of 500,000.

Adults: Long-term psychonosis units for six months to two years. In small home groups of 8–12 with experienced mature staff. Sexes are mixed. It is estimated that altogether approximately 48 beds will be necessary for a population of 500,000.

Adults: Night hospitals or hostels. Similar to those for adolescents.

Adults: Encephalonosis units. These should be provided in long-term and permanent mental hospital accommodation—again, in small units.

Aged: Assessment units. To be used when there is doubt concerning diagnosis, especially in neuropsychiatric problems. These are small units for short-term stay; 25 beds for a population of 500,000 will probably suffice.

Aged: Psychonosis units. These cater for the long-term rehabilitation of the aged over the age of 65. The sexes are not segregated. Stay should be for periods nearer six months than two years.

Dyadic units. These call for flexibility in the use of accommodation. They may accommodate husband and wife, or parent and children. Accommodation in the form of flatlets, or villas.

Family units. These are probably best supplied in the form of villas with central facilities for treatment and recreation. Indications for the admission of whole families are:

1. Distance makes out-patient therapy impossible.
2. A period of crisis.
3. Intensive investigation.
4. Research.

Five-day in-patient units. There is a very limited scope for these in the case of psychonotic patients of any age group. Returning to a disturbed family at weekends is rarely beneficial. Indeed, the in-patient units should give maximum concentration of care in the evening and at weekend—like any home.

Supporting services. In addition to night hospitals, there is a need for foster home placement, hostels, and special boarding schools for children and adolescents, and boarding-out care and hostels for adults and the aged.

Common features. It should be noted that certain principles apply for most of the above:

1. Treatment is on a long-term basis. It is not to be expected that the reintegration of personality can be effected quickly, as the therapy involves changing a process that has often been present for many years.

2. The therapy is one form of vector therapy. The harmful vectors in the family are replaced by beneficial vectors in the unit. Such a process is only possible if staff have the requisite personal qualities.

3. Employment, or attendance at school, in some cases can co-exist with therapy. Patients unable to work can attend a day hospital, or undertake sheltered employment within the hospital.

4. Sexes are not segregated. Marriages between disturbed people, however, are not encouraged except after a close examination of the two participants.

5. The vector process can be supplemented by benexperiential psychotherapy—individual, dyadic, family, and group—as well as by drug therapy.

6. It is clear that, except in the case of a diagnostic unit, much is to be gained by the units being placed on a pleasant annex of the main hospital outside, but not isolated from, a town. Isolation is a disadvantage to patients and increases the problems of staff recruitment.

Staffing. The success of in-patient units depends on staff selection more than upon any other single factor. Staff are likely to be successful if kindly, warm-hearted, unsentimental, intelligent and with a good sense of humour. These qualities usually go with stability and good relationships with their own parents in childhood and later. The dedicated, the sentimental and hypermoral are unlikely to be successful.

Professional staff can be shared with the out-patient service. The in-patient units should be in the charge of a responsible nursing officer, trained both in the mental and general hospital field. The nursing staff should be permanent and nurses in training should visit for observation only, this being an essential part of their training. Nursing assistants, recruited from the local community, can be invaluable in this work. In medium- and long-stay children's units, additional provision may be necessary for teachers for formal school subjects, while other units prefer to make use of local facilities.

Ratio of staff to patient is high and sometimes may need to be on a one-to-one basis. There is much to be said for project nursing whereby one member of the staff is responsible for a number of patients. Especially in the long-term units, time should be available for staff to keep in touch with discharged patients and there should be provision made for those patients who return to stay overnight. This is especially true of children and adolescents. Warm, genuine parent roles have been adopted by the staff and these cannot be put aside at the discharge of a young patient.

Treatment of children should go hand in hand with treatment of the parents and family. But this may be unavailing. Children should not be discharged to an unsatisfactory home. Hostel or foster placement is infinitely preferable. An interim assessment of results at the adolescent unit of the Institute of Family Psychiatry showed that those who did best were those who had spontaneously, or as a result of encouragement, severed links with disturbed families. This is in conformity with the right attitude to child-parent separation.

Layout. The layout should be as domestic as possible, with adequate facilities for indoor and outdoor recreation. Provision will also have to be made for a quiet room for study, interview rooms for professional staff, and, for children, accommodation for pets and a school room. Each unit is essentially a home.

Day hospital. Given a location near a town, it is possible to combine the day facilities for in-patients with the day hospital requisites of out-patients.

Staff

Usually the following clinical staff are employed in the out-patient service —psychiatrists, clinical psychologists, social workers, child therapists. For example, a case load of 400 families embracing over 1,000 individuals from a population of 250,000 requires a staff of 15 clinical workers in the out-patient service of the department noted here, there being five psychiatrists, three social workers, two clinical psychologists, five occupational therapists—all full-time. Such a staff complement does not allow all the families to receive the full range of treatment and, ideally, the number of staff should be larger. There is a complementary staff for research, administration, reception and portering. The in-patient service requires its own clinical and nursing staff.

Staff for a complete out-patient and in-patient service for a million people requires the minimum of 20 full-time psychiatrists of various grades of seniority, together with complementary staff of allied clinical professions and nursing staff. Four departments with integrated out- and in-patient services, serving a population of 250,000 each, are to be preferred, as they can then make links with community facilities with greater ease.

Much advantage comes from the same clinical workers remaining responsible for a family, should any of its members pass from the out-patient to the in-patient services, or vice versa.

In the recruitment of staff, emphasis should be placed upon the emotional stability of the applicants. Stability in a staff member is rewarding both to himself and to his patients, and even the best psychotherapy is seldom an adequate substitute for it.

The clinical director of a department of family psychiatry is usually a psychiatrist, who undertakes clinical responsibility for any patient referred to him; he has additional duties in relation to teaching, research, health promotion and advising the hospital authorities on matters appropriate to his field.

The clinical psychologist utilises a large number of psychological procedures for the assessment of children, parents and families. Discussion between the psychiatrist and the psychologist outlines the areas to be assessed. Thereafter, the psychologist selects his procedures and makes his report. A typical psychological report contains room for the findings; a systematic assessment of the patient in the test situation; a discussion of the results, including an estimate of their probable accuracy; the relation of the findings to any previous results and to the findings on other members of the family; recommendations for further assessments; and, usually, a concluding summary. Further discussions may reveal extra areas for assessment. Care is taken to prepare child, or adult, or family for the test situation. Experience has shown that an adequate rapport is essential to produce meaningful results and in the case of children it may be necessary for the child to attend for a number of occasions before testing commences or for a play room to be used as a milieu. Follow-up examination, at completion of treatment, can be valuable. In addition, the psychologist has teaching and research functions.

At one time, a social history was usually compiled by a social worker on the patient's first attendance. The traditional pattern of social history taking is giving way to a format which takes more into account the emotional experiences of the patient and the family. Great importance is attached to obtaining an adequate rapport with the patient, even at the cost of not obtaining a complete account during the first interview. To the social history from the patient is added relevant information from other agencies. But the social worker's greatest contribution comes in management, especially in vector therapy. Within and without a family there is a pattern of emotional forces (vectors) that bear on it for good or ill. The pattern of the forces can be ascertained and assessed and it can then be changed to the advantage of the family and child—vector therapy. This exacting, but rewarding task, requires not only individual and family case work, but also co-operation from a large number of family social agencies. A useful feature of the social work unit is an information cabinet containing particulars of statutory and voluntary agencies, welfare services and other relevant information. In addition, social workers are engaged in teaching and research.

Various patterns of co-ordinating the activities of staff members have been developed. The traditional practice in psychiatry was for all staff members to meet together in a large case conference. This, however, has certain disadvantages for day-to-day clinical work. It is time consuming, tends to promote a committee-patient relationship, often undermines the responsibility of each professional worker for his clinical work, and leads to group dependence. However, the value of the case conference as a teaching medium cannot be denied. The old-time traditional case conference is a major time waster and is a significant contributor to long waiting lists.

Another pattern employed is that of the small, brief case-conference procedure: the psychiatrist, social worker, psychologist and child psychotherapist concerned with a family meet informally together. Close collaboration over a period of time allows for many things to go unsaid. Decisions are rapidly arrived at, whilst each individual worker retains responsibility for his own contribution.

Yet another pattern is that of the psychiatrist meeting each member of the professional expert staff in individual interviews once a week. The advantage of this method is speed; one aspect of the case can be thrashed out thoroughly, and there is no wastage of time due to other professional workers standing by when discussion is irrelevant to their contribution. New cases can be quickly explored and decisions taken on treatment. There is also opportunity to discuss matters of common interest between the professionals.

Administrative co-ordination is also important, and this can be achieved by the staff meeting together once a week to co-ordinate appointments and to discuss matters of general interest.

A department cannot function without an administrative officer and an adequate number of personal secretaries, shorthand typists and clerical officers. A carefully selected receptionist with charm and poise is invaluable in the reception of patients. In addition a porter may be required for sundry duties, handyman work and moving play material in the play rooms. The cleaners complete the staff.

The administrative staff should be responsible for maintaining the waiting list, sending out appointments, maintaining records and card indexes, compiling statistics, requisitioning material, and the day-to-day upkeep of the building. In a hospital department they are responsible to the director of the department and to the hospital secretary.

RESEARCH

By its nature, family psychiatry offers new opportunities for research. Experiential psychopathology emphasises the importance of basing ideas and practice on real events, the facts of the situation, hard data. That is the foundation of effective investigation. It has not always been so. Reputations were made on ingeniously thought-out verbal concepts that rarely coincided with experience. They were uncritically accepted, as the beholders were ignorant of the knowledge that would allow them to correct the misconceptions. Concepts were dropped for no better reasons than those that justified their emergence. The next movement was hastily taken up. At times, practices bordered on the absurd and outdid phrenology (see the studies on body build), mesmerism, and divination. It has been particularly unfortunate that notions of psychopathology were based on fanciful verbal abstractions for, as therapeutic practice arose from them, it led to dangerous and inefficient practices that could not be corrected by an appeal to well-founded theory.

Naturally this field, like all other research areas, suffers and will continue to suffer from obstacles to progress that have been with us for all time. Pseudo intellectualisation will be confused with creativity. Mysticism, where knowledge is unclear, offers hope and appeals to the insecure, when an attack on ignorance alone offers true security. Vast reviews of the literature, spectacular exercises in "marking time," replace the more painful and daring pathways of creativity. Dependence on reference to others, the "name dropping" of science, raises doubtful and uncertain reputations to the status of gods; success is measured in terms of knowledge of these false prophets rather than in achievement of personal effort in creativity. Established opinion fights from entrenched positions against the threats of innovative thought. The unwary who seek out sponsors find themselves trapped in the repayments of sponsorship. Contemporary opinions, the "modern," are assumed to be the proven best when they may not only be false but be less certain that those previously held in history; this bespeaks a lack of a sense of history. Despite these evident pitfalls, the lessons of history show that progress is possible.

The position improves as researchers draw upon contributions from ethology, ethnology, experimental psychology, developmental psychology, and physiological psychology. Facts are now available and cannot be denied in any system of psychopathology. The field is complex and immense. Its immensity is not matched by available resources. Deficiencies in resources are due partly to the low priority given the field and partly to the fact that society can only deploy a small percentage of resources for its self-improvement. The complexity of the task is due to the difficulty of teasing out the fundamental causal psychic elements and in controlling, for the purpose of systematic investigation, the large number of variables. But as in other complex fields progress is still possible. It starts from careful observation by an observer truly knowledgeable about the field of exploration. Tentative speculations are proved or disproved. Slowly facts accumulate from which it is possible to make further testable hypotheses. Investigation proceeds a step at a time, moving on a small front, and rarely profits from large scale explorations which usually end with the identification of a number of correlates remote from the fundamental causal elements.

That useful hypotheses can only arise from an intensive knowledge of the field of study constitutes a compelling reason for clinicians to be concerned with clinical research. But it is obvious that research cannot be combined with a heavy clinical commitment, which is always given priority at the expense of research. For clinicians, clinical work is the easiest, teaching more difficult, and research most difficult. This is why so few undertake research and writing. A department is best served if clinicians with a special bent in clinical practice, teaching and research specialise in these fields; each is a special art. The researcher should carry a small clinical load to be explored in depth; this keeps him in touch with life experience, allows the inspiration of worthwhile hypotheses, and the continuous testing of speculation by reality.

The organisation of a department of family psychiatry must allow of the housing of one or a number of research units. Of course, each researcher needs a team of field workers, research administrative officers, typists, etc. Much routine work lies behind effective research in terms of careful culling of the literature, preparation of bibliographies, checking of references, reprint collecting, preparation of manuscripts, etc. Access to a computer seems essential for almost any research effort today other than case study procedure; it has proved to be often worthwhile, occasionally indispensable, but also often limited.

TEACHING

Three groups of recipients must be considered—professional staff, related professions, and the public—as illustrated by practice at the Institute of Family Psychiatry.

Learning continues after graduation in an ongoing process until retirement. Thus, even the most senior of clinical staff require orientation to the latest knowledge and techniques by participation and attendance at professional, national, and international congresses, together with visits to centres of relevant interest.

Trainees in each of the clinical specialties require in-service training with a programme of relevant theory and of supervised practice. In family psychiatry, there must be exposure to each clinical category—all age groups, and all parts of the family. Case conferences, discussion of sound and video recordings, and sharing in clinical procedures are valuable methods. Work should be in depth on a few families rather than superficial on a large number of families. Problem or hard-core families, while not very rewarding as therapeutic endeavours, are invaluable as teaching material; with them, psychopathology is writ large and is more obvious to the inexperienced. Role definition is important; it has become customary to blur the boundaries and almost lose one profession in another. The result is insecurity in day-to-day work because of unclear definition of duties and the provocation of trespass. The serious consequence is to make no-one master of his subject. This militates not only against the professions studying their field in depth—but, most importantly, against making advances in that field. Craftsmanship and expertise are matters of infinite appreciation. They are not often found as yet in the psychiatric field. Conferences and case discussions between a number of professions are useful only when the subject is of common interest and one on which each expert has the opportunity to express his particular skills. This calls for a careful selection of subject or the discussions become transactions between non-experts. While multidisciplinary meetings are a valuable fringe benefit to every profession, it is sometimes thought that they can replace training in the expertise of that subject. It has to be accepted as a practical reality that the most worthwhile transactions are between experts knowledgeable about one field.

Family psychiatry impinges on related professions; experts in these professions require an exposure to family psychiatry to allow them to be better practitioners in *their own fields*. It is the best practitioners who are able to limit themselves in this way. At the Institute of Family Psychiatry, the following have been found to be useful:

1. An introductory course of seminars with videotape teaching for medical practitioners for one week each year.

2. A similar annual course of seminars for psychiatrists.

3. An annual course of seminars for the nursing professions.

4. It is hoped to arrange further courses of seminars for a number of other related professions from time to time. At the moment, facilities allow only a generic course held for 22 Tuesdays pre- and post-Christmas each winter. This is an enormously valuable undertaking. It is offered free to members of all the helping professions—doctors, social workers, health visitors, teachers, clergymen, policemen, nurses, etc. Instead of giving a brief number of seminars covering the same ground to a number of disciplines, which is enormously time consuming, all can attend a course giving altogether nearly 100 seminars covering common ground. Members of each discipline can then go on to extend their expertise in their own field.

Experience seems to show that it is more effective to concentrate teaching on key personnel in the related professions, than upon members of the public; key personnel in their day-to-day work can informally influence public opinion.

Needless to say, the above requires time from senior and experienced tutors, visiting lecturers, a library, auditorium, seminar rooms, closed circuit television, a sound library, videotape library, film projection, etc. Studio facilities with technicians are essential in any unit of size.

REFERENCES

1. CAMMOCK, D. W., et al. (1961). The family's doctor. A report from the Research Committee of the North Midland Faculty of the College of General Practitioners. *Lancet, 1,* 213.
2. CROMBIE, D. L., and CROSS, K. W. (1956). The use of a general practitioner's time. *Brit. J. prev. soc. Med., 10,* 141.
3. Department of Health and Social Security (1973). *Children in Care in England and Wales, 1972.* London: H.M.S.O.
4. HORN, R. (1960). Personal communication.
5. HOWELLS, J. G. (1961). *Follow-up studies in child psychiatry.* Proceedings of 3rd World Congress of Psychiatry, Montreal.
6. LANGE, B., MOGENSEN, A., and FENGER, G. Nogle resultater ved intelligensundersøgelse afuudvalgte 10 års børn i en landbefolkning. *Nord. Psykiatr. Tss., 14,* 286–293.
7. Ministry of Health (1958). SAC (M. H.) (58)5. London: H.M.S.O.

NAMES INDEX

447

SUBJECT INDEX